Jesus and Christian Origins

Jesus and Christian Origins

Directions toward a New Paradigm

EDITED BY
Ben Wiebe

CASCADE *Books* • Eugene, Oregon

JESUS AND CHRISTIAN ORIGINS
Directions toward a New Paradigm

Copyright © 2019 Wipf and Stock Publishers. All rights reserved. Except for brief quotations in critical publications or reviews, no part of this book may be reproduced in any manner without prior written permission from the publisher. Write: Permissions, Wipf and Stock Publishers, 199 W. 8th Ave., Suite 3, Eugene, OR 97401.

Cascade Books
An Imprint of Wipf and Stock Publishers
199 W. 8th Ave., Suite 3
Eugene, OR 97401

www.wipfandstock.com

PAPERBACK ISBN: 978-1-5326-1483-5
HARDCOVER ISBN: 978-1-5326-1485-9
EBOOK ISBN: 978-1-5326-1484-2

Cataloging-in-Publication data:

Names: Wiebe, Ben, editor.

Title: Jesus and Christian origins : directions toward a new paradigm / edited Ben Wiebe.

Description: Eugene, OR : Cascade Books, 2019 | Includes bibliographical references and index.

Identifiers: ISBN 978-1-5326-1483-5 (paperback) | ISBN 978-1-5326-1485-9 (hardcover) | ISBN 978-1-5326-1484-2 (ebook)

Subjects: LCSH: Bible. Gospels—Criticism, interpretation, etc. | Oral tradition.

Classification: LCC BS2555.2 J44 2019 (print) | LCC BS2555.2 (ebook)

Manufactured in the U.S.A.   FEBRUARY 1, 2019

To mentors who prepared the way;
to friends and colleagues who encourage us and walk with us.

Contents

List of Contributors ix
Introduction vii

1. Doing New Testament History:
A Baseline for Studies - Martin Mosse 1
   Annex A: Notes and Resources for a New Testament Chronology 34
   Annex B: Paul's Mental Constitution 36

   Respondent: Ben Wiebe 41

2. Birger Gerhardsson and Oral Transmission in the Formation of the Gospel Tradition - Allan J. McNicol 67

   Respondent: Martin Mosse 87

3. Synoptic Gospels as Evidence of Jesus Remembered by Eyewitnesses - John Harrison 104

   Respondent: Allan J. McNicol 122

4. Reviving the Priority of John - Mark A. Matson 128

   Respondent: Jonathan Bernier 167

5. How and When the Four Gospels Became Scripture - Nicholas Perrin 172

   Respondent: Mark A. Matson 194

6. Ben F. Meyer and *The Gospels for All Christians* - Jonathan Bernier 201
   Respondent: Nicholas Perrin 224

7. The Sociological Contours of Pauline Christianity and Implications for the Bauer Thesis - Nicholas Perrin 230
   Respondent: John Harrison 246

Summary and Reflections - Ben Wiebe 256

Subject Index 267
Author Index 269

List of Contributors

Jonathan Bernier
Antigonish, Nova Scotia, Canada
St. Francis Xavier University
Lecturer

John Harrison
Oklahoma City, Oklahoma
Oklahoma Christian University
Professor of New Testament and Ministry

Mark A. Matson
Johnson City, Tennessee
Milligan College
Associate Professor of Bible

Allan J. McNicol
Austin, Texas
Austin Graduate School of Theology
A. B. Cox Professor Emeritus of New Testament

Martin Mosse
EMSWORTH, Hants UK
Retired

Nicholas Perrin
Wheaton Illinois
Wheaton Graduate School
Franklin S. Dryness Chair of Biblical Studies
    and Dean of the Graduate School

Ben Wiebe
Beamsville, Ontario, Canada
Union Biblical Seminary, Pune, India
Retired Teacher/Lecturer

Introduction

Ben Wiebe

Jesus called disciples to be with him and to follow him (Mark 3:13–18). Today the followers of Jesus live on six continents and in all parts of the world. They learn and speak of him in a thousand languages. They find orientation in their fears and hopes, creation and destiny hold together in Christ. In some ways whatever the case with Jesus, he will inevitably be known by the company he keeps. In the world beyond the circle of his followers, the name of Jesus may bring to mind both luminous acts of compassion and acts of willful to noxious evil. Whether in one case or the other, these acts take their place in history committed in the name of Jesus or in spite of it. Therefore it becomes a matter of critical discernment to ask about what in human response is in accord with Jesus Christ. The understanding that measures up to the gospel remains an important call and task. At the same time the variation and scope of Jesus' impact increases the challenge of making one's way to such an adequate understanding.

The focus in this volume is Jesus and Christian origins. It is evident that Jesus and the effects that follow from him are intricately bound up together in our world.

Jesus and the Discipleship Community

More specifically, Jesus can be fully understood only in the conjunction of his mission and the coming to be of the discipleship community. As it stands, there has been in NT studies a generations long aversion among scholars that issues in abstract consideration of Jesus, apart from his aims and the outcome of his mission, so as to exclude the complementary issue of the church. Or if it was noticed it was defined in limited "institutional" terms so as to rule out the evidence of Jesus' mission and the outcome of the discipleship community. In particular, this marked the Bultmann era. Bultmann, and those who followed in his wake, largely focused on the individual and personal decision, apart from Jesus' words and acts revealing purpose or the quest of concrete response.[1] What was the aim of Jesus' encounter in mission to Israel?

First, there is the now clearly acknowledged correlation of Jesus' intention and the "kingdom of God," and the more recently recognized correlation of the kingdom of God and the eschatological restoration of Israel. Already in 1925 Ernst Ludwig Dietrich published a philological study that drew attention to the major prophetic theme of the promise and the corresponding hope of Israel.[2] This basic theme of promise and restoration was developed by G. B. Caird.[3] "Your God reigns" is the proclamation of God acting for Israel's redemption (e.g., Isa 52:8-9). Ben Meyer developed the correlation between the biblical hope and the gospel theme of fulfillment, and so defined the aim of Jesus as the eschatological restoration of Israel.[4] Jesus does his work and makes his proclamation with a view to response and his proclamation finds its end in appropriate response. Thus, Jesus' enactment and proclamation of the kingdom of God called into being the community of the kingdom.

Second, concrete evidence of Jesus' purpose takes the form of Jesus choosing the twelve (Mark 3:13-19; Matt 10:1-4). This is recorded in all four Gospel accounts, in Acts, and in 1 Corinthians, with variations in the order of names but always adding up to twelve. In the context of

---

1. Bultmann, *Jesus and the Word*, 40-41, 51, 158-59. In studies of Jesus over the last century the conjunction of Jesus and church was often either ignored or marginalized at best. Yet in taking account of the origin and form of the NT texts, they were duly compelled to acknowledge the presence of the church. Beyond Jesus' expectation of the kingdom, for Bultmann the coming of the kingdom is not about events or persons in time and history, but the now (the present) in which the human being is called to decision. Following Bultmann, Norman Perrin in a similar vein defined the kingdom as a "symbol" (not in time or history) to speak of what every person "experiences in his own time" of God. See Perrin, *Language of the Kingdom*, 199.

2. Dietrich, *Sùb Sébut*.

3. Caird, *Jesus and the Jewish Nation*.

4. Meyer, *Aims of Jesus*, 127-28, 170-73.

lively expectation, for Jesus to appoint and send out the twelve is to make of them a "sign" of the eschatological restoration of Israel.[5] Jesus speaks of his followers as the "little flock" (Luke 12:32) reminiscent of prophetic texts about Israel of the messianic age (Mic 5:4; Isa 40:11; Ezek 34:12–14). The existence of the twelve itself is expressive of Jesus' purpose and as an appeal to the whole people of Israel.[6]

Transmission of the Gospel

This overview of Jesus and the kingdom community has established a specific direction in the field of Jesus studies. As a basic ascertainment it may serve as a baseline in gospel interpretation. It represents a turn from and advance beyond the gulf or "rupture hypothesis" between Jesus and Judaism on the one hand and between Jesus and the early Christian community on the other.[7] In recent decades, taking account of the Dead Sea Scrolls and other studies of Jesus in the context of Second Temple Judaism has helped to overcome the break between Jesus and Judaism.[8] While the break between Jesus and Judaism has been largely overcome, the perceived rupture between Jesus and early Christianity has continued even as contributions changing the landscape of Jesus studies are coming into place. Dunn, in his groundbreaking work *Jesus Remembered*, reframed the issue and moved beyond the rupture hypothesis. With respect to the stages involved, Willi Marxsen first expressed this in terms of three settings for the Jesus tradition: the setting of Jesus' ministry, the setting of the church, and the setting of the Gospels.[9]

The basic insight provided by Dunn is that NT material bearing on Jesus comes by way of the early church setting (mediated in that setting). The early Christians in their identity, teaching, and practice depended on Jesus' ministry setting so that the substance of the gospel tradition

---

5. The hope for the future including the restoration of Israel and of "the twelve" is maintained even in the Qumran community.

6. Bernier, *Quest for the Historical Jesus*, credits Ben Meyer with opening the way for this advance in overcoming the "rupture hypothesis."

7. Bernier, *Quest for the Historical Jesus*, 2–3.

8. The work of Hengel, *Judaism*; Sanders and Dunn, among others, has been basic in establishing the Jewish context of Jesus.

9. Marxsen, *Mark the Evangelist*, noted that "framework" is not to be overlooked (as in form history) but is important for reading the Gospel from the "historical standpoint," 22, 23. See also Bernier, *Quest for the Historical Jesus*, 2.

takes its distinctive shape from its antecedent dominical setting. It can therefore be said that the gospel tradition takes form in the church setting and the church setting is dependent on and in continuity with the setting of Jesus' ministry.[10]

As a consequence what follows is that the question about the gospel material and what comes from Jesus and what comes from the church appears to be misplaced. What we have is the mediated witness of the discipleship community. Yet in the form critical program the concern was to separate the two, based on the supposition that mediation by way of the early church setting presents a barrier to our knowing what is of Jesus. The critical question as posed was how do we distinguish what comes to us from which of the three settings? What in the end Dunn brings to the fore, following Meyer, is that the Jesus traditions mediated in the setting of the early church, including the Gospel accounts, presents not a barrier to, but a "conduit for genuine apprehension of Jesus of Nazareth."[11]

To reflect on baselines of NT studies is to think of reference points from which study can proceed (as in baseball the baselines do not prevent the game, they make it possible). There are certainly various lines of evidence that might serve as baselines for NT interpretation. History can serve as one of them. It is not simply a wax nose to be shaped to human whim or ideology. As such, it provides a frame for conversation across differences between various people and communities. History as reference to events of time and place provides the setting for discernment of meaning and truth.

Toward a New Paradigm

The aim of these chapters is to bring to light the conjunction between Jesus and Christian origins. To focus on the relation between Jesus and the church places the Gospels in the spotlight, to examine their character as Gospel accounts and their genre (purpose) with reference to biography and history.[12] The aim is to follow up on the substantive new work dealing

---

10. Bernier, *Quest for the Historical Jesus*, 3.
11. Bernier, *Quest for the Historical Jesus*, 4.
12. The work of scholars like Allison, *Constructing Jesus*, and Dunn, *Jesus Remembered*, at once stands in critique of the once dominant form-criticism and opens the way for new directions in Gospel studies.

with the Gospels in presenting the life and ministry of Jesus (biography), and of events in the past interpreted in the present (history).

In giving account of the literary features of the NT documents, a variety of approaches have been brought to bear. Beyond historical criticism, literary approaches have been developed, such as discourse analysis, genre criticism, certain kinds of rhetorical criticism, and reader response criticism. At the same time, these approaches alone from a more broad-based perspective of the NT are severely limited. For one, it is evident the NT documents have their origin and their reception not primarily as literature or rhetoric. That is rather like taking a brightly colored x-ray from the lab and hanging it in the hall to be observed as art. It can be interesting but it does not take account of its primary purpose or basic significance.

Amid the bewildering array of methods and approaches in NT studies there is an evident loss of orientation. The Gospels may be presented as "palimpsests." Jesus himself may be largely overwritten by certain group interests or by particular needs of the church. What the documents themselves say, as in Luke about various sources and ultimately apostolic source (Luke 1:1–4) or Paul and the common apostolic witness to Christ (1 Cor 15:1–11), may be discounted. Similarly, reception history and Christian witness beyond the NT period bearing on their origins may be overlooked. The aim here is to present a specific set of studies in order to illuminate some baselines for NT interpretation in the context of the early church.

There is important common ground among the writers of this book. But by design it represents an open conversation—each chapter is followed by a response. Perhaps this can contribute to a larger conversation and stimulate further thoughtful dialogue. It will be clear to the reader that there are differences of substance among the writers in some areas and certainly differences of emphasis in other areas. It is a conversation to illuminate baselines for interpretation with a view to discerning directions toward a new paradigm.

Overview of This Project

In what follows we proceed basically in three stages. History—from Jesus to the Gospels (the Fourfold Gospel); Unity and Diversity; and Identity and Structure of Apostolic Christianity. In chapter 1 Martin Mosse takes up history as context and baseline for NT studies. The question of the origin and authorship of the NT writings bears on their identity and so on their interpretation. To put it simply, taking account of the events about which the authors speak and the circumstances of their writing makes history essential for interpreting them. At the same time, differences in language and style have long been important, especially in the epistles, in judgments of authorship and origin. Mosse reviews the data for the authorship and chronology of the Acts of the Apostles and the Gospel of Mark; he then goes on to show how scholars have taken account or failed to take account of this evidence. Approaches to the NT documents and taking account of what Mosse calls the "external evidence" is a critical matter, and further discussed in the response. If scholars have largely focused either on the "internal" or the "external" evidence, in the response we take up the relation of the internal and the external evidence in dealing specifically with the origin of Mark. Pauline authorship of certain letters is evaluated from what we may know about Paul as a person and as an apostle, and with reference to the language and style of the letters (here mainly Ephesians).

In chapter 2 Allan McNicol examines the contribution of Birger Gerhardsson to Gospel studies, dealing specifically with how the Jesus tradition was transmitted and took form in the Gospels. Since the earliest days there have been sharp questions around the differences between the Gospel accounts. Today the further issue of memory and the reliability of the accounts is in the spotlight. Tradition was transmitted and took form in the Gospels. McNicol notes that in Judaism, along with a definite oral tradition, there was an emphasis on education of children and literacy. Beyond generalities about oral tradition, Gerhardson was concerned with the process in the Jewish setting and how transmission actually took place. An important question is raised about eschatology and time as it affects the transmission of Jesus' teaching.

In chapter 3 John Harrison reviews the evidence for eyewitness testimony in the Synoptic Gospels. In the context of the disciples hearing Jesus the question from Harrison is, what kind of teacher was Jesus and what level of memorization did he as teacher expect of the disciples? The difficulty as presented by Harrison is lack of consensus on the matter. He says it is one thing to assert memory and eyewitness testimony in the Gospel accounts; it is another thing to show this. What are the criteria to identify or ascertain this? Harrison understands the formation of the gospel tradition as mainly a collective communal development.

In response, McNicol questions the notion of transmission of the Jesus tradition as presented within the social science model of folkloric traditions in oral cultures. Instead, scholars like Gerhardsson and Rainer Riesner refer to the sacral community, for example Qumran, where knowing and reading certain texts is expected and has its own importance. The assumption may be that transmission of the gospel tradition in the communal setting will likely mean change or distortion. Actually, it may work the other way. A community receiving the tradition with care will have people who are aware and will not easily permit it to be invented or inverted.

In Chapter 4 Mark Matson presents a close study of the place of John in history and in relation to the three other Gospels. He does this as part of following up on the earlier landmark study by John A. T. Robinson, *The Priority of John*. For more than a century since the days of F. C. Baur and D. F. Strauss, John has been marginalized in terms of date, connection to history, the geographical setting of Jesus' life, and in terms of the aims of his ministry. The challenge in the study of John has been how to account for the important differences in order and content compared to the Synoptic Gospels and at the same time the common elements shared by the four accounts. Matson notes that over the last several decades there has been a serious rethinking of the historical value of John with reference to various features of the Gospel: John's Jewishness (which was diverse in the first century), the independent and coherent narrative account, the specific geographical references sustained by recent work in archeology, and so on. In response, Jonathan Bernier speaks mainly to affirm Matson's findings. And as it relates to the dating of John's account, Bernier thinks it may be time to follow up on Robinson's other work, *Redating the New Testament*. This would be a way to bring clarity and coherence to the dating of the NT documents, taking account of evidence from more recent studies.

In chapter 5 Nicholas Perrin, with reference to the supposed sociological and textual "fluidity" in the second century church, examines the evidence for the reception of the four Gospels in this period. This refers to the way in which the Gospels are cited but also to their being read in worship along with the Scriptures of the Old Testament. Toward the end of the second century, Irenaeus is clear in his affirmation of the fourfold Gospel. Perrin notes this reflects earlier history and acceptance of the "authority" of the four accounts that can be traced back to the beginning of the second century. This is evidenced in Justin Martyr and Tatian's

Diatessaron, the Muratorian Fragment, the Epistula Apostolarum, and the letter of II Clement. Perrin also deals with how the "authority" of the Gospels came to be recognized. In response, Mark Matson sifts the evidence Perrin has presented and concludes that as a whole the evidence is persuasive and that Perrin is sustained in his presentation. There is some ambivalence about the data from II Clement.

In Chapter 6, Bernier recognizes that Richard Bauckham's *The Gospel for All Christians* marks an important turning point in Gospel studies. Bernier aims to complement this work. He does so by setting Bauckham and Ben F. Meyer in mutual dialogue. In critique of "community criticism" as applied to the Gospels Bernier refers to a tendency going back to F. C. Baur and to portray Christianity "that is not Christianity, but multiple of Christianities, related if at all, via antagonism." In this case, Meyer brings context and a more precise formulation of "the unity and diversity" as it pertains to early Christianity. The work of Bauckham represents a shift toward a new paradigm; the attention is turned to the actual tradents and the origins of the Gospel accounts. Perrin, in response, has some questions but in the main perceives this as an important contribution. In particular the understanding as presented of unity and diversity of early Christianity, that is unity within diversity.

In the final chapter Perrin, in light of Bauer's thesis and the supposed diverse forms of Christianity, examines the structure of earliest Christianity as we know it from some of the main letters of the apostle Paul. He deals with the social, structural, and cognitive factors in discerning the identity of the church. The use of kinship language of brother and sister was not restricted by race, class, or geography, but obtained across the breadth of the community. This is evident when Paul refers to Apollos, who is not Corinthian, as "our brother" (1 Cor 16:12). Now it is true, as Harrison points out in response, this way of speaking was also used in wider society, as in the case of the people who asked Peter, "men and brethren, what shall we do?" after his address on Pentecost (Acts 2:37). It could also be used by certain guilds and groups. What is noteworthy is that in the church this language is not restricted to groups of common interest, rank, gender, or culture, but people share a connectedness that transcends all of these categories. It is thus an important indication, correlated with other factors, of what Perrin calls the "connectedness" of the church.

In his letters the apostle conveys a clear sense of the church in particular locations (e.g., Corinth, Rome) and at the same time of the more than local reality of the church. Evident already in the way the apostles exercise their authority and move from place to place; also simply in the way people move from one location to another, are welcomed and find a connection (e.g., Rom 16). For Perrin the authority of Paul as "apostle to the Gentiles" is a mark of structural unity. He speaks of Paul's "exclusive" authority as apostle to the Gentiles. Harrison questions this, Paul aligns himself with the other apostles in bearing witness to Christ (1 Cor 15:1–11) and apparently welcomes others to participate with him in work he himself began (e.g. 1 Cor 3:5–9, 21–25). So this calls for nuance; Paul certainly recognizes a specific and unique call as apostle to the Gentiles and as such served to bind them together in Christ.

Bibliography

Allison, Dale C. *Constructing Jesus: Memory, Imagination, and History*. Grand Rapids: Baker Academic, 2010.

Bernier, Jonathan. *The Quest for the Historical Jesus After the Demise of Authenticity*. London: Bloomsbury, T. & T. Clark, 2016.

Bultmann, Rudolf. *Jesus and the Word*. New York: Scribner, 1958.

Caird, G. B. *Jesus and the Jewish Nation*. London: Athlone, 1965.

Dietrich, Ernst Ludwig. *Sùb Sébut: Die eschatologishche Wiederherstellung bei den Propheten*. Giesen: Töpelmann, 1925.

Dunn, James D. G. *Jesus Remembered*. Grand Rapids: Eerdmans, 2003.

Hengel, Martin. *Judaism and Hellenism: Studies in Their Encounters in Palestine during the Early Hellenistic Period*. Translated by John Bowden. 2 vols. Philadelphia: Fortress, 1974 [1969].

Marxsen, Willi. *Mark the Evangelist: Studies on the Reduction History of the Gospel*. Translated by Janes Boyce et al. Nashville: Abingdon, 1969.

Meyer, Ben F. *The Aims of Jesus*. London: SCM, 1979.

Perrin, Norman. *Jesus and the Language of the Kingdom: Symbol and Metaphor in New Testament Interpretation*. Philadelphia: Fortress, 1976.

1

Doing New Testament History: A Baseline for Studies[1]

Martin Mosse

The Discipline of Ancient History

It is my thesis that New Testament history, and especially chronology, form a subset of the discipline known as ancient history, and require the mind and training of that discipline. A training in theology alone does not suffice. An ancient historian is someone who *thinks* like an ancient historian, which requires training and practice, not least in logical detective work. Similarly, a mathematician is one who *thinks* like a mathematician, which besides aptitude requires a stiff training plus the experience of solving a wide variety of problems.

I think that the distinction I am making underlies John Robinson's lament about the alarming change in attitudes to chronology that had already taken place in his day:

> [W]hat one looks for in vain in much recent scholarship is any serious wrestling with the external or internal evidence for the

---

1. I would like to thank my wife Barbara, together with David Kemball-Cook, James Bradby, Dr. Ben Wiebe, and my erstwhile tutor, Dr. Barbara Levick, Emeritus Fellow and Tutor in Ancient History at St. Hilda's College, Oxford, for their kind comments and criticisms while this chapter was being developed. I am especially grateful to Dr. Levick for having instilled in me long ago the virtues of Occam's Razor.

dating of individual books (such as marked the writings of men like Lightfoot and Harnack and Zahn), rather than an *a priori* pattern of theological development into which they are then made to fit.[2]

The difference of approach that he is highlighting is largely responsible for the wide divergence of dates for New Testament books that are conventional today from those that were traditional in, say, the late nineteenth or early twentieth centuries when entry into theological studies was commonly preceded by a study of the classics including ancient history.

In this chapter we shall consider four required competencies of a good New Testament historian, seeing first of all how they would help us to understand someone as complex as St. Paul. We shall then look at two major chronological conundrums, the dates of Mark and of the Book of Acts.[3] After offering our own account of these for readers to assess and criticize, we shall go on to examine those of four major New Testament scholars. Our aim will be to understand how their *thinking* has led to their conclusions, thereby opening up a dialogue that may lead to robust solutions capable of being understood and accepted by at least a substantial majority. If so, we shall be a step closer to a unified understanding of the New Testament. We shall conclude with a summary of lessons we may learn.

Qualities of a Good New Testament Historian

Stephen Neill and Tom Wright underline the apprenticeship required of anyone aspiring to become a New Testament historian:

> Historical research is always a difficult and delicate business. The difficulty is immensely increased, if the object of historical research is, as in the case of the New Testament documents, also the concern of faith. The only way to become an historian is through the handling and weighing of historical evidence. It would be an excellent thing if every scholar who wishes to approach the New Testament in the light of history could be required to win his spurs elsewhere in the wide fields of ancient history, and, only when his competence has been proved in the

---

2. Robinson, *Redating the New Testament*, 8–9.

3. For the incidental chronology supporting this chapter see Mosse, *Three Gospels*, and especially table A1-1, 292–302.

less difficult areas, to advance to the supremely difficult task of the historical reconstruction of the life of Jesus and of the story of the early Church.[4]

They go on to spell out the qualities that make "that rare bird, a real historian":

> To knowledge of facts and sources must be added three great gifts. First, the capacity of historical judgement—the delicate process of calculating exactly how much weight is to be attributed to each fragment of evidence. Secondly, historical imagination—the power to project oneself into the minds and thoughts of the men and women of a generation very different from our own. Thirdly, historical synthesis—the capacity to put together bits and pieces of historical evidence in such a way as to make a consistent and convincing whole.[5]

I see a need for four essential competencies, which I shall discuss in turn.

1. Psychology
2. Ancient sources, and how to handle them
3. Foundations of the discipline
4. Occam's Razor

Psychology

First, since history of any kind is about *people*, we need to develop a good understanding of the human *mind*: how it works—its psychology and what it can achieve. Without such an understanding of human spiritual development we are going to come to grief when we begin to engage with some of the great minds who are the object of our studies.

People change. They change their minds (think: Wittgenstein). They develop their ideas over time. Their personalities and spiritual understanding alter and grow. They are not always predictable. They are infinitely complex. They are self-contradictory. Most importantly, they are capable of entertaining two contrasting or even conflicting ideas at the same time. In the words of J. B. Lightfoot,

---

4. Neill and Wright, *Interpretation*, 300.
5. Neill and Wright, *Interpretation*, 304.

> Unhappily for criticism, but happily for humanity, history is not logically consistent. Men are not automata, which move on certain rigid and mechanical principles, but complex living souls with various motives, impulses, passions, reluctances.[6]

In the case of the truly great men and women of prayer—the saints and mystics—those towering spiritual geniuses who constitute a class of their own, the issue is magnified and we need to be doubly careful. The point is amply illustrated for our day by Thomas Merton's account of his own inner life:

> My ideas are always changing, always moving around one center, from somewhere else. I will always be accused of inconsistencies. I will no longer be there to hear the accusation.[7]

So changes in style and apparent conflicts of theology—so often adduced as evidence of plural or anonymous authorship—do not always support such claims.[8] They simply demonstrate that our texts were written by—often very remarkable—human beings.

It follows also that our research will take us nowhere very useful if we confine ourselves to the study of the *text* of the New Testament books, at the expense of the *people* who actually wrote them, whom it is today often unfashionable to identify. E. Earle Ellis comments wryly about this modern fad: "One must resist the modern tendency to assume that in early Christianity only unknowns could be authors."[9]

One might add also, to assume that only geriatrics could write gospels. Depersonalization is a risky habit.

Lightfoot's assessment of human nature in all its complexity allows for a very much more nuanced understanding of the New Testament

---

6. Lightfoot, *Apostolic Fathers*, part 2, vol. 1, 412, quoted in Neill and Wright, *Interpretation*, 52.

7. Merton, *Intimate Merton*, 265: January 25, 1964.

8. But sometimes they do. I am most grateful to Pheme Perkins for her extensive and detailed review of my book *The Three Gospels* in the *Review of Biblical Literature* in October 2009 with its accurate reporting of several of my chapters. However, it betrays strong evidence of dual authorship. When she (or whoever) castigates me for ignoring "the work of contemporary German exegetes and classicists," she seems not to have noticed the multiple references to both Martin Hengel and W. G. Kümmel throughout the book, which may be found from the second index. I actually corresponded with Professor Hengel in November/December 2006, less than three years before the great man's death. As for Professor Kümmel, his name is the first word of the main text on page one! The real Pheme Perkins would never have made a mistake like that.

9. Ellis, *Making of the New Testament*, 36.

than one often encounters in the textbooks. Indeed, it has been wisely said that an ability to cope with *paradox* is the hallmark of any mature religion. The tension between the sovereignty of God and the free will of man is an obvious case. Paul's "when I am weak, then am I strong" (2 Cor 12:10) is another. Without such illumination, exegesis tends to become somewhat one dimensional. Not least, as I shall argue, it is essential for understanding the life and ministry of Paul.

Ancient Sources and How to Handle Them

Second, the trained New Testament historian will be familiar with the history of the early Roman Empire—a specialist subject in its own right. Such familiarity, for instance, will enable him or her to pick up the nuances that assist in determining the date of Acts.[10]

Equally, they will not be confined to searching internally within the canon. Rather, recognizing that essential to New Testament chronology are the lives and careers of the people concerned, they will often have to mine the Early Fathers for their evidence—and must treat them with *respect*. All too often the testimony of the Fathers is arbitrarily dismissed with comments such as those with which Papias has been hounded for his testimony about Matthew:[11] "Papias is sand . . . the material about Matthew is valueless,"[12] "Papias' evidence is probably valueless,"[13] and—frighteningly!—"*[I]t will be most prudent to continue to treat the patristic witness with a pinch of salt.*"[14] Similarly, the testimony of Eusebius, who was a very conscientious historian,[15] is routinely ignored in some circles today. I doubt, however, whether the optimal approach to any historical problem is to jettison all the ancient evidence at the outset. The Fathers were better placed than ourselves by several centuries to know what was going on in the New Testament age. They are not always right and they often conflict; but equally, they are not summarily to be dismissed.

10. See the masterclass supplied by R. B. Moberly, "When Was Acts?," discussed below.
11. Papias *apud* Eusebius, *Ecclesiastical History* III.xxxix.16.
12. Goulder, *Luke*, 1:33.
13. Tuckett, *Q and the History*, 44n11.
14. Goodacre, *Synoptic Problem*, 81 (emphasis added).
15. The great German historian Eduard Meyer said of Eusebius that Luke "has found in him a successor who in many ways is of equal value," *Ursprung und Anfänge*, 1:3. Quoted in Neill and Wright, *Interpretation*, 306n3.

Foundations of the Discipline

Third, our historian will also be aware of the founding fathers of our discipline, those great historians of the past who have preceded us in our field and actually resolved problems that regrettably still raise their heads today. He (she) will know where we have come from. No one would think of embarking on a career in mathematics who was not already fully conversant with the work of, say, Sir Isaac Newton (1642–1727) on the binomial theorem and the calculus, or of Leonhard Euler (1707–83), whose celebrated identities epitomized the core of the mathematics of his day. Equally, no budding mathematician today seeks fame by trying to solve the three great classical problems bequeathed to us by the Greeks—squaring the circle, doubling the cube, and trisecting the angle—in each case using only a compass and straight edge. These were long ago proved to be impossible, and impossible they remain. Some results are here to stay, and we need to know them. I offer three examples from the study of New Testament history.

1. The Tübingen hypotheses. Few today, I suggest, would want to repeat the ultra-late dates for Acts (late second century) and the gospels (130–170) proposed by the German scholar F. C. Baur at Tübingen in 1845–47. These were decisively refuted by the detailed work of Lightfoot and Zahn on the letters of Ignatius and Clement of Rome, and are unlikely to return.[16]

2. Cadbury v. Hobart. Hobart's celebrated demonstration in 1882 that the medical language of Luke and Acts proves authorship by a physician, which convinced both Zahn and Harnack, was demolished by Cadbury's detailed critique in 1920.[17] As he showed, the so-called medical words are also to be found in non-medical authors, like Lucian and Josephus. This too is unchallenged today, even though Lucan authorship may certainly be maintained on other grounds.[18]

3. Date of the crucifixion. It seems to me that J. K. Fotheringham, writing in the pre-computer age, by a heroic computation correctly determined the date of the crucifixion to have been April 3, 33.[19]

16. See the exciting account in Neill and Wright, *Interpretation*, 59, who conclude that "it is not so often that a theory can be so completely overthrown."
17. Cadbury, *Style and Literary*, 39–72.
18. See Mosse, *Three Gospels*, chap. 10, "Authorship of Luke and Acts."
19. Fotheringham, "Evidence of Astronomy."

This conclusion has been confirmed and I would judge settled for all time by the Oxford physicists Colin J. Humphreys and W. Graeme Waddington, in the computer age.[20] April 7, 30 is to my mind now a lost cause.

These and other similar results constitute for me the foundations upon which our discipline is built.

Occam's Razor

Fourth, a vital element in the ancient historian's toolkit is Occam's Razor, *Entia non sunt multiplicanda praeter necessitatem* (Entities are not to be multiplied beyond what is necessary). This is another way of saying that we should always choose the simplest explanation for a matter in question that will do the job. It applies in all fields of human enquiry. Aristotle advocated it in mathematics. In science Einstein expressed it when he said, "The grand aim of science [is] to cover the greatest number of empirical facts by logical deduction from the smallest possible number of hypotheses or axioms."[21] C. H. Dodd applied it to his work as a theological scholar: "The best hypothesis is that which accounts for the largest number of known facts."[22] We should therefore exercise caution when we see the scholars of today treating it as optional or dispensable. As I have noted elsewhere in this volume, Occam's Razor lies at the heart of the case against Q: why postulate an entity for which there is no historical or archaeological evidence when a far simpler hypothesis (that Luke used a memorized version of Matthew) will do the trick?[23]

Occam's Razor expresses a faith that the world is marked by a certain order, and that right thinking will enable us to understand it. Conclusions obtained by Occam's Razor have a remarkable way of dovetailing when brought together.

---

20. Humphreys and Waddington, "Date of the Crucifixion."
21. Einstein quoted in Barnett, *Universe and Dr. Einstein*.
22. Dodd, "Mind of Paul II," 107.
23. See Mosse, *Three Gospels*, 6.

Paul the Apostle

Much of the above applies critically in the case of Paul, surely after Jesus the most powerful mind that we encounter in the pages of the New Testament. Fully to understand him we need to bring to the *text* of his epistles both the *chronology* of his career and the human *psychology* underlying it, as did Evelyn Underhill in her penetrating study of him almost a century ago, and after her, C. H. Dodd.[24] All too often in recent decades the study of Paul has concentrated on the text only, thus depriving us of any deep feel for the *man himself* and his developing ideas. Such an understanding will be essential in tackling questions of authorship.

As to *chronology*, I have suggested in annex A some guidelines for dating his epistles in terms of his captivities. On his *psychology* there is much to commend in Richard Dormandy's recent insightful and nuanced study of 2 Corinthians, *The Madness of St. Paul*, in which he makes a bold attempt to identify the apostle's mental states as a flesh and blood human being rather than a spiritual superman beyond analysis. He sees his subject at this time (early 56) as undergoing a severe spiritual depression, but finally emerging into a new dimension of God's *grace*, which was to inform his next letter, Romans.[25] Dormandy is in my judgment wholly justified in examining Paul through the categories of modern clinical psychology; and although I myself read the apostle a little differently,[26] future researchers will surely do well to follow his lead.

Dodd similarly held "that about the time when [Paul] wrote II Corinthians he underwent a significant spiritual experience which left its mark."[27] Tracing the development of Paul's teaching on topics such as eschatology and the law, he saw this process as reaching its culmination in this epistle. He perceived also a corresponding spiritual turning-point in the direction of *mysticism* occurring "somewhere about the time of II Corinthians."[28] The possibility of such transforming experiences needs to be taken into account when considering the authorship of later, disputed

---

24 Underhill, *Mystics of the Church*, 29–52; Dodd's two lectures on "The Mind of Paul" to be found in his *New Testament Studies*, 67–82, 83–128. Dodd accepts substantially the chronology of Eduard Meyer, *Ursprung und Anfänge*, 85.

25. Dormandy, *Madness of St. Paul*, e.g., 52–54, 68.

26. Dormandy's treatment of the "thorn" (*Madness of St. Paul*, 65–67) misses the pointers to *bipolar* disorder (see annex B).

27. Dodd, "Mind of Paul II," 84, referring back to "Mind of Paul I," 80–81.

28. Dodd, "Mind of Paul II," 113.

epistles such as 2 Timothy. For me the identification of this same critical episode in Paul's career proposed by both Dodd and Dormandy from their differing vantage points is highly significant, and we can build on it.

I have argued in annex B that, especially in 2 Corinthians, Paul exhibits and describes the characteristics of *mood disorder*, which today we call *bipolar*. However, a number of converging indications suggest that his two year captivity in Caesarea (summer 57 to summer 59, Acts 24:27) marked a watershed in his life, which I attribute to a major renewing and healing encounter with God in the solitude and silence of his cell, some two years or so after the mental and spiritual crisis perceived by Dodd and Dormandy in 2 Corinthians. There are changes to

1. his anticipated evangelistic program;
2. the style and content of his letters; and
3. his primary strategic goal.

Change of Evangelistic Program

In early 57 Paul, writing to the Romans during (probably) his third visit to Corinth, announces to them his plan to use his forthcoming first visit to Rome as a springboard for his next major missionary enterprise, to Spain. This major new departure will mark the intended end of his ministry in Asia and Greece, a turning westwards after so long in the east (Rom 15:23–29). But first he has some loose ends to tie up. He needs to return to Jerusalem in order to deliver the proceeds of the collection he has organized on behalf of its impoverished church. And already he anticipates trouble there before he can set out again. Returning then through his old stomping grounds in Asia, he calls in at Miletus to bid farewell to the elders of Ephesus (Acts 20:15–38). His mind is made up.

> Now I know that none of you among whom I have gone about preaching the kingdom will ever see me again. (Acts 20:25 TNIV)

Accordingly, around spring 57 we find him back in Jerusalem as planned (Acts 21:17). Then, famously, he is arrested and a chain of events follows that take him indeed to Rome in early 60—but as a prisoner rather than an evangelist. He does not get away, a free man again, until 62 or 63. And where did he go? To Spain, as announced? No, he never made it to Spain. There are no Spanish churches claiming Paul as founder.[29] Instead, contrary to his prediction of some six years before, he is next found back in *Ephesus*, where he has left Timothy, possibly for Epirus (1 Tim 1:3). Something significant happened between early 57 and 62 to change his mind.

Changes in His Letters

After Caesarea, Paul's pendulum temperament is no longer apparent in his letters. For instance, Hort in 1895 recognized in Ephesians that "the vehement moods of the earlier contests have subsided" and have been replaced by a "lofty calm." Hort ascribes this to a change within Paul's own mind, which he attributes to the "mellowing effect of years" and the "sense of dangers surmounted."[30]

I have argued elsewhere from considerations of Pauline chronology that Ephesians, Colossians, and Philemon, being the only prison epistles in which Paul indicates no prospect of a possible death sentence, were the product of his two years in Caesarea.[31] As any commentary will point out, the language and theology of the first two have become more elevated and abstract. There are novelties and differences of emphasis in matters of doctrine concerning marriage, the church, the apostolate, Christology, and so forth. Arguments rage as to whether differences as great as these could possibly be the work of the same man who wrote the undisputed earlier epistles such as Romans, which I date uncontroversially to early

---

29. Faint suggestions of a Spanish venture in the Fathers are almost certainly echoes of Rom 15. See Mosse, *Three Gospels*, chap. 11, annex A, "Did Paul Go to Spain?," 234–35.

30. Hort, *Prolegomena*, 152–53. On the authenticity of Ephesians see Mosse, *Three Gospels*, 216–19.

31. Contrast 2 Timothy and Philippians, both written from Rome c. 66, in which he recognizes a serious possibility of the death sentence. See Mosse, *Three Gospels*, 210–25 and 319–22. However, I have recently recognized that Paul's reference to "fellow-prisoners" (συναιχμαλώτους), Andronicus and Junia(s), in Rom 16:7 indicates a spell in prison before that letter was written in early 57. This will fit most easily into the "three years" spent in Ephesus recorded in Acts 20:31, which date to 52–55. However, I do not believe that any of the candidate letters Ephesians, Colossians, and Philemon was written at this time. Placing Ephesians before Romans is too high a price to pay.

57, shortly before the return to Jerusalem;[32] and Philippians, which I see as his last.[33]

Not least, the μυστήριον of God, which receives but three mentions in Paul's earlier letters,[34] now takes center stage,[35] with a new stress on the *principalities and powers* (ἀρχαὶ καὶ ἐξουσίαι)[36] to be found operative and indeed at war *in the heavenly realms* (ἐν τοῖς ἐπουρανίοις).[37] Paul is now thinking in terms of spiritual warfare on a cosmic level as never before.

Change of Evangelistic Strategy

Correspondingly, Paul has begun to aim higher in his missionary strategy. He appears to have acquired a new life goal. Beyond the business of founding and establishing churches, he is to preach to and, if possible, convert the Emperor. At that time the Christian Church and the Roman state presented no threat to each other. This could not last. Sooner or later there would be conflict—as happened when, after the Great Fire of Rome, Nero rapidly put the blame on the Christian Church and the persecutions began. There was everything to be gained by forestalling this if possible. So when finally put on trial before Festus in summer 59, he took his chance and used his Roman citizenship as a free passport into the Emperor's presence (Acts 25:12). Luke stresses that in the view of his judges, Festus and Herod Agrippa II, his appeal was unnecessary. Paul had done nothing worthy of death and could have been set free (Acts 26:31–32).[38] However, success in this jugular attack would have made the faith acceptable across the entire Empire, something that did not in fact happen until Constantine in 313.[39]

---

32. See Mitton, *Epistle to the Ephesians*, chaps. 2 and 3. For instance on pp. 9–10, he cites Sanday and Headlam's *International Critical Commentary on Romans*, "In the manner of style . . . Ephesians stands at the furthest possible remove from Romans."

33. See note 72.

34. 1 Cor 15:51; Rom 11:25; 16:25.

35. Eph 1:9; 3:3–4; 3:9; 5:32; 6:19; Col 1:26–27; 2:2; 4:3.

36. Eph 1:21; 3:10; 6:12; Col 1:16; 2:10–15. Hitherto we have only the isolated use of these two together at 1 Cor 15:24.

37. Eph 1:3–20; 2:6; 3:10; 6:12.

38. See also Acts 23:29; 25:25; 28:18.

39. This attempt to appear before Nero failed. There is no reason to believe that Paul was ever tried during his first detention in Rome (Acts 28:16–31; AD 60–62), there being no charge against him and no Jewish prosecutors to present it (Acts 28:21).

Comment

There do seem then to be converging indications that Paul underwent a considerable change to his inner life and temperament during his two years in a Caesarea jail, when he would have had no shortage of silence and solitude in which to wait upon God and be available to Him. Psychologically, this is not improbable.[40] It recalls the three solitary years in Arabia that followed his conversion, when he appears to have learned the content of the Christian gospel by direct revelation (Gal 1:16–18; most likely AD 34–36). The result in Caesarea was a major transformation that left him a man renewed, at peace with himself, *healed of his emotional extremes*, and ready for greater challenges—a healing for which he was not yet ready when he wrote 2 Cor 12. We look in vain for any manifestation of mood disorder in Paul's subsequent career, either in Acts or in his later letters.

So the many scholars who have concluded that several of his subsequent letters were written by a totally different man are right, but not as they believe: he *was* a different man. Granted, there is no one ancient text that declares this. I offer it under the terms of Occam's Razor, as a single hypothesis that is able to bring together, simplify, and explain a variety of hitherto seemingly disconnected phenomena about the apostle to the Gentiles.

I suggest then that this Caesarean transformation was the *culmination of a process of engagement with God*, traced so graphically by Dodd, which had been going on in his intellect in areas such as eschatology, the law, and the natural order ever since his conversion in 34 or 35 right up to the writing of 2 Corinthians. There is a coherence about this that suggests that in studying the mind of Paul we are actually observing the mind of God at work ("theology" indeed!). This process we might have

---

The show trial to which Luke's account has been building up for several chapters did not happen—this time. But Paul did not lose sight of his goal. The angel's promise that he would stand before Nero (Acts 27:23–24) stayed with him, and Luke on completing his work in 62 did not delete it. Paul considered it fulfilled not then but during his second and final Roman detention c. 66–67 (2 Tim 4:16–18), after which he saw his job as done (4:7). In the interim he reverted to peripatetic ministry at local church level, but not where he had originally intended.

40. See Maggie Ross's groundbreaking work *Silence* on the powerful effects of silence upon the inner life, as often urged in the Bible, which regularly speaks of "waiting on God" (as the older translations have it, in places like Ps 62:1 and Lam 3:25–28).

missed altogether without the well-worked chronology for which Robinson pleaded, and an accompanying grasp of human psychology.[41]

Unfortunately, in the decades that followed Robinson, scholarly interest in both of these fields was allowed to wane. Commentaries were written on Ephesians, for instance, in which the primary focus lay in source criticism of individual passages, while Paul himself receded into the shadows—sometimes being replaced by unknown imitators in the next century, non-persons, unknown to history and for whom a description of their mental and spiritual life and career history was not even attempted.

For reopening the study of the very human apostle himself in the light of modern psychology, breathing fresh life into him, we are very much in debt to Dormandy. The task now is to re-lay the groundwork relating to Paul's mind and career, in the hope of achieving a consensus from which we can then embark on a fresh appreciation of his epistles.

Let us now see how the same four competencies help us to establish the dates of Mark and the Book of Acts.

The Date of Mark

There are two clusters of dates offered today for Mark's Gospel. The first, and by far the more popular, relates to the death of Peter at the end of Nero's reign, and usually places Mark soon after it. I call these "late." The second, and very much the minority view today, places the writing of the Gospel in the reign of Claudius (41–54) or the later 50s. I call these "early." What ancient evidence has led to this dichotomy?

Most influential for the later date has been the survey of Irenaeus (c. 130–200) *Adversus Haereses* 3.1.1 reported in Greek in Eusebius' *Ecclesiastical History* V.viii.2–4:

---

41. So I question approaches like that of Pheme Perkins, who manages to insert an eight to fifteen year gap between Philemon (c. 54–55) and Colossians (c. 62–70), which were however manifestly sent on the same journey to the same *Colossae*, where dwelt the same *Archippus*, with the bearer accompanied by the same *Onesimus*, while the same signatories *Paul* and *Timothy* have with them the same *Mark, Aristarchus, Demas,* and *Luke*! Perkins, *Reading the New Testament*, 7–8. However, Colossae was by all accounts destroyed by the same Lycus Valley earthquake that as she rightly notes destroyed Laodicea in 60—after which it is not clear why anyone would want to send a letter there.

> Matthew composed his Gospel among the Hebrews in their own language, while Peter and Paul proclaimed the Gospel in Rome and founded the community. After their death (ἔξοδος)⁴² Mark, the disciple and interpreter of Peter, transmitted (παραδέδωκεν) to us in written form the things that were being preached (κηρυσσόμενα) by Peter. And Luke, who was Paul's follower, set down in a book the gospel which was being preached (κηρυσσόμενον) by him. Then John, the Lord's disciple, who had reclined on his breast, himself produced the Gospel when he was staying in Ephesus, in the province of Asia.

Even today, this passage is still seen by many as evidence that Mark wrote after the deaths of Peter and Paul (c. 66–67).⁴³ However, this view was decisively refuted in what is still the definitive commentary by John Chapman in 1905, often overlooked today.⁴⁴ By taking into account the Latin version of this text, which supplies the context that Eusebius has not quoted, Chapman demonstrates that so far from attempting to date Matthew, Mark, and Luke, Irenaeus is explaining how the preaching of the four apostles Matthew, Peter, Paul, and John was *transmitted* (παραδέδωκεν, not ἔγραψεν) to later generations in writing. Matthew and John wrote for themselves. But "the preaching of Peter has been preserved to us *after* his death by being written down [by Mark] *before* his death."⁴⁵ This is made evident by the continuous present participle (κηρυσσόμενα). And similarly with Paul and Luke, with their use of the participle (κηρυσσόμενον). "[T]here is no attempt to give any dates at all. The most that can be said is that all three Synoptists were thought by Irenaeus to have written before the death of St. Peter and St. Paul,"⁴⁶ while John wrote after Matthew, Mark, and Luke.

I know of no scholar who has read Chapman and not been persuaded by him. Most significantly, he persuaded no less an authority than Harnack.⁴⁷ To my mind this classic article of his constitutes one of the foundations of the subject such as I described above. It is to be lamented that both Chapman and Harnack are not more widely read today.

---

42. The suggestion that ἔξοδος at this point means "departure from Rome" is, I believe, an unnecessary confusion. See Chapman, "St. Irenaeus," 564.
43. For references see Mosse, *Three Gospels*, 227–28.
44. Chapman, "St. Irenaeus," 563–69.
45. Chapman, "St. Irenaeus," 567.
46. Chapman, "St. Irenaeus," 567.
47. Harnack, *Date of the Acts*, 130.

The only other notable passage from the Fathers claimed in support of the view that Mark wrote after Peter's death is the so-called anti-Marcionite (or Old Latin) Prologue to Mark, which reads:

> Mark declared, who is called "stump-fingered" (*colobodactylus*) because he had short fingers in comparison with the size of the rest of his body. He was Peter's interpreter. After the death (*excessionem*) of Peter himself he wrote down (*descripsit*) this same gospel in the regions of Italy.

Just what is meant by *descripsit*? *Writing* a gospel "in the regions of Italy" sounds a little curious, where "passed on" or "transmitted" would seem more natural. Further, a variant edition of the anti-Marcionite Prologue replaces *excessionem*, translated "death" above, by *discessum*, "departure" (from Rome). This also offers one of a variety of reports—such as Clement of Alexandria (c. 150–210), in his *Outlines*[48]—about Peter's reaction to the Gospel that Mark had written in Rome. Origen tells us that Mark wrote "as Peter instructed him,"[49] which seems to be more than is warranted. However apocryphal some of these may have been, *they could not have gained currency had it been known that Peter had died before Mark wrote.*

Further, Eusebius *EH* II.xvi.1 tells us that Mark went to Egypt with the Gospel he had already written, and founded churches in Alexandria. *EH* II.xxiv.1 reports that in the eighth year of Nero (62) Annianus was the first to succeed him there.[50] So he must have gone to Egypt with his written Gospel some years before 62; Eusebius' *Chronicle* gives the year as 43, which would seem to be too early. But whatever the year, it unquestionably precedes Peter's death.

All of this tells against taking the basic anti-Marcionite Prologue at face value. More probably, the author had access to a stream of tradition similar to that of Irenaeus (the relative dates are still disputed), in which a single word had altered or been misunderstood in the retelling (there are precedents). That the author is not merely paraphrasing Irenaeus is shown by *colobodactylus*, which clearly comes from another source.

---

48. Preserved in Eusebius, *Ecclesiastical History,* VI.xiv.5–7; cf. II.xv.1–2, which claims the support of Papias.

49. Cited in Eusebius *EH* VI.xxv.5.

50. Hengel, *Studies,* 6, sees in this a death notice for Mark. I doubt this. On the evidence of 2 Tim 4:11, which I accept as genuine, Mark was still alive in 65–66.

So far we have no strong ancient evidence that Mark wrote after Peter's death, and some significant indications to the contrary. Do we have any positive evidence to show he wrote before it?

We do indeed. In a well-researched section on events in the reign of Claudius, *EH* II.viii–xix, for which he claims among his sources Clement of Alexandria, Josephus, Justin Martyr, Irenaeus, Papias, and Philo of Alexandria, Eusebius tells us how Peter came to Rome and encountered Simon Magus (the sorcerer of Acts 8:4–24)[51] and the Jewish philosopher Philo. Within this, he has seamlessly embedded Clement's account,[52] endorsed by Papias, of how Mark came to write his Gospel at the behest of Peter's Roman hearers, who urgently wanted a written record of his preaching, in the light it would seem of Peter's imminent or recent departure. This passage is *prima facie* evidence for an early date for Mark, between 41 and 54, but seldom quoted by believers in a late date.[53] Its authenticity is not lightly to be impugned. For even if the encounters with Simon Magus and Philo (who is believed to have died c. 45–50) were apocryphal, they could hardly have gained credibility if the visit of Peter to which they are attached had never happened.

Further, near the end of this section on Claudius, Eusebius goes on to relate how "at this time . . . Claudius banished the Jews from Rome, and Aquila and Priscilla, with the other Jews, left Rome and came into Asia."[54]

This took place in 49, thereby reducing the upper limit for the writing of Mark. If he and Peter had arrived in Rome and sought to minister after that date, they would have been arrested.

How does this fit into what we know of the lives of Peter and Mark? The jigsaw was first assembled by Edmundson[55] in 1913, but not widely known until he was rediscovered by Robinson[56] in 1976. Briefly, in 42 Peter fled persecution in Jerusalem to "another place" (Acts 12:17). This may have been Caesarea, where he had friends in the household of Cor-

---

51. Eusebius *EH* II.xiv.6–xv.1. For references supporting this tradition see Ellis, *Making of the New Testament*, 365n42.

52. Eusebius *EH* II.xv.1–2, a rewording of Clement's original account reported in Eusebius *EH* VI.xiv.5–7. Eusebius probably also used Clement, *Outlines*, on 1 Pet 5:13, which tells very clearly how Mark wrote his Gospel in Rome at the request of Caesar's knights to enable them to commit to memory Peter's preaching to them there.

53. Hengel, below, is a striking exception.

54. Eusebius, *EH* II.xviii.9, ET Lake; cf. Acts 18:2; Suetonius, *Claudius*, 25.

55. Edmundson, *Church in Rome*, followed by Robinson, *Redating*, and others including Wenham, *Redating*.

56. Robinson, *Redating*.

nelius. Soon after, we find him in Antioch as related in Jerome's version of Eusebius' *Chronicle* for that year, which reads,

> Peter the Apostle . . . when he had first founded the Antiochean Church, is sent to Rome, where as bishop (*episcopus*) of the same city he continues preaching the gospel for twenty-five years.[57]

Jerome himself adds elsewhere the detail that Peter arrived in Rome in the second year of Claudius (42), that is, twenty-five years before Peter's death in the "last year" of Nero (67).[58]

By now we have reduced our bracket for the writing of Mark to 42–49. With the death of Herod Agrippa I in 44, it is now safe for Peter to return to Jerusalem, where we find Mark in 46 (Acts 12:25). If Mark remained in Rome to write his Gospel (apparently in the absence of Peter), Edmundson's estimate of 45 for that event looks very reasonable.[59] This has been confirmed independently by Crossley's detailed analysis of the attitudes to the Torah (Jewish Law) within Mark, which suggests a date *between the mid to late 30s and the mid 40s*.[60]

The association between Mark, Peter, and Rome has been challenged by modern scholars but is robust and emphatically survives the challenge. The German historian Eduard Meyer, one of the greatest ancient historians of all time, a rationalist and no card-carrying Christian believer, after examining Mark's Gospel, commented as follows:

> The conclusion we have won is of the highest importance. It is evident that for our history of Jesus we have by no means to reckon merely with representations of the second, sub-apostolic, generation, but are taken back far behind that into the midst of the first generation who personally had known him intimately (*genau*) and still preserved a lively recollection of him; and that these old recollections lie under our eyes in manifold forms. There is no ground at all for refusing to accept these oldest traditions as historically trustworthy in all essentials, and in their chronological ordering of the history.[61]

57. Edmundson, *Church in Rome*, 70, prefers "overseer" to 'bishop." This need not have required his continuous presence (see Acts 15:36, *episkepsōmetha*, which implies a traveling oversight).

58. Jerome, *de Viris Illustribus*, 1.

59. Edmundson, *Church in Rome*, 68.

60. Crossley, *Date of Mark's Gospel*, 208.

61. Meyer, *Ursprung und Anfänge*, quoted in translation by Gore, *Jesus of Nazareth*, 191.

Bishop Gore, who quotes this, describing Meyer in 1929 as "the greatest living authority on the history of antiquity as a whole," goes on to summarize:

> Thus in particular Meyer claims that we must accept as trustworthy the tradition of Papias . . . that Mark was the author of the second Gospel and that he had been the companion and interpreter (*Dolmetscher*) of Peter in his missionary journeys, so that it is obvious that "the foundation of our tradition goes back to Peter, and that Mark in a great part of his Gospel was reproducing Peter's own memories as to how things happened at the beginning, as Peter gave them to his converts."[62]

Mark 13:2, in which Jesus prophecies the destruction of the Temple, which happened in 70, gives us no help in dating the book. Jesus was just reporting what to him was patently obvious. That—as He might have concluded from the history of his people recorded in the Jewish Scriptures[63]—is the way the world is, and Jesus was astute enough to know it.

What is at stake here? First, if we are right then we can set aside the clichés to be found in almost any New Testament commentary, that our first written records of Jesus' ministry did not emerge until several decades after the resurrection; and that Paul was writing his epistles and indeed dead before any of the gospels was penned. Paul's First Letter to the Thessalonians was written around spring 50, five years after we have dated Mark.

Second, I have found no believer in a late Mark who is prepared to face up to its inevitable consequence: that not one of the Roman Christians who perished under Nero had ever seen even one single page of our canonical gospels. Whatever kept them going and held them together? Indeed, neither Peter nor Paul saw a gospel either, not even Luke's.

Third, the later we date our gospels, the less we can trust them to give an accurate picture of Jesus. The modern fashion for late dates is significantly at variance with the consensus that emerged from antiquity into the middle ages. According to the Prologue to Theophylact's *Commentary on the Gospels*, which is still highly regarded,[64] Matthew wrote

---

62. Gore, *Jesus of Nazareth*, 191–92.

63. See for instance 1 Kgs 9:1–9 where Solomon is given the terms under which he and his descendants would be allowed the continued use of the (first) Temple. A Jew of Jesus' day might well have seen in the destruction of the Temple by the Babylonians in 586 BC a fulfillment of God's word to Solomon (Jer 52).

64. Theophylact of Ohrid was born *c.*1050 and died after 1107. He had no

eight years after the Ascension (41), Mark after ten (43), Luke after fifteen (48), and John after thirty-two years (65). The ancients would doubtless have been mystified by the modern insistence upon late dates in defiance of all they have bequeathed to us.

The Date of Acts

Like Mark, there are early (c. 62 or later 60s) and late (80 onwards) dates for the Book of Acts. 62 is advocated here as being the year at which the narrative ends. Luke has brought it up to date, and stopped. Supporters of late dates today tend to argue from a prior belief in a late date for Mark, followed by a suitable interval to allow for the writing of Luke who unquestionably used Mark, and then went on to write Acts.

Whereas there is a plethora of information in the Fathers relating to the writing of Mark, for Acts there is less, so that we have to make more use of our knowledge of history. Our first ports of call are therefore the ancient historians. There are several who could be adduced to demonstrate not just the essential historicity of Acts, but also a detailed accuracy that is hard to account for in a document that had been written decades after its narrative ended. Among the most eminent is the Roman historian Sherwin-White:

> For Acts the confirmation of historicity is overwhelming. Yet Acts is, in simple terms and judged externally, no less of a propaganda narrative than the Gospels, liable to similar distortions. But any attempt to reject its basic historicity even in matters of detail must now appear absurd. Roman historians have long taken it for granted.[65]

Or one could quote Hemer on the "immediacy" of the later chapters of Acts,

> which are marked in a special degree by the apparently unreflective reproduction of insignificant details, a feature which reaches its apogee in the voyage narrative of Acts 27–28.... No writing up of a "typical" voyage scene could have embodied this natural integration.[66]

---

knowledge of Q.

65. Sherwin-White, *Roman Society*, 189.

66. Hemer, *Book of Acts*, 388. This book now surely serves as a baseline for all subsequent historical studies of Acts.

Or again we have the highly nuanced and refreshing account of the chronologist Robert B. Moberly, who presents a whole battery of details indicating the very closeness in time of the writing of the text to the events described.[67] For instance, references to Nero appear to indicate that he is still alive. Though he was universally damned after his death and spoken of as "Nero" by Pliny the Elder, Josephus, Martial, Juvenal, Tacitus, Suetonius, and others, rather than as "Caesar," "Acts had a habit of referring to Nero vividly, politely, hopefully, deferentially as 'Caesar'"[68] (Acts 25:8, 10–12, 21; 26:32; 27:24; 28:19). This would have been proper and natural if Nero were still alive, and unlikely if he were dead and universally vilified. It would incidentally indicate "in the present reign": after his death we would expect him to be called by name at least once.

Again, Moberly points out that Gallio (Lucius Annaeus Gallio, Acts 18:12–17, lesser known elder brother of the Stoic philosopher and statesman Seneca) and Felix (Marcus Antonius Felix, 24:1–27, brother of the prominent and wealthy Pallas), though readily recognizable under these familiar designations in Rome during the early 60s, would scarcely be household names among the Eastern Christians of Antioch or Ephesus during the Flavian decades.[69]

Much hangs on our understanding of the final verses (28:30–1). What happened next? Was this Paul's final detention, followed by his trial and death, as we are often told, or was he released with or without a trial? One difficulty is that taken on their own these verses give no indication that they refer to a *detention* at all. We see Paul preaching the kingdom in his own rented house "with all boldness and without hindrance" (TNIV). This is no way to describe a captivity! Eusebius interprets Acts in the same way:

> Luke also, who committed the Acts of the Apostles to writing, finished his narrative at this point by the statement that Paul spent two whole years (διετίαν) in Rome *in freedom* (ἄνετον), and preached the word of God *without hindrance* (ἀκωλύτως).[70]

In fact he records (*EH* II.xxii) two visits of Paul to Rome, and the writing of 2 Timothy during the captivity, which was the second, when

---

67. Moberly, "When Was Acts Planned?" I have presented a composite case in Mosse, *Three Gospels*, chap. 12, "Date of Acts."

68. Moberly, "When Was Acts Planned?," 8–9.

69. Moberly, "When Was Acts Planned?," 17–18.

70. Eusebius *EH* II.xxii.1.

Nero was more ferocious than at first. He is certain that Paul's martyrdom "was not accomplished during the sojourn [ἐπιδημίαν, not a word for a captivity] in Rome which Luke describes."[71] But he only holds it probable (εἰκότως) that Acts was written during the second stay, i.e., he does not claim to know. So Eusebius believes in an early date for Acts; I suggest he has chosen the wrong visit to Rome.

Of the five Captivity Epistles (Ephesians, Philippians, Colossians, 2 Timothy, and Philemon), only Philippians and 2 Timothy give any indication that Paul is facing a capital charge. They cannot therefore have been written during the two year sojourn of Acts 28:30, since Luke, as already noted, stresses that in Roman eyes he had done absolutely nothing worthy of death. This supports Eusebius' belief that there were *two* stays in Rome: the first recorded here at the end of Acts, which I believe produced none of our extant epistles; and the second reflected in 2 Timothy and Philippians, in which he is definitely facing a possible death sentence and putting a brave face on it,[72] and which we may associate with the strong tradition that he was executed in the "last year" of Nero, c. 67. *So Paul was released at some time during his first visit.*

When and why was he released? Crucially, no Jewish prosecutors had arrived from Jerusalem (Acts 28:21). Since Paul had committed no offence against Roman law, there was no case against him, and with no prosecutors there could therefore be no grand trial. There was no point in tying up a valuable Roman soldier (28:16) indefinitely to guard an innocent man. So (I propose) Paul was set free, not *after* the two year period as commonly assumed, but *before* it. Luke (mistakenly, as it turned out), seems to have thought this would be obvious to his readers. Whether or not there was a trial of any kind is unclear.[73]

If, therefore, we have convicted Luke on a minor charge of negligence, we have exculpated him from the far more serious and more frequent one of leaving us in mid-air, giving us no indication at all of Paul's fate at the end of the supposed first Roman captivity—was he tried or not, found guilty or not, executed or not, set free or not? This omission would

---

71. Eusebius *EH* II.xxii.7.

72. 2 Tim 4:6–8; Phil 1:20–24; 2:17; 3:10–11. It appears that 2 Timothy came first, since at 4:11 he asks Timothy to come to him; by Phil 1:1 Timothy has arrived.

73. However, Eusebius *EH* II.xxii.2 reports a tradition (λογός) that Paul had to defend himself on his first Roman visit (is this an echo of 2 Tim 4:16?), and states that probably (εἰκός) Nero was more lenient on his first defence (*EH* II.xxii.8). So he believes in two trials, but isn't sure.

be a damning indictment of a very capable historian, and has prompted all kinds of speculation about the critical incompleteness of Acts. But if the two years were spent in *freedom*, no such charge applies. Luke has neatly rounded off his book with the equivalent of "and they lived happily ever after." He's not going to carry on.

Eusebius does, however. As he tells us (*EH* II.xxii.2), Paul returned once more to the mission field, and is to be found in the East as documented in the Pastoral Epistles, 1 and 2 Timothy, and Titus,[74] particularly tackling problems in Ephesus, where he had long been expecting trouble (Acts 20:29–31).

From a literary point of view, the end of Acts is nevertheless a significant anticlimax. After taking several chapters to build up his narrative towards a *dramatic show trial* before the Emperor such as Luke clearly expected (as did even the angel of 27:23–24), he is disappointed at the end. If there was a hearing at all, it was no show trial before the Emperor. This has been likened to a gospel narrative that ended before the crucifixion. Something has not gone according to plan. Luke, if concluding his book in 62, has been disappointed in his hope, but does not see fit to rewrite his earlier narrative.[75] That is understandable in someone so scrupulous. But why would a later writer, who had not already penned the preceding narrative, deliberately build in such a crescendo only to disappoint us? This would be a dramatic folly of the first order. Why indeed would anyone in, say, 85, seeking to write a history of the early church, quite unnecessarily create such a literary disaster when under no compulsion to do so?

Again, why, writing after 70, would he stop at 62, knowing that Paul had some five or so years to run? Why would he have omitted the Great Fire of Rome in 64 and the ensuing Neronian persecutions that resulted in the martyrdoms of Peter and Paul, and the crisis of the church that followed (to which, I suggest, Hebrews bears witness)? Why omit the Jewish War of 66–70, ending in the catastrophic fall of Jerusalem in 70—the same Jerusalem that paid so great a part in the first half of his book, getting fifty mentions?

---

74. On the authenticity of the Pastoral Epistles see Mosse, *Three Gospels*, chap. 11, annex B.

75. In fact, Paul did get the show trial that Luke expected and the angel promised, but not until his next appearance in Rome (2 Tim 4:16–7), and it did not go the way Luke had hoped. But Paul insists that he has finished his appointed course (4:7), which for him included appearing before Nero.

In fact the first critical year for dating Acts is not 70 at all but 64, the year of the Great Fire of Rome, just after the narrative of Acts ends in 62. Until that time, as Acts demonstrates repeatedly, relations between the Christian Church and the Roman State had been thoroughly cordial. The Church was treated as a minor Jewish sect with all the deference that was traditionally granted to the Jews. Paul's Roman citizenship was his trump card, and he played it frequently. So we find the Roman authorities regularly rescuing him from the hands of the Jewish authorities who were responsible for all the persecutions described in Acts.

But 64 was a watershed. Nero wanted a scapegoat for the fire, and he wanted one fast.[76] So the Christians got the blame, and from then on for a very long time it was not safe to be a Christian in the Roman Empire. Paul's Roman citizenship did him little good when he was later arrested in (probably) Ephesus, c. 66. Yet not a shadow of this appears in Acts, in which the Roman presence was uniformly benign. Roman governors, officials, and centurions alike get a good press. Paul's evident expectation of a fair hearing by Nero in Luke's account owes nothing to that Emperor's posthumous reputation, when he was universally damned. Equally, there has been no rewriting to correct Paul's prediction that the Ephesians would never see him again (Acts 20:25). Yet, as is evident from the Pastoral Epistles, Paul did indeed return to Ephesus on leaving Rome in 62 or 63. Had Acts been written after Paul's death it would scarcely have included the falsified prediction.

What is at stake here? First, one of the main reasons for rejecting the Pastoral Epistles is that they find no context in Luke's history. But if Paul left Rome and lived another five years, we are compelled to reopen the question of their authenticity. And when we do so, we must remember the point made above, that contrasts, innovations of thought, and differences of style are not in themselves proof of a different author. Paul was a very unusual man who had, I have suggested, undergone a very unusual transformation.

We should also take account another point, made by E. Earle Ellis. He says that the assumption is regularly made that Paul either penned or dictated his letters word for word. On this assumption, using a few letters as touchstone, certain others are rejected. This is now recognized as mistaken in several important respects.

---

76. I owe this point to Dr. Barbara Levick, who thus rejects the modern notion, deriving from Edmundson, *Church in Rome*, 125-33, that the Roman persecutions began in 65.

1) Paul wrote his letters through secretaries who, in accordance with practice of the time, exercised a variable degree of freedom in their composition. Also, 2) for a number of letters he had co-senders who exercised some influence and, in one or two instances may have been co-authors of the letter. Consequently, vocabulary, idiom, and theological expression can no longer be used in any precise way to determine Pauline authorship of the letters ascribed to him.[77]

Second, the early dates for Mark and Acts that we have found by independent routes dovetail extremely well together. Since almost no one doubts that Acts was preceded by Luke, and Luke by Mark, we can place these three works very coherently between 45 and 62. Those who believe as I do that Luke made use of Matthew, and (with few dissenters) that Matthew also used Mark, can place all three Synoptics in this bracket.

We now consider how four different scholars have arrived at dates for Mark and Acts.

Raymond E. Brown

Consider now the position adopted by Raymond Brown in his highly regarded *Introduction to the New Testament*.[78] Professor Brown was extremely eminent in his field and without doubt represents mainstream thinking in New Testament scholarship today. On the date of Mark, he begins, "Among those who give credence to the Papias tradition,[79] the usual understanding is that Mark wrote just before or just after Peter's death and thus in the mid- or late 60s."[80]

Why is the "usual understanding" usual? Where is the historical evidence connecting in time the writing of Mark and the death of Peter? He does not tell us. After summarizing various scholars' conflicting opinions about the internal evidence, none of which constitute evidence themselves, he writes, tellingly, "If Mark was used independently by both Matt and Luke and they were written in the 80s or early 90s, as most scholars believe, a date beyond 75 seems unlikely."[81]

---

77. Ellis, *Pauline Theology*, 104.
78. Brown, *Introduction*.
79. Papias, quoting the ancient John, recorded in Eusebius, *EH* III.xxxix.15–6.
80. Brown, *Introduction*, 163.
81. Brown, *Introduction*, 164.

DOING NEW TESTAMENT HISTORY: A BASELINE FOR STUDIES 25

This is the only external evidence he provides, and after dismissing a claim about a supposed early fragment found at Qumran, he concludes, "Therefore, *there is widespread scholarly agreement that Mark was written in the late 60s or just after 70.*"[82]

Conversely, on the date of Luke/Acts, he writes, "That Luke used Mark is most plausible from internal evidence; and if Mark is to be dated in the period 68–73, *a date earlier than 80 for Luke is unlikely.*"[83]

So in terms of actual evidence presented, his argument is circular: he dates Mark by Luke/Acts and Luke/Acts by Mark. The late dates for Mark and Acts that he prefers stand or fall together. But which? Are there any considerations known to Brown that might help us to decide? The answer is yes. In a footnote to his section on dating Mark, he admits:

> The failure of NT works to make specific and detailed mention of the destruction of Jerusalem and the Temple is very hard to explain. J. A. T. Robinson, *Redating the New Testament* (London: SCM, 1976), has used this factor entirely too simply to date most of the NT before 70; *but we should not pretend to have a satisfactory answer.*[84]

So there we have it. There is a challenge to his late dates of which Brown is fully aware, and to which he knows no answer. So he relegates it to a footnote. When, some 90 pages on, he comes to date Luke/Acts, he repeats the caveat, again in a footnote:

> Nevertheless, we admit that the absence of an indisputable, clear, specific Gospel (or, indeed, NT) reference to the destruction of the Temple as having taken place remains a problem, since it should have had an enormous impact on Christians.[85]

So much for what he tells us. What does he not tell us? Beyond his passing reference to Papias, Brown makes no appeal to the *wealth of historical information about the origins of that Gospel*, which we have from the Early Fathers, and which, as we have seen, points strongly to an early Mark, while Peter was very much alive. Clearly this is something with which he does not wish to trouble his readers. Why? Perhaps because,

---

82. Brown, *Introduction*, 164 (emphasis original).
83. Brown, *Introduction*, 273 (emphasis original).
84. Brown, *Introduction*, 163n93 (concluding emphasis added).
85. Brown, *Introduction*, 273n102.

as Miss Prism cautioned of the fall of the rupee, "It is somewhat too sensational."

In consequence *Brown's case for late dates of Mark and Acts would be rejected after a moment's consideration by any court in the land.*

What else could he have done? In the words of Mary Douglas,

> There are several ways of treating anomalies. Negatively, we can ignore, just not perceive them, or perceiving we can condemn. Positively, we can deliberately confront the anomaly and try to create a new pattern of reality in which it has a place.[86]

Sadly, by simply ignoring the contrary data, Brown has passed up a valuable opportunity.

W. G. Kümmel

W. G. Kümmel, in his *Introduction to the New Testament*, develops his case for dating Mark, Luke, and Acts as follows.

1. On the origins of Mark he writes,

> That Papias asserts that Mark was written in Rome can be deduced from Eusebius only with great uncertainty (HE II.15.2), but Clement of Alexandria (Eus., HE VI.14.6) unambiguously asserts this tradition.[87]

However, he goes on,

> An early origin is improbable, because the development of the gospel tradition has already progressed far,[88] and Mark 13 shows traces of the threatening nearness of the Jewish war. Most scholars assign a date in the years 64–70, since the destruction of Jerusalem in the year 70 is mentioned not unambiguously, but some scholars consider a date after 70 more likely for the composition.... Since no overwhelming argument for the years before or after 70 can be adduced, we must content ourselves with saying that Mark was written ca. 70.[89]

---

86. Douglas, *Natural Symbols*, 38. Quoted in Fitzpatrick, *Fall and the Ascent*, 54.

87. Kümmel, *Introduction*, 97.

88. How far is "far"? How do you measure this by any canon beyond pure subjective guesswork? What control parallels enable us to assess it?

89. Kümmel, *Introduction*, 98.

No overwhelming argument? Is he serious? What is not overwhelming about Eusebius's long, continuous and well-researched section in *EH* II—whether or not it derives from Papias—describing in context how Mark in Rome came to write his Gospel, which, although Kümmel does not tell us, he repeatedly locates *in the reign of Claudius*?[90] As we have seen, this constitutes *prima facie* evidence of a very early date for Mark which needs to be either challenged or accepted. (Perhaps by "overwhelming" Kümmel meant "convenient." For whatever reason, like Brown after him, he did not find it convenient to pass on to his readers the fruits of Eusebius's research on this point.)

Clearly at this stage Kümmel does not believe that Mark 13 here represents the words of Jesus (to suggest otherwise would destroy the case for 64–70, which assumes Jesus could not himself have predicted the destruction of Jerusalem). Later on, discussing the date of Luke, he changes his mind:

> A prediction by Jesus of judgment on Jerusalem according to Mark 13:2 par. Luke 13:34f must be regarded as historical.[91]

So does this prediction in Mark represent the historical words of Jesus or not? Kümmel is unable to make up his mind. But the answer is critical for his date of Mark.

2. In dating Luke, he rejects the common belief that Luke and Acts were written in the late sixties:

> This date is scarcely compatible with Luke 1:1–4, however, since by the year 60 "many" gospel writings could not have been in existence, including Mark.[92]

So his date for Luke is going to lean heavily on his previous dating of Mark, itself highly fragile, to c. 70. He confirms this by contrasting Luke's treatment of the fall of Jerusalem with Mark's, which as we have seen has now become the historical words of Jesus. So accurate is the prediction in Luke, he maintains, that it can only have been a prophecy *ex eventu*. On this rests his dating of Luke to "between 70 and 90."[93]

---

90. Eusebius *EH* II. xiii.3, xiv.6 etc.

91. Kümmel, *Introduction*, 150.

92. Kümmel, *Introduction*, 150. At this point Kümmel has clearly forgotten his declared belief in Q, which he believes could have been completed by 50 (p. 71). As elsewhere, he adjusts his arguments to suit the current point at issue.

93. Kümmel, *Introduction*, 151.

As has been pointed out by others before me, the unspoken premise here that any accurate recorded prophecy must necessarily be *post eventum* is outrageous and provides no basis whatsoever for historical analysis. It is an intrusion of his personal philosophy. Such a view has been refuted succinctly by Austin Farrer who pointed out deftly that it leads to the "surprising joint conclusion (a) that people sometimes prophesy the future event; (b) that they are never right."[94]

3. Kümmel accepts the received view that Luke and Acts shared a common authorship. Under Luke he writes, "They undoubtedly belong together in language, style, and theological position."[95]

But under Acts:

> Since Acts . . . must have been written later than Luke, which was written after 70 . . . it could not have been written before 80; linguistic differences require a certain time lapse between the two writings by the same author. The attempts to assign the production of Acts to before the death of Paul are accordingly untenable. . . . The most likely assumption, therefore, is a date for Acts between 80 and 90, but a date between 90 and 100 is not excluded.[96]

This is a remarkable conclusion to draw from such astonishingly flimsy evidence. Any junior barrister of but six months' standing would have a field day here. Are Luke and Acts linguistically similar or are they linguistically dissimilar? In what respects? How can they be similar enough to guarantee common authorship, yet too dissimilar to have been written with less than ten years between them? Kümmel is trying to have it both ways. What examples illustrate this curious similarity/dissimilarity (none are suggested)? How does he manage to quantify this gap as approaching ten years instead of, say, five or twenty? Where has this method been used before, and with what success? *What indeed distinguishes it from pure guesswork?* It is hard to resist the impression that Kümmel is making up his arguments as he goes along, with no particular concern for consistency within his own document. (In one hundred years' time, will scholars propose multiple authorship for Kümmel's work? That is, the standard assumption that inconsistencies, apparent conflicts and changes of style within a single body of work demand that we postulate multiple

---

94. Farrer, *Study in St. Mark*, 358-59.
95. Kümmel, *Introduction*, 147.
96. Kümmel, *Introduction*, 188.

authorship—such as is commonly the fate of Paul—fails when we apply it to a case where we already know the answer.)

Martin Hengel

Very different is the late Martin Hengel's account of the origins of Mark in his *Studies in the Gospel of Mark*. In the section on "the tradition of the early church,"[97] he gives an excellent summary of the testimony of the Early Fathers on the writing of Mark's Gospel. His first two witnesses are Irenaeus and the anti-Marcionite Prologue, from both of whom he derives a date for Mark after the death of Peter. He sees these as representing the oldest and most reliable tradition. He goes on to discuss in some detail several different sources, starting with Clement of Alexandria at the end of the second century, who report what Hengel sees as the later tradition, that Mark wrote in Peter's lifetime in the reign of Claudius.

However, Hengel shows no knowledge of Chapman's convincing reinterpretation of Irenaeus discussed above. Without Irenaeus, Hengel's only support for a late Mark is the anti-Marcionite Prologue, which as we have seen is hardly strong enough to carry the weight placed upon it. *Every other source he cites tells in favor of an early Mark.* He is absolutely candid about the evidence for a Claudian Mark and the implications of this. This leaves him in a quandary. So—breathtakingly—he abandons the evidence of the Fathers altogether and pursues his case by examining the internal evidence on its own, centering on the relationship between Mark 13 and the politics of the era of the fall of Jerusalem. Finally he opts for the year 69.[98]

E. Earle Ellis

E. Earle Ellis, in his appendix on "The Date and Provenance of Mark's Gospel,"[99] has provided us with a master class in what Robinson, quoted above, called a "serious wrestling with the external or internal evidence for the dating of individual books." He accepts Chapman's interpretation of Irenaeus, affirming that "there are no patristic witnesses that date the

---

97. Hengel, *Studies*, 2–6.
98. Hengel, *Studies*, 28.
99. Ellis, *Making of the New Testament*, appendix 2.

origin of Mark's Gospel after Peter's death."[100] He accepts also the tradition in Eusebius and elsewhere that Peter opposed Simon Magus in Rome in the reign of Claudius,[101] dating the visit to the *end* of the reign, in 53–54. He accepts also Eusebius's account of how the Roman Church begged Mark to write them a record of Peter's preaching. But he rejects the implication, made explicit by Clement,[102] that Mark actually wrote it there and then. Instead he interjects a visit to Caesarea in 55–58, placing the writing of the gospel there. Then "in the mid-sixties [Mark] delivered it to churches in Italy."[103]

Against this I would urge:

1. Ellis underestimates the importance of Claudius's expulsion of "the Jews" from Rome in 49, which reverberates in Suetonius (*Claudius* 24.4), Eusebius (*EH* II.xviii.9), and in Acts 18:2, where Aquila and Priscilla are said to be among those exiled. Eusebius implies that it happened *after* the ministry of Peter and Mark. This suggests that the Roman visit took place *early* in Claudius's reign, or Peter and Mark would have been arrested at passport control. Slight confirmation of this is to be found in Eusebius' tradition that "Philo came to Rome in the time of Claudius to speak to Peter":[104] Philo is believed to have died by 50 at the latest. If this is correct it would also tell against Ellis.[105] It is in turn supported by the other traditions discussed above that Peter arrived in Rome in 42.

2. The interjection of a hiatus of some ten years between the Romans' request and its fulfillment, besides being intrinsically implausible does considerable violence to the text of Eusebius. The most natural reading of his account is that the writing of the Gospel followed directly on the request.

3. Ellis sees in Paul's delaying his first visit to Rome so as to avoid "building on another's foundation" (Rom 15:20) a possible reference to Peter.[106] This very credible idea has been inherited from

---

100. Ellis, *Making of the New Testament*, 365.
101. Ellis, *Making of the New Testament*, 365 and n. 42.
102. Clement, *Outlines* on 1 Pet 5:13.
103. Ellis, *Making of the New Testament*, 375.
104. Eusebius *EH* II.xvii.1.
105. However, on the face of it, Eusebius *EH* II.xvi–xvii suggests Philo may have lived a bit longer.
106. Ellis, *Making of the New Testament*, 367.

Edmundson, who argues that Peter is the only candidate of sufficient stature for such a compliment.[107] Given the uncontroversial date for Romans as (early) 57 this makes considerable sense on Edmundson's dating for Peter's first visit to Rome to 42–45; it makes very little sense on Ellis's date for that visit as c. 53–54: Paul has scarcely tarried at all. Yet in the interval since its founding and Paul's letter, the Roman Church had grown so much that their faith was "being reported all over the world" (Rom 1:8).[108] The longer interval is much more credible.

4. Given the explicit statement of Clement in his *Outlines* that Mark wrote in Rome, which supports the natural reading of Eusebius, the burden of proof lies upon those who would reject this. No ancient writer that I know of connects the writing of Mark to Caesarea.

5. Why did he need to go to Caesarea anyway? The obvious way to respond to such a request would be to write it there and then for the purpose for which it was requested—to enable the Roman Church to remember the preaching of the departing Peter, with which he was wholly familiar. To insert a ten year gap between request and delivery was hardly a gracious or helpful response! They would have been grateful for it rather earlier.

6. Ellis's account offers no space in Mark's life for a ministry in Alexandria.[109]

7. Ellis does not consider the implications of Mark's delivering his Gospel to Rome "in the mid-sixties"—that is, at the height of the Neronian persecutions. That would be a tale of heroism in itself. There is no dovetailing here.

In all, the Caesarea hypothesis conflicts with the patristic evidence and does violence to the natural reading of our texts. It is not supported by any ancient authority. It involves some very improbable behavior on the part of Mark. It solves no problem and is in fact redundant. So by Occam's Razor, it fails. The simplest hypothesis is that Eusebius, Clement, and (probably) Papias got it right. *Mark's Gospel was written in Rome*

---

107. Edmundson, *Church in Rome*, 27–29, 56.

108. I take founding to mean establishment as a structured community of believers. There will have been individual believers in Rome since the day of Pentecost (Acts 2:10).

109. Eusebius *EH* II.xvi, II.xxiv.1.

where Mark had attended Peter in the early years of Claudius's reign. So we have no good reason to reject our best estimate of AD 45 given above.

Ellis's dating of Luke/Acts to 63–64[110]—that is, soon after the διετια of Acts 28:30—does not differ significantly from our own.

Conclusion: How to Do New Testament History

We have now discussed two major cruces in New Testament chronology and the ways in which divergent solutions can arise, and the thinking behind them can be evaluated. In the course of doing this the following lessons in the practice of New Testament history have emerged.

1. Prove (test) all things for yourself (1 Thess 5:21). Ask awkward questions.

2. Do not follow the herd instinct. Do not be browbeaten by the untested claims of others who ask you to believe things they cannot justify. That "most scholars" believe something is not in itself evidence that the belief is true. Such a claim could equally well be a convenient way of claiming something that the writer wants you to believe but for which he (she) is too lazy to find any evidence. Beware of circular arguments.

3. Do not compartmentalize. Always consider what impact a new hypothesis will have upon your understanding of the rest of the New Testament and its world. How well does it dovetail with what you have already concluded?

4. Do not choose exotic or fancy solutions (like unevidenced multiple versions of the same document) when a more simple one will do. This is one thrust of Occam's Razor. Common sense is a very good guide.

5. Do not litter the first century with hypothesized documents that have no known author or have left no historical or archaeological trace. This again breaches Occam's Razor. It is not only messy; it is lazy. Instead, use your imagination and ask, from your knowledge of human nature, "What is going on here?"

---

110. Ellis, *Making of the New Testament*, 319, 391.

6. "One must resist the modern tendency to assume that in early Christianity only unknowns could be authors."[111] Or that only geriatrics could write gospels.

7. Do not underestimate the great New Testament historians of the past. Lightfoot, Chapman, Zahn, Harnack, Edmundson, Meyer, Dodd, and many others have plenty to teach us today. As in mathematics, we ignore to our serious loss the founding fathers of our discipline.[112]

8. There is something of value to be learned from practically everything we read. This may even be true of writers whose stance is inimical to our own.

9. Get acquainted with the early Roman Empire, preferably at degree level.

10. You must establish a sound chronology, or at least chronological skeleton, *before* beginning to expound.

11. Get to know well the Early Fathers, especially Eusebius. They may not always be right but they are nearly always illuminating. And they were very much more familiar with the age about which they write than we are.

12. Never underestimate the human mind and its ability to surprise us.

13. Never underestimate the diverse capabilities of truly great men and women.

---

111. Ellis, see note 9 above.

112. Interestingly, both Lightfoot (see Fahlbusch et al., *Encyclopedia of Christianity*, 5:422) and Edmundson (see Robinson, *Redating*, 349) studied mathematics during their university careers. Edmundson obtained a double first in the subject at Magdalen College, Oxford, gaining a university scholarship in it. Lightfoot was thirtieth wrangler of his year at Cambridge.

ANNEX A

Notes and Resources for a New Testament Chronology

One indispensable asset for the aspiring New Testament historian is a trustworthy chronological table. If you do not have access to such, you will need to create one of your own—a challenge that will abundantly repay the labor expended. I would suggest creating a spreadsheet within which to assemble your findings. Allow a column for recording a reference to the source or advocate(s) of the date chosen. The suggestions below are based on my own experience in compiling table A1–1 of *The Three Gospels*.

Enter as a skeleton the major external events whose dates are uncontroversial, such as the dates of Roman emperors and other rulers, Claudius's expulsion of "the Jews" from Rome, the Great Fire of Rome, the Jewish War, and the Fall of Jerusalem. Then for the events of Jesus' life and ministry we have as an essential basis:

- Ogg, *Chronology of the Public Ministry of Jesus*.

For the story of the early church in Acts, Eusebius and elsewhere, foundational are:

- Edmundson, *Church in Rome*
- Ogg, *Chronology of the Life of Paul*
- Hemer, *Book of Acts*

For dating the New Testament books the essential work today is still:

- Robinson, *Redating the New Testament*

I would strongly recommend here also:

- Harnack, *Date of the Acts*
- Edmundson, *Church in Rome*
- Humphreys and Waddington, "The Date of the Crucifixion"
- Wenham, *Redating Matthew, Mark and Luke*
- Moberly, "When Was Revelation Conceived?"

- Moberly, "When Was Acts Planned and Shaped?"
- Earle Ellis, *Making of the New Testament Documents*

You should also be asking, What can we learn from archaeology (for instance, the Gallio inscription and the Catacombs)? From external Christian sources like Eusebius and the Early Fathers? From Roman literature or Josephus?

In order to date Paul's letters we need to establish first the dates and locations of his various imprisonments. Then we may classify his letters in terms of those he wrote when free, and those from captivity; in the latter cases, where was he being held, and did he see himself as at risk of a death sentence? Who was with him when he wrote, and who would be present among the recipients?

From your table you can begin to tackle such questions as, Did Jesus die on April 7, 30, or April 3, 33? When was Paul converted? When did his three missionary journeys begin and end? When was he accompanied by Luke? Was there time in his life for his projected visit to Spain? How many times did Peter visit Rome? How many times did Paul visit Jerusalem? Are the three years of Paul's life spent in Arabia (Gal 1:18) distinct from or concurrent with the fourteen years that preceded his next visit there (2:1)? Can the Pastoral Epistles be fitted in anywhere or are they necessarily spurious? The list is long and the project utterly absorbing.

The ground you will have covered in creating such a table will give you an unrivalled platform from which you can begin to understand and expound the content of our texts. At the same time you will escape the charge spelled out in Robinson's lament quoted at the start of this chapter. Good hunting!

ANNEX B

Paul's Mental Constitution

Evelyn Underhill, writing in 1925, observed perceptively that Paul was "given to . . . alternate depression and exaltation."[113] Nor was she alone. C. H. Dodd in 1933 similarly observed how he was "a man of moods, with emotions readily aroused."[114] His "varying moods," he tells us, are betrayed by his letters, citing 1 Thess 2:17—3:5. And clearly Paul was indeed subject to temperamental extremes. Even when we first meet him, he is "breathing out murderous threats against the Lord's disciples" (Acts 9:1 TNIV).

In the 1950s such a temperament, unknown to the ancient world as such, came to be recognized clinically as *manic depression*. Nowadays, having been euphemistically renamed *bipolar disorder*, it is distinguished from *unipolar* depression by the manic "highs" experienced periodically by the sufferer. It is a most alarming and debilitating condition, characterized by rapid *mood swings* from one extreme to the other.[115] This seems to have been Paul's condition.

From what he tells us in 2 Cor 12:7-10, it is evident that Paul has a serious and chronic problem with *elation*—a dangerous exaltation of mood, precisely what we would today term *mania*. He attributes it to the "surpassingly great revelations" to which he was privy;[116] and we have no reason to doubt this. So Underhill writes of

> the persistent ill-health which accompanied [the revelations and visions] and was probably . . . a direct result of the psychophysical strain involved in his ecstasies.[117]

---

113. Underhill, *Mystics of the Church*, 40.

114. Dodd, "Mind of Paul I," 68.

115. To anyone who has no personal experience of bipolar disorder and would like a brief firsthand introduction I offer the Bipolar Disorder section of my website www.brainwaves.org.uk.

116. 2 Cor 12:2-4.

117. Underhill, *Mystics of the Church*, 42.

As Moses was warned, too much exposure to God can be highly dangerous (Exod 33:20). To protect him from such elation, ἵνα μὴ ὑπεραίρωμαι (v. 7, repeated for emphasis),[118] he is given a "thorn" (ἄγγελος Σατᾶν, angel of Satan, as he describes it), to prick his bubble and bring him back to earth again. This sudden deflation is precisely the effect associated with the downward mood swing today. It is not a pleasant experience, and Paul asks to be relieved of it, but is three times refused.

We are given a grandstand view of this process in action in the early chapters of the same epistle. Having set off on his own[119] from Ephesus for Macedonia in good heart (mid-55, Acts 20:1), he arrives in the Troad where, on not finding Titus as expected, he is hit by a powerful downswing (2 Cor 2:12–13), which leaves him at the very bottom of the pit:

> We were under great pressure, far beyond our ability to endure, so that we despaired of life itself. Indeed, we felt we had received the sentence of death. (1:8–9 TNIV; see also 7:9).

Unable to profit from the "open door" for evangelism presented there, and unsupported by friends, he flees to some in Macedonia (2:12–13). There he remains at rock bottom until Titus reappears, sending him back on an upswing to an exceptionally high emotional peak ("my joy was greater than ever," 7:6–7 TNIV). This is textbook bipolar, roller-coaster, behavior.

It is my contention, argued in the main text, that Paul was healed of this disability during his two year incarceration in Caesarea, not long after the spiritual crisis that both Dodd and Dormandy see in 2 Corinthians. In this reconstruction, the profound encounter with God that brought this about then overflowed into the letters to the Ephesians and

---

118. The emphasis is obscured by NIV and TNIV, which omit the repetition. The alternative rendering of ὑπεραίρωμαι as "proud" or "conceited," favored by many translators, leaves me baffled. Where else in Scripture does an encounter with God have this effect? On the contrary, time and again the subject is overcome, humbled, or given a sense of deep unworthiness: so Isaiah (6:5), Peter (Matt 5:8) and John (Rev 1:17). And in what way does the remedy meet the problem? References to an eye problem suggested by Gal 4:15 fail to convince.

119. We recall Jesus' instructions to his disciples during their missionary training that they should go out in pairs (Luke 10:1). Paul may not have heard this, but it might have saved him from this episode. Luke, his doctor, was last seen in Philippi (Acts 16:17), where he rejoins the party at Acts 20:5. Timothy has already been sent to Corinth with Erastus (Acts 19:22).

Colossians (and Philemon), far indeed in style and content from 2 Corinthians and Romans, which shortly preceded them.

Both Dodd and Underhill see in the "thorn" passage evidence that Paul was a *mystic*. The latter concludes her discussion of this passage as follows:

> If, then, we are to obtain a true idea of St. Paul's personality and the source of his amazing powers, we must correct the view which sees him mainly as a theologian and organizer by that which recognizes him as a great contemplative. For here we have . . . an immediate apprehension of the Being of God, such as we meet again in St. Augustine and certain mediaeval ecstatics.[120]

It is unfortunate that many commentators of today find so little of interest in Paul's inner life. So to depersonalize him risks seriously misunderstanding both the man and his writings, *affecting in no small way our judgment of authorship*. Revisiting Dodd and (especially) Underhill would provide a valuable antidote.

Bibliography

Barnett, Lincoln. *The Universe and Dr. Einstein*. New York: Morrow, 1957.

Brown, Raymond E. *An Introduction to the New Testament*. New York: Doubleday, 1997.

Cadbury, H. J. *The Style and Literary Method of Luke*. Cambridge: Harvard University Press, 1920.

Chapman, John. "St. Irenaeus on the Dates of the Gospels." *Journal of Theological Studies* 6 (1905) 563–69.

Crossley, James G. *The Date of Mark's Gospel: Insight from the Law in Earliest Christianity*. Journal for the Study of the New Testament Supplement Series 266. London: T. & T. Clark International, 2004.

Dodd, C. H. "The Mind of Paul I." In *New Testament Studies*, by C. H. Dodd, 67–82. Manchester: Manchester University Press, 1953.

———. "The Mind of Paul II." In *New Testament Studies*, by C. H. Dodd, 83–128. Manchester: Manchester University Press, 1953.

Dormandy, Richard. *The Madness of St. Paul: How St. Paul Rediscovered the Love of God*. Chawton, UK: Redemptorist, 2011.

Douglas, Mary. *Natural Symbols: Explorations in Cosmology*. London: Cresset, 1970.

---

120. Underhill, *Mystics of the Church*, 42. Underhill was particularly well qualified to make such a judgment having herself authored the definitive work, *Mysticism*, on the subject. See also Dodd, "Mind of Paul I," 70.

Edmundson, George. *The Church in Rome in the First Century*. London: Longmans, Green & Co., 1913.
Ellis, E. Earle. *The Making of the New Testament Documents*. Boston: Brill, 2002.
———. *Pauline Theology*. Grand Rapids: Eerdmans, 1989.
Eusebius. *Ecclesiastical History*. Books I–V. Translated by K. Lake. Loeb Classical Library 123. Cambridge: Harvard University Library, 1926.
Fahlbusch, E., et al., eds. *The Encyclopedia of Christianity*. Vol. 5. Grand Rapids: Eerdmans, 2008.
Farrer, Austin. *A Study in St. Mark*. Westminster: Dacre, 1951.
Fitzpatrick, Joseph. *The Fall and the Ascent of Man: How Genesis Supports Darwin*. Lanham: University Press of America, 2012.
Fotheringham, J. K. "The Evidence of Astronomy and Technical Chronology for the Date of the Crucifixion." *Journal of Theological Studies* 35 (1934) 146–62.
Goodacre, M. *The Synoptic Problem: A Way Through the Maze*. London: Sheffield Academic Press, 2001.
Gore, Charles. *Jesus of Nazareth*. London: Butterworth, 1929.
Goulder, M. D. *Luke: A New Paradigm*. 2 vols. Journal for the Study of the New Testament Supplement Series 20. Sheffield: JSOT, 1989.
Harnack, A. von. *The Date of the Acts and of the Synoptic Gospels*. Translated by J. R. Wilkinson. Crown Theological Library 33. London: Williams & Norgate, 1911.
Hemer, Colin J. *The Book of Acts in the Setting of Hellenistic History*. Edited by Conrad H. Gempf. Tübingen: J. C. B. Mohr (Paul Siebeck), 1989.
Hengel, Martin. *Studies in the Gospel of Mark*. Translated by John Bowden. London: SCM, 1985.
Hort, F. J. A. *Prolegomena to St. Paul's Epistles to the Romans and the Ephesians*. London: Macmillan, 1895.
Humphreys, Colin J., and W. Graeme Waddington. "The Date of the Crucifixion." *JASA* 37 (1985) 2–10.
Kümmel, W. G. *Introduction to the New Testament*, Revised ed. Translated by H. C. Kee. London: SCM, 1975.
Merton, Thomas. *The Intimate Merton: Thomas Merton's Life from His Journals*. Edited by Patrick Hart and Jonathan Montaldo. Oxford: Lion, 1999.
Meyer, E. *Ursprung und Anfänge des Christentums* (*Origin and Beginnings of Christianity*). Stuttgart and Berlin: Cotta, 1924.
Mitton, C. Leslie. *The Epistle to the Ephesians—Its Authorship, Origin and Purpose*. Oxford: Clarendon, 1951.
Moberly, Robert B. "When Was Acts Planned and Shaped?" *Evangelical Quarterly* 65.1 (1993) 5–26.
———. "When Was Revelation Conceived?" *Biblica* 73.3 (1940) 376–93.
Mosse, Martin. *The Three Gospels: New Testament History Introduced by the Synoptic Problem*. Milton Keynes, UK: Paternoster, 2007.
Neill, Stephen, and Tom Wright. *The Interpretation of the New Testament 1861–1986*. 2nd ed. Oxford: Oxford University Press, 1988.
Ogg, George. *The Chronology of the Life of Paul*. London: Epworth, 1968.
———. *The Chronology of the Public Ministry of Jesus*. Cambridge: Cambridge University Press, 1940.
Perkins, Pheme. *Reading the New Testament: An Introduction*. 3rd ed. New York: Paulist, 2012.

———. Review of Martin Mosse, *The Three Gospels: New Testament History Introduced by the Synoptic Problem*. *Review of Biblical Literature*, October 2009.

Robinson, J. A. T. *Redating the New Testament*. London: SCM, 1976.

Ross, Maggie. *Silence: A User's Guide*. Vol 1, *Process*. London: Darton, Longman and Todd, 2014.

Sanday, W., and A. C. Headlam. *A Critical and Exegetical Commentary on the Epistle to the Romans*. 5th ed. Edinburgh: T. & T. Clark, 1902.

Sherwin-White, A. N. *Roman Society and Roman Law in the New Testament*. The Sarum Lectures 1960–1961. Oxford: Clarendon, 2000.

Tuckett, C. M. *Q and the History of Early Christianity*. Edinburgh: T. & T. Clark, 1996.

Underhill, Evelyn. *Mysticism: The Nature and Development of Spiritual Consciousness*. 12th ed. Oxford: Oneworld, 1999.

———. *The Mystics of the Church*. London: James Clarke, 1925.

Wenham, John. *Redating Matthew, Mark and Luke*. Downers Grove, IL: InterVarsity, 1992.

New Testament Interpretation:
What Has Gospel to Do with History?

Respondent: Ben Wiebe

The basic thesis in this chapter from Martin Mosse is that interpretation of the New Testament documents requires taking account of their history. Some may question the position of Mosse at certain points; still, he presents a compelling case for the "external evidence" as essential to the whole of the evidence on the New Testament (NT) writings and specifically the origin of the Gospels.[1]

At first glance this may appear obvious, but as Mosse indicates the actual history has often been either overlooked or discounted. To interpret these books already calls for some awareness of their origin and their character. Clearly, reading them with understanding calls for us to see them in some kind of historical context. How did they come to be written? Are they simply literary works arising out of some social interest or some need in the life of the church? Genre matters. Are we to read a particular work as a novel, biography, history, or a travel guide? To read with understanding will require taking account of both the "external" and "internal" evidence for the identity and dating of the various NT writings. Among other things, this will necessitate the mining of the "ancient sources," the early church fathers, for evidence. This evidence is sometimes fragmentary, but often it is also found in cumulative and converging lines of evidence (for instance in Mark as the author of the Gospel so named).

---

1. Mosse, *Three Gospels*, has presented this at length in his monograph.

The Eclipse of the Gospel Accounts

With the rise of the Enlightenment consciousness, from the seventeenth century on people have come to the Gospels with varied assumptions. Certainly, for many it meant new questions about the Gospels; traditional authorship was questioned and alternative approaches were developed. This included the development of Gospel synopses to enhance the close study and comparison of the Gospels. Attention was focused on the "internal evidence" of the Gospels. This further intensified with the development of form-criticism beginning in the nineteenth and put into full effect in the twentieth century.[2] There is no real surprise that this was developed on the basis of certain assumptions, what is noteworthy is the particular assumptions that informed critical analysis:

1. Form-criticism aimed to discern and explain the pre-literary oral phase of the gospel tradition. Shortly after Jesus' crucifixion accounts of Jesus' sayings and actions were collected and handed on in the Christian communities. The first ones to tell stories and repeat sayings of Jesus were undoubtedly the witnesses to his ministry, elaborated and reinterpreted, and in the process taking on a form and substance of their own. The development through time was understood by comparison to folk tales.

2. The aim of form-criticism was the identification of extant forms in the Gospel accounts. Form-criticism was largely concerned with these forms communicated as isolated units in the way of sayings, parables, myths, and miracle stories.

3. This concern with particular forms was at the same time bound up with the concern of the *life setting* behind the forms, i.e., how they were used and developed in diverse settings in the church.

---

2. Strauss, *Life of Jesus,* called for "re-interpretation" of the Gospels, beginning with the determination of the extent to which they are historical. This put into question the Gospel accounts as they stand, in his dialectical criticism he already called for comparison of Gospel materials unit by unit. Schmidt, *Der Rahmen der Geschichte Jesu,* distinguished the editorial framework, which provided the chronological and geographical setting, from the units ("forms") that had been transmitted in oral form. Dibelius, *From Tradition to Gospel,* noted the specific types of gospel material, emphasizing the sermon as the main context for the gospel tradition, and as a base for the other forms. Bultmann, *History of the Synoptic Tradition,* beginning with the Synoptic texts, refined the aims of form-criticism.

4. The assumption was that in the early period the gospel tradition was passed on exclusively in oral form. Further, that the forms developed in anonymous communities; consequently, they were passed on as anonymous traditions. Unknown editors gathered the materials into larger rounded narratives or accounts.

5. In the end the concern of the form-critics was to determine the earliest form of a saying or story, and in this way to trace the content and the history of individual units of tradition. Embedded in the assumption of the form-critics was the idea that if they could unearth the original form of a saying or story, they would discover the authentic tradition about Jesus. What this would amount to was not all that clear, but the form-critics operating with these assumptions would thus uncover the "real Jesus"; for some a revolutionary, a kind of prophet, perhaps a teacher of wisdom, but someone other than the Jesus of the Gospels.

That is, the Gospels, written decades after Jesus' time, reflect more about the life of the church than they do about Jesus Christ.[3] This is not to say the Gospels were complete fabrications, but the assumption was that in order to get to the original content of the sayings or stories, and so to the real Jesus, we have to go behind the Gospels as they are. Form-criticism is closely tied to a particular hypothesis about the origin of gospel tradition and development of the church.[4]

What is postulated is a division between early Palestinian Christianity and the later Hellenistic (and Gentile) Christianity. Palestinian Christianity represented the early oral period of the gospel tradition that the form-critics wanted to recover.[5] In contrast, Hellenistic Christianity is the form developed beyond Jesus by interpreting and organizing the sayings and stories into the Gospel texts. The gospel tradition is received as a double reality. The aim of form-criticism was to separate the two levels. On one level the written Gospels represent "the original

---

3. Bultmann, *History of the Synoptic Tradition*. "The aim of form-criticism is to determine the original form of a piece of narrative, a dominical saying or a parable. In the process we learn to distinguish secondary additions and forms, and these in turn lead to important results for the history of the tradition." Again, he says the controversy stories about fasting or the Sabbath in Mark have their place in the "polemic" of the Palestinian Church and as such are "imaginary scenes illustrating in some concrete occasion a principle which the Church ascribed to Jesus" (6, 40, 41).

4. Wright, *New Testament*, 420.

5. Dibelius, *From Tradition to Gospel*, 5, 9, 39.

historical tradition" and on another second level they represent Christian interpretation and the work of the author. Based on these assumptions about how Christianity developed, the various units of tradition could be separated out and correlated with different stages of church life. This meant also to break the smaller units of tradition from their narrative context in the Gospels. Once isolated the form-critic was free to place the units in his own framework in accord with his supposition about the development of the tradition through the life of the church.

The basic point is that, as Mosse notes, this overlooks more than half the evidence. What accounts for the Gospels as literary wholes? Where are the people responsible for the tradition? Where are the eyewitnesses and the teachers representing the tradition? There is both the "external" and the "internal" evidence. More than that, it is to misconceive form-criticism itself, which was by design to function, as Morna Hooker noted almost five decades ago, as "a literary tool" and not a historical one.[6] It can deal with aspects of form but is not designed to determine the origins or the chronology of the gospel tradition. Form-criticism, focused on the text of the Gospels and operating with the attendant assumptions, discounted much of the internal and most of the external evidence for the origin of the Gospels.

Toward a New Paradigm

Critical questions arise at all the key points:

1. The idea that the gospel traditions originated in some pure form is little more than assumption. Indeed, there is reason to think that they existed in mixed forms from the beginning, in some cases delivered by Jesus in more than one form (unless we are to believe that Jesus could never present something more than once), or in the early church the received tradition could be performed in concise or more extended forms depending on the setting. James Dunn observes that sometimes the account in Mark is abbreviated in Matthew or Luke and sometimes material is added to make a further point (cf. Matt 14:28–31; 16:17–19).[7]

---

6. Hooker, "Christology and Methodology."; Hooker, "On Using the Wrong Tool."

7. Dunn, *Jesus Remembered*, 222–23. Sanders, *Tendencies of the Synoptic Tradition*, 272, has basically served to show that there "are no laws" of tradition determining the shape or extent of the various forms of the gospel tradition. Examining the manuscript

2. The notion in form-criticism that the gospel tradition developed with a bare memory of Jesus overlaid by extensive church interpretation and finally taking written form in the Gospel accounts needs to be reconsidered. Scholars of folklore in their study think of time over generations, even centuries; the time between Jesus and the Gospels is much shorter and falls within the generation of witnesses to Jesus.[8]

3. There is no basis for holding to a strict correlation between a form in the gospel tradition and some particular life setting. The same form can serve different purposes depending on context (cf. Matt 18:12–14; Luke 15:1–7).

4. The notion that these extant forms are communicated simply as isolated units is also questionable. To start with, it overlooks the inherent relation in their setting of sayings and actions within the Gospel narratives (e.g., a saying tied for its point to an action: Mark 2:5–12; 9:35–37; 14:22–24). The Gospel accounts are remarkably consistent in relating the teaching of Jesus to particular audiences, though one account may at certain points be more definite than another in audience identification.[9] Since sayings and actions have their meaning in context, to isolate them from their context is necessarily to reconstruct the meaning or data of a saying or action. Accordingly, as Vernon Robbins has noted, comprehensive understanding of Jesus' teaching "lies in methods which preserve and appreciate the fields of discourse which early Christians used to transmit the settings, action, and speech of Jesus." The narrative "frame" serves as the historical description and context for Jesus' teaching and actions.[10]

5. The idea that the Gospel tradition was simply transmitted in oral form in anonymous communities first of all overlooks the witness of the Gospels as we have them and the history of the early church.

---

evidence and looking further to the apocryphal Gospels he stated, "On all counts the tradition developed in opposite directions" (sometimes concise sometimes longer).

8. Hengel, "Eye-Witness Memory"; Various factors are recognized in the formation of the gospel tradition but the importance of the past and of memory is regularly overlooked. He goes on to say, "A further neglected factor in form-criticism, therefore, is personal memory, which can hold fast what is seen and heard for decades . . . 'institutionalized' in primitive Christian worship . . . in that 'the memory of Jesus' from his baptism by John to his passion and its interpretation was narratively proclaimed" (86).

9. Wiebe, *Messianic Ethics*, 141–42.

10. Robbins, "Pragmatic Relations," 35–62.

Where are the witnesses to the gospel and the teachers? The more we locate the gospel tradition in the context of social memory, of the community knowing itself to be dependent on decisive past events now carried forward in the gospel tradition (cf. 1 Cor. 11:23–26; 15:1–11; Luke 1:1–4), the more evident it becomes the form-critical approach fails in the account. There are two basic misunderstandings involved here.

First, this separation of the content of the Gospels is itself dependent on a quite specific assumption about the development of the Gospel tradition: It is no longer historically credible to simply set Judaism and Hellenism apart. The work of Martin Hengel has shown the complex reality of Judaism in interaction with Hellenism. In the Greek and Roman period over several hundred years Hellenism permeated all areas of life. From the middle of the third century BC, as Hengel notes, all Judaism must be recognized as Hellenistic Judaism.[11] Furthermore, within this setting the early church did not function in separated Jewish or Hellenistic (Gentile) compartments. Both Acts and Paul's letters show that Aramaic- and Greek-speaking members were present from the beginning in the church. People like Barnabas and John Mark moved in and between both groups. Gentiles were converted from the beginning (cf. Acts 6:5, 8–11). Paul in his letters is dealing with issues of fellowship between Jews and Gentiles in Galatia, Corinth, and Rome in the 50s and 60s. There is no indication of separate, not to say exclusive, Jewish or Gentile communities. This means the concern of the from-critical program to explicate the Gospel tradition by ascribing its main development to "Hellenistic Christianity" turns out to be an attempt to build on something that never existed.

The second basic misunderstanding in form-criticism is the idea that the Gospel traditions are largely the reflection of the diverse needs in the church and so the result of the interpretive work of the early church. First, there is a crucial distinction, largely overlooked in form-criticism, between events as the originating source for a tradition and the setting in which the tradition is enacted and passed on. The "forms" in the Gospel accounts, whether of parable or miracle, are at home in the setting

---

11. Hengel, *Judaism and Hellenism*, 1:103–6. Recent studies particularly in archeology would tend to qualify this; to some extent Greek culture was widely present but clearly within the ethos of Judaism (with Aramaic as the main language in use). Chancey, *Greco-Roman Culture*, 155–65.

of Jesus' ministry. And second, the fixed points in the NT actually go counter to the assumptions of form-criticism. Paul, in his letters dealing with the difficult questions faced in the churches, does not generally resort to quoting words of Jesus that could have supported him. When he does refer to Jesus' teaching, he does so clearly to distinguish between his own teaching and that of Jesus (1 Cor 7:10–13; 11:23–26). On the other hand, Paul refers to various conflicts and controversies that threatened the peace of the early church but that are without trace in the Gospels. For instance, circumcision was a fault-line threatening the unity of the church. This finds extensive reference in Paul's letters. This does not come up as an issue in any of the Gospel accounts. Questions about apostleship present in Paul's letters generated sharp controversy in the church. Apostleship is, of course, represented in the Gospels but not at all as an issue about authority in the church. The one occasion when apostolic authority comes up bears all the marks of the setting within the ministry of Jesus, twelve apostles associated with the twelve tribes of Israel, receiving the gift of the kingdom (still including Judas as one of the twelve so gifted! Matt 19:28; Luke 22:30). What is true for questions of circumcision and apostleship also holds for issues like tongues, justification, and the inclusion of Gentiles, slavery, meat offered to idols. In Paul's letters there are issues important in the early church but that are without trace in the stories and sayings of the Gospel accounts.

At this point form-criticism clearly fails. The Gospel accounts do not simply fuse the past of Jesus' ministry with the present of life in the church; nor do they separate interest in who Jesus was from who he now is as the risen Lord. The events and actions of the past in history have their distinct place and importance. In recognizing the past of Jesus' mission the early Church at the same time recognized its dependence and accountability to Jesus. This distinction between past and present becomes evident in the Gospel accounts by the way they present the story of Jesus. What we have in the Gospels, in accord with ancient biographical writing, is the indirect method of presenting his words and deeds and letting that speak for who Jesus is. As in the Gospel of Mark, the author assumes the readers know something (cf. Mark 1:1); they have received the basic proclamation about Jesus. In the Gospel, narrating the story of Jesus, the reference is to "Jesus" and not to the "Lord." For Luke, since we have both the Gospel and Acts, the distinction is concretely attested.

This becomes evident if we compare Luke 1–23 with Luke 24 and Acts. In the body of the Gospel "Lord" is used at times to refer to both

Jesus and to God but Jesus is not regularly addressed as Lord. Lord is not an abstract title to be filled with meaning drawn from elsewhere. It is with the events of the death and resurrection that Jesus is directly proclaimed as the Christ and acknowledged as Lord. It takes the narrative of Luke as a whole to convey what it means that Jesus is Lord. This holds for all the Gospel accounts, the early church in the post-Easter period specifically and boldly proclaims Jesus as Christ and Lord (cf. Acts 2:36).

From its beginning the church holds itself accountable to Jesus. So far from the church telling the story of Jesus retrospectively of their own Christian experience, that very experience "included as a pivotal point, the sense of dependence upon unique and unrepeatable events which had taken place earlier."[12] Indeed, one of the concerns inherent in the faith of the church is just this: to receive and remember faithfully certain things about and from Jesus (cf. Matt 23:8–10). The Gospels are not about something else extraneous to the narrative accounts, as represented in form-criticism. They are aimed to give account of the "thing" around which everything else revolves. They are not about some idea or abstract doctrine like Jesus as the example of love, or even the idea of the unity of the divine and the human (as represented in the work of David Friedrich Strauss). In accord with the evangelists, Jesus comes to fulfill the age long purpose of God, to bring the story of Israel to its intended climax.[13] The Gospels are narratives about Jesus, of actions and of events finding their fulfillment in history.

More specifically, this is part of the character of the Gospel accounts. They describe Jesus' activity within a particular temporal and geographical framework. The Synoptic Gospels concentrate on his activity in Galilee, John early on including Judea and Jerusalem. The accounts are about events that happened in the past. For example, the narrative of Jesus' movements and actions on the eastern shore of the Sea of Galilee and the Decapolis accounts for them in their time and place in history. This, at the same time, provides the historical setting for Jesus' teaching, calling disciples, and healing. The "forms" in the Gospel accounts, whether of parable or miracle, are at home in the setting of Jesus' ministry.[14] There

---

12. Wright, *New Testament*, 398.

13. Wright, *New Testament*, 397.

14. Casey, *Aramaic Sources*; in response to the notion that in many cases teaching or acts attributed to Jesus in the Gospel accounts have their origin in the interpretation of the church, shows that for example the teaching and healing in Mark 2:23—3:6 more precisely fits the *Sitz im Leben* of Jesus' ministry and not in the later time of the

is the inter-relation of past and present in the narrative about his actions in Galilee and the developing hostility that culminates in his crucifixion in Jerusalem. The Gospel accounts are indeed required to refer to Jesus' past history, to understand why and how he came to be crucified and also in order to comprehend the significance of the resurrection. That is, the Gospels embody both "the story and the significance of Jesus."[15] Past events are interconnected with the ongoing present of Jesus' mission.

Further, what follows is that the Gospels are not as such a direct proclamation of the Christian message. The message represented in the Gospels serves as the ground and context of the proclamation; as narrative accounts they present "wholes" culminating in the events of Jesus' death and resurrection. We see the church responding in various situations but substantial narrative traditions are not developed in making response. The Gospels present concrete narratives about Jesus. If we turn to other writings of the NT, we can say with equal certainty that the contrary holds: They are not aimed to present concrete narrative traditions about Jesus (as in Paul's letters). Outside the Gospels we have ethical instruction with allusions to the teaching of Jesus without narrative about Jesus, as in the book of James. In the Gospels we have extended narrative that can serve the purpose of ethical instruction (cf. Matthew), but no evidence that the need for ethical instruction led to the creation of narrative about Jesus. For the purpose of exhortation or apologetic, the church developed essential points and not complete narrative accounts (cf. the Gospel of John versus 1 John).[16]

Accounting for the variety in style and form of the Gospels, Mosse appropriately emphasizes the role of specific people in their production. They are identified with actual authors from the earliest time in the history of the church—not simply anonymous (see on Mark below). Furthermore, even the variations within the work of an author (Mosse highlights the letters of the Apostle Paul) compel us to recognize the "infinite complexity" of people to account for their writings. In NT criticism

---

church (189-92).

15. Stanton, *Gospels and Jesus*, 18.

16. Gerhardson, "Path of the Gospel," 77, underlined the point with reference to Luke, who knows well the life and work of Jesus, but he does not cite detail from that knowledge in Acts. We easily overlook the detailed knowledge he has of Jesus. Almost the same holds true in comparing the Gospel of John and 1 John. Sanders, *Jesus and Judaism*, in dependence on Gerhardson, has also highlighted this distinction of narrative in the Gospels and direct teaching in the letters (14).

it is regularly variations or differences that are made a basis for detecting different sources in a particular account. Fuller recognition of the complexity of people involved can lead to a greater awareness, with all their differences, of an underlying coherence or unity in the work of an author like Paul.

Not only are people complex, events we seek to understand also are often more complex than we realize. Indeed, when probed deeply, it seems there is always more to learn. So much so that some have raised questions on this account about the nature of history or historical events. The question may arise whether the events of the historical past are themselves "indeterminate and subject to variation with the passage of time."[17] Is it basically a matter of "perspective"? It is true that enquiry in the process of investigation will raise and seek to answer certain questions and thus will be limited and selective. Also, since history is not merely establishing some chronological items but is in part a question of meaning it differs from other fields of study. This is not to deny that events of the past are fixed; but it is to recognize that past is "so enormously complex that historians know only incompletely and proximately."[18] It remains that happenings of the past are fixed, but known only in part.

Paul's Aims and Purposes

The Apostle Paul, according to Mosse, represents a kind of test case of the complexity of people; real changes may take place in worldview, aims, and purposes. In the crucible of conflict and trial, scholars have discerned various changes in Paul so tested. It is appropriate to consider the effects of the apostle's challenges in relation to his aims and in relation to his writings. To start with, it is important to recognize with Mosse that to fully understand Paul and interpret the letters we need to bring a sense of the apostle, beyond a few items in a chronological list, and take account of his multidimensional character. In the effort to discern the mind of Paul, Mosse concentrates on II Corinthians in particular and on the two years of Paul's imprisonment in Caesarea (AD 57–59). I want to consider

---

17. Meyer, *Reality and Illusion*, 129.

18. Lonergan, *Method in Theology*, 220. Dunn, *Jesus Remembered*, refers to the important distinction for discernment between "probability" and "certainty" in matters of history (103–5).

the evidence for several of these changes in wider context, in some ways to complement and in some ways to qualify them.

Change of Evangelistic Program

On his return to Jerusalem, Paul is explicit in his farewell word to the Ephesian elders that he does not expect to see their faces again (Acts 20:25). But within the scope of Paul's activities, Mosse notes a change of plan. Before his imprisonment, he announced in his letter to the Romans his plan to visit Rome and from there to go on mission to Spain. There is no record of Paul going on to Spain. Instead, upon release from his first imprisonment, he apparently returned to Ephesus (1 Tim 1:3). This is evidence of something significant that happened in the years between AD 57 and 62 that affected a change of mind. Mosse anticipates that change with reference to the deep inner struggle of Paul reflected in 2 Cor 1:8–11.

What is the context for this? There had clearly been serious conflict in Corinth over leaders and, more basically, controversy about the shape of life and leadership in the community of Jesus the Messiah (2 Cor 5:11–15; 10:1–18). Paul faced the shocking reality of the church fragmented into various factions exalting different personalities in bitter competition among themselves. All this was counter to the love and unity of the reconciling work of Christ. Not only so, apparently it also involved some kind of attack on the apostle himself (2 Cor 10:1–2). Already in 1 Corinthians he had met with some of this (1 Cor 4:9–13). In this instance he counted on suffering for the sake of Christ. Here he is able to say, "That is to be expected by the follower of Jesus." In the second letter, as Mosse emphasizes, there is a change of mood. He has been so struck by events as to be overwhelmed—events about which he may leave some hints but does not describe. He was so crushed as "to despair of life itself" (2 Cor 1:8). This could be equated with deep depression or breakdown. I will leave aside the specific "diagnosis" of Paul's condition—it is not apparently an ongoing condition.[19] Even here in 2 Cor 1, in accord with what God has done in Christ, Paul takes up the dialectic of the cross and resurrection for his life and mission. The dialectic of the cross and

---

19. To take a point from Mosse, it may well be considered but people are complex; with limited information, and at this distance from Paul, I do not believe we are in a position to say more closely.

resurrection is the mark of authentic servants of the gospel, who are clay pots for the great treasure of the gospel (2 Cor 4:7). So Paul concludes, "We are afflicted in every way, but not crushed; perplexed but not driven to despair; persecuted, but not forsaken; always carrying in the body the death of Jesus, so that the life of Jesus may also be manifested in our bodies" (2 Cor 4:8–12).

He does not have to be the perennial optimist or a success all the time. In contrast to the Corinthians' expectations that he appear as the urbane or successful figure, Paul turns it around. He does so precisely in accord with the messianic meaning of power and authority (Mark 10:35–45). The apostle recognizes that this means not only telling people about the death and resurrection of Christ but also participating in this as one who belongs to Christ. Confidence in God provides for Paul "critical distance from himself and his hard experiences."[20] Accordingly, the main thing is not whether we live or die, for we belong to the Lord in either case (Rom 14:8–9).

The apostle acknowledges suffering for what it is; he cannot be placed in the camp with Stoics or the philosophers who emphasized self-sufficiency as their goal or those who would explain suffering as unreal, or that it could not affect the real inner self. Paul will have none of that; he acknowledges the deep challenges or struggles, and not simply struggles but also true joy (2 Cor 7:1–12). That, on the one hand, entails for Paul change reflected in early and later letters; on the other hand, there is a continuity in these letters that involves participation in the sufferings of Christ so that "the life of Jesus [resurrection] may also be manifested in our bodies" (2 Cor 4:8–12).

The Calm and Elevated Language in Ephesians, Colossians, and Philemon

Mosse highlights the character of these letters in connection with Paul's imprisonment in Caesarea. Differences in language and tone have been noted, compared to Paul's earlier letters, and then made a basis among scholars to call into question the authorship of these letters. These letters, though written from prison, present no indication of Paul facing a possible death sentence. For this reason, Mosse sees them as the product of his two year imprisonment in Caesarea.

---

20. Keck, *Paul and His Letters*, 121.

There is a notable and largely "general" tone particularly in Ephesians (in clear contrast to Philemon). The letter to the Ephesians and to the Colossians both carry much of the same teaching but in terms of address the letter to the Colossians presents a contrast, the apostle speaks directly and specifically to certain named people in Colossae (1:3-8; 4:7-17). Since Paul spent more than two years teaching and preaching in Ephesus (Acts 19:1-10) we would expect the apostle to speak even more directly and personally in the letter to the Ephesians. That we do not find this is in accord with evidence that "in Ephesus" in Eph 1:1 is not in some important early manuscripts of the letter. That would make it a general letter written as a kind of circular to be read in various churches, perhaps in the area around Ephesus. If the apostle is writing a general letter, in some cases to churches he has not seen, we would not expect him to deal with the specifics of the circumstances in Ephesus. Even in his own case, Tychicus will deliver the letter and speak directly for Paul, informing them about his situation (Eph 6:21, 22). It is a general letter by design.

The language of Ephesians and Colossians has been basic in setting them apart from other letters ascribed to Paul, not only the use of certain words and phrases, but also the use of words present in earlier letters of Paul but now used in new ways.[21] Terms like "mystery" used with reference to the unity of Gentiles with Jews in salvation (Eph 3:3-6; Col 1:26; cf. Rom 16:25-27). Then it is also used to refer to the reconciliation of all things in Christ in heaven and on earth (Eph 1:9-10). And quite differently, "mystery" is used to describe the unity in marriage as an image of the relationship of Christ to the church.[22] As used in Romans the term has distinctive emphasis with reference to a "hardening of Israel"; all the same in context it has to do with Jew and Gentile in relationship (11:25; 16:25-27). In Eph 3:3-6 mystery refers to the unity of Jew and Gentile in Christ, in Colossians it is associated with revelation and is used to refer more directly to Christ himself (Col 1:26, 27; 2:2, 3). Clearly the word can be used to refer to things in various connections in these letters; this is in

---

21. Kümmel, *Introduction*, 358-36. There is a need in taking account of the composition and language of various NT documents to reflect on what is meant by "author" in the first-century context. This is evident when in reading the letters we have specific reference to multiple authors (cf. 1 Cor 1:1; 2 Cor 1:1; Phil 1:1; 1 Thess 1:1) and also when amanuenses appear on the pages of the NT letters and speak for themselves (Rom 16:22). They could at times function as scribes simply taking down the words of an author and at other times contribute as co-authors. See Ellis, *Making of the New Testament*, 39-42.

22. Kümmel, *Introduction*, 358-361.

agreement with the use of the plural in 1 Cor 4:1 to refer to the "mysteries of God."[23]

What do we make of the general, more elevated style? The letters of Ephesians and Colossians carry an array of notes about peace and praise. A large number of possible fragments of hymns or prayers have been detected (Eph 1:13–14, 20–23; 2:4–7, 10, 14–18, 20–22; 3:5, 20–21; 4:4–6, 11–13; 5:2, 14, 25–17).[24] The exalted themes of reconciliation of Jew and Gentile, of peace and praise, will inevitably mark the style and language of the letters and help to explain their distinctive accents and their differences with other letters. When hymn or prayer fragments from Ephesians are compared with similar passages in Romans (cf. 8:38–39; 11:33–36) we find the same characteristic style.[25] Since a large part of the content, in particular of Ephesians, is prayer and hymn pieces, this can be expected to show up in elevated style and vocabulary.

Some, like Victor Paul Furnish, have further singled out "altered eschatology" in Ephesians as the most significant sign of a shift from earlier letters of Paul. Furnish makes the point that in Ephesians there is "no mention of Christ's return."[26] At the same time he perceives a clear reference to the expected return of Christ in Col 3:4. Widely recognized is a certain emphasis on the cosmic role of Christ in these letters (Eph 1:7–10, 20–22; Col 1:15–20). What is not to be overlooked, upon close reading there is actually a vital eschatology that marks the letters from beginning to end. Indeed, the cosmic reality is expected to be completed within the eschatological frame (Eph 1:9–10). To gather all things "in heaven and on earth" into one represents the working out of redemption in Christ (Eph 1:7–10; cf. Rom 8:22, 23, 38, 39; 1 Cor 8:5, 6). This eschatological emphasis is present in the great prayer, with hope at the center, that concludes chapter one ("so that, with the eyes of your heart enlightened you may know the hope to which he has called you," Eph 2:18). Again it is similarly present with reference to the Spirit that is "the pledge of our inheritance

23. Furnish considers these different uses in Ephesians of *mystery* and some other words and discounts the Pauline authorship. See "Ephesians." The word is not used in any of these letters to refer simply to one thing; the word occurs five times in 1 Corinthians, six times in Ephesians and four times in Colossians. It denotes something hidden now disclosed or revealed. What is evident is that there is continuity in the use of terms like mystery across the letters ascribed to Paul. It means this usage as a basis for calling Pauline authorship into question in the end does not hold up.

24. Barth, *Ephesians*, 1:6–8.
25. Barth, *Ephesians*, 1:5–8.
26. Furnish, "Ephesians."

and redemption as God's own people" (Eph 1:14; 4:30). This culminates in the note of hope; to belong to Christ and live for him is to "set our hope in Christ" (1:12; 2:12). It is therefore more than a little ironic that some will perceive a difference in wording but miss the basic theme of reconciliation and eschatology in continuity with the early letters to the Romans and Corinthians. There is indeed a calm and elevated tone that marks the later letters in accord with the notes sounded in them, and that may also be indicative of change toward more complete resolution of some earlier concerns for Paul; amid human machinations Paul can wait on God to work out his purposes for good. At the same time this holds true within a basic continuity of aims and purposes from the early to the later letters.

A Change of Evangelistic Strategy

The two year prison period in Caesarea, according to Mosse, resulted in a third change. The apostle "acquired a new life goal." His mission now, beyond planting and establishing churches, was to present the gospel to the emperor and if possible to convert him.

Reading in close context, how can we discern Paul's aims as we take account of his struggles and conflicts? What is clear is that the pursuit of his aims, as this issued in mission, took him into conflict (i.e., whether with opponents in Jerusalem or in Galatia). This means that his aims are not to be reduced to effects of his conflicts or struggles.

Specifically with reference to the meaning of his imprisonment culminating in his appeal to Caesar, what were the effects for Paul and for his aims in mission? What place was there for Caesar in Paul's thought and how does his appeal to Caesar figure in that? For Paul the gospel of Jesus the Messiah was creative of a particular community. They constituted a renewed people, a fellowship of "brothers and sisters," with mutual bonds with primary allegiance to Christ and to one another. People from all kinds of backgrounds, Jews and Gentiles, slave and free, rich and poor, male and female, made them a distinct community; men and women called together into a new social wholeness. This way of life realized in actual community constituted a challenge within the ancient world composed of various social groups torn by its own conflicts. It is then not surprising that, gathered in this way with a common allegiance to

Christ and to one another, this community would raise suspicions and sometimes hostility.

This is not yet to speak of Christian witness in worship of the one creator God in contrast to widely held views about the various gods and emperor worship itself. This witness included the understanding that the rulers are both appointed by and accountable to God. Israel waited in expectation upon God to fulfill his purpose with the conviction that God holds the nations to account, there will come a time when arrogant rulers will be judged. In the coming of Jesus there is a fresh affirmation of this but redefined in the shocking climax around the death and resurrection of Jesus. Though this did not come about as people expected, God acting for the redemption of Israel and so also for the nations, has happened in Jesus the Messiah. In accord with the message of the apostle, this can only mean that Jesus has been exalted as Lord, not only for the church but as the true Lord of all (Phil 2:1–11). The great turning point indeed happened with the death and resurrection of Jesus, but there is a "now" and "not yet" about this. Christ must "reign until he has put all his enemies under his feet" (1 Cor 15:20–28). For now this means that the creator God has put in place human authorities to limit or channel the powers of enmity and evil and to make space for the saving work of the gospel (cf. Rom 13:1–7; 1 Tim 2:1–7). In the same sphere where Caesar lays claim to divine honors and power as "Lord," to confess that Jesus is Lord means that Caesar is not.

Talk about righteousness, citizenship, kingdom of God, and at the same time proclaiming Jesus the Lord would certainly present a challenge in the face of Caesar's claims and assumptions. To say, as in Rom 13, "there is no authority except from God," and those authorities that exist have been "instituted by God" is already to deny the claim of Caesar. Within the scope of God's purpose for humans in his image there is a place for human authorities, subject to his oversight and ultimate judgements. In this light, Paul was prepared to bear witness before the various rulers including Caesar himself. This, I would argue, required no great change on the part of Paul in evangelistic strategy. The apostle to the nations was always open to the working of God to include them in witness to Jesus Christ and in reception of the gospel (Acts 26:12–29; Phil 1:12–14). Beyond this there is no indication from Paul of a specific plan or development aimed to convert the emperor. We do have the apostle, in accord with his call to go to Rome, ready to share the gospel with them. The center of the Roman world, the city of Rome was in some ways a climax for Paul in mission (Rom 1:8–13; 15:15–16). At the same time, Rome was a way-station, he looked to Spain as the main focus for further mission (Rom 15:22–26).

In context, after two years in prison Paul is handed on from Felix to Festus without any resolution in sight, with some Jewish elites scheming to have Paul transferred to Jerusalem and on the way to ambush and kill him (Acts 24:27—25:5). After the hearing, Festus apparently out of his depth on the issues between the Jewish leaders and Paul and wanting to keep favor with the Jews, holds out the possibility of sending Paul back to Jerusalem to be tried there. Without prospect of resolution there, Paul as a Roman citizen can appeal to Caesar, and he does (Acts 25:6–12).[27]

Mark: Genre and History

In his work on Mark and Acts, Mosse has sorted through much of the pertinent data bearing on the authorship and date for these writings. In the twentieth century, as scholars were largely occupied in form and redaction-critical studies of the Gospels, the external evidence was regularly dismissed or overlooked. The view developed in form-criticism that the Gospel writers mainly served as collectors of sayings and stories and strung them together turned out to be simply inadequate. Further, study of the Gospel accounts themselves opened out to new questions about original purpose, genre, and authorship. Mosse has focused on what he calls "external evidence" for the origin and dating of Mark. It is surprising how the external data has been either overlooked or discounted in major NT introductions and commentaries. I will respond in brief form on the relation between the "internal evidence" (the content and character of the account) and the "external evidence."

A Standard Account

We get a standard account from the *New Interpreter's Bible* in Pheme Perkins's commentary on Mark.[28] She cites Mark 13 as "the primary source of evidence" for many scholars that Mark composed his Gospel during or

---

27. Witherington, *Acts of the Apostles*, presents an illuminating discussion of the trial from the perspective of Roman authority and law, the Jewish leadership, and Paul, 717–25.

28. Perkins, *Gospel of Mark*.

shortly after the war with Rome and the destruction of the temple in AD 70. She is aware that on this basis a case can also be made for a connection to the earlier crises in AD 35–41 with the Emperor Caligula's order that an image of him be set up in the temple compound.[29] What is noteworthy is the possible evidence she is prepared to consider in arriving at a date for the Gospel of Mark. Perkins refers to early Christian witness on the origin of Mark but beyond that Perkins makes little more than passing reference to Papias and the tradition of Mark and the writing of the Gospel in association with Peter. Since Mark was a common name and he was associated with both Paul (Acts 12:12; 13:5, 13; Col 4:10; Phil 24) and Peter (1 Pet 5:13), she does not believe there is sufficient information to identify the author of the Gospel. She ends up with unknowns: unknown author, community of origin, and uncertain date of composition.

If Perkins is ambivalent about the date, she is more direct in her statement on the purpose of Mark. Perkins thinks the reference to "gospel" in Mark 1:1 signifies a comprehensive distinction of Mark's account from other types of writing. It "was not composed to record historical remembrances about Jesus."[30] The gospel in Paul's letters, she notes, refers to "the message of salvation" that Paul preached (Rom 1:1, 16; 1 Cor 4:15). Mark, she believes, retains *gospel* as a "preached message" (Mark 1:14–15). That is, Mark, by his opening words, indicates that what follows fills the role of earlier preaching.

Gospel and History

Here basic critical questions arise. Perkins is right, as far as it goes, to emphasize *gospel* to characterize Mark. But then the background for the term gospel (εὐαγγέλιον) sheds some light here. The word was used to denote good news in general and often news in particular of military victory.[31] It thus clearly intends factual announcement or proclamation

---

29. Perkins, *Gospel of Mark*, 684–85.

30. Perkins, *Gospel of Mark*, 518. It was Bultmann who most clearly set apart gospel from biography or history. This was taken to its conclusion by Mack in his work on Mark, *Myth of Innocence* (1988). According to Mack, Mark has taken up the Jesus story and turned it into a completely negative apocalypse. Like Bultmann before him, he presents Mark as combining two different streams from early Christianity (early Jewish and then Gentile). He ends up with a syncretism with little relation to Jesus himself (96–130).

31. To be sure the Gospels have their own focus—the good news of and about Jesus. The term *gospel* in Greco-Roman context concerned events, such as the accession

of events. What was the intention in the oral accounts about Jesus? Is there reason to think that gospel in some way excludes "historical remembrances" about Jesus? Ben Meyer's argument helps to illuminate this matter. He reviews thinking as it has developed in discerning the historicity of events. On one side there is simply credulous interpretation; on the other side is methodical skepticism. This regularly stifles historical investigation even before it can begin. Before the "demise" of "the criteria of authenticity" was recognized, Meyer pointed out their limited role in judgments of historicity, and the disappointment and skepticism that follows exaggerated expectations. Determination of what is so will hardly ever be a matter of a single question or consideration but will most often involve a larger frame of various data and converging lines of evidence. In the course of an investigation,

> the judgments . . . should, as far as possible, be independently verified. Independent verification follows either a direct or an oblique pattern of inference. . . . If the intention of the writer can be defined to include factuality and if the writer is plausibly knowledgeable on the matter and free of suspicion of fraud, historicity may be inferred.[32]

What is the pertinent direct or indirect information about the origin of the Gospel of Mark? On the threshold of Gospel interpretation the question may be stated in the following terms, "What does the writer intend to communicate about Jesus' life and teaching?" Specifically, with reference to history, the question can be formulated more precisely, "Does the writer intend to communicate truthfully about Jesus' life?"[33] What can be said about the origin and authorship of Mark? Someone at some time wrote the Gospel of Mark. He did so in the context of the primarily

---

or the military victory of the emperor. In first century Jewish context there is the "good news" of God's long-awaited victory over evil and the deliverance of his people (cf. Isa 52:7–12). Hengel, *Four Gospels*, refers to Mark as the "kerygmatic biography of Jesus." And he notes that ancient readers would "certainly also regard [it] as a biography" (63, 91). Perkins, *Gospel of Mark*, herself acknowledges that Greco-Roman readers would conclude that "Mark is an exercise in biography" (520). Inasmuch as it is focused on events (beyond simply the person of Jesus) it can also be said to be historiographical. Becker, *Birth of Christian History*, places Mark in the flow of ancient "historiographical writing." She states in the preface to the book that the line from Mark to Luke-Acts in their accounts of the beginnings of the gospel story "mark a transformation from narrative memory to full-fledged writing of history: this is the starting point of early Christian historiography" (Kindle edition).

32. Meyer, *Aims of Jesus*, 84–85.
33. Bernier, *Quest*, 44–45.

antecedent oral traditions about Jesus. Mosse presents the evidence from the early church that comes with some variation in detail, but with the largely consistent witness on the main point of Markan authorship for the Gospel.

Consider the Gospel of Mark as we have it. To begin with, we take note of the superscriptions the Gospels carry. With reference to the significance of these superscriptions, Martin Hengel writes,

> Sometimes there are still crude false judgments here. That may be connected with the fact that even in more recent editions of Nestle-Aland the textual evidence for inscriptions and subscriptions is in part quite incomplete.[34]

He notes that there is no record of the Gospels ever circulating as anonymous documents. Therefore, Hengel continues,

> These titles are widely attested in a variety of ways: by some of the earliest papyri, by reports in the second and third century church fathers, were already completely uniform in the second century.[35]

According to Hengel, if the Gospels had circulated anonymously or received their titles as additions in different communities—a title was needed to announce the reading in worship—this would inevitably have resulted in a diversity of titles, and how they received the titles they now carry would remain unexplained. But as it stands, there is no evidence of such anonymity. Instead there is the complete uniformity of titles from the earliest period, whether in Alexandria or Lyons, whether in Antioch or Carthage.[36] The contention that Mark, in association with the apostle Peter, composed the Gospel goes counter to the assumption in form-criticism and in much of modern scholarship. What the contention does is return attention to the role of real people as tradents involved in the process of Gospel formation. In place of a path now running out into a cul-de-sac it opens a new direction for Gospel study based on reference to events of the past and the memory of eyewitnesses (cf. Luke 1:1–4).

The main eyewitnesses would have been able to reflect on not only particular sayings or incidents related to Jesus but on the whole scope of his ministry. This in general is reflected in the Gospels. The Gospel

---

34. Hengel, *Four Gospels*, 48.
35. Hengel, *Four Gospels*, 48–53.
36. Hengel, *Four Gospels*, 54.

accounts begin with John the Baptist and conclude with the resurrection. Matthew and Luke provide introductions or prologues, as in John, to the story as a whole. The awareness of the whole of Jesus' ministry is specified in the first chapter of the Acts of the Apostles. In the selection of another to fill the place of Judas, the candidate must be a person who has "accompanied us during all the time the Lord Jesus went in and out among us, beginning from the baptism of John until the day that he was taken up from us—one of these must become a witness with us to his resurrection" (Acts 1:21–22). This spells out the qualifications for the work of the apostolic witness to Jesus: specifically to be able to bear witness to the resurrection but also to have been with Jesus "from the beginning." This is further confirmed in the summary of Peter's message later in Acts with the same notations on the scope of Jesus' ministry and the witness linked specifically to the resurrection (Acts 10:35–42).

This understanding of the disciples especially called as witnesses to Jesus is certainly not limited to Luke. In John, Jesus promises the coming of the Spirit to those who will testify to Jesus. And furthermore on the point here, "You also are to testify because you have been with me from the beginning" (John 15:26–27). It is noteworthy that Luke and John are in agreement on the qualifications of these witnesses to Jesus as those who have been with Jesus from "the beginning" and called to bear witness to his resurrection. In further direct confirmation, the specific authority of the apostles who had been eyewitnesses of the whole ministry of Jesus was recognized in the early Christian community (cf. Acts 2:42; 1 Cor 15:1–11). With this basic ascertainment in place, often simply overlooked, we are prepared to consider the evidence for this witness represented in the Gospel accounts.[37]

With reference to Mark's Gospel, the first disciple named right after Jesus begins his ministry is Peter. Jesus, passing along the Sea of Galilee, comes upon Peter and Andrew fishing. "Jesus said to them, 'Follow me and I will make you fish for people.' And immediately they left their nets and followed him" (1:16–18). The name "Simon" is highlighted—the name is repeated for emphasis. This is followed later by the significant act of Jesus in changing his name to Peter (Mark 3:16). Mark's narrative toward the end of his account is concise, with the note that all the male disciples deserted Jesus at his arrest. But at the very end the women at the empty tomb received the message that Jesus has been raised and the

---

37. Bauckham, *Jesus and the Eyewitnesses*, 24.

command to go to tell Jesus' "disciples and Peter that he is going ahead of you to Galilee; there you will see him, just as he told you" (16:7). Bauckham rightly refers to "the rather surprisingly specific mention of Peter (who after all was one of the disciples)."[38] This most likely points ahead to the appearance of Jesus specifically to Peter as indicated by both Paul (1 Cor 15:5) and Luke (24:34). Mark's reference to Peter sets him in a preeminent light at the end just as at the beginning. "The two references form an inclusio around the whole story, suggesting that Peter is the witness whose testimony includes the whole."[39]

If the use of the inclusio is designed to indicate that Peter was the main source behind Mark's account, it is in coherence "with the remarkable frequency with which his name occurs in Mark."[40] Luke, in his own way, supports Mark's reference to Peter. He does not locate the references in just the same way; still Peter is the first disciple individually named in Luke (Luke 4:20), and at the end Luke does not have the name of Peter in the message of the angels as Mark has it. Instead, he refers retrospectively to Jesus' appearance to Peter and so makes him the last to be named (Luke 24:34). Luke thus acknowledges, in confirmation of Mark, the important place of Peter in the apostolic witness to Jesus and as a source for his Gospel account.

What is the coherence between "internal" and "external" evidence for the origin of Mark? If we take up the early Christian witness the evidence points consistently to Mark as the author in association with Peter, serving as Peter's interpreter, writing down what he heard in Peter's preaching. In citing early Christian evidence about the origins of Mark's Gospel, Perkins only makes reference to Papias. And she fails to take full account of the statement of Papias; she minimizes it as a statement in defense of "the apostolic origin of the Gospel."[41] Comparing Mark with other Gospels and with what is found in Q, she believes that Mark used various sources in a way that discounts Peter as source. So she asserts, where is the evidence?[42] More to the point, she overlooks the range of

---

38. Bauckham, *Jesus and the Eyewitnesses*, 125. Hengel, *Four Gospels*, 82.
39. Hengel, *Four Gospels*, 82.
40. Hengel, *Four Gospels*, 82.
41. Perkins, *Gospel of Mark*, 517.
42. Perkins, *Gospel of Mark*. There seems little reason to discount Mark as author simply because he is described in association with both Paul and Peter at some point. More important, if Mark as author had access to various sources of the gospel tradition and he used them, how does that negate Peter as a primary source? She is skeptical

evidence from the early Christian witnesses that Mosse presents, including Justin Martyr, Irenaeus, Clement, and Origen.

The Papian data and the history of the Markan account are further established in that, what is otherwise largely supposition, the Gospel has strong traces of its origins from a predominantly oral context. We should note what is actually said by Papias on this point,

> And Mark, having become Peter's interpreter, wrote accurately but not in order the things that the Lord spoke or did, insofar as he remembered. For he had not heard the Lord or followed him, but as I said, Peter, who taught according to need without making as it were an arrangement of the oracles of the Lord. Therefore Mark did nothing wrong in writing down single points as he remembered them, for his plan was to leave out nothing or to misrepresent what he had heard.[43]

Papias is concerned to receive firsthand witness. In the case of Mark, if Papias had been concerned simply to exalt the Markan account he could have attributed it directly to Peter. Mark is not one of the original witnesses but, as an "interpreter" of Peter, is in position to convey the original witness of Peter. Papias is writing in the awareness that he yet has access to people who have heard the apostles (the "living memory" of the original witnesses). He is living in a setting in which the oral and written communication co-existed; the written supported the oral—the written often produced for the purpose of oral communication.[44]

---

about the early multiple witnesses to Mark as author in association with Peter; skepticism it seems can be selective. She shows little or no reserve about her ability to isolate various layers of tradition in Mark based on reference to Q and "variants" of tradition in Mark (surely at least an equally formidable task!) (517).

43. Eusebius, *Eccl. Hist.* 3.39.15.

44. Casey, *Aramaic Sources*, 136–37, 259–60, presents convincing evidence that Mark in part includes Greek in translation from Aramaic materials originating prior to c. 40. Whether Mark was the first to write a Gospel or not, there is no convincing reason to deny he had access to earlier written notes or accounts, including Aramaic sources. Papias has been read as discounting written sources. First, the main concern for him seems to be to receive the living witness of those who followed Jesus, "and if any of those who followed the elders might come, I would ask about the words of the elders, what Andrew or Peter or Philip or Thomas or James . . . had said. . . . For I do not suppose things which come from books would help as much as a living and abiding voice." At the same time, that he did not simply aim to discount writing is evident in that he himself engaged in writing his own exegetical volumes on the Word of the Lord. *Eccl.Hist.* 3.39.4.

If we consider closely the relation between the Markan account and the patristic data, we have indications pointing to it as a work in translation. We think of Peter operating largely in Aramaic and we have Mark's account in Greek. Probably Papias thought of Peter mainly using Aramaic, with some knowledge of Greek that Mark helped to clarify and communicate to Greek speaking audiences.[45] All this is in accord with the earliest witness to the origin of Mark as a work involving translation. On the basis of the "internal evidence" of Mark as we have it, if Mark was the first of the Gospels to be written it emerged most immediately from the context in which the Jesus tradition was treasured and carried the stamp of its original Aramaic setting. If we did not have Papias' statement on the origin of Mark what would we assume about the Markan account? Since Mark was written in Greek some work of translation from Aramaic to Greek was clearly carried out. This is much as Papias described the process of Mark writing his account.[46] This also fits with the tradition of Peter and Mark in Rome in a church that apparently originated in Jewish sections of the city with a largely Hellenist background. Thinking with Mark's account, the internal evidence fits with the external data from the early church on Markan origins.

Conclusion

The background for Mark writing the Gospel is Second Temple Judaism, with Scripture as central to community life, a community that in this period produced an array of writings including the documents of the Qumran community. This is a context where oral and written communication coalesced and existed quite happily together. Mark, in the context of the Christian community handing on the gospel (orally and supported by various "written Jesus traditions"), in writing the Gospel was acting in accord with the long history of writing down what God had

---

45. Casey, *Aramaic Sources*, 1–72, 76, considers the history of the study of Aramaic as it has developed in NT scholarship (with special reference to the Dead Sea Scrolls), and specifically in Mark, Casey examines key terms and full statements indicative of the Aramaic background. How communication from Aramaic to Greek worked out concretely with people is concisely indicated by the example of Josephus, well educated and part of a Judean priestly family—he learned Greek but it was his second language, and he relied on stylistic help when he wrote in Greek (C. Ap. I. 50, also AJ I.7; XX.263–5). That Peter and Mark were at some time together in Rome is the implication from 1 Pet 5:13. This holds whether we believe the letter to be from Peter or not.

46. Bernier, *Quest*, 139.

done with his people and now in Jesus Christ. This Gospel comes to us in the ordinariness of Jesus as servant riding on a donkey, not to impose but to open up a way of life.

Bibliography

Barth, Markus. *Ephesians 1–3*. Vol. 1. New York: Doubleday, 1974.
Bauckham, Richard. *Jesus and the Eyewitnesses: The Gospels as Eyewitness Testimony*. Grand Rapids: Eerdmans, 2006.
Becker, Eve-Marie. *The Birth of Christian History: Memory and Time from Mark to Luke-Acts*. New Haven: Yale University Press, 2017.
Bernier, Jonathan. *The Quest for the Historical Jesus after the Demise of Authenticity*. New York: Bloomsbury, 2016.
Bultmann, Rudolf. *The History of the Synoptic Tradition*. Oxford: Blackwell, 1968 (1921).
Casey, Maurice. *Aramaic Sources of Mark's Gospel*. Cambridge: Cambridge University Press, 1998.
Chancey, Mark A. *Greco-Roman Culture and the Galilee of Jesus*. Cambridge: Cambridge University Press, 2005.
Dibelius, Martin. *From Tradition to Gospel*. Cambridge: James Clarke, 1971 (1919).
Dunn, James D. G. *Jesus Remembered*. Grand Rapids: Eerdmans, 2003.
Ellis, E. Earle. *The Making of the New Testament Documents*. Leiden: Brill, 1999.
Eusebius, *Eccl. Hist.*
Furnish, Victor Paul. "Ephesians." In *Anchor Bible Dictionary*, edited by David Noel Freedman et al., 535–42. New York: Doubleday, 1992.
Gerhardsson, Birger. "The Path of the Gospel Tradition." In *The Gospel and the Gospels*, edited by Peter Stuhlmacher, 75–96. Grand Rapids: Eerdmans, 1991.
Hengel, Martin. "Eye-Witness Memory and the Writing of the Gospels." In *The Written Gospel*, edited by M. Bockmuehl et al., 70–96. Cambridge: Cambridge University Press, 2005.
———. *The Four Gospels and the One Gospel of Jesus Christ*. Translated by John Bowden. Harrisburg: Trinity, 2000.
———. *Judaism and Hellenism: Studies in Their Encounter in Palestine during the Early Hellenistic Period*. 2 vols. Philadelphia: Fortress, 1974.
Hooker, Morna D. "Christology and Methodology." *New Testament Studies* (1970) 480–87.
———. "On Using the Wrong Tool." *Theology* 75 (1972) 570–81.
Keck, Leander E. *Paul and His Letters*. Philadelphia: Fortress, 1989.
Kummel, W. G. *Introduction to the New Testament*. Nashville: Abingdon, 1975.
Lonergan, Bernard. *Method in Theology*. New York: Herder, 1972.
Mack, Burton L. *The Myth of Innocence*. Minneapolis: Fortress, 1988.
Meyer, Ben F. *The Aims of Jesus*. London: SCM, 1979.
———. *Reality and Illusion in New Testament Scholarship*. Collegeville, MN: Liturgical, 1994.

Mosse, Martin. *The Three Gospels: New Testament History Introduced by the Synoptic Problem*. Milton Keynes, UK: Paternoster, 2007.

Perkins, Pheme. *The Gospel of Mark*. Edited by Leander E. Keck. The New Interpreter's Bible 8. Nashville: Abingdon, 1995.

Robbins, Vernon. "Pragmatic Relations as a Criterion for Authentic Sayings." *Focus and Facets Forum* 1.3 (1985) 35–62.

Sanders, E. P. *Jesus and Judaism*. London: SCM, 1985.

———. *The Tendencies of the Synoptic Tradition*. Society for New Testament Studies 9. Cambridge: Cambridge University Press, 1969.

Schmidt, Karl L. *Der Rahmen der Geschichte Jesu*. Berlin:Trowitzsch, 1919.

Stanton Graham N. *The Gospels and Jesus*. Oxford: Oxford University Press, 1989.

Strauss, David Friedrich. *The Life of Jesus Critically Examined*. Translated by George Eliot. London: Chapman, 1846 [1835–36].

Wiebe, Ben. *Messianic Ethics: Jesus' Proclamation of the Kingdom of God and the Church in Response*. Scottdale, PA: Herald, 1992.

Witherington, Ben. *The Acts of the Apostles*. Grand Rapids: Eerdmans, 1998.

Wright, N. T. *The New Testament and the People of God*. Minneapolis: Fortress, 1992.

2

Birger Gerhardsson and Oral Transmission in the Formation of the Gospel Tradition

ALLAN J. MCNICOL

THOSE OF US WHO spend considerable time pondering the texts of the canonical gospels generally have a working perspective on how they developed. This would include views on how the παραδόσεις "traditions" about Jesus the Nazorean were formulated and utilized in the written gospel accounts, somewhat akin to what we have in our possession today.[1] From this very generalized working position numerous perspectives emerge and clutter the landscape. A good place to gain an initial appreciation for the complexity of the issue of the origin of the Gospels is to engage in a serious study of the Synoptic Problem.[2] There, one will be confronted with a bewildering array of differing views about these matters.

Yet fascination with what possibly can be known about the life of Jesus and the earliest decades of the Christian movement remains. Somewhat akin to issues faced by critical scholars of the Qur'an, we sense that

---

1. Gospel criticism in the last several decades was characterized by a massive expansion of scholarship featuring non-canonical accounts of Jesus' teaching such as the Gospel of Thomas. Since I count myself among those who accept the position that these works came after the canonical gospels and reflect considerable dependence upon them. I do not intend to move into a discussion about them in this essay. A mainstream work on this issue may be consulted profitably in Goodacre, *Thomas and the Gospels*.

2. Foster, *New Studies, and the Synoptic Problem*.

what happened in the earliest days of the Christian movement is critical for gauging its essence; but, at the same time, these early decades seem stubbornly resistant to supplying a coherent picture of what took place that even approximates a consensus.

For most of the history of Christianity its adherents have been able to live with these points of uncertainty. The attacks on the inconsistencies in the gospel accounts by Celsus and Porphry in the second and third centuries of our era stung deeply.[3] Ultimately, however, they had no permanent effect in suppressing the growth and influence of Christianity in the latter days of the Roman Empire. But the posthumous publication of the writings of Hermann Samuel Reimarus (1694-1768) was a different matter. Reimarus flatly contended that such critical doctrines for Christianity as the death of Jesus constituting an atonement for sin, references to Jesus' resurrection, and expectations of his imminent return to consummate his kingdom were products of the early church and could not be anchored historically in Jesus' earthly life.[4] The importance of this material was underscored by Gotthold Lessing, the influential publisher of Reimarus's works. In his own famous contribution to philosophical theology he contended that there was a massive "ditch" or gulf between the accidental contingent truths set forth by historians in their reconstruction of the past and the necessary results of rational thought that only a good philosopher could establish on the basis of reason.

Thus, by the time of the end of the Enlightenment there was embedded in Western critical thinking a deep suspicion about the ultimate validity of historical research—especially with respect to earliest Christianity. It was inevitable that this ethos would have a deep impact on attempts by biblical scholars to assemble assured knowledge of the process of the transmission of the sayings and deeds of Jesus and the formation of the gospel tradition. Some of this skepticism became so extreme that in the nineteenth century there was a school of thought that denied the existence of Jesus altogether. More reasonably, however, continued attempts to bridge "Lessing's ditch" spawned a massive industry attempting to place historical research about the earthly Jesus on solid ground.

---

3. Dungan, *History of the Synoptic Problem*, 59-64, 89-97. However, these venomous attacks did frame questions that still arise from time to time and that remind readers about some inconsistencies of these works.

4. See Talbert, *Reimarus*, 27-28, 61-269. Readers should be aware that this English translation is only part of the larger Reimarus corpus.

Nevertheless, to this day, the authenticity and reliability of much of this scholarship is still frequently brought into question.

A new twist on the difficulties facing critical historical study of the Gospels has recently come to light in an analysis by Bart Ehrman, a well-known scholar of early Christianity.[5] The general tone of Ehrman's polemic deepens the Reimarus/Lessing assault. It shifts the focus of the assault against the results of historical study from general questions about the dependability of this kind of research by later histories back to questions about the people who first recorded this material. Instead of wondering how this research fits into the mold of rationality, Ehrman has questioned the reliability of the memory of those who witnessed Jesus' ministry and transmitted the tradition about him. He asks whether humans have the capacity, after having witnessed an earlier significant event, to recall it later, accurately, in vastly different settings.

Ehrman assembles a considerable body of social-science data analysis of experts of oral testimony given in legal trials, and material from other settings to make a case that human recollection of momentous or stressful situations in the past is often deeply unreliable. He then slips over easily to reflect on how this research may be used to call into question the status and reliability that many attribute to the veracity of the arguments given in the biblical Gospels.

Ehrman reminds us that, at the very least, the present received text of the Gospels was not in place before a generation after Jesus had passed; it was also composed in a different setting. Given the present state of research on memory, Ehrman concludes that the burden of proof of the Gospels being reliable accounts of what actually happened in Jesus' day shifts to those who make these claims.[6]

Regardless of how far one wishes to follow Ehrman's line of thinking it is clear that he has reopened a foundational question with respect to the status of study of the earliest constructs of the gospel tradition. Even with the simplest models of how the words and deeds of Jesus were transmitted before the final text of our Gospels, there were several distinct and important stages in the transmission of these events. The assault on "memory" itself is troubling, for it appears to weaken every link in the chain of transmission. In the middle of this maze one may well ask,

---

5. Ehrman, *Jesus Before the Gospels*. Since an earlier well-researched book, *The Orthodox Corruption of Scripture*, Ehrman has built a career calling into question what many have reckoned as the assured results of research in this area.

6. Ehrman, *Jesus Before the Gospels*, 242.

"Have we made as much progress in bridging 'Lessing's ditch' as is often thought?"

The Contribution of Birger Gerhardsson

In the modern era no one has given more attention to the issue of the transmission of the earliest Jesus tradition than Birger Gerhardsson.[7] He has taken the position that it is not enough to be content with setting forth generalities about how traditions about Jesus emerged in this earliest era of Christianity. Rather, he has probed for more specificity about how this actually took place. At its core, Gerhardsson's work instituted a new approach. For example, on the matter of the transmission of the Jesus tradition he argued that it was critical to give careful attention to analogies of how the words of revered teachers on sacral matters were transmitted in first century Israel for this was the closest parallel to the immediate context of Jesus' ministry.

Such an approach put him at odds with the majority of New Testament scholars of the mid-twentieth century. The background of most of these scholars was in the classics of the Greco-Roman world. They utilized the traditional classical approaches to this literature in their study of the writings of early Christianity. On the other hand, Gerhardsson argued that this was the wrong place to begin. Gospel literature must be assessed primarily within its dominant Jewish cultural framework. This was the place where one may expect the legacy of a wisdom teacher like Jesus the Nazorean would begin to be preserved and promulgated.[8]

---

7. I first met Gerhardsson at an international symposium on the gospels in Jerusalem in 1984. Since then I continued to interact with him until several years before his death in 2013. For those who did not know Gerhardsson personally it should be stressed that one could not overstate how deeply he was hurt by what he considered to be the misconstrual of the work of his doctoral dissertation. As a result, I have never known anyone who so rigorously explained the general direction and purpose of his later publications and why they contributed to his total project. A typical expression of this concern can be found in the later publication of the original translation of his seminal dissertation into English in 1964. I refer to Birger Gerhardsson, *Memory and Manuscript*, with a foreword by Jacob Neusner. The attention that Gerhardsson gave to the reception history of his work is aptly illustrated in the preface of this work, ix–xxiv. Also noteworthy is Neusner's foreword, xxv–xlv, which functions as a scholarly act of atonement for an earlier caustic review. Since the entire book is an easily accessible form of Gerhardsson's dissertation for most English readers it is the version I will quote in this essay.

8. This remains a somewhat minority position although the extensive scholarly

Consequently, Gerhardsson began his study of the Jesus tradition by engaging in an exhaustive evaluation of the educational process at work in late Second Temple Judaism. Here he found a starting point. Anything that was relevant for understanding what Jesus could have appropriated from this cultural heritage could be carefully reviewed as a potential source for shedding light on how the Jesus tradition was transmitted. Furthermore, an essential presupposition was that similar practices in the later Rabbinic era with its far greater volume of source material often had their roots in practices operative in Jesus' own time. He reckoned that this also needed to be carefully studied.

This project proved to be a massive undertaking and continues to be developed and expanded by contemporary scholars.[9] In one brief essay, of course, it is not even possible to give an adequate summary of Gerhardsson's total project.[10] Rather, I intend to focus on several key aspects of Gerhardsson's work that pursues one central question. Keeping in mind certain issues raised by Ehrman about the historical validity of the Jesus tradition I wish to inquire into what extent does Gerhardsson's contribution still provide an acceptable foundation for the ordinary person to have confidence that the Gospels give us an authentic picture of Jesus.[11] I realize that important related issues such as memory, orality, and the complicated issue of the format of the earliest traditions themselves are closely intermingled with my goal. Nevertheless, I desire that the basic issue of historicity remains central.

Procedurally, I will attempt to bring into focus several areas of Gerhardsson's work on transmission of the earliest Jesus tradition. One area,

---

publication by Bruce Chilton is a notable exception.

9. The important work of Riesner, *Jesus als Lehrer* is an excellent example of further expansion of Gerhardsson's work on the educational levels of first-century Galilee and Judea. Later editions of Riesner's original work have followed in 1984 and 1988 and a substantial revision is promised. References in this essay come from the original edition.

10. An entire book of essays dedicated to dialogue with certain aspects of Gerhardsson's work has fairly recently been published. cf. *Jesus in Memory*. This, in itself, is an ongoing tribute to the significance of Gerhardsson's work.

11. Here I do not wish to stake out a literalist position on the historicity of the Jesus tradition similar to the earlier work of Riesenfeld that Ehrman, *Jesus Before the Gospels*, 66–71, caricatures. cf. Riesenfeld, *Gospel Tradition*. The Synoptic Gospels clearly present many accounts of the same incidents that anchor them in diverse settings, wording, and outcomes. I do argue that by following some of Gerhardsson's procedures of searching for the formation of tradition in Jesus' Jewish social world constitutes the best way one can come to solid ground for accepting their basic historicity.

surprisingly overlooked, I believe, validates the essential historicity of this tradition. Second, I will attempt to distinguish between the enduring features of Gerhardsson's strategy and those that are more open to question. A final summary of where we stand in light of Gerhardsson's work on historicity will constitute the conclusion.

The Complexity of the Process of Transmitting the Jesus Tradition

The Question of Orality

Any attempted reconstruction of the Jesus tradition must take into consideration the indisputable reality of the place of orality in its earliest stages.[12] Indeed sometimes people refer, questionably I believe, to Gerhardsson's work as "The Oral Tradition Hypothesis." If one means by this that special attention should be given to the earliest phase of the development of the Jesus tradition I have no problem with the terminology. However, to state the obvious before one goes much further, a basic problem must be confronted. Tradition that is oral only exists in a theoretical sense because of the intrinsic nature of oral performance. In the ancient world each oral presentation was an event in and of itself. Consequently, aside from some private notes, memories perhaps preserved in later writings, or sundry descriptions of actual oral performance, not much that is reliable can be retrieved by historians. Thus, at the outset the question of how one can go about characterizing the oral tradition that preceded the written Gospels appears to be an elusive and, perhaps, insoluble question. Orality *per se* would appear to be a dead end unless it is qualified by a supplemental definition. I would argue that when I refer to "oral tradition" I am simply talking about "a communal recollection of an authoritative body of teaching/deeds of Jesus." There is little doubt that something like this had to occur in the earliest stages of the Gospel tradition.

What Precipitated the Tradition?

This raises another initial question. Why, in the first place, did there exist a tradition associated with Jesus the Nazorean? He came from an obscure

---

12. Eve, *Behind the Gospels*, 1–8.

village under Roman occupation in a part of the land that had a checkered history. Given his marginal economic background situation and his scandalous death it would seem hardly likely that anyone would be motivated to engage in the collection and transmission of the sayings and deeds of this "teacher of parables." The Gospel accounts (especially Matthew and Luke) narrate events that took place in Jesus' ministry outside of Jerusalem. Under what circumstances could the work of this itinerant teacher be granted such respect? Surely one must conclude only if something extraordinary was developing around him!

This is precisely what Gerhardsson claimed actually happened. In this connection he often drew attention to an earlier statement by Gerhard Kittel to the effect that Jesus' teaching had enormous power. According to Matt 23:8-10 Jesus was reckoned by his community to be the only teacher.[13] This emphasis on his authoritative word permeates Matthew and in the crescendo of 28:20 is reckoned as the foundational teaching for all later followers. Gerhardsson argued that this was not only an emphasis of Matthew but reflects the belief that Jesus had given a body of teaching on divine authority that was accepted by other early Christian leaders. In the early years of the church important figures like James and Paul, perhaps not always in agreement, shared a perspective that a body of common tradition reaching back to Jesus existed and served as an authoritative norm for church life.[14] Indeed, somewhat later, one pre-

---

13. Kittel, *Die Probleme des palästinischen*, 69. cf. Gerhardsson, *Memory and Manuscript*, 332-33. See also Byrskog, *Jesus the Only Teacher*, 12-15, 20-24. The latter writer, deeply knowledgeable of Gerhardsson's work, documents this connection and made it central to an important monograph.

14. Gerhardsson, *Origins of the Gospel Traditions*, 29-41, lays out the evidence for Paul as a transmitter of a body of Jesus tradition. He makes a key observation. "As an old Rabbinical student, Paul would be familiar with the current manner of transmitting sacral traditions about Torah among the Jews. A tradition was simply passed on either in a written text or orally. If the latter, one had to know it by heart. It was written upon his mind."

With respect to the epistle of James, Gerhardsson, *Origins of the Gospel Traditions*, 38-39, relates an occasion that was influential in developing his views on oral tradition. While reading Dibelius's commentary on James he came to the conviction that the famous German scholar had overlooked an important fact. James is a paraenetic letter based on presumed available knowledge of a separate body of the sayings of Jesus. Early Christian paraenesis, primarily, was grounded in the latter (i.e., a transmitted body of sayings and deeds of Jesus). Therefore, contrary to the form-critics, Gerhardsson came to realize "that the words of Jesus in the Synoptic Gospels cannot have had their primary *Sitz im Leben* in early paraenesis." This opened the door for Gerhardsson to conclude that much of the Jesus material that found its way into

sumes, it would function as a major source for much of the material in our received Gospel accounts. This brings us to the heart of his proposal. Granted that Gerhardsson's dismissal of the form-critics has validity, it is a fact that a body of Jesus tradition must have begun to emerge as early as the time of his Galilean ministry. What remains to be addressed is how reliable was that body of tradition?

The Reliability of the Earliest Jesus Tradition

It is at this point that one encounters the most discussed feature of Gerhardsson's proposal. He presumed that from the outset of Jesus' ministry, along and in connection with his announcement of the coming of the kingdom, Jesus developed a deliberate strategy to transmit the main body of his teaching to an inner core of his disciples. Furthermore, the obvious model that he would use was the one he could draw from the surrounding cultural practices of transmitting sacral material on authoritative Rabbinic teaching on Torah through a strict emphasis on memorization.

Even though there were those who believed Gerhardsson drew most of his evidence from the procedures of later Jewish academies, his work on the methodology of transmission of sacral tradition in Jesus' time has been validated by specialists in this field.[15] As already noted more recently it has been supplemented by the contribution of Rainer Riesner.[16] The latter's work is especially important because it provides extensive insight into the literary level of the average person of faith around Jesus.

Gerhardsson, along with many others, had noticed that from the Exilic period there was a major shift on the part of the Jewish community to preserve its identity (Ezra 7:10, 21–26).[17] After the later incursions of Hellenism into Jerusalem and the setting up of the gymnasia in the holy city this movement gathered momentum (1 Macc 1:14; 2 Macc 4:9). Jews who sought to maintain their traditions and derided Gentile lifestyles

---

the Synoptic Gospels had an existence distinctly separate from the regular paraenesis given by teachers in the later communities of Jesus. Therefore, the form-critics were wrong when they claimed most of the Jesus tradition was birthed in the paraenesis of early Christian assemblies. The basic authority of Jesus' works came from a different source that may well have preceded much of the later paraenesis in preaching and letters.

15. Cf. Neusner's foreword in Gerhardsson, *Memory and Manuscript*, xxv–xlvi.
16. Riesner, *Jesus als Lehrer*.
17. Gerhardsson, *Origins of the Gospel Traditions*, 13.

developed alternative places of learning that focused on deepening their knowledge of Torah.[18] Riesner supplemented Gerhardsson's work by tracing the development of a close connection between learning and piety (1 Enoch 83:1; Jub 7:38; 4 Macc 18:10–19).[19] Through his extensive research on family life and the importance of participation in synagogue activities by the pious, Riesner demonstrated that the drive for preservation of the identity of the people of God accelerated the passion for widespread literacy—even among the marginalized.[20]

The results of Riesner's research are impressive. One still hears of scholars who contest the existence of synagogues in the land until well into the first century. This is despite the growing accumulation of a mass of archaeological evidence to the contrary. More widely argued is the claim that only a small percentage of the people in the land were literate enough to facilitate reading and transmission of texts.[21] I find the latter claim highly questionable. For reasons stated above the people of God were strongly motivated to instruct their children to read the Torah aloud in their religious conventicles. Given the task of mastering what was even for them an ancient linguistic text this would be quite an accomplishment. Moreover, recitation would also entail memorization.[22] This capacity to work with written texts seems to be a fair representation of the culture in which Jesus was raised and began his ministry of announcing the coming of the kingdom of heaven. Thus, scholars like Eric Eve overstate when they assert that the kind of transmission of tradition envisioned by Gerhardsson by the earliest followers of Jesus could only be carried out by educated elites.[23] I believe that Jesus, as with many of his followers, had the capacity to deal with written texts. There is evidence in the Gospels that he thought deeply about the biblical story of Israel and devised a strategy for how, in light of the coming kingdom, he saw himself within that story. That being said, most of Jesus' teachings that made their way into the Gospels focus on his elaboration of the nature of

---

18. Gerhardsson, *Origins of the Gospel Traditions*, 15.

19. Riesner, "From the Messianic Teacher," 406–7.

20. Riesner, *Jesus als Lehrer*, 123–245.

21. Eve, *Behind the Gospels*, 10–13. Eve primarily appeals to the work of Keith, *Jesus' Literacy*, 71–85.

22. Riesner, "From the Messianic Teacher," 414, states, "The Sabbath readings from the Hebrew Old Testament normally had to be learned by heart in order that they could be recited without errors or pauses."

23. Eve, *Behind the Gospels*, 40.

the kingdom. If coherence is a test of reliability, then what shows up in the Synoptic Gospels does seem to receive a high passing grade.

The following evidence underscores this claim. Jesus is widely remembered as a teacher of wisdom (Matt 12:42; 23:27–31). For most scholars the Synoptic accounts of his gathering of a community of close inner-group disciples (the Twelve) appears to stand on firm historical ground. Indeed, the Gospels take it for granted that his disciples shared many similar features with the disciples of John the Baptist and the Pharisaic teachers (cf. Matt 9:14–17; Mark 2:18–23; Luke 5:33–39). It would not be an overstatement to say that the community of Jesus and his disciples gave every appearance to most people of the time as being a *Heburah*.[24] As such, they did not function like traditional oral societies but lived as a community that was functionally literate.

Thus, I come to the point that I described earlier as "often overlooked." It is within the borders of this community, overwhelmingly evident in the Gospels, that Jesus fashioned the bulk of his teaching into *meshālim*: a body of "parabolic like" teaching.[25] The point that is often overlooked is that it has such a consistent and unified form that it must be shaped by the views of one person. In my judgement herein rests the chief argument for the reliability of the earliest Jesus tradition.

Rainer Riesner has counted approximately 246 independent units of Jesus' teaching that have been preserved in the Gospels.[26] He considers that approximately 80 percent of these units are brief collections of Jesus' sayings (λογία), usually in some form of *parallelismus memborum* that have literary features often similar to those attributed to the biblical prophets.[27] Characteristic of this teaching are attempts to highlight

---

24. Stendahl, *School of St. Matthew*, 31.

25. Gerhardsson, "Secret of the Transmission," states precisely that the carriers of this teaching "handled and transmitted an oral tradition, most of which was not of a rigid halachic type but of a haggadic type (*māshāl*—and *ma'saeh*), less precisely formulated but still in principle memorized."

26. Riesner, "From the Messianic Teacher," 417. cf. Riesner, *Jesus als Lehrer*, 392–93. Curiously, the latter furnishes 247 as the number. My own study of the evidence is that Riesner's exact figure is too precise. The number of pericopes (even if restricted to Jesus verbal tradition) is variable and often depends on a particular source hypothesis. A check of published synopses reveals massive differences in the number of pericopes identified. However, the critical issue is not the exact number of units in the transmitted material, but whether they have identifiable forms and structures. Here Riesner seems to be on more solid ground.

27. Riesner, "From the Messianic Teacher," 418–19.

some features of the kingdom of God that have been described as "brief, pointed and pregnant."[28] In their entirety (both shorter and longer forms) these units are sometimes designated as *meshālim*, "parabolic," even though, for most later in conventional discussion, it is usually the longer units that have become known as "the parables."

In significant ways the shorter units do differ from the longer ones stylistically. Their use of particular literary features such as rhythm, theme, alliterations, assonances, paranomasia, and word plays as carefully formulated summaries of the λογία are usually a more prominent feature of the text than the wording of the longer parables.[29] These brief λογία and χρεῖαι appear to be used in a way to create the maximum ease for oral delivery. This, along with the more extended parables, is characteristic of many public speakers and convincingly brings us as close as possible to the form and content of Jesus' teaching.

This evidence that Gerhardsson (later supplemented by Riesner) has gathered is very significant. As noted, I believe it is often overlooked because it provides proof for the habitual style of one person in shaping a message; and most likely that person was Jesus the Nazorean. Nevertheless, in my judgment it goes too far to say that the formulation of these short pithy sayings is evidence of a deliberate attempt by Jesus to fashion for use a collection of sacral tradition that he called for his present and future followers to memorize. More likely, as with any skillful orator, Jesus crafted his sayings to create a sense of urgency so that his hearers would understand his message about the demands of the kingdom in a time of crisis. They were remembered because of both the power of their delivery and the tenor of the critical time. That they came from a charismatic teacher, no doubt, was a contributing factor.

To be sure, given the importance of memorization in the ancient world, as well as throughout most of the history of education, there is no doubt that Jesus demanded that some things be remembered. Such matters as the "Our Father" prayer (Matt 6:9-13; Luke 11:2-4) and charges to the disciples on mission would seem to fit into this category. However, it is interesting to note that even here, the received Gospel tradition fails to preserve these traditions with the precise exactness Gerhardsson attributed to the carriers of oral Torah.[30]

---

28. Gerhardsson, *Origins of the Gospel Traditions*, 70-71.

29. Riesner, "From the Messianic Teacher," 418.

30. A similar point may be made with respect to the words of bestowal at the Last Supper where one may suspect the wording was critically important for the

Thus, in light of both the context of Jesus' mission (eschatological fervor) and the massive instances of widespread verbal variation in *meshālim* preserved in the Synoptic Gospels, serious questions can be raised about what level of emphasis Jesus placed on memorizing his teachings with verbal exactitude. It has always struck me that, from the beginning of the Jesus movement, unlike Islam, earliest Christianity had no misgivings about translating the words of Jesus into a multitude of different languages. There was nothing sacred about maintaining the actual words of Jesus in their original linguistic expressions. Indeed, people still argue whether he spoke mainly in some form of Hebrew, Aramaic, or both! Add to this the fact that we have hardly any of this preserved since we are dependent for access to these sayings through Greek texts; then, and only then, can one begin to appreciate the magnitude of the task of reconstructing the earliest tradition.

To be sure, I agree with Gerhardsson that from the beginning a loose corpus of the words of Jesus began to be put into place. The form-critics, because of their theories, were wrong to charge that only some words and phrases of Jesus were accidentally preserved. Certainly Gerhardsson was also correct in allowing "for some variability in the process of oral formation," and in other texts such as the birth and temptation narratives one can agree that they were scribal creations.[31] This is not to forget the incorporation of the Passion account, which must have been put together in the early years of the Christian movement. But at the end of the day his strong emphasis on the proto-rabbinic model of transmission, especially with respect to memorization, probably over stressed because of his reaction to the form-critics, takes him too far in the direction of a formal reconstruction of Jesus' sayings and deeds. But this is not to deny that from the beginning the transmitted material had its own integrity. Gerhardsson was right about that.

Although it is exasperating to prove, it is probable that various segments of the Jerusalem community in the early days after Jesus took a lead in formulating further these words and deeds into a structured body of tradition.[32] Before this time it would seem likely that significant re-

---

earliest followers of Jesus (viz., Matt 26:26–29; Mark 14:22–25; Luke 22:19–20; 1 Cor 11:23–25).

31. Eve, *Behind the Gospels*, 38.

32. Gerhardsson's treatment of Paul's reverence and utilization of the tradition of Jesus, cf., *Memory and Manuscript*, 262–323, articulating the view that Paul himself, once a Proto-Rabbinic Jew, could have read this transmitted material in a more

membrance of Jesus' ministry was maintained in circles that were more widespread than Gerhardsson presumed. In addition to the Twelve, there were members of his own family who became believers, as well as other close family friends (e.g., Mary and Martha at Bethany).[33] In addition, various coteries of disciples who remained in one place had to be reckoned as important sources of information about him.[34] These may well have provided important source materials for the later composers of the Synoptic Gospels. Only after the departure of Jesus and the emergence of important figures in the restored community centering in Jerusalem would the Jesus community be in a position to engage in some assessment of these sources. Unfortunately, this is one of those places where there is little or no information in our literary sources about the status of the tradition. All we can say is that Paul utilized a version of it as authoritative and, most likely, other leaders did so as well.

Gerhardsson's Proposal: A Retrospective View

Luke 1:1 claims that others previously had sought to compile a διήγησις "narrative account" about matters concerning Jesus before his historical work. On this and other grounds it seems probable that both oral and written sources on Jesus circulated from a very early time. But how and in what form? Determining the content and manner of the transmission has often moved scholars close to a counsel of despair. E. P. Sanders is typical of reflection on this question.

> The problem of the transmission of the material remains opaque. We cannot solve it, but we should explore in slightly more detail the question of oral tradition.[35]

In short, there had to be a transmission of this material; but how was it accomplished?

Despite Sanders's pessimism Gerhardsson's proposal remains fruitful. If Jesus is remembered as a teacher how, in his culture, would one

---

traditional fashion is a worthwhile point to ponder. On this he may well be correct.

33. Richard Bauckham has frequently made a case for the importance of Jesus' family and close friends providing important eyewitness details on Jesus' life and ministry. See Bauckham, *Jesus and the Eyewitnesses*, 39-66.

34. Bauckham, *Jesus and the Eyewitnesses*, 358-411, also reminds us of the Johannine testimony that must be factored into this synthesis.

35. Sanders and Davies, *Studying the Synoptic Gospels*, 137.

expect that the information he imparted be passed on to others? Gerhardsson's answer was disarmingly simple: the same way as in the wider Jewish culture—by authoritative transmission in oral form involving massive repetition.[36]

In retrospect, Gerhardsson's accomplishments can be summarized as falling into three major areas.

First, Gerhardsson undermined forever the dominance of form-criticism in Gospel studies. Now that there were other viable models of accounting for the transmission process of the Jesus tradition the shine came off the luster of form-criticism and many of its weaknesses became more readily apparent.[37] Instead of viewing the Jesus tradition as a series of complicated layers that had to be carefully stripped away by experts to rediscover the pearls of a few original words of the teacher, Gerhardsson showed that it was possible to determine much more of what Jesus was saying and doing.[38] This, in itself, was a significant achievement.

Second, through his research on the *meshālim*, expanding on his first achievement, Gerhardsson was able to trace a substantial amount of the material attributed to Jesus back to the actual historical context of his ministry. With respect to the longer narrative *meshālim* Gerhardsson was able to claim,

> The narrative *meshālim* of the Synoptic Gospels have been "actualized" on their way from Jesus to the evangelists' Gospels. But the alterations of the texts do not seem to have been very great. The more developed theological topics and terms of early Christianity have not entered the narrative *meshālim* noticeably.[39]

There we have it. Through careful literary analysis of the structure of the actual sayings attributed to Jesus one can learn much about the actual source of the tradition. With respect to the question of the historicity of the Jesus tradition this is a significant result.

Much of my own academic research has involved the study of the Synoptic Problem. I continue to be nervous when I engage people who make sweeping statements about the Synoptics while freely admitting that they have never taken their Synopsis and worked through these texts unit by unit. Contrariwise, Gerhardsson examined the entire body of

---

36. Byrskog, "Introduction," in *Jesus in Memory*, 5–6.
37. Tuckett, "Form Criticism," 23.
38. Tuckett, "Form Criticism," 23–27.
39. Gerhardsson, "Illuminating the Kingdom, 290.

texts carefully and determined convincingly that there was more there than the fragments of a constantly reconfigured set of texts. He has given solid evidence that the structure of what he calls the *meshālim* bears the imprint of a single author.

Third, it is true that much of Gerhardsson's work can only be accepted if it is granted that a circle in the movement that Jesus started had basic literacy skills. Gerhardsson contributed much to this debate by insisting that the heart of Jewish life in this period centered around the study of sacred texts and listening to them being expounded in communal gatherings. To a major degree Gerhardsson assumed this was the case (viz., the Qumran discoveries began to be published during his formative academic years). This is an instance where earlier intuitions are now being vindicated.[40] It is important to note that it does appear that the literary level of leaders of the Jesus movement can be assumed to be high enough to refute the idea that it functioned only at the less ambitious level of most ancient oral societies.[41] Indeed, whether it be short collections or some form of aids to memory it seems most likely to follow that there were some literary analogues to the process of oral transmission within the Jesus tradition from the beginning.[42] There are still many questions here but the weight of evidence is trending toward the perspective espoused by Gerhardsson.

Despite the prescient work of Gerhardsson in placing the spotlight on the significance of controlled oral transmission for reconstruction of the sayings and deeds of Jesus significant issues still remain to be adequately addressed. Chief among them is the issue of the reliability of the memory of those who transmitted the tradition. In a way, Gerhardsson

---

40. Riesner, *Jesus als Lehrer*, 119–245; Riesner, "From the Messianic Teacher," 406–14. Also some useful material can be found in Fiensy and Strange, *Galilee*, 129–46, 253–58.

41. Gerhardsson, "Secret of the Transmission," 14, states, "I cannot . . . see that the Israel of NT times can be characterized as an oral society." This is why I prefer to call Gerhardsson's work an 'Oral Transmission' thesis and I seek to differentiate it from the recent widespread revival of various forms of mainstream theories about oral tradition. cf., Kelber, *Oral and the Written Gospel*; Dunn, *Jesus Remembered*. As is well known, the latter work is heavily indebted to theories of oral tradition espoused by K. E. Bailey. For a recent update on the status of this active movement see Rodriguez, *Oral Tradition*. Much of this work is very technical and sophisticated but it operates from different premises and presuppositions than those espoused by Gerhardsson. At the ground level it presumes that the Jesus community had close affinities with conventional ancient oral societies.

42. Gerhardsson, "Secret of the Transmission," 14–16.

finessed this question by claiming that Jesus followed strictly the scribal method of passing on teachings about Torah. Although this did not demand inflexibility in memorization of a text it put considerable emphasis on retaining the essence of what was being communicated. But today even this methodology is questioned with respect to its ability to recall accurately events of the past. Again, have we really advanced beyond Reimarus and Lessing?

There is a point when extreme skepticism descends into chaos and unreason. We may be close to reaching it here. Even a scholar such as Bart Ehrman, renowned for stressing the uncertainty of much historical judgment, recognizes that a body of tradition of some kind existed from the earliest days of the Jesus movement.[43] Although I have different reasons, I concur with Ehrman that Gerhardsson's wholesale appropriation of a rabbinic model of transmitting tradition is not the most fruitful part of his suggestions on tradition. There is little or no evidence in the texts that Jesus carefully imitated these procedures. The highly charged eschatologically oriented message of Jesus can hardly be conceived as being compatible with such a procedure. And, finally, the parallels between the Synoptic Gospels are not close enough to suggest that the carriers of the Jesus tradition were accustomed to following such a model. I conclude that Jesus and his community had some awareness of these particular scribal models but did not directly appropriate them.

As a way out of this maze I would suggest a path forward may be found in using selectively what social-scientists call "social memory."[44] To a major extent it is reasonable to conclude that from the beginning the formation of the Jesus tradition was a social or collective enterprise carried out by an inner core group of followers. Social scientists have noted that this kind of enterprise is characterized by a number of special features. Used carefully, "social memory" insights can produce a plausible model that supplements our knowledge about the formation and transmission of the Jesus tradition.

Social memory is the belief that the collective memory of a particular group (viz., the inner core of Jesus' disciples) produced a coherent frame that could legitimately function as the basis for shaping the narrative of the Jesus tradition. No doubt there were many people who treasured personal reminiscences in being with Jesus or seeing something that he did.

43. Ehrman, *Jesus Before the Gospels*, 65–66.
44. For a cogent overview of collective or social memory, see Eve, *Behind the Gospels*, 86–107.

Yet, as opposed to merely keeping these recollections in their minds in an unstable and fragmentary order (something akin to a dream sequence), something else was necessary to provide coherence to the developing narrative.[45] A key element of social memory is that it is primarily reconstructive rather than reproductive of a narrative.[46] It was the persistent existence of the Jesus community that finally molded the narrative frame and structure that resulted in the Jesus tradition. Commencing with the work of the Twelve the belief that the Kingdom was near provided a touchstone around which both personal reminiscences and communally shaped collections of Jesus' teachings were gathered and molded to provide a unified functional way to enable the Jesus community to look at the world. In this context an authoritative social memory develops and a tradition begins to grow and be transmitted.

Eve points out that as the narrative expands various devices emerge to facilitate transmission of this narrative tradition.[47] Thus, the social memory is maintained and provides growing coherence and confirmation of the tradition. The advantage is that since this is a collective narrative it cannot easily be manipulated to invent or invert sayings and accounts of Jesus without communal input. Granted, this is a different model than what Gerhardsson advocated, but in my judgment, understood conservatively, it is a more plausible explanation for the earliest formation of the Jesus tradition. From the beginning, as Luke 1:1–2 narrates, there were eyewitnesses. For reasons including translations from Semitic languages, accounting for an emerging Christology and the incorporation of the Passion narrative, it is not possible to reconstruct the *ippsisima verba* of Jesus. Nevertheless, careful study of the Synoptic traditions confirm that what underlies their diverse wording and order of presentation is a very solid recollection of the social memory of a major body of his earliest teaching by followers.[48] Therefore, the Gospel narrative is not dependent upon the fallible memories of individual followers.

This tradition was no doubt clarified by early ecclesiastical leaders in Jerusalem and elsewhere and eventually served as a foundational

---

45. Eve, *Behind the Gospels*, 93.

46. Eve, *Behind the Gospels*, 93.

47. Eve, *Behind the Gospels*, 96–98. Here he refers to such things as the application of schemata to interpret the significance of information that was encoded in the past; and "keying": the telling of one story in sequence to validate another.

48. cf. Tuckett, "Form Criticism," 24.

resource for the writers of the Gospel accounts. But how that took place is another story for a different day!

Conclusion

It is now slightly more than fifty years since Birger Gerhardsson's now classic *Memory and Manuscript* began to seriously engage the attention of Gospel scholars in Europe and North America. Retrospectively, what became widely known as his "oral tradition thesis" lit a spark that ignited a new interest in oral tradition among Gospel scholars. Despite the fact that Gerhardsson's thesis has serious critics, as a part of Gospel studies, the study of oral tradition took off in new directions and has become a burgeoning industry.

In one form or another works on the transmission of the earliest oral traditions about Jesus raise questions about the reliability of the history narrated. In this essay I have sought to show that Gerhardsson's model of transmitting oral tradition, drawn from a proto-rabbinic model with its strong emphasis on memorization, has problems in explaining the formation of the gospel tradition. On the other hand, the often overlooked massive body of *meshālim* that characterizes the received teaching of Jesus, which Gerhardsson carefully drew from the Gospels, is strong evidence that many sayings in the Gospels represented the work of a single teacher, and that teacher would be no other than Jesus the Nazorean. This body of evidence seems to underscore the essential historicity of a body of tradition that undergirds the Synoptic Gospels.

Gerhardsson is to be commended for laying the groundwork for our understanding that the subsequent early Christian narrative was drawn by Jesus' disciples out of the core of his teaching. This was the basis for its authoritative status in the early Christian communities. Recent research in social memory provides deeper insight into how the Christian narrative was formed from this body of tradition. Herein rest the essential elements of the argument that the transmission of the earliest Jesus tradition confirms the claim that Christianity is a historical religion.

Bibliography

Bauckham, Richard. *Jesus and the Eyewitnesses: The Gospels as Eyewitness Testimony.* Grand Rapids: Eerdmans, 2006.

Byrskog, Samuel. *Jesus in Memory: Traditions in Oral and Scribal Perspectives.* Edited by Werner H. Kelber and Samuel Byrskog. Waco: Baylor University Press, 2009.

———. *Jesus the Only Teacher: Didactic Authority and Transmission in Ancient Israel, Ancient Judaism and the Matthean Community.* Coniectanea Biblica New Testament Series 24. Stockholm: Almquist & Wiksell, 1994.

Dungan, David L. *A History of the Synoptic Problem: The Canon, the Text, the Composition, and the Interpretation of the Gospels.* New York: Doubleday, 1999.

Dunn, James D. G. *Jesus Remembered.* Vol. 1, *Christianity in the Making.* Grand Rapids: Eerdmans, 2003.

Ehrman, Bart D. *Jesus Before the Gospels: How the Earliest Christians Remembered, Changed, and Invented Their Stories of the Savior.* New York: HarperCollins, 2016.

———. *The Orthodox Corruption of Scripture: The Effect of Early Christological Controversies on the Text of the New Testament.* New York: Oxford University Press, 1993.

Eve, Eric. *Behind the Gospels: Understanding the Oral Tradition.* Minneapolis: Fortress, 2014.

Fiensy, David A., and James Riley Strange, eds. *Galilee in the Late Second and Mishnaic Periods.* Vol. 1. Minneapolis: Fortress, 2014.

Foster, P., et al., eds. *New Studies in the Synoptic Problem: Oxford Conference, 2008: Essays in Honour of Christopher M. Tuckett.* Bibliotheca Ephemeridum Theologicarum Lovaniensium 239. Leuven: Peeters, 2011.

Gerhardsson, Birger. "Illuminating the Kingdom: Narrative Meshalim in the Synoptic Gospels." In *Jesus and the Oral Gospel Tradition*, edited by Henry Wansbrough, 266–309. Journal for the Study of the New Testament, Supplement Series 64. Sheffield: JSOT, 1991.

———. *Jesus in Memory: Traditions in Oral and Scribal Perspective.* Edited by Werner H. Kelber and Samuel Byrskog. Waco: Baylor University Press, 2009.

———. *Memory and Manuscript: Oral Tradition and Written Transmission in Rabbinic Judaism and Early Christianity with Tradition and Transmission in Early Christianity.* Grand Rapids: Eerdmans, 1998.

———. *The Origins of the Gospel Traditions.* Philadelphia: Fortress, 1979.

———. "The Secret of the Transmission of the Unwritten Jesus Tradition." *New Testament Studies* 51 (2005) 1–18.

Goodacre, Mark S. *Thomas and the Gospels: The Case for Thomas's Familiarity with the Synoptics.* Grand Rapids: Eerdmans, 2012.

Keith, Chris. *Jesus' Literacy: Scribal Culture and the Teacher from Galilee.* Library of New Testament Studies 413. London: T. & T. Clark, 2011.

Kelber, Werner. *The Oral and the Written Gospel: The Hermeneutics of Speaking and Writing in the Synoptic Tradition, Mark, Paul and the Q.* Bloomington: Indiana University Press, 1997.

Kittel, Gerhard. *Die Probleme des palästinischen Spätjudentums und das Urchristentum* Stuttgart: Kohlhammer, 1926.

Porter, Stanley E., and Bryan R. Dyer, eds. *The Synoptic Problem: Four Views.* Grand Rapids: Baker Academic, 2016.

Riesenfeld, Harald. *The Gospel Tradition.* Philadelphia: Fortress, 1970.

Riesner, Rainer. "From the Messianic Teacher to the Gospels of Jesus Christ." In *Handbook for the Study of the Historical Jesus,* edited by T. Holman and S. Porter. Leiden: Brill, 2011.

———. *Jesus als Lehrer.* WUNT 2.7. Tübingen: Mohr Siebeck, 1981.

Rodriguez, Rafael. *Oral Tradition and the New Testament: A Guide for the Perplexed.* Bloomsburg: London, 2014.

Sanders. E. P., and Margaret Davies. *Studying the Synoptic Gospels.* London: SCM, 1989.

Stendahl, Krister. *The School of St. Matthew and Its Use of the Old Testament.* Ramsey: Sigler, 1991.

Talbert, Charles H., ed. *Reimarus: Fragments.* Translated by Ralph S. Fraser. Philadelphia: Fortress, 1970.

Tuckett, Christopher. "Form Criticism." In *Jesus in Memory: Traditions in Oral and Scribal Perspectives,* edited by W. H. Kelber and S. Byrskog, 21–38. Waco: Baylor University Press, 2009.

Historicity and the Jesus Tradition

Respondent: Martin Mosse

Classification of Gospel Research

McNicol's chapter, "Birger Gerhardsson and Oral Transmission in the Formation of the Gospel Tradition," brings a thoughtful emphasis on the historicity of the Synoptic Gospels. His conclusion that "the transmission of the earliest Jesus tradition confirms the claim that Christianity is a historical religion" marries well with conclusions I have reached on very different grounds.[1] McNicol is asking, "What possibly can be known about the life of Jesus and the earliest decades of the Christian movement?"

What kinds of research are open to us in order to answer this? There are two dichotomies according to which Gospel research may be usefully classified. The first relates to the *types of researcher* in terms of the type of evidence they work with. The second distinguishes two essential *types of transmission*. We may describe them respectively as follows.

Types of Researcher

A. Those who typically look first of all for their information *internally*, within the Gospels. The source critics and form-critics have traditionally operated like this, characteristically by making *textual* comparisons between them, the tool of choice being the parallel

---

1. For "Jesus tradition" I am following the definition given by Michael F. Bird, *Gospel of the Lord*, 3, who gives it as "the body of oral tradition transmitted in the early church which rehearsed the words of Jesus and stories about Jesus."

synopsis. They have often been uncomfortable with research into the historical individuals involved as either transmitters or authors, and with the detailed chronology that accompanies this. It is routine in such circles to deny traditional authorship of the Gospels, however strong may have been the belief of the Fathers.[2] So as the author of the third Gospel, St. Luke is replaced by "the anonymous author of Luke/Acts."

B. Those who typically look for *personal* and *historical* information about the individual transmitters and authors, and the chronology of their lives and movements, which are mostly to be deduced from *external* sources such as the Book of Acts or the Early Fathers. This is the province of ancient historians, whom I have described in chapter 1, and with whom I number myself.

As an illustration, researchers of type A are likely to concern themselves more with the gospel message, the *kerygma*; type B, more with the *keryges*, those who proclaimed it. But it must be stressed that boundaries can overlap. So type A researchers, besides scrutinizing the text of the Gospels, will also want to consider the first century environment in which transmission took place. Conversely, researchers of type B, though primarily focused on evidence external to the Gospels, will not want to omit any historical or chronological indications that may be gleaned from within the Gospels themselves.[3]

B. H. Streeter in his foundational work *The Four Gospels* (1924) managed to combine both types A and B, but his successors have tended to concentrate rather more upon the internal relations between the Gospels (type A), often at the expense of historical research (type B). Richard Bauckham's *Jesus and the Eyewitnesses* (2006) marked something of a swing of the pendulum back to historical research into the contributions

---

2. "The form-critics did not think much of the information which the ancient church provides concerning the concrete persons behind the Gospels, not even of the personal reference in the New Testament. . . . This depersonalization has had a contagious effect right into the present." Gerhardsson, *Reliability*, 74.

3. So for instance in attempting to date Matthew, they will note his statement that Judas's blood money was used to buy the potter's field, which was used as a burial place for foreigners, and is still called the Field of Blood, ἕως τῆς σημερον, "to this day" (27:8). Likewise, the tomb guards were instructed to blame the disappearance of Jesus' body on the disciples who stole it, "and this story has been widely circulated among the Jews to this very day (μέχρι τῆς σημερον)" (28:15). Both of these suggest that Jerusalem was still standing when Matthew wrote, before the ensuing diaspora.

made to the creation and transmission of the Gospels by recognized individuals.

Types of Transmission

The second dichotomy classifies source theories according to the *type of ancestry* they ascribe to the Gospels, that is, the mode through which the Jesus tradition is deemed to have taken [and] been *transmitted*. The basic alternatives are:

1. *Oral transmission*, according to which the Jesus tradition is held to have been passed on primarily by word of mouth before being crystallized into writing. Classically, this was by no means exclusively the territory of the form-critics, and hence of Gerhardsson and McNicol after him. They have found much of their material within the Gospel text (as type 1: for instance Gerhardsson's work on the *meshālim*), and from the nature of oral transmission generally, especially in the Jewish environment.

2. *Written transmission*, by which the elements of the Jesus tradition were put into writing before the emerging of our present Gospels. Candidate proto-gospels have been proposed at various times, such as the Matthean λογια, "Ur-Marcus," Proto-Luke, and Q. This is the battlefield on which the conflict between advocates of Q and alternative hypotheses like those of Farrer[4] and his successors has been played out.

Although for both dichotomies the boundaries between these classifications may be fluid, when trying to understand the genesis of our Gospels, they do help to understand how conflicts between rival approaches and theories can arise. Indeed, it is often in the combinations and overlaps between them that interest arises.

Advocates of Q (type 1) subsequent to Streeter, and many of their opponents, have concentrated almost exclusively on minute examinations of the Synoptic text, with little or no consideration of history. Type 2 opponents of Q, by contrast, have justly made much of the fact that so far not a shred of anything that could be identified as coming from Q has ever been unearthed by the archaeologists; and that no mention of this supposedly lost text has ever been found in the considerable volume of

---

4. Farrer, "On Dispensing with Q."

writings bequeathed to us by the Early Fathers, who give no indication of having even heard of this sacred document or possessed it, still less of having lost it.[5]

Historicity of the Gospels

McNicol is pessimistic as to how much can be known about New Testament history:

> We sense that what happened in the earliest days of the Christian Movement [is] critical for gauging its essence; but, at the same time, these early decades seem stubbornly resistant to supplying a coherent picture of what took place that even approximates a consensus.

And again:

> Determining the content and manner of the transmission has often moved scholars close to a counsel of despair. E. P. Sanders is typical of reflection on this question. "The problem of the transmission of the material remains opaque. We cannot solve it, but we should explore in slightly more detail the question of oral tradition."

McNicol reports fears that New Testament or at least Gospel history has been discredited, and it is because of this that he has concentrated his researches *within* the Gospels: type 1 making up for a failure of type 2. But has it? He lists some of the most notable pessimists.

The "inconsistencies in the Gospel accounts" found by Celsus and Porphyry present no serious obstacle to the practiced historian. We see this every day whenever two different eyewitnesses report the same news incident.[6] We have no difficulty in handling this. On the contrary, if all the Gospels, for instance, gave identical accounts of the resurrection, the

---

5. I once asked Professor Larry Hurtado after a public lecture, was there, among all the thousands of fragments of the New Testament and early Christian writings that archaeologists have unearthed, any single scrap that could ever be claimed as coming from Q? He replied that he was himself a believer in Q as the best solution to the Synoptic Problem; nevertheless, the answer to my question was no. Contrast the Gospel of Thomas, which had been known of long before it was discovered in 1945, because assorted references to and quotations from it are to be found in the Fathers.

6. This is no newly recognized phenomenon. "Different eyewitnesses give different accounts of the same events, speaking out of partiality for one side or the other or else from imperfect memories." Thucydides, *History of the Peloponnesian War*, 1.22.3.

naysayers who today make hay of the divergences between the evangelists would soon be talking the language of conspiracy as some do anyway.

Reimarus and Lessing are welcome to their views on what the Gospels *mean*. But their "philosophical theology" has very little bearing on the historical investigation of how they came to be. To this a "good philosopher," for all his or her "rational thought," will contribute very little unless he or she has some detailed understanding of first century history and how to research it.

As to the "ultimate validity of historical research," this too depends not a little on who is doing it. People do historical research all the time. Most of us have no serious problem with this. We accept that the validity of their work depends upon the quality of the researchers. Were that not so, and as a matter of principle all history were routinely discarded as untrustworthy, no one would do such research because no one would pay for it. This is a smokescreen.

McNicol writes also of the post-Enlightenment, nineteenth century "school of thought that denied the existence of Jesus altogether." Such people still survive today. Many of them are sixth formers.

Ehrman's work on memory has been criticized on its own ground. Anthony le Donne, for instance, writes,

> Oral cultures have been capable of tremendous competence. The human mind can remember vast amounts of information with great accuracy when it remains active and fluid. The oral culture in which Jesus was reared trained their brightest children to remember entire libraries of story, law, poetry, song, etcetera.[7]

Again, Ehrman's attack on memory assumes there were no early written records of Jesus' ministry. Alan Millard, in keeping with McNicol's proposition that "a circle in the movement which Jesus started had basic literacy skills," argues for wider literacy in first century Palestine than used to be believed, making a case for "written notes of [Jesus'] individual sayings, or a collection of some, and reports of remarkable events"; so that "some, possibly much, of [the Evangelists'] source material was preserved in writing from [Jesus' lifetime], especially accounts of the distinctive teaching and actions of Jesus."[8] Similarly, Michael Bird argues that "the Jesus tradition was carried in a mix of oral and textual media beginning in Jesus' own lifetime all the way through to the Gospels

---

7. Le Donne, *Historical Jesus*, 70, quoted in Bird, *Gospel of the Lord*, 4.
8. Millard, *Reading and Writing*, 223–24.

and beyond,"⁹ including the use of "notebooks" forerunners of the codex, such as may have been designated by the "books" (βιβλια) and "parchments" (μεμβράνας) that Paul left behind at Troas (2 Tim 4:13).¹⁰

A Parallel from the Greco-Roman World

McNicol reports Gerhardsson's dismissal of scholars whose background lay mostly in the classics of the Greco-Roman world and "utilized the traditional classical approaches to this literature in their study of the writings of early Christianity." I plead guilty to having such a background myself, and would defend it. The qualities of a good ancient historian[11] are indeed transferable from one culture to another, and lessons learned in a familiar culture can often serve as a control for testing judgments we make in another.

The great Roman historian A. N. Sherwin-White, lecturing in 1961–62, tackled this very question in a salutary passage headed, "The Historicity of the Gospels and Graeco-Roman Historiography," which I would commend to anyone working in this field.[12] He discusses the impact of modern day source criticism when applied to Greco-Roman historians such as Thucydides, Polybius, Livy, Tacitus, Suetonius, and Herodotus in their records of such figures as Peisistratus, Caius Gracchus, Tiberius, and Hipparchus, considering bias and distortion during the process of oral tradition. Even though in such cases our sources are not just one or two generations after the events they describe, but much more often two to five *centuries*, he concludes that

> a hard core or basic layer of historical truth can be recovered even from the most deplorable of our tertiary sources. . . . The refinement of source-criticism has not led to the notion that knowledge in ancient history is unattainable.[13]

Sherwin-White expressed himself amazed at the conclusion of the form-critics that the historical Christ is unknowable and that the history

---

9. Bird, *Gospel of the Lord*, 45.
10. Bird, *Gospel of the Lord*, 47.
11. See my section "Qualities of a Good New Testament Historian" in chapter 1.
12. Sherwin-White, *Roman Society*, 186–93.
13. Sherwin-White, *Roman Society*, 186.

of his mission cannot be written. For that to be credible we would need much later dates for the Gospels than could be the case:

> The tests suggest that even two generations are far too short a span to allow the mythical tendency to prevail over the hard historic core of the oral tradition.[14]

Again,

> It can also be suggested that it would be no harder for the Disciples and their immediate successors to uncover detailed narratives of the actions and sayings of Christ within their closed community, than it was for Herodotus and Thucydides to establish the story of the great events of 520–480 BC. For this purpose it matters little whether you accept the attributions of the Gospels to eyewitnesses or not.[15]

New Testament Chronology

This last point raises the question, what were the dates of the Gospels? It is a question too often passed over. And there's the rub. We cannot even begin to determine the reliability of transmission of the Jesus tradition without first establishing the *intervals across which that transmission is deemed to have taken place*. If we are going to cross a bridge it helps to know where it starts and where it ends. We must define the problem before we can solve it. And for this we need to know our chronology. Type 1 research on its own will not suffice.

Ehrman's "reminder" that, in McNicol's words, "at the very least, the present received text of the Gospels was not in place before a generation after Jesus had passed," on which rests his skepticism over the Gospels, falls at this fence, although it would still command widespread acceptance today. Since J. A. T. Robinson's groundbreaking *Redating the New Testament* appeared in 1976,[16] the movement for revising downwards the dates of the Gospels, Acts, and other parts of the New Testament has been gaining traction. Robinson has been followed, among others, by John Wenham in 1992[17] and E. Earle Ellis in 1999.[18] The challenge that

14. Sherwin-White, *Roman Society*, 190.
15. Sherwin-White, *Roman Society*, 191.
16. Robinson, *Redating the New Testament*.
17. Wenham, *Redating*.
18. Ellis, *Making of the New Testament*. I have offered my own contribution in

he famously threw down—"One of the oddest facts about the New Testament is that what on any showing would appear to be the single most datable and climactic event of the period of the fall of Jerusalem in AD 70, and with it the collapse of institutional Judaism based on the temples never once mentioned as a past fact"[19]—continues to be a thorn in the side of any scholar seeking to maintain conventional late dates, and to my knowledge has never been satisfactorily answered.[20]

As I have argued in chapter 1, there is a very strong case, originating from Edmundson,[21] that Mark, the first Gospel, was written c. 45, just twelve years after the crucifixion. It is difficult to see much memory-induced distortion taking effect in that interval, even without Sherwin-White's affirmations. Ehrman need not trouble us.

Also in chapter 1 I argued briefly that Acts is to be dated to AD 62 where it ends,[22] with Luke's Gospel, making good use of Mark, around AD 60. Matthew also used Mark, and there is a strong case for the Farrer Hypothesis (see below) that Luke redacted Matthew. So all three Synoptics can be placed with a high probability between AD 45 and AD 60 that is to say, *pace* McNicol, all were *completed* "before a generation after Jesus had passed."[23] But the knock-on effects on present understandings of New Testament history, and of the development of Christian theology and Christology, are potentially massive.[24]

Mosse, *Three Gospels*. *Pari passu*, the date of Papias's writings was being brought down from Lightfoot's estimate of 130 to c. 95–110, thus increasing our confidence in his accounts of gospel dates: see particularly Yarbrough, "Date of Papias." This has now acquired widespread acceptance, making more credible the much maligned (see chapter 1) Papias's information about the origins of the Gospels.

19. Robinson, *Redating*, 13.

20. See my comments on Raymond E. Brown's difficulties in his *Introduction to the New Testament* in chapter 1 of this volume.

21. Edmundson, *Church in Rome*, 1913.

22. See Hemer, *Book of Acts*; also the chronologist Moberly, "When Was Acts Planned?" I have combined the arguments of Hemer and Moberly with others of my own in chapter 12 of *The Three Gospels*.

23. The arguments supporting all this chronology are laid out in full in Mosse, *Three Gospels*.

24. The ancestor of late dates for the Gospels and Acts is F. C. Baur (1792–1860) and the Tübingen school that followed him, who supplied second century dates for them all. Although these have now been totally discredited, there are still those for whom lateness holds a glutinous attraction in its own right. See Ellis, *Making of the New Testament*, Appendix VI, "Ferdinand Christian Baur and His School." The exciting tale of how the Tübingen hypotheses were then refuted by the detailed work of

The failure here is a failure of historical scholarship, and begins to explain the despair of McNicol and others over the lack of reliable historical evidence for the period in question. As he tells us, "To this day, the authenticity and reliability of much of this scholarship is still frequently brought into question." The problem is not one of evidence, but a *shortage of top class historians*, prompting Stephen Neill and Tom Wright to lament that Eduard Meyer (1855–1930) and J. B. Lightfoot (1828–89) were the "only two great historians" in the whole history of modern scholarship who "have concerned themselves with the events of the first Christian century."[25] We need better historians.[26] Edmundson might well be among the candidates.

Transmission

Looking now at possible modes of transmission that led to the writing of our Gospels, we can usefully take a leaf from Gerhardsson's book by investigating the practices and understandings of the time, in this case by considering how the early church saw the process.

Irenaeus (c. 130–200) supplies a valuable clue. In a passage preserved for us by Eusebius, which I have discussed in chapter 1, he gives his account of how the gospel was preserved:

> Matthew composed his Gospel among the Hebrews in their own language,[27] while Peter and Paul proclaimed the Gospel in Rome and founded the community. After their death Mark, the disciple and interpreter of Peter, transmitted to us in written form the things that were being preached by Peter. And Luke, who was Paul's follower, set down in a book the gospel which was being preached by him. Then John, the Lord's disciple, who had reclined on his breast, himself produced the Gospel when he was staying in Ephesus, in the province of Asia.[28]

Lightfoot and Zahn on the letters of Ignatius and Clement of Rome is expounded by Neill and Wright, *Interpretation*, 51–59.

25. Neill and Wright, *Interpretation*, 306–7.

26. As Gerhardsson puts it, "What is needed is a more sober approach to history," (*Reliability of the Gospel Tradition*, 40).

27. Matthew's Gospel does not appear today to have been written in Hebrew or Aramaic and then translated into Greek. For a possible explanation of the origins of this view of Matthew see Mosse, *Three Gospels*, chap. 4.

28. Irenaeus, *Adversus Haereses* 3.1.1, quoted in Eusebius's *Ecclesiastical History* V.viii.2–4.

What matters to Irenaeus is that the Gospels his generation received had pedigrees that could be traced back to *either the apostles themselves, or to a very close associate of theirs.*

We find the same in a much debated passage in Eusebius, where he quotes from Papias's own record of how he kept abreast with both original and current church teaching, taking trouble to obtain the most authentic account that he could:

> Yet Papias himself, according to the preface of his treatises, makes plain that he had in no way been a hearer and eyewitness of the sacred Apostles, but teaches that he had received the articles of the faith from those who had known them, for he speaks as follows: "And I shall not hesitate to append to the interpretations all that I ever learnt well from the presbyters and remember well, for of their truth I am confident. For unlike most I did not rejoice in them who say much, but in them who teach the truth, nor in them who recount the commandments of others, but in them who repeated those given to the faith by the Lord and derived from truth itself; but if ever anyone came who had followed the presbyters, I enquired into the words of the presbyters, what Andrew or Peter or Philip or Thomas or James or John or Matthew, or any other of the Lord's disciples, had said, and what Aristion and the presbyter John, the Lord's disciples, were saying. For I did not suppose that information from books would help me so much as the word of a living and surviving voice." (*EH* III.xxxix.2–4 tr. Lake)

I have discussed the details of this elsewhere.[29] My present point is that Papias's discriminating search for the truth about Jesus led him to enquire about the most reliable sources, that is, *either the apostles themselves, or others who had learned from them*: in both cases, prominent church leaders and, apparently, as many as possible, thus guaranteeing the integrity of the tradition. We find the same emphasis on the earliest church leaders in Paul, for whom the church had been "built on the foundation of the *apostles and prophets*, Christ Jesus being the cornerstone" (Eph 2:20). Then *Paul* in turn passed on his knowledge to *Timothy*, budding leader of the next generation, expressing his concern for the *next two generations* after him (2 Tim 2:2). This is very different from the form-critical model of anonymous oral transmission, developing separately in isolated communities, that Gerhardsson did so much to refute.

---

29. Mosse, *Three Gospels*, 109–12.

This then is the passing down of the Jesus tradition from one generation of recognized church leaders to the next and is one model of transmission that we can identify from history. It does not compel the strong emphasis on controlled memorization that Gerhardsson adopted from rabbinic practices, of which McNicol writes that it "is not the most fruitful part of his suggestions on tradition." Rather, its fidelity is maintained by these *identifiable church leaders* who stand as the guarantors of its content. As Gerhardsson himself tells us, in standard practice,

> the message was presented as an eyewitness account. In the first phase the object was to produce witnesses; in the second, to find witnesses to what the witnesses had said.

So we have "Mark, the interpreter of Peter," "Polycarp, who was a disciple of John," and "the elders, the disciples of the Apostles."[30]

Richard Bauckham's groundbreaking book *Jesus and the Eyewitnesses* takes this point even further.[31] Bauckham maintains that the accuracy of many of the Gospel stories will have been assured by *eyewitnesses* such as Jesus' family and close friends. Some stories may have originated with participants named in them, who will have been guarantors of its accuracy for as long as they were alive.[32] Oral tradition, then, got off to a good start.

On the Book of Acts, researched by Luke, one of the finest historians of the classical world, Sherwin-White commented,

> For Acts the confirmation of historicity is overwhelming.... But any attempt to reject its basic historicity even in matters of detail must now appear absurd. Roman historians have long taken it for granted.[33]

Acts abounds in historical information, often in microscopic detail, about the life and growth of the early church in the first thirty years of its existence, which is abundantly coherent. I do not recognize in it McNicol's comment given above that "these early decades seem stubbornly resistant to supplying a coherent picture of what took place," although

---

30. Gerhardsson, *Memory and Manuscript*, 283.

31. Bauckham, *Jesus and the Eyewitnesses*, 39–66.

32. Bauckham, *Jesus and the Eyewitnesses*, 47, suggesting Cleopas, the women at the cross and the tomb, Simon of Cyrene and his sons, and the recipients of Jesus' healing miracles.

33. Sherwin-White, *Roman Society*, 189. The full quotation is given in chapter 1 of this volume.

anyone who relegates its date to, say, 80 or later, rather than 62 as suggested above, may well underestimate its value. But its emphasis on the *dramatis personae*, the speed of communications between the churches to which Paul's letters also bear witness, and the extraordinary accuracy of its account of the Roman state, make it a fascinating and valuable resource for the inquiring historian.[34]

The "well-rounded" feel of many Gospel pericopae does not require an explanation in terms of frequent reshaping by communities over decades as per the form-critics. Frequent retelling by the apostles themselves and others in the early years, notably in Jerusalem, works very well.

Conclusion

The above considerations give us ample confidence that we have in the Gospels a reliably preserved historical record of the life, teachings, death, and resurrection of Jesus of Nazareth. I am very happy therefore as a self-confessed type 2 researcher to find my own conclusions supported by Allan McNicol who, researching from what I would describe as a type 1 perspective, has very significantly rediscovered within the Gospel texts the person of Jesus.

Epilogue: Transmission and the Synoptic Problem

Let us finally consider how assumptions about transmission have affected the debate about the Synoptic Problem. Q is habitually arrived at as a deduction from the written texts of Matthew, Mark, and Luke. There are two fallacies here.

First, this ignores the existence of the *oral tradition*, which can have affected the redacting process at any stage.[35] Matthew, Mark, and Luke do not form a closed system, as would be required for the deduction of Q to be valid. In the rival Farrer Hypothesis, Luke, while working on Mark and Matthew, could have incorporated unknowable material from the

---

34. See for instance the long and accurate catalogue of official titles cited by Rackham, *Acts of the Apostles*, xlv. Also Mosse, *Three Gospels*, 240–42.

35. As for example Catchpole, *Quest for Q*, chap. 1, "Did Q Exist?" where the possible effect of oral tradition is ignored throughout. Likewise, Tuckett has in my judgement seriously undermined his own case for Q in chap. 1, "The Existence of Q," of his *Q and the History of Early Christianity*, by his repeated failure to take due account of the role of oral tradition.

oral tradition, which as a first rate historian he had researched (much of "Special Luke," L, material, such as the Parables of the Prodigal Son and the Good Samaritan, is nowadays thought to have been orally transmitted). *Without knowing the exact content of the oral tradition to which Luke had access we can arrive at no valid deduction of Q.*

Second, hypotheses of the Farrer type have been damned since Streeter on account of the curious way in which Luke in redacting Matthew appears to have redistributed some of his material. In Streeter's celebrated put-down,

> A theory which would make an author capable of such a proceeding would only be tenable if, on other grounds, we had reason to believe he was a crank.[36]

This again rests on a false premise that Farrer himself surmounted. His historic paper of 1955 did not propose that Luke was working on a written text of Matthew at all, as Q champions have commonly portrayed him, but on a *memorized* version.[37] He was not thumbing forwards and backwards through a scroll of Matthew while redacting Mark, but *reproducing what he found in his memory*. So any peculiarities of order may simply reflect the way Luke's recollective processes worked; including even the possibility of plain *memory failure* (here is a genuine question for Ehrman!).[38]

There could in fact be any number of reasons why Luke ordered his Gospel as he did. Perhaps he *was* a crank! In which case, Streeter's case collapses and Farrer wins outright. Alternatively, maybe Luke was unwell at the time and unable to concentrate; or perhaps he was worried sick there in Rome about the way Paul's trial was going to work out; or heartbroken, after having just broken up with his girlfriend. Rather more likely, Luke could have been following a perfectly reasonable rationale that simply escaped Streeter and his successors.[39] It matters not. Once we

---

36. Streeter, *Four Gospels*, 183.

37. So for instance, "St. Luke had read St. Matthew, but decided to work direct upon the more ancient narrative of St. Mark for himself. He does his own work of adaptation, but small Matthean echoes keep appearing, because St. Luke is after all acquainted with St. Matthew." Farrer, "On Dispensing with Q," 61.

38. There is, after all, excellent precedent for recording the Jesus tradition from memory, but not in order, *ou mentoi taxei*: see John's account of how Mark penned the teaching of Peter, as reported by Eusebius, *EH* III.xxxix.15.

39. So for example Drury, *Tradition and Design*, 128–29.

have admitted with Streeter that Luke was a real flesh and blood human being with a psyche of his own, Q is doomed.

This reduction of the Synoptic Problem to questions about the working of Luke's mind illustrates the point that, try as you may, *you can never eliminate* people *from Gospel studies*. They always pop up somewhere else. This is why I urged in chapter 1 that *the New Testament historian needs a good grasp of human psychology*. Depersonalization, to use Gerhardsson's word, which lies at the very heart of the Q hypothesis, is never going to work.

But it is part of Q culture that the author of Q is no historical being. One should never even ask who wrote it, still less venture an answer, which might threaten to tie the hypothesis in with recorded history and so become testable.[40] Even dates for Q are hard to come by. Q's supposed author is in fact a veritable Melchizedek, "without father or mother, without genealogy, without beginning of days or end of life" (Heb 7:3 TNIV), the original ghost writer!

What is going on here? Reality itself is personal. Putting it theologically, in the Genesis story, humanity is personal because it was made in the image of a personal Reality. So to exhaust human beings of their personal qualities will always end in a nonsense. It can't be done.

Indeed, it is the attitude to the personal that ultimately distinguishes researchers of type 1 from type 2. That is why his emphatic reintroduction of the personal makes Richard Bauckham's *Jesus and the Eyewitnesses* so significant.

Even the physical process of redaction required by the Q hypothesis is problematic. It requires the unknown redactors who created the original scrolls of Matthew and Luke to have been manipulating scrolls of both Mark and Q at the same time as that on which they were writing, rather like juggling three rolls of wallpaper. We recall the view of Streeter himself that "both Matthew and Luke would have needed rolls of fully thirty feet long."[41] This will have been very difficult in an age that had no writing table.[42] I have not seen any Q theorist explain just how it was done.

Lastly, I do not share McNicol's enthusiasm for taking a synopsis and working through its texts "unit by unit" as a necessary prelude to tackling

---

40. So Tuckett's *Q and the History* is notable for the extreme paucity of its references to anything resembling recorded history. Eusebius merits just one entry, 339.

41. Streeter, *Four Gospels*, 169.

42. Wenham, *Redating*, 204–7. Derrenbacker, "Greco-Roman Writing," 66–7, 82.

the Synoptic Problem. According to Parker, in his landmark book *The Living Text of the Gospels*,[43] the value of the synopsis for such purposes is overrated because it cannot display the Synoptics' complex interactive textual history. Not even our most authoritative and recent Greek New Testament edition offers us the "unique autograph" or "published" text that such a study would require. In reality, "recovery of the original text is a task that remains beyond all of us."[44] Besides unintentional errors in the copying process, copyists may from the very start have *intentionally* changed the wording of the texts before them in order to achieve harmonization, "the most frequent kind of corruption in the Gospels," affecting particularly the Codex Bezae. Copyists have held

> an attitude which assumes the essential unity of the separate Gospels which treats them as *needing* harmonization. While source criticism requires the separation of the several strands into their constituent threads, the harmony weaves them together into a cord.[45]

So there was most probably from very early on, long before our earliest manuscripts, a *plurality* of readings. Parker concludes that "there are often as great, if not greater, variations between the manuscript copies of each Gospel" as there are between different Gospels.[46] What we have is a genuine problem of transmission, not this time of the sayings and deeds of Jesus, but of the text of the documents written about him. Parker argues for a "three-dimensional" model of repeated cross-fertilization between the Gospels during transmission. Because of this he maintains that *the evidence of the Gospel texts does not permit a documentary solution to the Synoptic Problem* by determining the relationship between Matthew and Luke.[47] Consequently, those whom McNicol castigates for "admitting that they have never taken their synopsis and worked through these texts unit by unit" have saved themselves a great deal of unnecessary hard labor.

That is to say, not only are the arguments for Q fallacious; we do not even possess, and cannot obtain, the raw material to which they are supposed to refer.

---

43. Parker, *Living Text*.
44. Parker, *Living Text*, 204.
45. Parker, *Living Text*, 120.
46. Parker, *Living Text*, 197.
47. Parker, *Living Text*, 121.

Bibliography

Bauckham, Richard. *Jesus and the Eyewitnesses*. Grand Rapids: Eerdmans, 2006.

Bird, Michael F. *The Gospel of the Lord: How the Early Church Wrote the History of Jesus*. Grand Rapids: Eerdmans, 2014.

Brown, Raymond E. *An Introduction to the New Testament*. New York: Doubleday, 1997.

Catchpole, David R. *The Quest for Q*. Edinburgh: Clark, 1993.

Derrenbacker, Robert A., Jr. "Greco-Roman Writing Practices and Luke's Gospel: Revisiting 'The Order of a Crank.'" In *The Gospels According to Michael Goulder: A North American Response*, edited by Christopher A. Rollston, 61–83. Harrisburg: Trinity, 2002.

Drury, John. *Tradition and Design in Luke's Gospel*. London: Darton, Longman and Todd, 1976.

Edmundson, George. *The Church in Rome in the First Century: An Examination of Various Controverted Questions Relating to Its History, Chronology, Literature and Traditions*. Bampton Lectures 1913. London: Longmans, Green and Co., 1913.

Ellis, E. Earle. *The Making of the New Testament Documents*. Boston: Brill, 1999.

Eusebius. *Ecclesiastical History*. Books I–V. Translated by K. Lake. Loeb Classical Library 123. Cambridge: Harvard University Library, 1926.

Farrer, A. M. "On Dispensing with Q." In *Studies in the Gospels: Essays in Memory of R. H. Lightfoot*, edited by D. E. Nineham, 55–88. Oxford: Blackwell, 1955.

Gerhardsson, Birger. *Memory and Manuscript: Oral Tradition and Written Transmission in Early Christianity* with *Tradition in Rabbinic Judaism in Early Christianity*. Grand Rapids: Eerdmans, 1998.

———. *The Reliability of the Gospel Tradition*. Peabody, MA: Hendrickson, 2001.

Hemer, Colin J. *The Book of Acts in the Setting of Hellenistic History*. Edited by Conrad H. Gempf. Tübingen: J. C. B. Mohr (Paul Siebeck), 1989.

Le Donne, Anthony. *Historical Jesus: What Can We Know and How Can We Know It?* Grand Rapids: Eerdmans, 2011.

Meyer, E. *Ursprung und Anfänge des Christentums* (*Origin and Beginnings of Christianity*). Stuttgart and Berlin: Cotta, 1921–23.

Millard, Alan. *Reading and Writing in the Time of Jesus*. The Biblical Seminar 69. Sheffield: Sheffield Academic Press, 2002.

Moberly, Robert B. "When Was Acts Planned and Shaped?" *Evangelical Quarterly* 65:1 (1993) 5–26.

Mosse, Martin. *The Three Gospels: New Testament History Introduced by the Synoptic Problem*. Milton Keynes: Paternoster, 2007.

Neill, Stephen, and Tom Wright. *The Interpretation of the New Testament 1861–1986*. 2nd ed. Oxford: Oxford University Press, 1988.

Parker, D. C. *The Living Text of the Gospels*. Cambridge: Cambridge University Press, 1997.

Rackham, R. B. *The Acts of the Apostles: An Exposition*. Westminster Commentaries. London: Methuen, 1901.

Robinson, J. A. T. *Redating the New Testament*. London: SCM, 1976.

Sherwin-White, A. N. *Roman Society and Roman Law in the New Testament*. The Sarum Lectures 1960–1961. Oxford: Clarendon, 2000.

Streeter, B. H. *The Four Gospels: A Study of Origins*. London: Macmillan, 1924.

Tuckett, C. M. *Q and the History of Early Christianity: Studies on Q*. Edinburgh: T. & T. Clark, 1996.

Wenham, John. *Redating Matthew, Mark and Luke*. Downers Grove, IL: InterVarsity, 1992.

Yarbrough, Robert W. "The Date of Papias: A Reassessment." *Journal of the Evangelical Theological Society* 26 (1983) 181–91.

3

Synoptic Gospels as Evidence of Jesus Remembered by Eyewitnesses

JOHN HARRISON

Is it possible to detect in the Gospels specific items that can only come from the memory of eyewitnesses? This paper engages with the arguments of this recent claim that one can and sketches why it is less certain that specific details in the text are better explained as evidence of eyewitness memories.

Several broad declarations about Jesus and the Gospels have general consensus among historical Jesus scholars as accurate remembrances of Jesus: 1) He existed; 2) he was an agrarian Galilean Jew living under Roman occupation; 3) he preached and taught;[1] 4) Jesus had followers/disciples who were taught by him and observed him teaching others; 5) Jesus taught things and acted in ways that attracted opposition from other Jews (e.g., Pharisees, temple, and Roman authorities); 6) Jesus was crucified in Jerusalem; 7) after his death some of his eyewitnesses (most likely those who formed a more intimate group of disciples) orally dispensed what they remembered of his teachings and actions to a second generation of disciples/believers; 8) after a few decades, during which time the Pauline corpus recalls explicitly a few things that Paul was taught Jesus said (e.g., 1 Cor. 7:10–11; 11:24–25), Gospels were produced that reported the sayings of and narratives about Jesus; and 9) Gospels were composed by

---

1. Dodd, "Jesus als Leherer und Prophet," 67–86. Bultmann, *Die Geschichte der synoptischen Tradition*, 52.

individuals who had a vested interest in the promotion of Jesus as the Messiah Son of God.²

Within the items in this broad sketch of what scholars accept as certain that were remembered are two debated issues. First, how *accurately* was the "Jesus tradition" (both the things Jesus said as well as did) remembered by those followers/disciples who were eyewitnesses as they re-performed their memories for new disciples prior to the production of the Gospels or pre-gospel texts? Second, which media and performance methods were used in the transmission of his life during the formative stages? With regard to this second issue, as Terence Mournet has observed, once scholars broke free from the singular model of Bultmann's form-critical approach as *Kleinliteratur*, with its primary focus on the traditioning activities *after* the initial formative period, it wasn't long before a multiplicity of interacting "media models" became viable: "oral tradition from the mouth of Jesus; written notes (notebooks); formalized didactic activity; written *logiai* collections; the informal circulation of sayings, traditions, and teachings of and about Jesus; and the recirculation of the oral Jesus tradition back into written texts."³ The multiplicity of media has made answering this second question of media use during the formative period even more challenging.

But one point can be safely assumed. Jesus' disciples did not wait to recall Jesus' teachings and deeds until after his death. As others have noted, disciples are remembering Jesus' ministry.⁴ Equally safe to assume, the disciples needed to remember Jesus' teaching in service of their own need to utilize that material in their preaching. Byrskog describes the scenario clearly when he states, "From early on, the preaching was not

---

2. Among Sanders's "indisputable facts" about Jesus and his followers are: 1) Jesus' baptism by John the Baptist; 2) in addition to preaching, Jesus practiced healing; 3) Jesus not only called disciples but had twelve specific ones; 4) Jesus confined his activity within the land of Israel; 5) Jesus had some controversy with the temple; 6) Jesus was crucified by Roman authorities; 7) after his death his followers continued a movement that centered on him; and 8) some non-Christian Jews persecuted the early movement. Sanders, *Jesus and Judaism*, 11.

3. Mournet, "Jesus Tradition," 41. On the reason why Bultmann did not focus on the earliest formative period of oral traditions, Kirk, "Memory," 155–72, 248–55, 155–56.

4. Gerhardsson stated, "Turning to Jesus' oral teaching, we must reckon with the fact that he used a method similar to that of Jewish—and Hellenistic—teachers: the scheme of text and interpretation. He must have made his disciples learn certain sayings off by heart; if he taught, he must have required his disciples to memorize." Gerhardsson, *Memory & Manuscript*, 328.

merely a matter of conveying separate words and deeds of Jesus, but of speaking about history as story. The narrativization of the past started immediately, as soon as the disciples heard and observed Jesus."[5] Jesus' disciples are hearing and seeing, remembering and reflecting, and then performing in proclamation what they have seen and heard.

However, what is not self-evident in this reconstruction is to what level of memorization Jesus anticipated or expected his disciples to learn his teaching in order to re-perform them. As disciples are "narrativizing" their memories, are they expected to recall with detailed accuracy or are they capturing the gist of his teachings? Scholars focused on the oral tradition of Jesus material are back to the earlier form-critical, redaction-critical question of how much of Jesus' teaching (but now prior to the Gospels) had to be remembered *ippsima verba* and how much of it could be sufficiently performed reflecting the *ippsima vox* of the teacher to still be considered "authentic" or "reliable."

The near universal agreement that Jesus taught is complicated by the fact that there is no consensus among historical Jesus scholars on the type of teacher Jesus was. For some scholars Jesus taught like the Cynics.[6] For others, he taught like an eschatological or a millenarian prophet.[7] Still for others, Jesus' teaching needs to be seen in parallel to the activities of a charismatic leader[8] or a political revolutionist[9] or even a Pharisee or a rabbi.[10] Identifying *what kind* of teacher Jesus was would greatly effect what one might expect about the delivery method of his teaching and the expectation he had for the level of memorization from his disciples of that teaching.

The Jesus tradition was clearly formed by people who, to use James Dunn's concept, were "impacted"[11] by what they saw Jesus do and what they heard him say. But acknowledging that eyewitnesses are somehow at the source of the Jesus tradition does not indicate what they understood as the appropriate and responsible method(s) of passing the narrative that impacted them on to others. Did Jesus himself expect (even train!) his students to observe a formally controlled memorization of his teachings,

---

5. Byrskog, "Transmission of the Jesus Tradition," 1465–94, 1494.
6. Crossan, *Historical Jesus*.
7. Allison, *Jesus of Nazareth*.
8. Hengel, *Charismatic Leader*.
9. Horsley, *Jesus and the Spiral of Violence*.
10. Gerhardsson, *Memory & Manuscript*.
11. Dunn, *Jesus Remembered*.

as Harald Riesenfeld[12] and his student Birger Gerhardsson argued? When they re-performed his teaching, did they think they were expected (even obligated) to repeat in as much detail exactly what they had heard? Or, is it more probable that his teachings were "informally controlled"? Were the eyewitnesses allowed to be creative, as Werner Kelber,[13] Kenneth Bailey,[14] and Dunn contend, and change details, even substantive portions, while maintaining a stability of the essence of what Jesus taught? If anything was changed would they have thought that the teaching or story was no longer "authentic" or "legitimate"?

The Gospels portray Jesus as a teacher of different groups of people. He spoke to large crowds of agrarian Galilean Jews in the open, to smaller groups in synagogues, and even on occasions to Gentiles. He taught in individual homes, sometimes around a meal, and on occasion in the temple precincts. Also all four Gospels attest to Jesus teaching his closer circle of followers. This broad framework of Jesus as someone who was remembered as a teacher is not really debatable.

But while Jesus was doing all of this teaching to these various groups, even among his inner circle of disciples, was anyone taking dictation? Gerhardsson argued that it is likely that eyewitnesses did write down Jesus' words and actions very soon after they were performed, similar to what was done by students of the post-70 rabbis.[15] But his thesis is not convincing for several reasons. First, the evidence cited to argue Jesus' Jewish students taking notes comes from rabbinic evidence that is late and seems insufficiently analogous. Jesus, unlike the rabbis, never tries to align his teaching within a particular stream of teachers or tradition. He did not see himself as one who belonged to a "school" of interpretation as many appear to do. Second, as is often noted, even by those who argue for the employment of written notes, in the first century Jewish and Greco-Roman environment, the "living voice" (*viva vox*) was preferred to what was written.[16] Additionally, even if Jesus had counted among his

---

12. Riesenfeld, "Gospel Tradition," 1–29. That Jesus acted like a rabbi and taught his disciples to remember *verbatim* his teachings is assumed by Taylor, "Memory," 479.

13. Kelber, *Oral and the Written Gospel*.

14. Bailey, "Informed Controlled Oral Tradition," 34–54; Bailey, "Middle Eastern Oral Tradition," 363–67.

15. Gerhardsson, *Memory & Manuscript*, 160–70, notes the evidence compiled by Strack, *Einleitung in Talmud und Midraš*, 16 (English).

16. Gerhardsson notes the rational criticism of writing expressed by Plato, *Phaedr.*, 275; Aristeas 127; and Papias in Eusebius, *Hist. Eccl.* III.39, 157n6. He also speculates that the Pharisees may have been opposed to writing down oral traditions

disciples people who were literate enough to act as scribes, the work of scribes is done in the service of oral memory. Writing's primary function was to serve oral performances. For example, Colossians, and the supposed letter to the Laodiceans, is expected to be read to (not read by) the congregation (Col 4:16).[17] The author of Revelation acknowledges a blessing upon the one who reads aloud (most likely imagining an oral performance) for those who will hear and take the prophecy to heart (Rev 1:3). Alan Kirk notes that scribes are not mere "copyists" in the service of a literate culture. Rather, he states, "The scribe grasped the manuscript text not just as a visual but as an auditory entity, even preponderantly so."[18] Third, while the idea of disciples literate enough to make notes is at least conceivable (e.g., a tax-collector),[19] the primary spokespersons of the community, Peter and John, are remembered in Acts as being "illiterate" (ἀγράμματοί) and "uneducated" (ἰδῶται) people (Acts 4:13).[20] What should also be pointed out is that a major motif of the disciples' responsibility in performing Jesus tradition in Acts and the Johannine corpus is in their role as "witnesses" of Jesus.[21] This image stresses the concept of the oral performance of the tradition rather than a formal method of controlled dictation to scribes. Though it is certainly true that the image does not demand an either-or scenario where one media is performed at

---

because of their reverence for the written Torah, 158. This aversion to writing what is transmitted orally certainly appears later in the Babylonian Talmud, b.Tem. 14b, Byrskog draws attention to the claim of Eusebius (*Hist. Eccl.* 3.39.40) that Papias in the second century preferred to hear from those who had heard from the eyewitnesses of Jesus, Byrskog, "Transmission of the Jesus Tradition," 1481).

17. καὶ ὅταν ἀναγνωσθῇ παρ' ὑμιν ἡ ἐπιστολή

18. Kirk, "Manuscript Tradition," 220. Kirk's conclusion here stems from the work of Chaytor, *From Script to Print*; Clanchy, *From Memory to Written Record*; Junack, "Abschreibpraktiken und Schreibergewohnheiten"; Sweeny, *Full Hearing*; and Doane, "Oral Tests."

19. Here it would be helpful to make a distinction, as some have done, between different types of literacy (e.g. signature, phonetic, craft, or scribal). See Kirk, "Memory," 158.

20. If ἀγράμματοί is rendered "unlearned" or "unschooled" and ἰδῶται is taken as "ordinary," the emphasis of these two words still suggest that Peter and John were not known to have any scribal education that would explain why they could be bold and confident before their inquisitors who had received education in reading and writing the Scriptures. For the use of these terms during this period, see van der Horst, "Hellenistic," 42; and for explanations of its use see Kraus, "Uneducated," 434–49.

21. Dunn, *Jesus Remembered*, 177. Acts 1:8; 2:32; 3:15; 5:32; 10:41; 13:31.

the exclusion of the other, the point is that the image of being witnesses places more emphasis on the oral performance of the tradition.

If written dictation is less plausible as a medium by which Jesus' disciples reviewed and discussed what Jesus actually said and did, they undoubtedly utilized their memory. Consequently, it is important to inquire, what exposure would Jesus and his disciples have had to the activity of memorization? What effect did living in a primarily oral culture have on the continued re-performance of memorized material?

I start examining the question of the role of memory among Jesus' eyewitnesses by stating what is surely obvious. Jesus' disciples were not recalling things in isolation. Eyewitness testimony of Jesus' actions was a group activity.[22] The implication of this observation is that from the very beginning of the process of remembering, it is done in community. Yes, eyewitnesses of Jesus are present in the community. Their presence is noted by several authors. Luke claims that his investigation into the accounts of things that were fulfilled was focused on that which was "handed down to us by those who from the first were eyewitnesses and servants of the word" (Luke 1:1-2). The author of John's Gospel claims his account comes from the written testimony of the unnamed "disciple whom Jesus loved" (John 21:24), who was an eyewitness of events (at least from the point in the narrative [John 13:23]) when the character appears in Jerusalem at a meal soon before Jesus' arrest and crucifixion. Paul also notes, in his letters to the Corinthians, the presence of eyewitnesses in passing down the tradition of testimony of seeing the resurrected Jesus (1 Cor 15:1-8).[23] Nevertheless, while eyewitnesses were certainly present giving their accounts as they recalled them, it is probable that the entire community process helped to give the memories of these eyewitnesses their shape and potential stability. Rather than focused on word for word reproduction as the measure of accuracy, eyewitnesses are more likely to have had their memory fashioned into something that expresses meaning

---

22. Dunn, *Jesus Remembered*, 240.

23. It is not clear what Paul, in his first letter to the Corinthians, is explicitly referencing when he cites that some commands (prohibition against divorce) are the Lord's (7:10-11), and another command (remaining married or single) is not (1 Cor 7:25). Is Paul referencing direct communication from Jesus or a tradition of Jesus' teachings? The same caution could also be applied when Paul references what he received from the Lord about eating bread and drinking wine in remembrance of Jesus (11:23). Again, is this account of the last supper a direct communication from Jesus or is Paul alluding to what the community has passed down?

and significance (i.e., "impact") upon groups as a whole in their various and diverse contexts.

If the memory of the disciples during the ministry of Jesus is the genesis of the Jesus tradition that comes to be performed later after Jesus' death, can their memory be detected in the formation of the traditions that are written down in the Gospels? This is what is sometimes claimed. For example, Dunn states, "What we have in the Jesus tradition [that is the tradition we see now in the Gospels] is the consistent and coherent features of the shared impact made by his deeds and words, not the objective deeds and words of Jesus as such. What we have [in the Gospels] are examples of oral retelling of that shared tradition, retellings which evince the flexibility and elaboration of oral performances."[24] But the question is, how are these "consistent and coherent features" identified as belonging to the "shared impact"?

What is generally not debated is that Jesus' life, teaching, actions, and death would have been remembered by eyewitnesses in at least broad terms. What is questioned is the degree to which his teachings and actions were memorized and performed with accuracy and able to survive through the process of multiple and various sharings in the communities spread throughout much of the Greco-Roman world. What is most probable is that the testimony of eyewitnesses is received in a community that serves to establish coherence as well as stability and diversity in expressing that testimony. It was shared with a second generation of believers in the way they had received those teachings informally (albeit authoritatively)

---

24. Dunn, *Jesus Remembered*, 241. It is not Dunn's contention that eyewitnesses are always incapable of recalling the very words they heard. His point is that the evidence of the Gospels show there were features in a tradition that had impact upon the eyewitnesses. These eyewitnesses later recalled those events or teachings with a freedom to develop their accounts beyond any exact replication and would not have thought of their responsibility as reproducing verbatim every detail of what was witnessed or heard. Eyewitnesses were motivated by the perpetuation of the original impact of the overall sense of Jesus' actions or teaching onto new audiences, not attempting to recall every exact word spoken or action performed by their teacher. The Gospels are evidence of variations in the way Jesus traditions are passed on. If the overall meaning or significance of the teaching and/or action is conveyed, these variations are performing responsibly in what would have been expected within an oral cultural setting. Regarding Dunn's comment on the "objective deeds and words of Jesus," which I take to mean "the actual deeds and words of Jesus," the early Jesus community performing the sayings and deeds of the risen Christ, even with the presence of eyewitnesses in their midst, are not engaging in a type of historiography that an ancient historian might have hoped to represent as they report the observations of eyewitnesses they interviewed.

from Jesus. Afterward, those believers memorized and performed collectively what they had heard from these eyewitnesses and passed them on informally. These would be creatively performed through their own abilities to cast traditions into stories that would provide meaning and significance for others.

The most likely scenario is that memorization of Jesus' tradition was done "within a frame of variation."[25] Byrskog correctly presents cautions about how the differences of details in the traditions preserved in the Gospels should be evaluated. They are not evidence against the practice of memorization. Rather, those differences demonstrate "that different people could choose to memorize the same thing in different ways and that memorization, while maintaining its distinctive preservative character, was never an entirely passive enterprise isolated from the social environment and activities of the larger group."[26] Again, just as the question was raised with Dunn's statement, how is one to determine that what shows up in the Gospels is evidence of what was passed down to be memorized? While it is not inconceivable that the Jesus tradition is heard by believers, recalled through new performances through various successive stages[27] until it is written down and then utilized by a Gospel author, what features in a particular tradition are clearly indicative of originating from eyewitness memory and then through various successions of the memory of subsequent believers? To put it more concisely, what features in the Gospels would constitute clear evidence justifying the classification of that tradition as eyewitness memory? A historian's work on the Gospels has to have criteria to judge a claim that an action of Jesus could or could not have happened or that a saying attributed to him could or could not have been spoken. If a historian wants to utilize the "criterion of memorization," how is she or he to identify features as coming from eyewitness memory rather than arising out of one of the multiple informal re-performances of a story that could have been created?

One of the key theses of Richard Bauckham's *Jesus and the Eyewitnesses: The Gospels as Eyewitness Testimony* is that Jesus traditions originated with and were formed by individuals who were known to be eyewitnesses of Jesus' ministry.[28] Opposing the idea of Dunn and others,

25. Byrskog, "Transmission of the Jesus Tradition," 1487.
26. Byrskog, "Transmission of the Jesus Tradition," 1487.
27. At times these performances would have likely been carried out in the presence of eyewitnesses but also in most cases it would not have been.
28. Bauckham, *Jesus and the Eyewitnesses*.

particularly form-critics, that the Jesus traditions were the product of a community that collectively shaped the traditions in order to address communal interests, Bauckham contends that details about and within the tradition reflect the type of elements an eyewitness would remember rather than what would be preserved by a community for its use. More specifically, Bauckham argues that while some details could be mis-remembered or distorted—in other words there was variability in oral performances—the basic framework of the incident could be recalled with stability.[29]

> This continuity of tradition before and after the resurrection was made possible by the eyewitnesses, who themselves saw their stories in a new light after the resurrection, but whose memories already had a degree of stability that severely limited the degree to which they were changed by further interpretative insight. We return to a point made earlier: that the stereotypical form of each tradition would already have been relatively fixed in the eyewitness's memory after only a short period of frequent rehearsal.[30]

Bauckham criticizes Dunn for his inability or unwillingness to "take seriously a role for the eyewitnesses once their testimony had been absorbed into the oral tradition."[31] Instead of envisaging eyewitnesses to Jesus' teachings and actions as having to take a back seat to the tradition formed by the various Jesus communities, Bauckham accepts traditions that the Synoptic authors themselves would have heard from eyewitnesses "rehearsing" their own recollections on many occasions. For example, Mark heard Peter and Luke talk to eyewitnesses. He "takes seriously" the role of eyewitnesses by conjecturing that the authors of the Gospels would not be content to simply record the communities' remembrance of Jesus material. Instead, they would have striven to "get closer to the source if possible."[32]

29. Kirk prefers "multiformity" over "stability," Kirk, "Manuscript Tradition," 216.
30. Bauckham, *Jesus and the Eyewitnesses*, 355.
31. Bauckham, *Jesus and the Eyewitnesses*, 292.
32. Bauckham, *Jesus and the Eyewitnesses*, 292. Bauckham does acknowledge that both Gospel authors and re-performances of Jesus traditions were not always attempting to preserve exact replicas of previous memories nor should it be expected that the eyewitnesses, other tradents, or the Gospel authors themselves were infallible when it comes to recalling the tradition. Bauckham, "In Response," 235. Some of the differences that occur in the sayings material are due to "variability normal in oral performances of a tradition, especially narrative, and 'deliberate alterations or additions,' and

Bauckham predicates these points on the understanding that memorization must operate as a control.³³ But what is "controlled memory"? The concept arises out of two of Bauckham's convictions. First, similar to Gerhardsson's thesis, he envisions that eyewitnesses of Jesus would have taught students in a formal manner to memorize what the eyewitnesses recalled.³⁴ It would then be expected that these students would later become the authorized community teachers of those eyewitnesses' accounts. This reconstruction of Jesus' teaching activity recalls the question I raised earlier as to the kind of teacher Jesus is imagined to have been. Do all teachers teach with the same assumptions about what they are doing? Does an apocalyptic, prophetic, itinerant person proclaiming the imminent kingdom of God teach followers in the same fashion as a rabbi who gathers students for the purpose of studying the Scriptures and passing down the oral tradition in perpetuity? Do the eyewitnesses see themselves as alternative rabbis using their formal methodology but now in service to Jesus Messiah? Or do they see themselves as an eschatological community,³⁵ called into existence in the last days, and now preparing

---

changes by the Gospel authors 'in order to integrate the traditions into the connected narrative of their Gospels'" (Bauckham, *Jesus and the Eyewitnesses*, 286). It should also be noted that Bauckham is not claiming his method gets us from the testimony of the eyewitnesses to the historical Jesus. When responding to Byskog's criticism that Bauckham's approach fails to do so, Bauckham responds by pointing to his earlier statement that "the historical Jesus *is* in fact the testified Jesus" (Bauckham, *Jesus and the Eyewitnesses*, 160), and that there is no such "uninterpreted Jesus," that is uninterpreted by the eyewitnesses. Further clarifying his original intent, Bauckham states that what he is attempting to show is that despite the denial by a number of Gospel scholars that reliable eyewitness testimony can be found in the traditions used by the Gospel authors, scientific studies amply demonstrate that such testimony can indeed be reliable (Bauckham, "In Response," 229-30). For a more recent response to Bauckham, see Dunn, "Eyewitnesses," 213-29.

33. Bauckham, *Jesus and the Eyewitnesses*, 293.

34. Bauckham does note that Gerhardsson's earlier work can be faulted on several accounts. First, he assumed "too much continuity between Pharisaism and rabbinic Judaism." Second, he assumed that it was "pharisaic tradition that would have been the most obvious model for early Christianity to follow." Third, Gerhardsson exaggerated the ridged control of the tradition (Bauckham, *Jesus and the Eyewitnesses*, 250-51). But it is also fair to note that Gerhardsson later recognized that flexibility in rabbinic halakha could explain changes and development in gospel traditions and that the evangelists themselves had flexibility in the sources they used (Bauckham, *Jesus and the Eyewitnesses*, 251).

35. I use the term "eschatological" to refer to the notion that God will in the future bring an "end" (ἔσχατος) to the present age, which is currently characterized as unfulfilled promises made to Israel. God will replace it with the "age to come," which

themselves and others in an ad hoc informal manner for the near arrival of God's kingdom? What overall image is attested in the whole of the New Testament as to the kind of performer Jesus was? Does the evidence suggest he was like a rabbi and his disciples were like rabbis-in-training? Doesn't the overall image of Jesus point to him as an eschatological figure (i.e., anticipated Messiah) who is announced and acted and is going to act in order to bring about the kingdom of God imminently?

The second conviction in Bauckham's theory of "controlled memory" is that the testimony Papias gives points to a preference for the remembered words of named eyewitnesses rather than information from others is the same preference under which the Gospel authors operated.[36] But it is important to bear in mind that, even if Eusebius's account of what Papias actually claimed is reliable, memory is a mental construct. In every act of remembering an event, the person and/or group doing the remembering is reconstructing the past into something new (i.e., not the actual event itself). Allison correctly points out that memory is not only reconstructing the past, it is "reproducing" it by use of imagination.[37] So even if the Gospel authors, as Bauckham contends, preferred the testimony of eyewitnesses, what the eyewitnesses are remembering may be part recollection but it will be performed utilizing their imagination. Therefore, any specific feature in the text one might cite as evidence of what an eyewitness actually saw and heard is dubious because eyewitnesses themselves are capable of adding features that were not actually witnessed.

Kloppenborg further notes another set of problems with Bauckham's speculation about what the authors of the Gospels would or would not be content with in terms of accurate tradition. First, Bauckham assumes that the Gospels' authors had the ability to distinguish between firsthand testimony and the memory of that testimony by other firsthand eyewitnesses and those they had performed their memory to. In other words, if a firsthand eyewitness performs the memory of a different firsthand eyewitness, how does a Gospel author distinguish between the memory this eyewitness is performing and what she or he actually saw or heard? Second, Bauckham does not argue why we are to believe that even at

---

will bring about the restored glory of Israel on earth and the restoration of the earth itself to its originally intended purposes. It is a restoration that will be self-evident to all because it will include the unquestionable intervention of God's power.

36. Bauckham, *Jesus and the Eyewitnesses*, 294–95.
37. Allison, *Constructing Jesus*, 197.

the stage of the earliest performances of these memories they were not already under the influence of communities's standards for such memories.[38] Memories of Jesus did not exist in a vacuum. Performances will be influential but will also be influenced by the hopes, aspirations, and longings of the community to address them and their concerns. With no argument for why these memories were free at the very beginning from such influences, it is more reasonable to expect that they were influenced as other performed memories would have been.

At the heart of the debate is the question whether "memories," either from an individual or a community, are reliable?[39] While everyone recognizes that people can and do have "false memories" of events they did not experience and that memories are characteristically selective and interpretive and frequently prone to distortion, Bauckham builds his case that the Gospels are preserving accurate eyewitness memory upon the work of several psychologists who have identified certain events that are more likely to be remembered by eyewitnesses with greater accuracy.[40] Those events are characterized as unique, significant to the individual, personally impactful at a highly emotional level, or including vivid/visual imagery. But this observation still doesn't lead us to distinguishing what features in a written text come from eyewitness memory. It only states what an eyewitness more likely wants to remember.

Bauckham, perhaps anticipating such an objection, contends then that the character of these "recollective" memories frequently include these features: irrelevant details, a point of view is taken of either how the memory was originally experienced or how an external observer might experience it, not include exact dates, and are highly reliable in

38. Kloppenborg, "Memory," 296.

39. Allison lists nine ways, based on the work of a wide range of memory studies, that demonstrate why memories are frequently deemed unreliable. 1) They are reconstructed using the imagination; 2) post-events frequently influence a person's recollection of it; 3) people often project their present circumstances and biases onto their memories; 4) over time memories become less distinct, reducing details; 5) memories are sometimes distorted by sequential displacement; 6) both individuals and collective memories will structure those memories so that they advance particular agendas; 7) collective memories will not rehearse memories that are not in agreement with the memory approved by the group; 8) memories of events told by storytellers tend to be ordered with clearer narrative structures and stereotyping of characters; and 9) there is no reliable process of adjudicating the accuracy of a memory. See Allison, *Constructing Jesus*, 2–10.

40. The psychologist Bauckham relies on is Brewer, "What Is Recollective Memory," 19–66.

terms of the "gist" or "broad outline" of the event.⁴¹ This last so-called "feature" can be corroborated by recognizing at least one ancient source stating that those passing on sayings primarily held themselves accountable to the "sense" of the saying rather than a verbatim reproduction. In his *History*, Thucydides remarks on the difficulty of repeating with strict accuracy the exact words of a speech and that instead what he has done has been to preserve the "general sense" (ξυμπάσης γνώμης) of what was actually spoken.⁴² But granting that ancient eyewitness memory is reliable in terms of the broad outline of an event doesn't help the historian who is trying to distinguish in the Gospels what "broad outline" is coming from that eyewitness memory or coming from the performance of a tradition that had become impactful for a particular Jesus community. "Broad outlines" are not the exclusive property of eyewitness testimony.

The last observation Bauckham makes about the accuracy of ancient memory is that recollective memories are more likely to retain what was originally said by eyewitnesses when they are frequently rehearsed by the eyewitnesses. Bauckham, however, does not sufficiently explain how he knows that frequently rehearsed ancient stories are providing recollective memories with what was presumably originally said by eyewitnesses. Yes, there were likely occasions where an eyewitness is present when the memory of the community is being orally performed and could and would conceivably address some feature of inaccuracies in the performance. But it is not self-evident that an eyewitness (or several) requires the performance of something they said or reported be replicated as they would have recalled it. Rather, Bauckham's observation primarily argues for what is habitually found to be more powerfully impactful upon audiences. In other words, frequently rehearsed stories can just as easily elaborate and improve upon a story with new particulars for the sake of maintaining continuity with the impact the story/tradition had previously made.⁴³ Adding new items to a story or a tradition (such as the

---

41. Bauckham, *Jesus and the Eyewitnesses*, 330–35. Bauckham's point here is that the cumulative evidence of the Jesus tradition (e.g., Jesus preached that the kingdom of God was near) are particulars that show up in various traditions (e.g., miracles stories, parables, sayings, etc.) that can provide assurance in the broad outline of the eyewitness testimony about Jesus.

42. Thucydides, *Hist.* 1.22. See Allison, *Constructing Jesus*, 28n113, who translates ξυμπάσης γνώμης as "general drift." For a more detailed analysis of Thucydides' claim to report "what the situation called for," see Wilson, "What Does Thucydides Claim?" 95–103.

43. My point is not that every single tradition (whether presented as a paraphrase

name of a character) does not invalidate it or mean that the performer is irresponsible or deceptive. The continuity required is to the sense or meaning of the tradition as representing truthfully who Jesus actually is (i.e., God's anointed who brings God's kingdom to earth) and/or what he taught his disciples to do (e.g., prepare themselves to enter that kingdom through faithful obedience to God's law (i.e., bearing fruit of righteousness) as interpreted by God's anointed.

Bauckham takes his list of identity markers that are characteristic of accurate individual or community memory and attempts to demonstrate how they work at identifying material in the Gospels as coming from eyewitness memory. For instance, Jesus was remembered as a healer and an exorcist. Disciples who witnessed these events would have had a generic memory of their performance. But the ones that were passed down and eventually ended up in the Gospels have "specific features that are central, not merely peripheral, making them memorable as specific events."[44] In other words, the "reliability" or "accuracy" of the eyewitness testimony about Jesus' healings and exorcisms is not a matter of replicating verbatim what was said or done. Instead, Bauckham acknowledges that a memory's accuracy is indicated by central, unchangeable features that constitute the meaning of the teaching or event.[45] Still, Bauckham doesn't inform the historian how she or he will be able to tell if any central, specific details that are memorable in a particular account are the exclusive features of an eyewitness memory and could not have come from communities who have discovered how to tell a story so that it will be impactful. A story teller could certainly have features in a story they have created that would also be central, specific, and memorable.

The recent works of Bauckham, Dunn, and others are serious challenges to historical Jesus and Gospel scholars. They are certainly correct to contend that eyewitness testimony played a preservative role in relaying accurate details about the life of Jesus and that the memory of those eyewitnesses should not be dismissed for an uncritical preference for

---

or summary as Paul may have done in 1 Corinthians or as a quote or story as in the Gospels) is confined to *only* what was impactful to the community but that every tradition would have been vulnerable to the possibility of retaining only what was impactful just as they could possibly retain particulars that had come from eyewitness testimony. Claiming a particular in a tradition as *more likely* coming from an eyewitness account could certainly be reasonable supposition, but it is not the case that any particular in a tradition could have only come from an eyewitness's testimony.

44. Bauckham, *Jesus and the Eyewitnesses*, 342.
45. Bauckham, *Jesus and the Eyewitnesses*, 346.

the creative activity of Jesus communities. They have raised important questions about the assumptions scholars work under about how Jesus traditions were remembered and the media used to re-perform those memories during the formative pre-Gospels period. Scholarly work in ancient memory studies and orality opens up new possibilities of reimagining and reconstructing scenarios in which the Jesus tradition may have flourished. However, what has yet to be demonstrated by Bauckham is exactly how scholars are to distinguish in the Gospels themselves a detail that could only (or even most probably) originate from an eyewitness and not from the traditioning/story-telling activities of early communities of Jesus followers spread throughout the Mediterranean world. Lists of what eyewitnesses tend to want to remember and lists about details they do and don't remember may be parallels to the memorizing activity of the eyewitnesses of Jesus. But still, they are no more probable than creative performances of story-tellers who know that an impactful story is more truthful and reliable than accurate history.

So if form-critic theories postulating that Synoptic traditions were created by communities apart from the participation of any controlling influence by eyewitnesses is wanting, and if eyewitness testimony cannot be discerned conclusively from the Synoptic Gospels after pointing to specific details as more likely the provenance of an account from an eyewitness, then what paradigm should a Gospel and historical Jesus researcher pursue? If the researcher should not go down the hyper-skeptical path of attributing the origin of the majority of traditions to the nearly complete fabrication of the faith communities or go down the tradition-trusting path of attributing the origin of the Gospels to the controlling influences of eyewitnesses, then what path remains?

Scholars will inevitably continue to advance theories and arguments attempting to make clear sense of the existing material's origins and continue to question which explanations more satisfactorily account for all the relevant data. The framework I believe best serves those investigations acknowledges the activity of both formally and informally controlled story-telling in predominately oral culture, both in urban and rural contexts. Focusing on the how and why diverse types of stories are told, whether they are claimed to be based on memories or not, will assist researchers in interpreting the rhetorical effectiveness of what already exists in the Gospels rather than attempting to identify what existed behind them. Aiming to isolate specific traditions as originating either directly from Jesus of Nazareth himself or his eyewitnesses is hoping to hit an elusive target. However, aiming to identify how traditions in the Synoptic Gospels are continuing to perpetuate the potential impacts story-telling about Jesus (whose source is likely never to be determined with certainty) may have had can open new avenues where scholarly investigation holds more promise for reconstructing the manner in which and purposes for which the Synoptics were formed.

Bibliography

Allison, Dale C. *Constructing Jesus: Memory, Imagination, and History*. Grand Rapids: Baker Academic, 2010.

———. *Jesus of Nazareth: Millenarian Prophet*. Minneapolis: Fortress, 1998.

———. "Memory, Methodology, and the Historical Jesus." *Journal for the Study of the Historical Jesus* 14.1 (2016) 13–27.

Bailey, K. E. "Informed Controlled Oral Tradition and the Synoptic Gospels." *Asia Journal of Theology* 5 (1991) 34–54; reprinted in *Themelios* 20 (1995) 4–11.

———. "Middle Eastern Oral Tradition and the Synoptic Gospels." *Expository Times* 106 (1995) 363–67.

Bauckham, Richard. "In Response to My Respondents: Jesus and the Eyewitnesses in Review." *Journal for the Study of the Historical Jesus* 6 (2008) 225–53.

———. *Jesus and the Eyewitnesses: The Gospels as Eyewitness Testimony*. Grand Rapids: Eerdmans, 2006.

———. "Review Article: *Seeking the Identity of Jesus*." *Journal for the Study of the New Testament* 32 (2010) 337–46.

Brewer, W. F. "What Is Recollective Memory?" In *Remembering Our Past: Studies in Autobiographical Memory*, edited by D. C. Rubin, 19–66. Cambridge: Cambridge University Press, 1996.

Bultmann, Rudolf. *Die Geschichte der synoptischen Tradition*. 4th ed. Göttingen: Vandenhoeck & Ruprecht, 1958.

Byrskog, S. "The Transmission of the Jesus Tradition." In *Handbook for the Study of the Historical Jesus*, edited by Tom Holmén and Stanley E. Porter, 1465–94. Leiden: Brill, 2011.

Chaytor, Henry J. *From Script to Print: An Introduction to Medieval Vernacular Literature*. Cambridge: Cambridge University Press, 1945.

Clanchy, Michael T. *From Memory to Written Record: England 1066–1307*. Oxford: Blackwell, 1993.

Crook, Zeba R. "Collective Memory Distortion and the Quest for the Historical Jesus." *Journal for the Study of the Historical Jesus* 11 (2013) 53–77.

Crossan, John Dominic. *The Historical Jesus: The Life of a Mediterranean Jewish Peasant*. San Francisco: Harper, 1991.

Doane, Alger N. "Oral Tests, Intertexts, and Intratexts: Editing Old English." In *Influence and Intertextuality in Literary History*, edited by Jay Clayton and Eric Rothstein, 75–113. Madison: University of Wisconsin Press, 1991.

Dodd, C. H. "Jeaus als Leherer und Prophet." In *Mysterium Christi*, edited by G. K. A. Bell and D. Adolf Deissmann, 67–86. Christologische Studien britischer und deutscher Theologen. Berlin, 1931.

Dunn, James. "Eyewitnesses and the Oral Jesus Tradition: In Dialogue with Birger Gerhardsson and Richard Bauckham." In *The Oral Gospel Tradition*, by James D. G. Dunn, 213–29. Grand Rapids: Eerdmans, 2013.

———. *Jesus Remembered: Christianity in the Making*. Vol. 1. Grand Rapids: Eerdmans, 2003.

Eusebius. *The Ecclesiastical History*. Translated by Kirsopp Lake. Loeb Classical Library. Cambridge: Harvard University Press, 1980.

Gerhardsson, Birger. *Memory & Manuscript: Oral Tradition and Written Transmission in Rabbinic Judaism and Early Christianity*. Grand Rapids: Eerdmans, 1998.

Hengel, Martin. *The Charismatic Leader and His Followers*. Edinburgh: T. & T. Clark, 1981.

Horsley, Richard A. *Jesus and the Spiral of Violence: Popular Jewish Resistance in Roman Palestine*. San Francisco: Harper, 1987.

Junack, Klaus. "Abschreibpraktiken und Schreibergewohnheiten in ihrer Auswirkund auf die Textüberlieferung." In *New Testament Textual Criticism: Its Significance for Exegesis: Essays in Honor of Bruce M. Metzger*, edited by Eldon Jay Epp and Gordon Fee, 277–95. Oxford: Clarendon, 1981.

Kelber, Werner H. *The Oral and the Written Gospel: The Hermeneutics of Speaking and Writing in the Synoptic Tradition, Mark, Paul, and Q*. Bloomington: Indiana University Press, 1983.

Kelber, Werner H., and Samuel Byrskog, eds. *Jesus in Memory: Traditions in Oral and Scribal Perspectives*. Waco: Baylor University Press, 2009.

Kirk, Alan. "Manuscript Tradition as a Tertium Quid: Orality and Memory in Scribal Practices." In *Jesus, the Voice and the Text: Beyond the Oral and the Written Gospel*, edited by T. Thatcher, 215–35. Waco: Baylor University Press, 2008.

———. "Memory." In *Jesus in Memory: Traditions in Oral and Scribal Perspective*, edited by W. H. Kelber and S. Byrskog, 155–72. Waco: Baylor University Press, 2009.

Kloppenborg, John S. "Memory, Performance, and the Sayings of Jesus." In *Memory in Ancient Rome and Early Christianity*, edited by Karl Galinsky, 286–323. Oxford: Oxford University Press, 2016.

Kraus, Thomas J. "'Uneducated,' 'Ignorant,' or even 'Illiterate'? Aspects and Background for an Understanding of *ΑΓΡΑΜΜΑΤΟΙ* (and *ΙΔΙΩΤΑΙ*) in Acts 4.13." *New Testament Studies* 45 (1999) 434-49.

McIver, R., and M. Carroll. "Experiments to Develop Criteria for Determining the Existence of Written Sources, and Their Potential Implications for the Synoptic Problem." *Journal of Biblical Literature* 121 (2002) 667–87.

Mournet, T. "The Jesus Tradition as Oral Tradition." In *Jesus in Memory: Traditions in Oral and Scribal Perspective*, edited by W. H. Kelber and S. Byrskog, 217–23. Waco: Baylor University Press, 2009.

Neusner, Jacob, trans. *The Babylonian Talmud: A Translation and Commentary*. Vol. 21, *Tractate Berhorot, Tractate 'Arakhin, Tractate Temurah*. Peabody, MA: Hendrickson, 2005.

Plato. *Euthyphro, Apology Crito, Phaedo, Phaedrus*. Translated by Harold North Fowler. Loeb Classical Library. Cambridge: Harvard University Press, 1999.

Riesenfeld, H. "The Gospel Tradition and Its Beginning." In *The Gospel Tradition*, by H. Riesenfeld, 1–29. Philadelphia: Fortress Press, 1970 [1957].

Sanders, E. P. *Jesus and Judaism*. Philadelphia: Fortress, 1985.

Strack, Hermann L. *Einleitung in Talmud und Midraš*. 5th ed. München, 1930. Eng. ed. *Introduction to the Talmud and Midrash*. New York: Meridian, 1959.

Sweeny, Armin. *A Full Hearing: Orality and Literacy in the Malay World*. Berkeley: University of California Press, 1987.

Taylor, W. S. "Memory and the Gospel Tradition." *Theology Today* 15 (1959) 470–79.

Thucydides. *History of the Peloponnesian War*. Translated by Charles Foster Smith. Loeb Classical Library. Cambridge: Harvard University Press, 1956.

van der Horst, Pieter W. "Hellenistic Parallels to Acts (Chapters 3 and 4)." *Journal for the Study of the New Testament* 35 (1989) 37–46.

Wilson, John. "What Does Thucydides Claim for His Speeches?" *Phoenix* 36 (Summer 1982) 95–103.

Synoptic Gospels as Evidence of Jesus Remembered by Eyewitnesses

Respondent: Allan J. McNicol

This carefully written essay seeks to engage recent claims that eyewitness memory of Jesus' ministry was an important contributing factor in the formation of the Jesus tradition that undergirded the canonical Gospels.[1] It is clear that if one seeks to do historical research on the "real Jesus" then defensible assessment of these traditions embedded in our Gospels (especially the Synoptics) must become a priority. However, since the Enlightenment this research has reached little consensus. To this day it continues to be plagued by irreconcilable theories. Recently, the emergence of the discipline of social memory studies has sparked new interest in what can be known about these matters.

In the opening paragraph of this essay the author asserts that it is one thing to make a claim for the presence of "eyewitness testimony" as being central to the integrity of the earliest traditions about Jesus in the Christian Community and quite another for this to stand up to scrutiny. A major reason for this equivocation is because the author of the article considers that another issue has surfaced that is more foundational. It centers around the importance of memory. Can "memories" of any kind, even those of an individual (perhaps even an eyewitness) or ones that emerge and were entrenched within communities of believers be reckoned as capable of being accorded the status of providing reliable

---

1. Here the author has especially in mind the work of Bauckham, *Jesus and the Eyewitnesses*. Harrison probably worked from the first edition in 2006. The second edition is a reprint of the first edition with several extra chapters added that mainly reinforce what was said earlier and respond to critiques. Observations and reference to Bauckham's work in this response come from the second edition.

information about Jesus? For scholars and historians of antiquity, current research on memory by social scientists is making this a difficult proposition.[2]

Nevertheless, at the outset I would like to make this observation: It still is reasonable to conclude that important figures in the early church such as Peter, James, and John would have had a major say in the form and content of the earliest remembrances about Jesus. No one doubts that they were eyewitnesses and participants in Jesus' ministry. They were remembered as important figures in the church until close to the time of the production of the Gospels a generation after Jesus. Their recollections and memories of what Jesus said and did, as well as some within his own earthly family must have had a special place in the life of the early church. Vincent Taylor's often quoted dictum about form-critics needs to be heeded, for he claimed that if they were correct in their published views about the chaotic development of the tradition, then the original eyewitnesses must, like Jesus, have been translated to heaven because their imprint no longer could be seen.

The Gospels do sometimes claim contact with sources of eyewitness testimony (Luke 1:1-2; cf. John 13:23; 21:24). Nevertheless, it is curious that the canonical gospels have very few, if any, expressions such as "according to Peter," or "the disciples recollect." So it is apparent that a set of serious questions can be raised about the connection between the original eyewitnesses and what appears in the Gospels. I am convinced that some eyewitnesses of Jesus' ministry must have had significant influence and control over these traditions, but I do concede that questions remain as to how this influence was exercised.

These sorts of questions come close to the center of concerns addressed by the author of this article to which I am furnishing this response. At the outset it can be stated that he agrees that nineteenth to twentieth century research has not answered such questions and that convincing research still needs to be carried out.

The Setting of the Transmission of the Jesus Tradition

I have a point to make that I believe stands as the heart of my response. I would like to query Harrison's claim that the transmission of the Jesus

---

2. Here I have in mind the work of such scholars as Halbwachs, *On Collective Memory*; and Assmann, *Cultural Memory*.

tradition occurred in a "predominantly oral culture." My chief interest in Gospel studies remains the Synoptic Problem. Research on this issue has been around for a long time. But even before the modern era of Synoptic Problem research began in the nineteenth century a series of romantic literature writers were active. They were busily involved in development theories about the canonical Gospels being the products of a vital ancient oral folkloric culture. This terminology persistently raises its head from time to time in Gospel studies. In my view it is seldom profitable. Whether it be form-criticism, oral traditional literature as championed by such scholars as Albert Lord, or Werner Kelber's radical distinctions between oral transmission and written Gospel, the term "oral culture" has tended to muddy the waters of Gospel studies. Now I am afraid that, likewise, mixing research on the transmission of the Jesus tradition with certain kinds of social memory theory will not end well.

To be sure, oral transmission of the Jesus tradition was a staple of its earliest period. But here we need to make a clear distinction. The main people involved in the earliest transmission of the Jesus tradition did not live in a dominantly oral culture such as the ones that most social memory practitioners of folk culture presume. In these cultures only a miniscule percentage of people could read or write. They portray a culture of memorization with few benefits and a host of shortcomings as the central reality of daily life. But what if these situations were a far cry from the culture in which the earliest transmission of the Jesus tradition took place?

What if the transmission of Jesus' sayings and deeds was not primarily in a folkloric culture but a religious one undergirded and suffused with Jewish piety? As carefully staked out by scholars such as Rainer Riesner, there is evidence that Jesus' family was primarily Hasidic in origin although not directly existing within the fold of other groups such as the Qumran community. Jesus probably had a similar level of education and interests as other marginalized pietists within Israel in this era. As well as work, the daily routines of his later followers would center around prayer, reading Scripture, and transmission of Jesus material within some institutional framework that they would be responsible for maintaining. I do not believe this text-centered existence, typical of other esoteric communities in Palestine in this era, can be labelled as "predominantly oral culture." Certainly it was not folkloric. Rather, I would prefer to call it a version of Jewish sacral communitarianism. The leaders and probably many others of influence could read and write because that was central to their *raison d'être*.

The Preservation of Jesus Material by Eyewitnesses

In keeping with the title of Harrison's article, Bauckham's massive work on *Jesus and the Eyewitnesses* looms strongly in the discussion. To an ordinary person (ancient or modern) if it could be shown definitively that the original witnesses of Jesus' sayings and deeds continued to exercise a dominant role in their transmission then the case for historical integrity would be enhanced. Not only does Bauckham argue that eyewitnesses were sources of central information for the process of transmission but that the core accounts of the canonical Gospels are actually based on their direct eyewitness testimony.[3]

Eric Eve handily notes that Bauckham presents four basic "strands" of argumentation for his position.[4] First, using mainly a form of literary argumentation heavily dependent upon perceived "inclusios" at the beginning and end of the Gospels he attempts to show that all the Gospels claim to embody authoritative eyewitness testimony from foundational leaders. Second, he uses the fragments of Papias to build a case that the words of an eyewitness (in this case, John) authoritatively overshadowed all others. Third, he seeks to describe what he believes is the most plausible frame in which to place the oral transmission of eyewitness testimony. Fourth, much of the book engages in a comparative study of names. Bauckham compares the names of persons in the New Testament with comparative names of persons found in ancient sources from the same time period and place. The result reveals a strong overlap and thus he concludes that this serves to validate the historicity of the Gospel accounts.[5]

I am convinced that the first, second, and fourth "strands" are interesting but do not deal directly with the key issue of the nature of the transmission of the earliest Jesus tradition.[6] This leaves the third "strand" to supply the crucial information to warrant the conclusion that these

---

3. Bauckham, *Jesus and the Eyewitnesses*, 264–89.
4. Eve, *Behind the Gospels*, 143–44.
5. Eve, *Behind the Gospels*, 144.
6. Eve, *Behind the Gospels*, 144.

accounts show evidence of direct eyewitness testimony by the main group carriers.

Not surprisingly, Harrison concludes that Bauckham's claims are more asserted than shown. Firm criteria for direct eyewitness testimony are lacking. But one must be careful when one raises the question about points of comparison. Eyewitness testimony may not necessarily have to be compared with "multiple informal re-performances" of a story that would have been "created," or even "traditioning/story-telling" activity. Again, I am bothered by a tendency to automatically draw models for transmission of Jesus tradition from conventional oral culture models.

I have spent all of my life in Christian communities and I am well aware that certain preachers and teachers do dominate the tone and ethos of what is reckoned as normative in most local faith constituencies. Before print culture this must have been even more apparent. I am arguing that if the earliest communities of Jesus' followers functioned in a similar way to other esoteric Jewish sacral bodies of believers of the time, then distinctions between original eyewitnesses and later oral transmitters would not be as rigid as later scholars presume. In a dynamic learning community where literacy was presumed for the community to function, the words of key leaders would be treasured (either through the keeping of notes or memory). The reference to Acts 4:13 should not be seen as a counterpoint to this claim. As with the observant Jewish community that nourished the Gospel of John, the earliest followers of Jesus were just as literate as their opponents. They were branded as "common" and "uneducated" because they simply did not accept the teaching of the mainstream synagogues. Nevertheless, what was put in its place was just as sophisticated and carefully stated. The differences between these groups were more in matters of class rather than ability to read or write.

Conclusion

I appreciate very much the balanced and fair appraisal Harrison has made of Bauckham's magisterial work. In the main I would agree with his conclusion that Bauckham has not shown conclusive proof that the canonical Gospels leave compelling literary evidence of the direct imprints of eyewitnesses of Jesus' ministry controlling the tradition. A lot happened in that first generation.

My major disagreement, as is so often in these matters, is in the area of methodology. As I view the essay, Harrison has assessed Bauckham's work from the perspective of contemporary orality studies—especially those that are informed by recent studies of memory by social scientists. I believe that this move places Bauckham in the wrong stream of Gospel studies. He is more in the Gerhardsson/Riesner stream of scholarship, which argues for a different *Sitz im Leben* for the transmission of the Jesus tradition. Here, the Jesus tradition has become anchored within a small sectarian sacred community that treasures original eyewitness memories that continue to be transmitted under the guidance of established leaders. This is a different model and understanding of the role of memory than that which is purveyed by contemporary social media critics who operate out of a model drawn from oral folkloric cultures. Bauckham overstates the evidence of the control of the eyewitnesses but he is on the right track in describing the dynamic process of maintaining the tradition.

I would like to make one final observation that connects with this debate. Studies of social memory are important. But I note two critically related areas of the transmission of the Jesus tradition that are often overlooked in this context. First, who will continue to do the linguistic work on establishing what the original Jesus tradition looked like? It is needed. Second, would the conclusions of the social media critics be the same if Mark's Gospel was not the first as they seem to universally presume? There is still work to be done!

Bibliography

Assmann, Jan. *Cultural Memory and Early Civilization: Writing, Remembrance, and Political Imagination*. Cambridge: Cambridge University Press, 2011.

Bauckham, Richard. *Jesus and the Eyewitnesses: The Gospels as Eyewitness Testimony*. 2nd ed. Grand Rapids: Eerdmans, 2017.

Eve, Eric. *Behind the Gospels: Understanding the Oral Tradition*. Minneapolis: Fortress, 2014.

Halbwachs, Maurice. *On Collective Memory: The Heritage of Sociology*. Edited by Donald N. Levine. Chicago: University of Chicago Press, 1992.

4

Reviving the Priority of John

Mark A. Matson

THE POSTHUMOUS PUBLICATION OF John A. T. Robinson's final work, *The Priority of John*, appeared in 1985.[1] Like so many works by Robinson, this book was, and remains, controversial. Certainly it was "swimming against the tide." *The Priority of John* as a major study challenged the common assumptions held by scholarship and the church about the nature of the Fourth Gospel. Certainly a large body of evidence had already been produced that challenged the opinion that the Gospel of John was late, secondary, and derivative of the other Gospels. But Robinson's book added new life to rethinking the relationship of John to the Synoptics, its relationship to the historical Jesus, and its development as a narrative about Jesus.[2]

In the thirty-plus years since Robinson's work, there have been relatively few works that have dealt directly with the issue of John's dating, either relative to other Gospels or absolutely.[3] A significant number of articles, however, have addressed issues that do relate to the dating of John: the narrative unity of the Gospel, the question of sources behind John and especially the question of a "signs gospel," the historical value of material in the Gospel, the relationship of John to the Synoptic Gospels,

---

1. Robinson, *Priority of John*.

2. I had offered a previous assessment of the state of scholarship a number of years ago. See Matson, "Current Approaches," 73–100.

3. Of particular note, though, is Berger, *Im Anfang war Johannes*, and a collection of articles from a 2000 Symposium on Johannine priority: Hofrichter, *Für and Wider die Priorität des Johannesevangeliums*.

and issue of the "Jews" in John, along with many more issues. Despite a significant amount of continuing research that calls into question the view that John's Gospel is "secondary" in nature to the Synoptics, and thus also called into question the basis for its late dating, many summary treatments of John continue to assume that John is late and secondary as a window to Jesus' life and ministry.

In this essay I wish to return to Robinson's core thesis in light of the last thirty years of research, and pose the question again about John's unique character, its relationship to other Gospels, and most especially the dating of John relative to the other Gospels. It is my thesis that Robinson was correct in his argument that John has a "priority": Certainly that John is not dependent or secondary to any of the other Gospels, and further that in many ways John offers information about Jesus' life and ministry that is likely superior to that in the Synoptic Gospels.[4] In the short compass available here it will not be possible to provide extensive arguments or a full representation of research. Rather, the purpose here is to review the key issues that involve the dating of John and offer some observations about John, observations that confirm Robinson's overall perspective, though not perhaps on every point. In other words, it is time to revisit, in a positive appraisal, Robinson's view on John.

Background: The Development of Modern Views of John's Gospel

Before taking up Robinson's arguments, it is worthwhile to review the landscape of Johannine studies. Robinson's book was revolutionary in part because it was so contrary to what had become a more or less accepted understanding, if not even an orthodoxy, about John's origin, composition, and relationship to the other Gospels.

Up until the nineteenth century, John was generally considered to be one of the Gospels written by an eyewitness— the Apostle John. While the differences between John and the Synoptics were noticed quite early in the church, and created some questions about its place in the developing canon of the New Testament, these differences were generally

---

4. It is important to note that Robinson never argued for John's absolute chronological priority. In fact, he held it likely that John was written over a period of time, and so the final product might have been later than some other Gospels. But Robinson was arguing that John was never "secondary"—that is, that it stood in an independent trajectory, and had equal or better claim to a historical connection to Jesus.

resolved in favor of it offering simply a difference in purpose. This was perhaps stated in the most classic way by Clement of Alexandria who deemed the Fourth Gospel a "spiritual Gospel." And while most of the church fathers assumed John was written last among the Gospels, it was often considered to be authoritative on historical issues, or at least on the larger framework of Jesus' life. Thus, even in the nineteenth century Friedrich Schleiermacher, one of the leading figures in "higher criticism," was convinced that John had a superior claim to a historical perspective on Jesus:

> The Gospel of John everywhere presents itself as one originating from an immediate eyewitness. In contrast with this the others' compilation [of their narratives] from single elements is subject to comparable doubt. All three, without exception, are seen as coming to us second hand.[5]

This changed, however, with David Strauss's dramatic book published in 1835, *The Life of Jesus Critically Examined*. Although a student of Schleiermacher, he questioned the historical validity of much of John's account of Jesus, arguing that John's account is but a more developed form of "myth" than the Synoptics. And this critical view of John was further supported by F. C. Baur who, in 1847, argued that John's Gospel had no interest in providing a historical account, but is controlled throughout by an ideological tendency.[6] More specifically, between them Baur and Strauss developed four primary arguments for discounting John, arguments that reinforced one another:

1. John is thoroughly theological.
2. John is primarily the product of a Hellenistic environment, not the original Palestinian environment in which the events related took place.
3. John is dependent on the Synoptic Gospels. As a result its presentation is second-hand, derivative, and less reliable.

---

5. Citation from Strauss, *Christ of Faith*, 41. See also Schleiermacher, *Life of Jesus*, 223: "It is a fortunate circumstance that in our task of recreating the life of Jesus, we are not compelled to regard the narrative in the Gospel of John also [i.e., as compared to Synoptics] as derived from second or third hand sources, as altered in many ways, and as no longer reliable."

6. Baur, *Kritische Untersuchungen über die kanonischen Evangelien*, 239.

4. John is a late Gospel. Since it was written most distant from Jesus' life, it cannot be counted on to provide reliable information about Jesus.

But while some of these early critical approaches to John continue to appear in New Testament introductions, there have been some important developments in the scholarly approach to John in the early and mid-twentieth century. The idea that the Gospel of John was of Hellenistic origin was certainly dominant well into the middle of the twentieth century.[7] But the discovery of the Dead Sea Scrolls in the 1950s, and the subsequent revision of views of Judaism, has largely undermined this view.[8] And, while there are still some who argue that John was aware of and used the Synoptic Gospels, perhaps the majority view tends to be either agnostic or skeptical of this.[9] Yet, while the Synoptic Gospels may no longer be seen as the central source of John's information, other sources for John have been suggested that have become more important in scholarly discussions. Moreover, major theories have been advanced about John's compositional methods that involve complex multi-stage socially interactive processes.

The first of these approaches, John's use of sources, finds its primary genesis in the work of Rudolf Bultmann. Bultmann, in his landmark

---

7. This idea of John's Hellenistic origin perhaps reached its zenith with Bousset, *Kyrios Christos*, 236: "Thus the Johannine writings with their view that one acquires life by means of the vision, with their concepts of the miracle working word, of faith, knowledge, truth, light and darkness, light and life, are rooted in the soil of Hellenistic mythicism." But it continued on for quite some time, and certainly influenced Bultmann.

8. See Keener, *Gospel of John*, 1:154–58, for a thoughtful discussion concerning the Hellenistic milieu in which the Gospel was written and how that might affect our understanding of its influence.

9. For example, a sampling of modern New Testament introductions and commentaries shows that reliance on Synoptics and/or sources is often rejected, but a late date is often retained. Introductions: Johnson, *Writings of the New Testament*, 466, John is late first century, but does not use sources; Ehrman, *New Testament*, 172, John does not use Synoptics but uses other sources; Burkett, *Introduction*, 217, John shows some knowledge of the Synoptics, but it is not its primary source, which includes the Signs source; Brown, *Gospel According to John*, xxxiv, John begins with a core narrative independent of the Synoptics, but it goes through multiple revisions, so is quite late; Schnackenburg, *Gospel*, 1:42 and n. 64, is independent of the Synoptics, though perhaps assumes some knowledge of them, perhaps uses a signs source, dating is relatively late; Keener, *Gospel of John*, opts for independence from the Synoptics (40–42), and for lack of use of sources (37–39).

commentary published in 1941, argued that underneath the text of John were a variety of sources that could be detected and separated.[10] Notably, Bultmann argued that four primary influences could be detected: 1) a *semeia-quelle*, or signs source, that provided the miracle stories; 2) a passion source, similar to the passion stories in the Synoptics; 3) an *offenbarungsreden*, or revelation discourse source; and 4) the hand of an ecclesiastic redactor that shaped the material prior to the final publication by the author of John.[11] While much of this theory, notably the gnostic orientation and even existence of the revelation discourse source, has been cast in doubt in the intervening years, the existence of some variety of sources remains a topic in Johannine studies. In particular, the existence of a signs source has been argued by Robert Fortna and Urban von Wahlde, among others.[12] Notably, von Wahlde has very recently published a new three-volume commentary on the Johannine corpus in which he refines his earlier source hypothesis in terms of a three-stage rewriting/editing process, the earliest stage of which is somewhat like a semeia-gospel.[13] In addition to the signs source, an independent origin for the logos-prologue is also often asserted, perhaps with it being a late addition to the Gospel. In the same vein, the epilogue (chapter 21) is often seen as a late addition, perhaps by another hand.

The second influential critical approach to John involves the hypothetical engagement of the author(s) with an audience among whom, and for whom, the Gospel was written. Undoubtedly the origination for this approach comes from J. Louis Martyn, with his *History and Theology of the Fourth Gospel*.[14] This highly influential work suggested that the Fourth Gospel was rhetorically engaged at a different level than the core narrative. That is to say, the narrative is operating at two levels: the main level, the core narrative of Jesus, is a story that relates Jesus' life as a series of miraculous events leading up to his passion. But at a second level, often involving disputes with "the Jews," the narrative is reflecting on current events in the Johannine community that is quite distinct from

---

10. Bultmann, *Gospel of John*.

11. A thorough analysis of Bultmann's theory of sources and editing can be found in Smith, *Composition and Order*; Bultmann's Literary Theory.

12. Fortna, *Gospel of Sign*; von Wahlde, *Earliest Version*; Nicol, *Sēmeia*; Teeple, *Literary Origin*.

13. von Wahlde, *Gospel and Letters*.

14. Martyn, *History and Theology*, 47–66.

the life of Jesus. Martyn argues that it is on this second level much of the rhetoric of the Gospel is focused.

The clearest example, and the one that serves to set out this hermeneutical approach to John, is found in John 9, the story of the man born blind. The series of critical exchanges between the man's parents and the Pharisees points to a situation that could not, according to Martyn, have fit in Jesus' lifetime. The parents are afraid to even claim their son's healing because, as the Gospel states, "they were afraid of the Jews, for the Jews had already agreed that anyone who confessed Jesus to be the Messiah would be put out of the synagogue" (John 9:23). Martyn argued that this disagreement fit better the situation sometime after AD 80, when the Jews met in Jamnia and began to develop rabbinic Judaism. Indeed, he sees behind the term ἀποσυνάγωγος in 9:23 a situation that only arose after the inclusion of the *birkhat ha-minim*—the cursing of the minim—in the eighteen benedictions recited in the synagogue:

> For the apostates let there be no hope. And let the arrogant government be speedily uprooted in our days. Let the Nazarenes [Christians][15] and the Minim [heretics] be destroyed in a moment. And let them be blotted out of the Book of Life and not be inscribed together with the righteous. Blessed art thou, O Lord, who humblest the proud.[16]

What is particularly important about Martyn's approach is the view that the gospel text has been redacted at various places to accommodate historical situations that are contemporaneous with the audience of the Gospel, here imagined as a unique community. This perspective has proliferated with a number of studies that hold the "Johannine community" to be a central element in understanding the Gospel: Oscar Cullman's *The Johannine Circle*; Alan Culpepper's *The Johannine School*; and most importantly, Raymond Brown's *The Community of the Beloved Disciple*.[17] The element that binds all these studies together is that the Fourth Gospel is seen as a product of a sectarian group that is distinct from other branches of Christians, and, especially in Brown's fully developed thesis,

---

15. The term here is "nozerim." It is translated by Martyn as "Nazareans" and hence he can use the gloss "Christians." Kimelman, "Birkhat Ha-minim," 232–44, provides ample evidence that this may, in fact, refer to Nazoreans—a Jewish Christian sect in the third century, which links very well with the few Talmudic uses of the term.

16. As found in Martyn, *History and Theology*, 62. This is the Cairo Geniza form of the twelfth benediction.

17. Cullmann, *Johannine Circle*; Culpepper, *Johannine School*; Brown, *Community*.

the life of the Johannine community can be traced through a series of crises that are represented in the text of the Gospel by means of crises in Jesus' ministry. In these analyses, then, the Gospel narrative is as much about the Johannine community as it is about Jesus. The hermeneutical focus moves from the sources behind the Gospel to a series of redactional glosses in the text that reflect then-current situations in the life of the community.

While it is always dangerous to assume a consensus on any aspect of gospel scholarship, it does seem that perspectives on John contained in New Testament introduction textbooks would include some or all of the following, either explicitly or implicitly:[18]

1. John is still considered to be a late Gospel, probably being completed in the second century, or at earliest 90 CE.[19]

2. John's overall construction is seen as theological and shows signs in this theological construction of some very late ideas. On the one hand, the idea that Greek religion or philosophy influenced John's theology (i.e., that either a descending-ascending God or a logos-theology were influenced by either Platonism or Stoicism) has generally waned. Yet for many New Testament scholars, the existence of John's "high" Christology of a preexistent Christ is still often considered to be a late theological development.[20]

3. The events recorded in John have been shaped by events within a Johannine community, including conflicts with developing rabbinic Judaism.[21]

4. While some of the sources, such as the *semeia* source, might be early, these have been thoroughly mixed-up with, and overshadowed by, the addition of subsequent material—either other sources (e.g.,

---

18. Many of these issues are presented as more or less accepted scholarly ideas in standard New Testament textbooks. I reviewed sections on John in Powell's *Introducing the New Testament*, Ehrman's *New Testament*, and Burkett's *Introduction* for these issues and they are referenced below. While they each have distinctive discussions of John's origin, many of the points below are noted or assumed in their textbooks, as noted below.

19. Powell, *Introducing the New Testament*, 176; Ehrman, *New Testament*, 183; Burkett, *Introduction*, 216.

20. Burkett, *Introduction*, 220.

21. Powell, *Introducing the New Testament*, 176; Ehrman, *New Testament*, 179; Burkett, *Introduction*, 224.

revelation-discourse material) or the anachronistic overlay of later crises in the church.[22]

5. Some still at least imply that John is dependent on the Synoptic Gospels for the core narrative, or at least for parts of it (e.g., the passion narrative).[23]

6. The lateness of John, and its peculiar community-sectarian formation, raises serious questions about any information about Jesus that is presented in the Gospel.

Revisiting John's Priority

It is against this set of underlying arguments presented above that Robinson was arguing in his 1985 book. The central matter with which he took issue was the assumption of lateness and secondariness of these various perspectives presented for John's Gospel. In essence, he was arguing that John is not dependent on other sources, but rather it contains primary, original testimony to the Jesus event. Moreover, he argues that John is not secondary because of its theological sophistication, or because of its difference from the Synoptic Gospels. Instead, he argues that for a variety of reasons John's Gospel should re-enter the discussion as a primary source of information about Jesus, both with reference to the course of his ministry as well as his teaching. Yet Robinson does not argue for an absolute priority, or an absolute early dating. Instead, he sees John as both early and late, and in many ways parallel to the Synoptic tradition (with Mark being developed by Matthew and Luke), which has direct information that is shaped over time. So he can argue that John is both an alpha and omega of the Jesus tradition, though not perhaps the alpha.[24]

Since much has happened in scholarship in the last thirty years, I will not simply retrace Robinson's arguments. But I will follow the major contours of his thought, which I think is still generally valid, and here sketch out a number of issues that contribute to an overall assessment of John's priority. This includes a number of features that support a historical priority (not absolute priority, but often relative priority over the

---

22. Powell, *Introducing the New Testament*, 175–76; Ehrman, *New Testament*, 17–24, Burkett, *Introduction*, 216.

23. Burkett, *Introduction*, 217.

24. Robinson, *Priority of John*, 33.

Synoptics), as well as interpretational issues that go some distance to locating John's Gospel more securely in the early gospel category. The discussion that follows is not meant to be comprehensive by any means. Instead, examples of key issues will be presented and discussed, in order to give an overall picture of some of the trends in scholarship and some of the more recent developments that point toward John as an early and independent source of information about Jesus and his teaching.

But it is worthwhile to state more specifically what I am arguing for, not just what I am arguing against. I hope to engage in this article many of the following issues, and to suggest that these conclusions below about the Gospel of John are worth considering:

1. John is not dependent on the Synoptics, but rather independent.
2. Indeed, a strong case can be made that John has been a source for at least Luke, which would place it earlier than 85 CE, and perhaps even earlier.
3. The question of sources behind the Gospel is still a live question, but the Gospel we have does show a remarkable literary cohesiveness. This is to say, identifying sources is not essential to understanding John's message.
4. John is of course Hellenistic, since the entire Mediterranean basin was Hellenistic. But John is thoroughly Jewish, and reflects Jewish practices and ideas and is perhaps the most consonant with Jewish thought.
5. The continued advancement of archaeology has demonstrated time and again that John's information about Palestinian geography has very often been as strong, or stronger, than the other Gospels.
6. In many ways, John may represent historically superior accounts, and certainly gives us a second major perspective on Jesus.
7. The historical evidence for reading John on two levels is weak, and this alone undermines Martyn's whole approach to the Gospel. A two-level narrative that incorporates a much later historical situation is unlikely.
8. The community approach to explaining Gospels in general, and John in particular, is flawed and I think at best is questionable.

9. John is, however, clearly written from a post-resurrection perspective, and this perspective interprets Jesus' words, especially in his long dialogues and monologues.

10. The Gospel of John is, of course, theological, and yet we see that all the Gospels are theological. This merely means "distinctive."

All of this points to, or is supportive of, a certain "priority" for John. Perhaps it is not *the* earliest Gospel, though it may be *among the earliest*, but certainly it is an independent (and unique) one that provides a valuable and at times superior witness to Jesus.

Issues Related to John's Priority

John's Independence (And Even Priority)

John's dependence on the Synoptic tradition was a central element of the nineteenth century depreciation of John. And one can certainly see a certain logic to it. Once literary relations became the dominant way of explaining the relationship between the Synoptic Gospels—whether by means of the two-document hypothesis (Mark + Q), or the Griesbach hypothesis (or now with the even-more-recent Farrer hypothesis)—it seems natural to ascribe a similar process for the Synoptic relationship to John. They all are, after all, narrative accounts of Jesus' life, and share some striking similarities in the passion narrative and even some similarities in selected stories, like a feeding of the 5,000 or a temple cleansing or an anointing of Jesus. And yet, apart from the similar ways John and the Synoptics begin and end, there is very little point-to-point similarity. Certainly in both the ministry of Jesus begins with his baptism at the hands of John the Baptist (although John the Baptist's continued role and connection to early disciples is markedly different in the two traditions), and both sets of narratives end at approximately the same place—a resurrection of Jesus after his death. And both narratives do have a feeding of 5,000. Yet aside from these similar tag points, other potentially similar parts of Jesus' life are very different: the temple incident (temple "cleansing") is located very differently, miracles are very different, and even the geographical focus of the ministry is different.

It is this lack of specific similarity between John and the Synoptics that prompted two early twentieth-century writers to challenge the presumption of literary connection. Indeed, these two very short books, one in German and one in English, still provide the basic common sense arguments against any literary relationship. Both took as their starting point the significant number and degree of differences between John and the Synoptics.

Hans Windisch raised the first serious objections to a Johannine reliance on the Synoptics in a small book published in 1926 with a provocative title: *Johannes und die Synoptiker: Wollte der vierte Evangelist die älteren Evangelien ergänzen oder ersetzen?*[25] (Did the fourth Gospel supplement the older Gospels, or replace them?) Windisch examined four possible explanations for the relationship between John and the Synoptics: 1) independence; 2) supplementation theory (the primary theory offered by church fathers); 3) interpretation theory (in which John is providing an interpretation of the Synoptics); and 4) replacement theory. Windisch severely critiques the supplementation theory, arguing that the Gospel of John can hardly be seen as simply supplementing, since similar events take place in such radically different ways. For instance, the difference in the calendar sequence in the passion narrative can in no way be explained as a supplement: Jesus dies on a different day in the Jewish lunar calendar; the final meal is not a Passover meal. The very different placement of the temple incident—early in the Jesus active ministry for John, and late in the ministry for the Synoptics—can hardly be seen as a supplement. Nor, indeed, can many of these differences be explained as an interpretation. Not only are the events often told in radically different ways, but no attempt at offering an explanation of the differences is offered. While Windisch allows that independence is a possible explanation, he finds instances where there are some similar events that are told very differently. These occasional, and yet to Windisch quite distinctive, linkages between John and the Synoptics suggest for him another explanation. For Windisch, the only reasonable explanation for the differences between John and the Synoptics, if John knew the Synoptics, is that he must have intended to displace them, to replace the Synoptic story with a new story—the Fourth Gospel account. For instance, the temple cleansing must have taken place either in the beginning of Jesus' ministry or at the end. John's placement at the beginning was, for Windisch, a clear replacement of the order of events leading to a different story entirely. And this explanation would function equally for many other events in the gospel narrative.

25. Windisch, *Johannes und die Synoptiker*, 1926.

Percival Gardner-Smith approached the same issue as Windisch, but in an entirely different way. In 1938, with apparently no knowledge of Windisch's earlier book, he published a short 100-page monograph entitled *St. John and the Synoptic Gospels*.[26] Gardner-Smith's thesis was deceptively simple: given the large number of differences between the Gospels, and the relatively few points of contact, is it easier to explain this set of facts by means of John's dependence on the Synoptics, or by John's independence of them? For Gardner-Smith, after exploring a number of similarities and differences, the answer was clear: John was literarily independent of the Synoptics, and any overlap in the Gospel accounts can be accounted for by means of oral accounts or eyewitness memory. That is, the few similarities are precisely what one might expect from two independent accounts of an historical event.

Although coming from very different perspectives, these two short books had an effect on the course of scholarship, and by the early 1960s a new critical consensus seems to have been emerging which saw John as literarily independent of the Synoptics. C. H. Dodd's second major work on John, *Historical Tradition in the Fourth Gospel*, underscored this shift in a scholarly center of opinion.[27] The Louvain school under the influence of Frans Neirynck pushed back against this emerging consensus, and produced a veritable library of articles arguing that John is dependent on all the Synoptic Gospels.[28] And yet more and more scholars doubted Johannine dependence on the Synoptics.

Much of the discussion on the relationship of John and the Synoptics focused on the larger scope of the narrative, often comparing Mark and John. But there was another wrinkle in the John-Synoptic relationship that became a side topic of discussion: the unique relationship between John and Luke. Here there were a significant number of minor details, which added up cumulatively to offer a significant problem for the independence theory. Perhaps a few examples would help capture the kind of linkages one finds between Luke and John. 1) In John's version of the anointing of Jesus, Mary took ointment and anointed Jesus' feet instead of his head, and then wiped his feet with her hair. The distinctive features of a woman anointing his feet and wiping them with her hair is also found in Luke, although it is not the traditional anointing at

---

26. Gardner-Smith, *St. John*.
27. Dodd, *Historical Tradition*.
28. For instance, see Neirynck, "John and the Synoptics."

the end of Jesus' ministry (there is none in Luke), but a sinner woman who slips into a meal Jesus has with Simon the Pharisee. 2) Only in Luke and John does Pilate declare Jesus innocent three times, do the crowds call out for Jesus' death with a distinctive double-cry "crucify, crucify," and does the narrator relate that it is the right ear of the soldier that is cut off at the arrest. 3) Only in Luke and John do the disciples go to the empty tomb, though in John both Peter and the Beloved Disciple race to the tomb, while in Luke we only hear about Peter peering into the tomb—though later in the Emmaus report the disciples who went to the tomb are reported in the plural; and furthermore, only in Luke and John does Jesus appear to the disciples in closed rooms. I could go on; the list is extensive.[29] The standard argument has been that John must have relied on Luke. But there is a curious feature here—where Luke and John agree is precisely where Luke varies the most from the Markan story line. In other words, it seems that Luke may have been pulled away from the Markan version by another account—a Johannine account. My dissertation was an attempt to test that theory in the passion account, and found it a highly plausible, even likely, explanation.[30]

A more recent effort to address the similarities between the Synoptics and John seeks a more nuanced relationship. Paul N. Anderson in general has posited the independence of John, and yet sees certain connections between John and Mark such that at an early stage of writing John was influenced by Mark, and perhaps the Gospel was an effort by an eyewitness to address missing items from Mark.[31] In this scenario, John and Mark are both quite early, and yet Anderson allows a certain priority to Mark's Gospel, even while finding John in general reflecting a direct, original, and often historical, perspective on Jesus.[32]

---

29. I have developed a comprehensive list of the various similarities between Luke and John noted by various scholars. See Matson, *In Dialogue*. See also on this Shellard, *New Light on Luke*.

30. Matson, *In Dialogue*. See also Matson, "Influence of John.

31. This basic idea is best addressed in Anderson, "Mark and John," 175–88. It is also advanced in Anderson, *Fourth Gospel*.

32. In addition to Anderson, Brown late in his career also suggested that in addition to an overall "independence" there may have been some "cross-influence" of Mark on John, perhaps at the very early (oral) stage. See Brown, *Introduction*, completed posthumously by Moloney, 101. He also sees such cross-influence between John and Luke in the later stages of development.

So what should one's conclusion be about John's relationships to the Synoptics?[33] I would suggest that the strongest position is that John's Gospel represents an independent account of the ministry of Jesus. Windisch's critique of the relationship is, for me, critical: If John used the Synoptics, he intended to displace the other accounts; there is no other reasonable way to explain the differences. And yet, contra Windisch, John seems to show little sign of a consistent anti-Synoptic agenda. But if John is an independent story, based on an independent oral and/or eyewitness tradition, we can account for the few similarities between Mark and John as coming from common events. The strong set of relationships between Luke and John I would suggest a reverse order—that Luke, who clearly used many sources in compiling his Gospel,[34] had John among them and was influenced at critical points in his narrative.

Now if this is correct, then the first leg of John's "secondariness" within the canon of Gospels is either gone or severely weakened. If John is not derived from the other Gospels, it could be as early as Mark (or earlier), and offer equally vital perspectives on the life of Jesus.

Is John Fragmented or Incoherent? Sources and Literary Styles

For much of the twentieth century, a large part of scholarly discussion of John has focused on the question of sources behind the Fourth Gospel. The most significant efforts in this vein have come from Rudolf Bultmann,[35] Robert Fortna,[36] and Urban C. van Wahlde,[37] although numerous others have sought to explain John by some combination of sources, dislocation of material, or re-editing of material by a later hand. And certainly the existence of a "second ending" of the Gospel at chapter 21, seemingly as a postscript, does suggest some more complex form of composition—at the very least the possibility that the author took up his pen a second time to add these final verses. Others point to the hymnic

---

33. The best discussion of this relationship, including the shifts over time, is found in Smith, *John among the Gospels*.

34. See, for instance, Luke's own prologue where he points to multiple narratives already in existence.

35. Bultmann, *Gospel of John*.

36. Fortna, *Gospel of Signs*.

37. von Wahlde, *Gospel and Letters*.

prologue as an indication of a late addition, and thus evidence of a complex editorial process.

But why have source theories been so attractive to scholars with the Gospel of John? In part it may be the influence of Synoptic Gospel scholarship relative to the interrelationships of the Gospels, which has posited "sources" as the default explanation for all Gospel writing. Yet John has little of the apparent indications of sources, i.e., common material found in other Gospels, which begs for the explanation of a literary relationship. Still, John does present some tensions in the narratives that might indicate the existence of editing or pasting of material. These tensions are called *aporias*, or inconcinnities: places where there is a shift in geography or logic or chronology which stands out in the flow of the story. For instance, the resumption of the story in chapter 21 after what seems to be a decisive conclusion is an *aporia* begging for explanation. Or consider the geographical location of the feeding miracle in chapter 6: chapter 5 contains a lengthy dialogue that takes place in Jerusalem, yet chapter 6 begins rather abruptly in Galilee, with Jesus "crossing over to the other side of the Sea of Galilee." Why the sudden transition? The alternation in the Gospel between activities of Jesus (often in relatively few, but noteworthy, "signs") and lengthy discourses has led many to assume that a simpler Gospel of Signs has been absorbed and modified by the later addition of controversies and discourses.[38]

The effort to isolate sources in John has used a number of methodologies. Early efforts identified stylistic differences in the various sections of John, but Eduard Schweizer's and Eugen Ruckstuhl's major studies of John's vocabulary and style have demonstrated a unity of style throughout the Gospel.[39] Later efforts have seen theological tensions and ideas that present "patterns" that point to sources, while the sources themselves have been thoroughly massaged by a later editor, thus removing stylistic differences.[40] Certainly one can imagine the Gospel arising from the use of sources, with successive efforts in absorbing material that then resulted in a final edited Gospel. But such a perspective must be based on some clear indication of sources and the use of sources. How definitive are the criteria for such *aporia* and/or theological and stylistic differences? Often

---

38. So, following Fortna, Miller, *Complete Gospels*, 175, as a distinct source that they publish as a Gospel in their compendium of Gospels.

39. Schweizer, *Ego eimi*.

40. So, von Wahlde, *Gospel and Letters*.

the *assumption* of sources remains, even while clear evidence of them proves more elusive.

The rise of narrative criticism, however, has cast new doubt on the value of source theories for explaining the Fourth Gospel. Simply put, the Fourth Gospel has its own, yet very effective narrative strategy for telling the story of Jesus. The number of scholars attending to various kinds of narrative-centered research on John is growing and presenting different explanations for what have often been seen as difficult sections in John.[41] Attending to the narrative structure of John often explains some of the difficult features in the Gospel.

This paper cannot offer a full review of narrative approaches to John; I will, however, present a couple of examples of how narrative readings may offer alternative explanations for some of the difficulties in the Fourth Gospel. I have tried to show in a couple of articles how the "temple cleansing" in John serves a critical narrative function in the Gospel in two ways. First, the conflict with the Jews—which is the core "plot" feature in the Gospel—is introduced very early in this pericope and sets the stage for a pattern of conflict that follows throughout the Gospel.[42] As a result, the placement of the temple incident is part of the larger narrative construction, not a haphazard *re-placement*. While the temple incident in the Synoptic Gospels seems to precipitate the push to arrest Jesus, John's Gospel instead has Jesus "indicted" well before he enters Jerusalem in the final Passover Week. Secondly, the narrative time perspective by which the Gospel is told, one that is overtly from the perspective of the resurrection often as "recollections," is also introduced here.[43] The temple incident, then, establishes a narrative pattern that coheres with the rest of the Gospel.

---

41. For instance, Moloney's three-volume commentary on the Gospel of John focuses on just such a narrative task. In the introductory matter to his first volume, *Belief in the Word*, he engages just this issue with a section entitled "Synchronic or Diachronic?" While Moloney accepts the possibility of a complex process of growth of the Gospel, he also accepts its basic narrative unity: "Yet whoever may have been responsible for the final shape of the Gospel consciously took stories from the recorded memory of the community and laid them side by side to form the Gospel. This process may have been repeated many times until our Gospel was eventually produced. Because of this process, the final product, even though it sometimes has untidy seams, is thoroughly Johannine in all its parts" (3).

42. Matson, "Temple Incident," 145–54.

43. Matson, "Time to Tell" paper presented at the 2003 SBL Meeting.

One *aporia* that has been noted is the notice that Mary is the one who anointed Jesus' feet, which occurs anachronistically before that event happens (John 11:2). To source critics of John, this is an example that the author was referring to an event from another source, and that an editor has rearranged material from that source without fully attending to all the chronological links. Thus, this reference to an event in the future, reported here in the past tense, is out of place—an *aporia*. But is that the only explanation? In a subsequent paper on John's use of time, I noted that John throughout the Gospel engages in such "proleptic" statements—comments that anticipate a later event.[44] This occurs not only with the anticipation of Mary's footwashing/anointing, but that a subsequent anointing passage then further alludes to a still-later footwashing episode. Such proleptic narrative constructions also are found with respect to Satan's future role in Jesus' betrayal, reported as a "past fact" numerous times early in the Gospel. We find similar proleptic references with respect to John the Baptist, Nicodemus, and the resurrection itself. The reference to Mary's future anointing role is, then, part of the narrative pattern of John's Gospel. Is it an *aporia*, an inconcinnity; or is it rather a part of John's careful narrative anticipation?

In other words, many narrative interpretations find the Gospel is indeed more unified than source critics had recognized. While this does not invalidate source theories, it does raise questions about how earlier scholars read the Gospel with an eye to problems: are the problems really problems, or are they simply features common to a complex narrative? John clearly has constructed his Gospel from a post-resurrection perspective, which assumes certain actions had already happened. Similarly, John's Gospel betrays a definite self-selection of events for rhetorical purposes: "Jesus did many other signs in the presence of his disciples, which are not written in this book. But these are written so that you may come to believe that Jesus is the Messiah, the Son of God" (John 20:30). Thus, John's Gospel shows signs of very definite theological and narrative organization, which at times uses temporal or logical disjunctions to drive the story forward.

For many, the presence of the prologue and chapter 21 both speak to multiple editions of the Gospel. Yet even here the narrative approaches to the Gospel provide a corrective against a methodology that easily finds sources and discontinuity in the Fourth Gospel. Perhaps under the

---

44. Matson, "Foreshadowing and Realization."

influence especially of Alan Culpepper's narrative analysis, the role of the prologue as integrally connected to the rest of the Gospel has gained substantial traction.[45] Luke Timothy Johnson has summarized the perspective of many Johannine scholars: the prologue anticipates many of the main themes of the Fourth Gospel, and "gives explicit expression of the constant assumption behind the deeds and works of Jesus," such that "everything in the FG presupposes this highly explicit framework."[46]

One final note is worth making here about the seeming inconcinnities in the Gospel. While source critics have found numerous problems or seams in the Gospel, surprisingly few naïve readers of the Gospel notice these problems. The Gospel of John is a favorite first Gospel for young Christians, and rarely are problems in reading noted. This suggests that the *aporias* that may be in the story are functional, or at least are not problematic at a narrative level.

John's Jewishness

Part of the reason for rejecting John's historical validity in the early critical period was a belief that John's difference from the Synoptics was due to a significant difference in the culture that had influenced the composition of the Gospel. Put simply, many argued that John was a product of a Hellenistic environment, remote from Palestine, while the Synoptic Gospels portrayed a more Palestinian environment, and thus were considered to be closer to the life and times of Jesus. Indeed in the early twentieth century both B. W. Bacon and the early work of C. H. Dodd, as well as Rudolf Bultmann, sought to find theological influence for John's ideas from thought worlds separate and distinct from Palestinian Judaism.[47] Sometimes these were suggested as Gnostic influences, or following the similarity of key terms with Philo, the syncretizing Platonism of the Hellenist world. Such cultural influences, and the remote location suggested by such influences, contributed to the idea that John was late and secondary to the Synoptic Gospels.

---

45. Culpepper, *Anatomy*; and Culpepper, "Pivot of John's Prologue," 1–31. A very careful narrative analysis of the prologue, linking it to various sections of the Gospel, can be seen in Staley, "Structure of John's Prologue," 241–64. A more recent discussion of the place of the prologue in John's larger gospel can be seen in Voorwinde, "John's Prologue," 15–44.

46. Johnson, *Writings of the New Testament*, 474–75.

47. Bacon, *Gospel of the Hellenists*; Dodd, *Fourth Gospel*; Bultmann, *Gospel of John*.

These studies often shared a view that somehow Palestine, and Palestinian Judaism in particular, was in some way sequestered from the influence of Hellenism, even after four centuries of Hellenistic political, economic, and cultural domination. Even while noting that, linguistically, John's Gospel shows signs of extensive Semitic influence, still the Hellenistic-influenced Judaism supposedly reflected in the Fourth Gospel was imagined as a separate kind of Judaism from Palestinian Judaism. A major corrective to this view of Palestinian provincialism has come in recent years, especially forged by Martin Hengel's magisterial two-volume work, *Judaism and Hellenism*. As Hengel notes in his conclusion, "The distinction between 'Palestinian' Judaism and the 'Hellenistic' Judaism of the Greek-speaking Diaspora, which has been customary for so long, now becomes very questionable."[48]

But even leaving aside the ubiquity of Hellenism in the Levant, we might also inquire about those elements in John that are deemed foreign to Judaism. The prologue of John has often been noted as being a late addition to the Gospel because of its non-Jewish "elements." The prologue's focus on an apparent second divine figure—a Logos—who shares some of the attributes of God, including creation of the world, has been suggested to be alien to Jewish thought. And we might add another feature from the prologue that has been seen as non-Jewish: the strong dualism of the Gospel, in which such oppositions as "light and dark," "flesh and spirit," and "truth and falsehood" all seem to participate in a worldview that is not shared by rabbinic Judaism. Yet the documents from Qumran have opened up a view of Second Temple Judaism that now suggests extensive diversity, including ethical dualism. In fact we tend now to use the term "Judaisms" to speak of the Second Temple period, because in fact there was great diversity. For instance, from Qumran we find a Judaism that is every bit as dualistic as John is, and in similar ways—a fact that James Charlesworth and others first noted some forty years ago.[49] The more we explore the many facets of Judaism in the Second Temple—from Qumran to Enochian literature to the extensive variety of wisdom literature—the more we find ways in which John fits into the mosaic of Judaism in the time period.

The "logos" theology of the prologue, in which the word is a co-participant with creation, can also be seen to have deep roots within

---

48. Hengel, *Judaism and Hellenism*, 311.
49. Charlesworth, "Critical Comparison."

Jewish theology. Certainly the opening verse, "in the beginning," echoes the opening line of Genesis. While many have traced the "logos" idea to various aspects of Hellenistic philosophy, including Stoicism and Philo's use of such philosophy in interpreting the Old Testament, the wisdom writings of the Old Testament themselves seem to be a more appropriate background for John's use. In Prov 8, Wis 7, and Sir 24, wisdom is personified in a way that is very suggestive of the use in John's prologue. Wisdom is seen as a participant in creation, as mediating in significant ways God's role in the world, and in Sirach wisdom is portrayed as "tabernacling" with Israel, all of which have echoes in John's prologue.[50] Rather than some strict "source relationship," or the intermediation of a hymn to wisdom that provided a basis, it might best be seen here, as Daniel Boyarin suggests, as a midrash of Genesis 1 and wisdom texts.[51] Or, to use a more modern form of literary interpretation, John's prologue is engaging in extensive intertextual dialogue with Gen 1 and with wisdom texts. What is clear, though, is that the prologue is thoroughly steeped in Old Testament images.

The Gospel of John is, indeed, a rich tapestry of discussions and comments that are constantly engaging the Old Testament Scriptures. Recent scholarship has been focusing on this intertextual engagement between the Gospels and the Old Testament, and certainly John is no exception. A taskforce at the annual meeting of the Catholic Biblical Association has focused for a number of years on the use of the Old Testament in John, and a volume of these papers is forthcoming soon. Richard Hays, in his new volume *Echoes of Scripture in the Gospels*, notes that while the number of explicit citations to Scripture are fewer in John than other Gospels, there is an extensive use of images and figures from the Old Testament, as well as some specific verbal echoes.[52] For instance, John's reference in 3:14 to, "And just as Moses lifted up the serpent in the wilderness, so must the Son of Man be lifted up," alludes to the story of the bronze serpent in Num 21. But it may also allude to Isaiah's reference to the Suffering Servant (Isa 52:13). Allusions to the Scriptures abound throughout the Gospel, as do references to Old Testament figures in debates.[53]

---

50. Ashton, "Transformation of Wisdom," 161–86.

51. Boyarin, "Gospel of the Memra."

52. Hays, *Echoes of Scripture*, 284.

53. An additional fine study that shows the extensive use of OT Scripture in John, often in allusive form, is Peterson, *John's Use of Ezekiel*. Another good example of an image that dominates the Gospel is the temple. Coloe, *God Dwells With Us*, has

Perhaps most important in questions about John's "Jewishness" is the terminology of Jesus' main opponents throughout the Bible: "the Jews." It has often been argued that this objectification of Judaism as "they" points to a time when Christianity had already split from Christianity. But more recent studies have raised real questions about being too hasty in our assumptions about Judaism or the way the term "the Jews" is used in John. A number of literary studies of John have begun to appreciate the way that John uses the term "the Jews."[54] Indeed, as an example, while "the Jews" do serve as the archetypical opponents of Jesus, Jesus also can claim that "salvation is from the Jews" (John 4:22). As Adele Reinhartz, herself a Jewish Gospel scholar, and others have pointed out, the term "the Jews" is a fundamental part of the narrative structure of John.[55] That is, that in the dualistic presentation of John's Gospel, in which belief is set in stark opposition to unbelief, truth to falsehood, and life to death, those who do not believe that Jesus is who he said he was—the very representative of God—are indeed "dead"; they have already been judged. "The Jews" are the literary representation of that opposition, that unbelief.[56] To speak of the Jews opposing Jesus confirms the prologue's statement, "He came to his own, and his own did not know him," and is part of the essential literary fabric of the Gospel. But this literary depiction need not reflect a later time of the separation of Judaism from Christianity—and the opposite of "the Jews" in John is not "the Gentile." Thus, this term is part of the larger literary and theological framework of the Gospel, but does not necessarily reflect a retrojection of later controversies about religious differences.

At the same time, John's story of Jesus is on the surface the one most thoroughly engaged *with* Judaism. The narrative is constructed around multiple Jewish festivals, and indeed his frequent presence in Jerusalem where most of the critical discourses take place is not accidental—it is precisely because of these festivals. And many of his controversies—at Passover and at Tabernacles—reflect features that are part of the very fabric of the festival celebrations.[57] To add to this literary focus on Jew-

---

devoted significant attention to the way the temple image functions in the Gospel.

54. See for instance Johnson, "Salvation Is From the Jews," 83–100.

55. Reinhartz, "'Jews' and Jews in the Fourth Gospel." In this same volume are a number of other essays that address the issue of Judaism in John. See also Reinhartz, "Judaism in the Gospel of John," 382–93.

56. Ashton, "Identity and Function," 40–75.

57. See Keener, *Gospel of John*, 722 and 739 for discussion of the Jewish practices of the Water Drawing Ceremony (and the rich intertextual engagement with Scripture)

ish life, many of the geographical features unique to John are now being confirmed—which is to say John reflects intimate details of the land of Israel, particularly Jerusalem, that suggest a proximity to Judaism, not a distance.

So, to summarize an important point, and one that is all too often overlooked: John, far from being distant from the Judaism of Jesus' time, shows time and again a close, perhaps the closest, reflection of Judaism and Jewish thought. As Raymond Brown notes in his *Introduction*, "A large number of scholars are coming to agree that the principal background for Johannine thought was the traditional Judaism of the first century A.D."[58]

Geography and John

One aspect of Robinson's argument for the priority of John involved the re-evaluation of the geographical details in the Fourth Gospel. As he notes, there is a long history of skepticism about geographical details in John.[59] As part of the skepticism of John's connection to the actual ministry of Jesus, various geographical references in the Fourth Gospel were taken to be manufactured by John, often as part of an attempt to create a symbolic portrayal of Jesus' ministry. For instance, the healing at the pool of Bethesda in chapter 5 was seen as contrived, since Bethesda means "house of mercy" and so fits the action of healing Jesus performed there. But despite the skepticism, examination of the geographical references in John is a prime example of the movement in scholarship on John. Paul Anderson notes, for instance, "There are more archaeological, topographical, and apparently historical materials in John than in any other Gospel or even in all three combined."[60] Indeed, a survey of topographical details in John show the vast majority of geographical locations in John have been confirmed by archaeological findings, as will be touched on below.

The case of the pool of Bethesda serves to exemplify well the rethinking about John and geography that is taking place. The location for the healing that John describes in chapter 5 has been verified as a real

---

and the lighting ceremony in the Sukkoth festival.

58. Brown, *Introduction*, 132.
59. Robinson, *Priority of John*, 50.
60. Anderson, "Aspects of Historicity," 587.

pool in the time of Jesus, and archaeological data fit the description that John's Gospel offers. There is a large pool northeast of Jerusalem, near the location Nehemiah had identified as the "Sheep's Gate" in the wall surrounding the city.[61] Like John's rather detailed description, this pool does have five porticos around it (made possible by a portico that divides two connected pools). The lower pool appears to have been used as a *miqvah*, complete with steps that would assist people entering the pool for cleansing, and the upper pool likely functioned as an *otzer* for the larger pool.[62]

But the situation of the pool of Bethesda is by no means unique. Urban von Wahlde evaluated what is currently known about the sizeable number of geographical details in John, many of which had been viewed skeptically by scholars. Yet the vast majority of these geographical references have either been verified or seem to fit well with what we know of the region. Many locations were unique to John, and thus were viewed with particular skepticism: places like Sychar, a village near Jacob's well near ancient Shechem that is referred to in John 5, or the town of Ephraim, or Cana in Galilee. Yet in each case a combination of literary and/or archaeological evidence offers relatively firm support for John's descriptions. While Shechem was destroyed by John Hyrcanus in 107 BCE, in the nearby region of Jacob's well and Mt. Gerizim there are numerous patristic references to a Sychar near Neapolis (a new city founded by Vespasian near Shechem in 72 CE), as well as a reference to a Sakir in the same region in the book of Jubilees and in the Talmud. These descriptions fit well with the present town of Aschar. Thus, there is a strong likelihood that the author of John was reporting with some accuracy the linkage of Jacob's well, Mt. Gerizim, and a town of the Samaritans called Sychar. In a similar way, the finding of stone jars in both Kefr Kenna and Kirbet Qana, two of the most likely sites for John's town of Cana, certainly seems to add at least the reasonableness that small mountain communities in Galilee were concerned about Jewish purity rules. And while this does not verify with complete certainty that John's description of Cana is accurate, it at least goes a long way to adding credibility to John's overall geographical presentation.

Many more examples could be offered, but von Wahlde's careful assessment should be consulted for full details. The point of the examples offered here, and as von Wahlde's larger and much more detailed

---

61. Neh 3:1, 32; 12:39.

62. Von Wahlde, "Pool(s) of Bethesda," 11–136. See also, von Wahlde, "Archaeology," 561–66.

discussion shows, the Fourth Gospel's representation of the physical space in the region—around Jerusalem, near the Praetorium, in small towns in Judea, Galilee, and Samaria—is being found time and again to be accurate, or at least appropriate, to what we know of the region and the geographical concepts of the time. The author of the Fourth Gospel, then, is reflecting real and accurate information about the region, information that suggests more than a second-hand reporting. While this does not certify the events in the Gospel as accurate, or that the author was an eyewitness, it does challenge the perspective that the author was removed from the events by geography and time.

Baur's and Strauss's main argument was that John could not be trusted to provide historical data about Jesus. And indeed most of the work on the historical Jesus has focused heavily, often exclusively, on the Synoptic Gospels. And yet in the last couple of decades significant rethinking has taken place about the historical value of many of the features of John's Gospel. Because scholars have begun to recognize John's Jewishness, especially in light of our understanding the diversity of Judaism in Jesus' time, and because they are recognizing other features such as geographical features sustained by archaeology, a new interest in John's contribution to history has arisen.

The John, Jesus and History section at the Society of Biblical Literature annual meeting has become one of the best attended sections, and has produced now three volumes of collected papers that testify to a renewed interest in John as a primary source for historical understanding of Jesus. This section was begun in 2002, and in the fourteen years of its existence numerous papers (five dozen was the count at the end of 2009, with at least five more years of activity to come) have been delivered, often with responses, from a variety of perspectives. Increasingly, John is being viewed as at least a potential source for valuable historical data about the life and teaching of Jesus. Paul Anderson summarized at the midpoint of the project some of the results thus far. His summary includes these points, along with others:

1. As opposed to being a "spiritual gospel," the Fourth Gospel clearly shows a historical interest.
2. "A good quantity of the distinctive material in John makes particular contributions to our understanding of Jesus and his mission."
3. Close examination of John uncovers a good amount of primitive undeveloped material.

4. Archaeological and topographical details in John cast valuable light on the historicity of the Fourth Gospel.
5. John's chronological plausibility deserves a new look.[63]

At the very least, the essays presented in this SBL section suggest that John may hold significant historical value, though of course it must be evaluated critically and compared with the Synoptic and other data. A couple of examples should suffice to suggest the relative value of John in historical reconstruction:

John Meier's multi-volume work, *A Marginal Jew*, is a good example of where John's historical contribution is appreciated on a selective basis. When Meier examined the issue of John the Baptist, John's baptism, and Jesus' relationship to John the Baptist after his baptism, the Fourth Gospel was taken seriously as a possible source of historical material. Only John's Gospel reports Jesus having a parallel baptizing ministry with John the Baptist, and only John suggests that the earliest disciples of Jesus were initially disciples of John the Baptist. After an extensive discussion of available information and theories on John the Baptist's relationship to Jesus, Meier concludes:

> So strong was the impact of John on Jesus that, for a short time, Jesus stayed with John as his disciple and, when he struck out on his own, he continued the practice of baptizing disciples. While the last two points are not as certain as the fact of Jesus' being baptized, I think the criterion of embarrassment, applied to the Fourth Gospel, makes them fairly probable, especially since they are supported by the criterion of coherence as well. That some of Jesus' early disciples also came from John's may be less certain, but the criterion of embarrassment also seems to apply here. At the very least, if we grant the historicity of Jesus' being baptized, his spending time with John, and his continuing the practice of baptism in his own ministry, then the further point of his drawing disciples from among the Baptist's followers coheres well with these three points.[64]

An example of contested chronology also, I think, offers substantial evidence for John's superiority in historical presentation.[65] In an article

---

63. Anderson, "Aspects of Historicity," 379-86.
64. Meier, *Marginal Jew*, 129.
65. While my main example here is the Passion dating, it is worth noting that earlier in the *JJH* volume, McGrath offers compelling reasons for choosing John's

for the John, Jesus, and History seminar noted above, I offered a study of John's account of the Passion chronology.[66] As is well known, John's Passion chronology is at odds with the Synoptic traditions, and in a way that is frankly impossible to reconcile. Either John's Gospel is correct, or the Synoptic Gospels are correct. Using a variety of data, including worship practices in the early church, other external evidence, as well as the tendencies of the various gospel authors, I argued that John's Passion dating is both plausible and probable.

More examples could be offered of course. But what these do suggest is that increasingly scholars are willing to consider the Fourth Gospel as a source of historical data for constructing a picture of Jesus. And often the Gospel of John is found to provide accurate material, or to at least offer a compelling alternative to the Synoptic portrayal.

Writing History/Theology on Two Levels?

Perhaps no single book has been as influential on the course of Johannine studies as J. Louis Martyn's study, *History and Theology in the Fourth Gospel*.[67] Martyn proposed that parts of John's Gospel did not originate from, and indeed were not truly about, Jesus' life. Rather, they are intrusions of events in the life of the Johannine community retrojected onto the gospel story. In other words, the history of the Johannine community has merged with the gospel story, and the Gospel itself becomes a commentary on the historical period in which the Gospel is written. The decisive narrative unit for Martyn is John 9, the healing of the blind man.[68] Martyn finds the references to the Pharisees seeking to expel people from the synagogue (ἀποσυνάγωγος) for following Jesus is not plausible in the time of Jesus and thus reflects a time after the Council of Jamnia (c. 80 CE to the close of the first century). He further suggests that the adoption of the *birkhat ha-minim*, the curse on the *minim* or heretics, to the Jewish eighteen benedictions came about during the period. He thus reads John

---

chronological placement of the Temple Cleansing over the Synoptic chronology. See McGrath, "Destroy This Temple," 39–41.

66. Matson, "Historical Plausibility," 291–312.

67. Smith, "Contribution of J. Louis Martyn," 1–23.

68. The issue of expulsion from the synagogue (found with reference to a neologism of John, *aposynagogos*) occurs in three places in John: John 9:22; 12:42; and 16:2. The clearest situation though is in John 9, where most of the discussion has centered.

on two levels: the level of the narrative, a story of Jesus, and the level of the history of the community.

On the face of it, this rendering of John 9 (along with John 12 and 16) has significant implications for the writing of the Gospel. Certainly it places the composition after 80 CE, and more likely in a period closer to 90–100 CE, giving enough time for the initial rupture between Judaism and Christianity to take place. Indeed, the proposal by Martyn may be one of the main reasons why the Fourth Gospel is still seen as late and secondary. Not only does this theory postulate a post-80 CE date, it also presumes a number of issues that further affect the reading of the Gospel and supporting a late reading. First, it presumes that Judaism and Christianity have suffered a breach, a "parting of the ways," that began in this later period. Second, and linking to an issue discussed above, Martyn's reading of the Gospel in light of this supposed historical situation already implies that the Gospel cannot be read as coherent; in his reading, the events in the Gospel must have transpired in the following order: chapter 9, 12, 16, 5, and 7.[69] So, while developed around a different basis, Martyn's work follows Bultmann's basic idea that the final Gospel does not follow the original diachronic order. This view that the Gospel is anachronistic also supposes its later and secondary final composition. Third, and perhaps most importantly, Martyn's approach placed the community of the author, the "Johannine community," in the center of hermeneutical approaches to the Gospel.

From Martyn's view of the intertwined nature of the Gospel and the life of the community in which it was written has arisen a veritable cottage industry of reading John as an expression of its community. For Johannine studies this has had particularly important results, and Martyn's book provided a hermeneutical springboard for using it in subsequent interpretation. Raymond Brown's attempt to sketch the historical relationship between community and texts—both of the Gospel and the epistles—has in particular extended the influence of Martyn's basic "two level" reading strategy.[70] Moreover, traces of historical events that ostensibly affected this community could be found in various episodes in the Gospel. And the majority of commentaries of John assume precisely this central role of a Johannine community, which shows how influential this has been.

---

69. Klink, "Expulsion from the Synagogue," 106.

70. Brown, *Community*.

Yet significant, and I think persuasive, objections have been raised against this primary thesis of Martyn's in two different areas: historical and literary. There has been an extensive scholarly discussion on these issues, and so we can here only touch on some key items.[71] First, the idea of the formal adoption of the *birkhat ha-minim* by a Jewish council, especially toward the end of the first century, has in my estimation been completely demolished. Reuven Kimmelman has pointed out that we have no evidence of the *birkhat ha-minim* in Jewish benedictions before the third century, no evidence of it being extensively used even then, and indeed no evidence even of a Jewish council at Jamnia, especially not one that had any authority over nascent rabbinic Judaism.[72] For others, notably Daniel Boyarin, the focus on a council at Jamnia itself is a much later construction in rabbinic Judaism, and this raises further questions about the historical core of Martyn's thesis. So Boyarin argues, "There is every reason to doubt that the *birkath hamminim*, the so-called curse of the heretics, was formulated under Gamaliel II at Yavneh or that it existed at all before the end of the second century."[73] Boyarin further argues that the word *min/minim* first entered the religious discourse in the second century in the Mishna, and that the idea of a "heresy" or "*min*" as a religious division is late; up to this time *hairesis* maintained its earlier meaning of a group of people with common ideas. While Boyarin argues that the cursing of the heretics, David Instone-Brewer hypothesizes that eighteen benedictions were introduced earlier at Jamnia. While this is likely not correct, his construction does offer another aspect that undermines Martyn's thesis. If the eighteen benedictions are an early element in Jewish liturgy (earlier than Jesus believers), then by necessity this would mean that the *minim* would have referred more to intra-Jewish conflict between various groups within Judaism, rather than a conflict with what was now becoming a separate group.[74] As a result, Klink follows this possible scenario and finds the use of ἀποσυνάγωγος in the Fourth Gospel might well describe a feature that fits Judaism before 70 CE, even perhaps in the time of Jesus, and not an anachronistic use at all.[75] In other words, instead of it reflecting a late conflict of Jews vs. Christians, it might

---

71. Or more on the historical issues in particular, see Bernier, *Aposynagogos and the Historical Jesus*.

72. Kimelman, "Birkhat ha mimim," 226–44.

73. Boyarin, "Justin Martyr Invents Judaism," 431.

74. Instone-Brewer, "Eighteen Benedictions," 25–44.

75. Klink, "Expulsion from the Synagogue," 116–17.

indicate the existence of internal tensions between various factions in Judaism quite early.

Secondly, more recent narrative studies of John have suggested that the "aposynagogos" did not play as important a role in John's Gospel as Martyn maintained. Adele Reinhartz has shown that the tensions between Jesus and the Jews in the Fourth Gospel are remarkably rich and complex, and that subsequent to the account in John 9, the Jews and Pharisees are viewed more positively and they are portrayed interacting constructively with early believers in Jesus; this subsequent positive portrayal would seem to be impossible if the major breach Martyn proposes between the church and synagogue had occurred. In other words, Reinhartz argues that the two-level reading of John proposed by Martyn simply does not work that well when the entire Gospel narrative is considered.[76]

But Martyn's theory also and perhaps more importantly, presumes that the Gospel of John is written for, and within, a community that has experienced some kind of trauma similar to a major breach with Judaism. Thus, even if the exact cause of the breach with Judaism is not the introduction of the *birkhat ha-minim*, there may still be some major event or series of events that is reflected in John 9, 12, and 16. Thus, some scholars who have found little evidence for the *birkhat ha-minim* in the first century still would press some other major dissension between Jewish communities and the Johannine churches.[77] Thus the larger issue is the connection between the experiences of the author's "community" and the narrative world of the text. The narrative of Jesus, so it is proposed, reflects in its portrayal of the life of Jesus the events that have happened subsequent to that.

But the validity of these "community" readings, either with respect to John or other Gospels, has been questioned in recent years. Certainly the use of such purported communities as a hermeneutical key to interpreting the Gospels became very popular in the last half of the twentieth century. But how valuable are they? Dwight Peterson, in his examination of "communities" in interpreting Mark, has shown that it provides no

---

76. Reinhartz, "Johannine Community."

77. Note, for instance, that Anderson, even while viewing John as having historical value and perhaps being an early counterpart to Mark, still uses the community model as a basic hermeneutical approach, and while not buying into the *birkhat ha-minim* origination, finds some vague disruption between John's community and Judaism reflected in the Gospel. See Anderson, "Mark, John and Answerability," 233–34.

clear objective basis for interpretation.[78] That is, each interpreter constructs slightly different communities ostensibly on the basis of the text, and then in circular fashion, interprets the Gospel according to their constructed community. But no two interpreters arrive at the same community. In an important collection of essays edited by Richard Bauckham, *The Gospels for All Christians?*, the idea of a Gospel being written within and for a community is challenged.[79] Bauckham, in the lead essay in the book, raises the question of why, given the emphasis on the oral presence, an author would write for his own church community. Or, put differently and taking into account the nature of almost all the writing in the New Testament, he notes, "The obvious function of writing was its capacity to communicate widely with readers unable to be present at its author's oral teaching."[80] This volume edited by Bauckham, and a follow-up volume edited by Edward Klink, has sparked a vigorous debate about communities and their relationship to Gospel production.[81] All of this is a healthy push-back on the use of "the community" as a conceptual, and largely hypothetical, basis with which to build an interpretive structure. In the case of the Gospel of John, the community concept has led to debatable ideas about early Christianity in which Johannine Christians were somehow cut off from, even hermetically separated from, other Christian movements. Is that, indeed, the case? Just as the recent discussions on John's Jewishness have implied stronger links to the life of Jesus, perhaps questioning the role of "communities" in shaping the narrative of the Fourth Gospel will allow us to reconsider it as a vital reflection of the earliest memories of Jesus. Is it plausible that intra-Jewish religious conflict at the time of Jesus might be reflected in John's Gospel? The answer to this is at least a tentative yes by Bernier, and suggests again the possibility, even probability, that John provides a "priority" perspective of Jesus' life rather than reflecting later conflicts in John's community.

---

78. Peterson, *Origins of Mark*.
79. Bauckham, *Gospels for All Christians*.
80. Bauckham, "For Whom Were Gospels Written," 29.
81. Klink, *Audience of the Gospels*.

Early High Christology: John's Theology—Not Necessarily "Developed" or Late

Perhaps the most consistent argument lodged against John is that its theology is highly developed and thus is late. This is often also connected to the idea that has been written under a theological influence alien to or separate from Judaism—particularly the features in John of a descending/ascending God and the explicitly divine nature of Jesus. This is, of course, closely related to a belief discussed above, that the Gospel is Hellenistic in thought.

While this has been an argument proffered for some time, it gained substantial popularity under the general influence of the early twentieth century Religionsgeschichtliche studies, particularly Willem Bousset's very influential work *Kyrios Christos*.[82] Without going into an extensive discussion here, Bousset argued that there was a fundamental difference between Palestinian Christian concepts and Hellenistic Christian concepts, and that the latter's views of Jesus as being divine—seen especially in the title of "kyrios, Lord" assigned to Jesus—come from the Hellenistic religions, particularly the Caesar and Isis cults as well as the Asclepius cult, not from the Old Testament or Judaism. According to Bousset, these Hellenistic ideas were introduced in the Hellenistic Christian environment, and then found their way into the Gospels.[83] Bousset found John, then to be an expression of the pervasive influence of the Hellenistic Christology on the gospel narrative, the complete assimilation of the "myth" with the story of Jesus. But the myth remains totally alien to the Palestinian Jesus: "The Christian confession is summarized in the solemn sentence that Jesus (Christ) is the Son of God, the confession with which the Gospel concludes. There can be no doubt at all that this here has metaphysical significance quite alien to all Jewish messianology."[84]

Bousset's influence has been substantial, but much recent research has critically undermined it. For instance, the early dating of key Christological hymns such as in Phil 2 and Col 1, as is commonly held, pushes back the time for any putative influence of Hellenistic "divine Christ" myths on New Testament material. In the past decade, moreover, what would seem to be a death-knell for Bousset's position was sounded by Larry Hurtado's research into Christ devotion. Beginning first with *One*

---

82. Bousset, *Kyrios Christos*.
83. Bousset, *Kyrios Christos*, 129–52.
84. Bousset, *Kyrios Christos*, 213.

God, One Lord: Early Christian devotion and Jewish Monotheism in 1988, and then with the even more influential *Lord Jesus Christ: Devotion to Jesus in Earliest Christianity* in 2003, Hurtado has offered compelling, and I think thoroughly convincing, evidence that devotion to Christ, *which implied His divine nature*, is found in every stratum of early Christian writings: in Paul, in the Synoptics, as well as in John.[85] It is not always contained in overt Christological discussions, but often in the actions of the early Christians—in worship, prayers, and benedictions. Christ devotion, which presumes a shared honor that alone had been reserved for God, suggests that Christ too is divine. As a result, John's perspective on Jesus is not entirely unique or even necessarily more developed. John's prologue, in which the Logos participates with God in creation, is not remarkably different from the Christ-hymn in Col 1 on this issue. And again, is not John's prologue statement about the Word "becoming flesh" similar in essence to the Christ-hymn in Philippians in which Jesus, who having the form of God, emptied himself and was born in human likeness?

More specifically, in John Jesus asserts a relationship with God that could be challenging to Jewish monotheism, and many would argue that it is here surely that the lateness of John is to be found. But once again recent studies are providing a greater context for how these dialogues might be perceived within first century Jewish culture.

First, and most recently, I would cite a general audience book by Daniel Boyarin, perhaps one of today's most significant Talmudic scholars, entitled *The Jewish Gospels*.[86] Boyarin argues that Jews in the first century had a variety of ideas of a "second figure in heaven" that would fit well within and explain the various Gospels' description of Jesus in divine terms. In other words, from ancient Judaism's perspective, the Gospels' representations are not that unusual. Boyarin, for instance, goes to great lengths to point out that the significant divine title for Jesus is not "son of God," but rather "son of Man," which he argues evokes Dan 7 in which "one like the son of man" is given dominion and power alongside God. Moreover, Boyarin points out that other figures in Jewish writings had occupied similar status verging on "second figure in heaven": the Great Angel, Michael, Enoch, and Metatron.[87]

85. Hurtado, *One God*; cf. also Hurtado, *How on Earth did Jesus Become God*.

86. Boyarin, *Jewish Gospels*.

87. So, in addition to the short treatment in *Jewish Gospels*, see Boyarin, "Beyond Judaisms"; and Boyarin, "Gospel of the Memra," 243–84.

Similarly, in a published dissertation dealing with John's argumentation in the dialogues, James McGrath explores the ideas of divine elements in Jesus' argumentation. He, too, finds that the issue of Jesus claiming divine prerogative was not as fundamentally controversial as it may seem. There was common acceptance that God could and did send agents that could claim full divine authority. That is, "the Johannine conflict with 'the Jews' over Christology was not about Jesus performing divine functions *per se*. If Jesus was God's appointed, subordinate, obedient agent, then he could clearly do such things legitimately. The problem is that the Jews do not recognize *Jesus* as God's agent."[88]

In other words, taking Boyarin's and McGrath's studies together, some scholars are coming to recognize that Jesus' claim "to do the works of my Father" are not as alien within first century Judaism as was previously thought. And thus, taken with other studies, John's Christology need not be seen as either alien within the diverse landscape of early Jewish theology, nor specifically a sign of late development. Or, to put it bluntly, perhaps John's Christology is no higher than elsewhere in the Gospels, and perhaps not even remarkable within the diversity of ancient Judaism.

Conclusion

Beginning with Strauss and F. C. Baur, the status of John as a witness to Jesus has been undermined in the New Testament scholarship. It has been marginalized in terms of its date, in terms of its connection to the history and the geography of the life of Jesus, and in terms of its portrayal of the aims of Jesus' ministry. It has been considered a late, theologically driven production of the church, constructed over successive iterations, derivative of other portrayals of Jesus, and reflecting as much the life and times of the church as the life of Jesus. But is this scholarly assessment correct? Already J. A. T. Robinson believed that some push back against this "consensus" was necessary. And research, both with respect to history and also with respect to narrative theory and the hermeneutical role of communities in gospel writing, has continued to chip away at this common understanding of John.

Both the chronological lateness and the secondary value of the Fourth Gospel, often assumed more than argued for on the basis of

---

88. McGrath, *John's Apologetic Christology*, 77.

features that have been noted above, came to be almost the accepted position. But the ground has shifted. Now in each case more recent research seems to give more value and credence to John's status as an early and independent witness to Jesus:

1. While previously John was often assumed to be dependent on the Synoptics, the arguments for such dependence are slim. While not universal, the dominant view of John's relationship to the Synoptics is one of independence. If John is independent, one major argument for its lateness is removed.

2. Beginning with Bultmann, John was increasingly seen as made up of a patchwork of sources. Moreover, either the insertion of source material or the moving around of various parts of John—later editorial activities—created a number of *aporias*. This explanation, while still offered by some, is less common now due in part to stylistic analyses that portray a more coherent Gospel, at least stylistically. Moreover, narrative studies offer other explanations for some of the *aporia*. That is to say, the Gospel is increasingly seen as stylistically coherent and marked by a unified narrative structure. Again, a move away from sources and multiple editions removes common arguments for John as late or secondary.

3. In the approaches to John in the earlier half of the twentieth century, Hellenism was seen as a major way of explaining John's distinctiveness. But increasingly scholars are appreciating John's thoroughgoing Jewishness—its rich intertextual use of Old Testament Scriptures, its narrative structured around Jewish festivals, and the rich use of images and figures from the Old Testament. This, again, removes a major reason for seeing John as late and secondary.

4. Earlier views of the Fourth Gospel imagined that John's extensive references to places in Judea and Galilee might have been constructed to fit theological issues, or simply made up. As more information becomes available about the geography of Palestine in the first century, John's portrayal is found to be generally reliable.

5. Over the last decade a substantial number of scholarly papers have addressed John's historical representation. While major areas of disagreement remain about John's historical value (as there are also with the other Gospels), very often John's Gospel fits well with historical reconstructions of various aspects of Jesus' life and ministry.

Certainly John presents a quite distinctive portrayal of Jesus. Yet John is increasingly recognized as offering valuable data for the reconstruction of the history of Jesus.

6. A major influence on Johannine scholarship for the last fifty years has been J. Louis Martyn's two-level reading of John. This reading has both a historical core (the expulsion from the synagogue) and a hermeneutical emphasis (a combination of community reading and two-level reading of the narrative). The historical core of Martyn's thesis has lost credibility and has been largely undermined. Although the hermeneutical model is still maintained by many, I think it rests on fundamentally unsound principles. Insofar as it is maintained, it may be the most significant reason for continuing to consider John as late and secondary, and increasingly it is being questioned.

7. The "high Christology" of John, along with distinctive theological features (e.g., dualism) have often been used to consider John both late and secondary to the Synoptics. With the documents from Qumran, and a reevaluation of Judaism, has come a greater appreciation for certain features in John. More importantly, the growing awareness of early high Christology in the last few decades has led to a rethinking of John's place in theological development.

Much rethinking and reappraisal is taking place in the world of Johannine scholarship. As seen above, in many ways various "assured results" of scholarship are being examined anew. The various arguments for considering John to be secondary to the Synoptics for an understanding of Jesus, his ministry, or his own engagement with Judaism of the first century are increasingly being shown to be less than compelling. As a result, the assessment that John is less reliable is increasingly being questioned. And with it, perhaps also the dating of John will be questioned. It is becoming harder and harder to put John's composition late. While it is very difficult, if not impossible, to establish absolute dates for the composition of any of the Gospels, it is time to reconsider John's relative dating to the other Gospels.

Bibliography

Anderson, Paul N. "Aspects of Historicity in the Fourth Gospel: Consensus and Convergences." In vol. 2 of *John, Jesus and History*, edited by Paul N. Anderson et al., 379–86. Atlanta: Society of Biblical Literature, 2009.

———. "Aspects of Historicity in the Gospel of John: Implications for Investigations of Jesus and Archaeology." In *Jesus and Archaeology*, edited by James Charlesworth, 587–618. Grand Rapids: Eerdmans, 2006.

———. *The Fourth Gospel and the Quest for Jesus: Modern Foundations Reconsidered*. London: Contiuum, 2006.

———. "Mark and John—the Bi-Optic Gospels." In *Jesus and the Johannine Tradition*, edited by Robert Fortna and Tom Thatcher, 175–88. Louisville: Westminster John Knox, 2001.

———. "Mark, John, and Answerability: Interfluentiality and Dialectic between the Second and Fourth Gospels." *Liber Annuus* 63 (2013) 197–245.

Ashton, John. "The Identity and Function of the Ἰουδαῖοι in the Fourth Gospel." *Novum Testamentum* 27 (1985) 40–75.

———. "The Transformation of Wisdom: A Study of the Prologue of John's Gospel." *New Testament Studies* 32 (1986) 161–86.

Bacon, B. W. *The Gospel of the Hellenists*. Edited by Carl H. Kraeling. New York: Henry Holt, 1933.

Bauckham, Richard. "For Whom Were Gospels Written?" In *The Gospels for All Christians*, edited by Richard Bauckham, 9–48. Grand Rapids: Eerdmans, 1998.

———, ed. *The Gospels for All Christians*. Grand Rapids: Eerdmans, 1998.

Baur, F. C. *Kritische Untersuchungen über die kanonischen Evangelien, ihr Verhältniss zu einander, ihren Charakter und Ursprung*. Tübingen: Verlag und Druck, 1847.

Berger, Klaus. *Im Anfang war Johannes: Datierung und Theologie des vierten Evangeliums*. Stuttgart: Quell, 1997.

Bernier, Jonathan. *Aposynagogos and the Historical Jesus in John: Rethinking the Historicity of the Johannine Expulsion Passages*. Leiden: Brill, 2013.

Brown, Raymond. *The Community of the Beloved Disciple*. New York: Paulist, 1979.

———. *An Introduction to the Gospel of John*. Edited by Francis J. Moloney. New York: Doubleday, 2003.

———. *The Gospel According to John*. Vol. 1, *Chapters 1–12*. Anchor Bible 29. New York: Doubleday, 1966.

Boyarin, Daniel. "Beyond Judaisms: Metatron and the Divine Polymorphy of Ancient Judaism." *Journal for the Study of Judaism* 41 (2010) 323–65.

———. "The Gospel of the Memra: Jewish Binitarianism and the Prologue to John." *Harvard Theological Review* 94 (2001) 243–84.

——— *The Jewish Gospels: The Story of the Jewish Christ*. New York: New Press, 2012.

———. "Justin Martyr Invents Judaism." *Church History* 70 (2001) 427–61.

Bousset, Wilhelm. *Kyrios Christos*. Nashville: Abingdon, 1970.

Bultmann, Rudolf. *The Gospel of John: A Commentary*. Translated by G. R. Beasley-Murray et al. Philadelphia: Westminster, 1971.

Burkett, Delbert. *An Introduction to the New Testament and the Origins of Christianity*. Cambridge: Cambridge University Press, 2002.

Charlesworth, James H. "A Critical Comparison of the Dualism of 1QS 3:13–4:26 and the 'Dualism' in the Gospel of John." In *John and the Dead Sea Scrolls,* edited by James H. Charlesworth, 76–106. New York: Crossroad, 1990.

Coloe, Mary. *God Dwells With Us: Temple Symbolism in the Fourth Gospel.* Collegeville, MN: Liturgical, 2001.

Cullmann, Oscar. *The Johannine Circle.* Philadelphia: Westminster, 1976.

Culpepper, R. Alan. *Anatomy of the Fourth Gospel.* Philadelphia: Fortress, 1983.

———. *The Johannine School.* Society of Biblical Literature Dissertation Series 26. Missoula: Scholars, 1975.

———. "The Pivot of John's Prologue." *New Testament Studies* 27 (1980) 1–31.

Dodd, C. H. *The Fourth Gospel.* Cambridge: Cambridge University Press, 1953.

———. *Historical Tradition in the Fourth Gospel.* Cambridge: Cambridge University Press, 1963.

Ehrman, Bart. *The New Testament.* 4th ed. New York: Oxford University Press, 2008.

Fortna, Robert. *The Gospel of Signs: A Reconstruction of the Narrative Source Underlying the Fourth Gospel.* Society for the New Testament Studies Monograph Series 11. Cambridge: Cambridge University Press, 1970.

Gardner-Smith, Percival. *St. John and the Synoptic Gospels.* Cambridge: Cambridge University Press, 1938.

Hays, Richard. *Echoes of Scripture in the Gospels.* Waco: Baylor University Press, 2016.

Hofrichter, Peter, ed. *Für and Wider die Priorität des Johannesevangeliums.* Hildesheim: Olms, 2002.

Hurtado, Larry. *How on Earth Did Jesus Become a God?* Grand Rapids: Eerdmans, 2005.

———. *Lord Jesus Christ: Devotion to Jesus in Earliest Christianity.* Grand Rapids: Eerdmans, 2003.

———. *One God, One Lord: Early Christian Devotion and Jewish Monotheism.* Minneapolis: Fortress, 1988.

Hengel, Martin. *Judaism and Hellenism.* Philadelphia: Fortress, 1974.

Instone-Brewer, David. "The Eighteen Benedictions and the Minim before 70 C.E." *Journal of Theological Studies* 54 (2003) 25–44.

Johnson, Brian D. "Salvation Is From the Jews." In *New Currents Through John: A Global Perspective,* edited by Francisco Lozada and Tom Thatcher, 83–100. Atlanta: Society of Biblical Literature, 2006.

Johnson, Luke Timothy. *The Writings of the New Testament.* 3rd ed. Minneapolis: Fortress, 2010.

Keener, Craig. *The Gospel of John.* Peabody, MA: Hendrickson, 2003.

Kimelman, Reuven. "Birkhat Ha-minim and the Lack of Evidence for an Anti-Christian Prayer in Late Antiquity." In *Jewish and Christian Self-Definition,* edited by E. P. Sanders, 232–44. London: SCM, 1981.

Klink, Edward, III. *The Audience of the Gospels: The Origin and Function of the Gospels in Early Christianity.* London: T. & T. Clark, 2010.

———. "Expulsion from the Synagogue? Rethinking a Johannine Anachronism." *Tyndale Bulletin* 59.1 (2008) 99–118.

Martyn, J. Louis. *History and Theology of the Fourth Gospel.* 3rd ed. Louisville: Westminster John Knox, 2003.

Matson, Mark A. "Current Approaches to the Priority of John." *Stone-Campbell Journal* 7 (2004) 73–100. Reprint: *Evangel* 25 (2007) 4–14.

———. "Foreshadowing and Realization: Key Elements in John's Narrative Construction." Unpublished SBL presentation. https://www.academia.edu/33148261/Foreshadowing_and_Realization_Key_Elements_in_Johns_Narrative_Construction.

———. "The Historical Plausibility of John's Passion Dating." In vol. 1 of *John, Jesus and History*, edited by Paul N. Anderson et al., 291–312. Atlanta: Society of Biblical Literature, 2009.

———. *In Dialogue with Another Gospel? The Influence of the Fourth Gospel on the Passion Narrative of the Gospel of Luke*. Society of Biblical Literature Dissertation Series 178. Atlanta: Society of Biblical Literature, 2001.

———. "The Influence of John on Luke's Passion: Toward a Theory of Intergospel Dialogue." In *Für und Wider des Johnnesevaneliums*, edited by Peter Hofrichter, 183–94. Hildesheim: Olms, 2002.

———. "The Temple Incident: An Integral Element in the Fourth Gospel's Narrative." In *Jesus in Johannine Tradition*, edited by Robert Fortna and Tom Thatcher, 145–54. Louisville: Westminster John Knox, 2001.

———. "A Time to Tell." Unpublished paper presented at the 2003 SBL Meeting. https://www.academia.edu/1173334/A_Time_To_Tell_Narrative_Time_and_The_Gospels.

McGrath, James. "Destroy This Temple: Issues of Historicity in John 2:13–22." In vol. 2 of *John, Jesus and History*, edited by Paul N. Anderson et al., 35–43. Atlanta: Society of Biblical Literature, 2009.

———. *John's Apologetic Christology*. Cambridge: Cambridge University Press, 2001.

Meier, John P. *A Marginal Jew*. Vol. 2, *Mentor, Message, and Miracles*. New York: Doubleday, 1994.

Miller, Robert, ed. *The Complete Gospels: Annotated Scholars Version*. Sonoma, CA: Polebridge, 1992.

Moloney, Francis J. *Belief in the Word*. Eugene, OR: Wipf and Stock, 1993.

Neirynck, Frans. "John and the Synoptics." In *L'Evangile de Jean: Sources, rédaction, théologie*. Louvain: Louvain University Press, 1977.

Nicol, William. *The Sēmeia in the Fourth Gospel: Tradition and Redaction*. Supplements to Novum Testamentum 32. Leiden: Brill, 1972.

Peterson, Brian Neil. *John's Use of Ezekiel: Understanding the Unique Perspective of the Fourth Gospel*. Minneapolis: Fortress, 2015.

Peterson, Dwight N. *The Origins of Mark: The Markan Community in Current Debate*. Boston: Brill, 2000.

Powell, Mark Allan. *Introducing the New Testament*. Grand Rapids: Baker Academic, 2009.

Reinhartz, Adele. "'Jews' and Jews in the Fourth Gospel." In *Anti Judaism and the Fourth Gospel*, edited by Reimund Bierenger et al., 213–30. Louisville: Westminster John Knox, 2001.

———. "The Johannine Community and Its Jewish Neighbors." In vol. 2 of *What Is John?*, edited by Fernando Segovia, 111–38. Atlanta: Scholars, 1998.

———. "Judaism in the Gospel of John." *Interpretation* 63 (2006) 382–93.

Robinson, John A. T. *The Priority of John*. London: Meyer Stone, 1985.

Ruckstul, Eugen. *Die literarische Einheit des Johannesevangeliums : der gegenwärtige Stand der einschlägigen Forschungen*. Göttingen: Vandenhoeck et Ruprecht, 1988.

Schleiermacher, Friedrich. *The Life of Jesus*. Translated by S. Maclean Gilmour. Philadelphia: Fortress, 1975.

Schnackenburg, Rudolf. *The Gospel According to St. John*. Vol. 1. New York: Crossroad, 1990.

Schweizer, Eduard. *Ego eimi: die religionsgeschichtliche Herkunft und theologische Bedeutung der jo-hanneischen Bildreden, zugleich ein Beitrag zur Quellenfrage des vierten Evangeliums*. Göttingen: Vandenhoeck & Ruprecht, 1939.

Shellard, Barbara. *New Light on Luke: Its Purpose, Sources, and Literary Context*. London: Bloomsbury T. & T. Clark, 2004.

Smith, D. Moody. *The Composition and Order of the Fourth Gospel: Bultmann's Literary Theory*. New Haven: Yale University Press, 1965.

———. "The Contribution of J. Louis Martyn to the Understanding of the Gospel of John." In *History and Theology in the Fourth Gospel*, by J. Louis Martyn, 1–23. Louisville: Westminster John Knox, 2003.

———. *John Among the Gospels*. 2nd ed. Columbia: University of South Carolina Press, 2001.

Staley, Jeff. "The Structure of John's Prologue: Its Implications for the Gospel's Narrative Structure." *Catholic Biblical Quarterly* 48 (1986) 241–64.

Strauss, D. F. *The Christ of Faith and the Jesus of History: A Critique of Schleiermacher's Life of Jesus*. Philadelphia: Fortress, 1977.

Teeple, Howard. *The Literary Origin of the Gospel of John*. Evanston, IL: Religion and Ethics Institute, 1974.

Voorwinde, Stephen. "John's Prologue: Beyond Some Impasses of Twentieth-Century Scholarship." *Westminster Theological Journal* 63 (2002) 15–44.

Von Wahlde, Urban C. "Archaeology and John's Gospel." In *Jesus and Archaeology*, edited by James Charlesworth, 523–86. Grand Rapids: Eerdmans, 2006.

———. *The Earliest Version of John's Gospel: Recovering the Gospel of Signs*. Wilmington, DE: Michael Glazier, 1989.

———. *The Gospel and Letters of John*. Vol. 3. Grand Rapids: Eerdmans, 2010.

———. "The Pool(s) of Bethesda and the Healing in John 5: A Reappraisal of Research and of the Johannine Text." *Revue Biblique* 116 (2009) 11–136.

Windisch, Hans. *Johannes und die Synoptiker: Wollte der vierte Evangelist die älteren Evangelien ergänzen oder ersetzen?* Leipzig: Hinrichs, 1926.

Reviving the Priority of John

Respondent: Jonathan Bernier

It is not easy to respond to contributions that lack any substantive difficulties, but unfortunately that is exactly what I am called upon to do here. Matson's contribution aims to revisit J. A. T. Robinson's argument in his posthumous work, *The Priority of John*.[1] More specifically, Matson aims to situate that work in relation to more recent developments in Johannine scholarship. His mastery of the literature and its relevance for revisiting Robinson's argument renders it virtually impossible to find fault with his contribution. Most "faults" would be on the level of quibbles, and as far as I can tell none of these would impact the overall argument that Matson develops, namely that Robinson was correct to argue that Johannine tradition and theology are generally coeval with Synoptic tradition and theology. As such, I find it useful to respond by developing the implications of Matson's contribution for Robinson's arguments in his better-known work, *Redating the New Testament*.[2]

Although *Redating the New Testament* is perhaps best known for Robinson's argument that the entirety of the New Testament corpus was written prior to 70 CE, as the only critical monograph addressing the dates of the entire New Testament corpus published in the twentieth-century it would constitute a significant scholarly contribution even if it did not argue for such a "low" chronology. In this earlier work, there were already intimations of what Robinson would later develop in *Priority*, which is in a certain sense an expansion of chapter 9 of *Redating*.[3] In this earlier work, Robinson offers 40–65+ as a date for John's Gospel, with

1. Robinson, *Priority of John*.
2. Robinson, *Redating the New Testament*.
3. Robinson, *Redating the New Testament*, 254–311.

the former date intended to suggest that the development of Johannine tradition and theology began c. 40, and that from this development something recognizable as our gospel emerged by the late-60s. The relevance of Matson's contribution for our understanding of *Redating* is that it demonstrates that more recent scholarship would tend to strengthen rather than weaken the antecedent possibility for such an early dating.

One fruit that results from a careful reading of *Redating* is the recognition that one can rarely consider the dates of any given text in the New Testament corpus in isolation. Matson's argument that Luke's Gospel used John's as a source thus becomes of significant interest. On its own, this is simply a relative date. It becomes the grounds for an absolute date once we define the date for either Luke's Gospel or John's. At first glance, Matson's source-critical argument regarding Luke's Gospel and John's, if accepted, creates a significant problem for Robinson's chronology as argued in *Redating*. Robinson dates Luke's Gospel to c. 57–60, and indeed given that he argues strongly that Acts was written prior to Paul's death in the mid-60s he cannot date the first half of Luke-Acts much later than c. 60.[4] In fact, Robinson's *terminus ante quem* (time before which) for Luke's Gospel is similar to, albeit not quite identical with, the *terminus post quem* (time after which) for John's: on his understanding, the Lukan Gospel must have been written sometime before Paul was executed in the final years of Nero's reign, and the Johannine Gospel sometime after Peter was executed during the same approximate period (cf. John 21:18–19). If we accept Matson's argument for the literary priority of John's Gospel over Luke's, must we then reject Robinson's arguments regarding the dates of these texts?

Perhaps with some irony, precisely to the extent that one emphasizes that John 21 is a late addition to the gospel, one minimizes the extent to which the reference to Peter's death in 21:18–19 can be used as a *terminus post quem* for the balance of the gospel. One could plausibly argue that while John 1–20 predates Luke's Gospel, John 21 was added sometime after the Lukan evangelist completed her or his work c. 60. Conversely, precisely to the extent that John 21 is seen not as secondary but rather original to John's Gospel one does lose the capacity to accommodate Robinson's chronology to Matson's source-critical argument regarding Lukan priority, but one also loses one of the primary arguments used for the relatively late date of John's Gospel, namely the (dubious) supposition

---

4. Robinson, *Redating the New Testament*, 86–117.

that the addition of chapter 21 points at a process of composition that could not have been completed in the time span allowed by a pre-70 date.

The possibility that John 1–20 predates Luke's Gospel while John 21 postdates raises a reality to which Robinson will advert throughout his corpus, namely that the history of the gospel tradition is almost certainly messier than our nice graphs, with neat lines between complete texts (extant and hypothetical) would tend to suggest. In addition to situating Luke's Gospel in the late-50s and arguing that John's Gospel resulted from an extended process of development dating from c. 40 to c. 65, Robinson suggests that Matthew's Gospel was the result of an extended process of development dating from c. 40 to c. 60 and Mark's Gospel a comparable process from c. 45 to 60. Instead of imagining an artificially neat relationship among literary artifacts, Robinson imagines a more realistically complicated relationship among actual persons working over the course of decades; in principle, this relationship involves not just the evangelists, but also any and all Christian groups with which they were associated. As Robinson himself suggests, "The gospels as we have them are to be seen as parallel, though by no means isolated, developments of common material for different spheres of the Christian mission, rather than a series of documents standing in simple chronological sequence."[5] The Matthean tradition likely did not begin to develop only after the Markan Gospel was written. Even if one were to argue that the various gospel traditions developed—or at the very least achieved something like the textual form known to us—sometime later than Robinson suggests, one is left with the reality that in temporal terms their developments almost certainly overlapped to a significant extent.

Cumulatively, Robinson's work calls out for us to develop workable accounts of these parallel though by no means isolated developments. Bauckham's edited volume *The Gospels for All Christians*[6] represents a significant breakthrough in developing such an account, because the critical focus upon distinct gospel communities—which Matson rightly recognizes as an effectively obsolete mode of scholarship—can only be sustained as long as one maintains the illusion of not just isolated but in fact hermetically sealed ancient Christian communities (an illusion dispelled every time that one talks—as one inevitably must—about the relationships among either gospel texts or the communities in question).

---

5. Robinson, *Redating the New Testament*, 94.
6. Bauckham, *Gospels for All Christians*.

But *Gospels for All Christians* is but a start, and hardly constitutes an adequate account in and of itself (nor does it pretend to). As a Lonergan scholar alongside a New Testament one, I have found the thought of the Jesuit philosopher and theologian Bernard Lonergan to be particularly useful in thinking through the messiness.[7] In particular, I have found his thinking about the dialectical nature of development to be particularly stimulating.[8]

Ormerod has recently and succinctly defined Lonergan's "general notion of development" as something that "involves a dialectical tension between transcendence and limitation. Within this general notion there are *integrator functions*, which are principles of limitation, providing integration and harmony, and *operator functions*, which transform the present situation in the direction of some normatively defined transcendence."[9] Let us suggest that in the development of the gospel tradition the integrator function was the preexisting Jewish tradition(s) inherited by the first Christians, the operator function the early Christian experience of salvation, and the direction toward which the situation moved was the then-emerging Gospel tradition. For our purposes, what matters most is the operator, *viz.* the early Christian experience of salvation, a term that I borrow from the Lonerganian New Testament scholar Ben F. Meyer.[10] Through their encounters with Jesus, both earthly and risen (in whatever material terms this risen-ness might have entailed), and with their newly nascent communities, early Christians were able to overcome what Lonergan describes as alienation, defined as the refusal to work toward becoming the best version of oneself, i.e., that version of the self that is attentive, intelligent, reasonable, and responsible.[11] This experience of becoming reconciled with oneself constituted a powerful impetus for rethinking the Jewish tradition. Through this process of rethinking, the early Christians employed various imageries to articulate this experiential dimension, including for instance the language of the logos found in John 1. Such a process eventually cumulated in our gospels, among other texts.

---

7. Bernier, "Twelve on the Way to Nicea."

8. Cf. Lonergan, *Insight*, 489–92, 553–617; Lonergan, *Method*, 124–25, 220–49; Lonergan, *Triune God*, 29–255.

9. Ormerod, *Re-Visioning the Church*, 64.

10. Cf. Meyer, *Early Christians*, 174–81.

11. Lonergan, *Method*, 54, 333– Robinson, *Redating the New Testament*, 38.

Now, one need not embrace this particular experiential account of what existentially drove the development of the gospel tradition. Yet, if one is bring to completion the promise of Robinson's work, one must develop a comparable experiential account that can explain why the early Christians felt the need to produce the gospels in the first place. It is precisely Robinson's insistence upon the messiness of gospel development that demands such an account, for such messiness urges us to move from textual relationship to human operations. By demonstrating the extent to which Robinson's understanding of specifically Johannine origins holds up, Matson has implicitly emphasized the need for such an account. Matson's contribution calls attention to what most diligent readers of J.A.T. Robinson's literary corpus tend to discover: the presence of a lively mind, which New Testament scholarship neglects at the very real risk of intellectual impoverishment.

Bibliography

Bauckham, Richard, ed. *The Gospels for All Christians: Rethinking the Gospel Audiences.* Grand Rapids: Eerdmans, 1998.

Bernier, Jonathan. "The Twelve on the Way to Nicea: Gospel Narrative and the Prehistory of Dogma." Paper presented at the Lonergan Research Institute, Toronto, ON, October, 2017.

Lonergan, Bernard. *Insight: A Study in Human Understanding.* Edited by Frederick E. Crowe and Robert M. Doran. 5th ed. Collected Works of Bernard Lonergan 3. Toronto: University of Toronto Press, 1992 [1957].

———. *Method in Theology.* Edited by Robert M. Crowe and John D. Dadosky. 3rd ed. Collected Works of Bernard Lonergan 14. Toronto: University of Toronto Press, 2017 [1972].

———. *The Triune God: Doctrines.* Edited by Robert M. Doran and H. Daniel Monsour. Translated by Michael G. Shields. Collected Works of Bernard Lonergan 11. Toronto: University of Toronto Press, 2009 [1964].

Meyer, Ben F. *The Early Christians: Their World Mission and Self-Discovery.* Wilmington, DE: Michael Glazier, 1986.

Ormerod, Neil. *Re-Visioning the Church: An Experiment in Systematic-Historical Ecclesiology.* Minneapolis: Fortress, 2014.

Robinson, John A. T. *The Priority of John.* London: Meyer Stone, 1985.

———. *Redating the New Testament.* London: SPCK, 1976.

5

How and When the Four Gospels Became Scripture

Nicholas Perrin

IN RECENT YEARS, A number of scholars writing on the topic of Christian Origins have alleged not only a profound sociological fluidity between proto-Orthodox Christian sects (i.e., communities that the third-century Origen would have recognized as comprising the "Great Church" [*Contra Cel.* 5.59]) and heterodox sects, but also a corresponding textual fluidity, that is, a scenario in which scribal adherents would revise their received textual traditions freely while incorporating others. Of course this is not intrinsically unlikely. For when we think of "textual tradition," we may be contemplating, on the one hand, an authoritative, well-circumscribed, and carefully preserved scribal deposit resistant to revision in principle; or we may equally imagine, on the other hand, a provisional set of writings of equally provisional content, which the receptor community may at will liberally adapt, extend, or negate, either by revising the original text or by creating altogether new texts designed to supplant what has gone before. There are also, of course, shades between these two extremes, but what we're after here is a generalized description of the early Christian communities' attitude toward their inherited texts. What was the ascribed status of these texts? And what level of authority did these same texts attain in the eyes of those who preserved and employed them?

In this essay, I seek to take a step toward answering such questions by revisiting the history behind the authority and canonicity of the four now-canonical gospels (Matthew, Mark, Luke, and John). Of course, this is a well-trodden path: the history of the canon has been a very long-running discussion. But given the current emphasis on textual fluidity in second-century Christianity, it will be useful to reconsider the historical evidence for the four gospels' reception in that period.[1] My essay consists of three parts. In the first part, I will survey the standard late second-century witnesses (Irenaeus, Tatian, the Muratorian Fragment, and Justin) to the authority of the four gospels that would come to be included in the Christian canon. Then, paying special attention to the *Epistula Apostolorum* and *2 Clement*, in parts two and three, respectively, I maintain the possibility that the early church recognized an authoritative four-fold Gospel canon as early as the beginning of the second century, not long after the Gospels were composed. Finally, having offered a plausible explanation for the "when?" of the four-fold Gospel canon, I offer my own suggestions—assuming the validity of my argument—regarding the "how?" of the Gospels' scriptural status.

Irenaeus, Tatian, the Muratorian Fragment, and Justin

In reconstructing the history of the canon, we are grateful for whatever firm milestones we can uncover. Therefore we are glad to possess Irenaeus's brief but well-known discussion of the four gospels in the third book of his five-volume *Against Heresies*. The passage reads as follows:

> So firm is the ground upon which these Gospels rest, that the very heretics themselves bear witness to them, and, starting from these [documents], each one of them endeavors to establish his own peculiar doctrine. For the Ebionites, who use Matthew's Gospel only, are confuted out of this very same, making false suppositions with regard to the Lord. But Marcion, mutilating that according to Luke, is proved to be a blasphemer of the only existing God, from those [passages] which he still retains. Those, again, who separate Jesus from Christ, alleging that Christ remained impassible, but that it was Jesus who suffered, preferring the Gospel by Mark, if they read it with a love of truth, may have their errors rectified. Those, moreover, who follow Valentinus, making copious use of that according to John, to illustrate their conjunctions, shall be proved to be totally in error by means of this very Gospel, as I have shown in

---

1. Such "current emphasis" is perhaps best exemplified by Watson, *Gospel Writing*.

the first book. Since, then, our opponents do bear testimony to us, and make use of these [documents], our proof derived from them is firm and true.[2]

For our purposes, the passage is important in at least two respects. First, Irenaeus clearly identifies the four gospels as authoritative for faith and life. Second, the Bishop of Lyons also faults heretical teachers for appropriating a single gospel only then to go on to distort its meaning. Irenaeus's objection suggests that by c. 180 CE (the conventional later dating for his *Against Heresies*) the four Gospels had already circulated broadly and had become, in part or as a whole, a fundamental reference point for intersectarian dialogue. In short, despite the differences between the Ebionites, the Marcionites, the Valentinians, the Christological separatists (Cerinthians?), and Irenaeus's own constituency, *Adv. Haer.* 3.11.7 provides clear evidence that these groups not only shared a common interest in the person of Jesus but also regarded at least one of the four Gospels as authoritative. This is confirmed by extant Gnostic texts that pre-date *Against Heresies* and make authoritative use of at least one Gospel or another.[3]

Even if at the time of Irenaeus's writing the so-called heretical sects were still evolving in their beliefs, their gatekeepers would have been naturally inclined to preserve some continuity with the sect's original sources and interpretative practices. Thus, Irenaeus's complaints regarding the sects' isolative and distortive use of the gospels can hardly be a response to a set of new developments. Given the radical difference between Irenaeus and his opponents (at least on his report), not to mention the absence of any hint that *Adv. Haer.* 3.11.7 is introducing a *novum* into the churches' reading practices, it is also implausible that the bishop wrote *Against Heresies* as way of implementing a drastically new policy calling for an unexpected break with the sectarians he names. Irenaeus did not precipitate the divide between proto-orthodoxy and the competing sects but rather decisively cemented it. Despite the long-standing dispute between Irenaeus (and his forebears) and his opponents (and their forebears), the involved parties shared common ground in the gospels *qua* authoritative texts.

In the next section of his argument, the Bishop of Lyons returns to his criticism of the heretics for their limiting themselves to one gospel

2. *Adv. Haer.* 3.11.7.
3. See Tuckett, *Nag Hammadi*.

over and against the rest. The better way, he insists, is to embrace all four together—no less, no more:

> The Gospels could not possibly be either more or less in number than they are. Since there are four zones of the world in which we live, and four principal winds, while the Church is spread over all the earth, and the pillar and foundation of the Church is the gospel, and the Spirit of life, it fittingly has four pillars, everywhere breathing out incorruption and revivifying men.[4]

While some have made a field day out of belittling Irenaeus's words for their seemingly specious logic, such evaluations are invariably blinkered by an epistemological short-sightedness that fails to appreciate his theocentric starting points (unfathomable as this might seem for us post-Enlightenment folk). For the bishop, the "four zones" of geographical creation are relevant on account of the double typology between, on the one hand, Adam and old creation, and on the other hand, Christ and new creation, precisely as these have been marked out by the four gospels—a correspondence to which his audience would have probably assented without even arching an eyebrow. Likewise, with intimations of 1 Tim 3:15, the gospel story "fittingly has four pillars (*styloi*)," on analogy with the four-sided tabernacle of the Mosaic era that was also supported by posts or pillars (*styloi*).[5] The unstated assumption seems to be that just as God's presence was circumscribed by the posts of the Mosaic tabernacle, now the divine presence, having appeared in the person of Jesus, is contained not in any one of the four Gospels but in the interstitial cultic space between them. From Irenaeus's viewpoint, the geometrical analogy between the four-sided creation/temple and the four-fold Gospel is not a matter of happenstance but divine necessity. Just as it was virtually inevitable for Jesus to have appointed twelve apostles, corresponding to the twelve tribes of Israel; so too the four corners of creation, together with the four sides of the temple, practically demanded that there be four gospels—again, no more and no less.

Due to its odd resonance in modern ears, Irenaeus's famous statement regarding the necessity of four Gospels has been regularly interpreted as a nonsensical and (therefore) utterly desperate attempt to corral believers to a redefined faith, one which henceforth would be limited to a closed set of authoritative sources regarding Jesus: the four-fold Gospel.

---

4. *Adv. Haer.* 3.11.8.
5. Exod 26:15, 16, 17, etc.

However, the strength of this interpretation is undermined by two considerations. First, if we fail to be impressed by Irenaeus's argument (for reasons I have just described), this is no grounds for assuming that Irenaeus's first readers would have registered the same skeptical response. In fact, given the high-stakes, it is very unlikely that a rhetorician of Irenaeus's caliber would have attempted to score the clinching goal through some improbable trick play easily resisted by any half-witted audience members. We hardly have warrant at any rate for conjuring a scenario in which a beleaguered bishop, a day late and a few arguments short, pulls from out of his sleeve a wildly innovative but hardly compelling set of claims. Second, it cannot be ruled out that Irenaeus's argument is in fact one with which his readers would have been at least vaguely familiar. For all we know, in other words, *Adv. Haer.* 3.11.8 may be preserving something like an episcopal stump speech, regularly delivered by Irenaeus himself in his official iterations or indirectly by his ecclesial reports within the leadership structure. In this case, the Bishop of Lyons is merely reiterating a standard biblical-theological warrant for a well-ensconced liturgical practice that already privileged the four gospels.

That the four-fold canon is no Irenaean novelty is corroborated not least by the earlier publication of Tatian's *Diatessaron*, usually judged to have been written around 173 CE.[6] Having converted to the faith under Justin Martyr while in Rome, Tatian was determined to bring the gospel to his homeland of Assyia, and to that end composed a unified gospel harmony, weaving together Matthew, Mark, Luke, and John. Tatian is important in the history of canon not only because he uses John as the organizing framework for his harmony (thereby calling into question the old supposition that the Great Church was receiving John's gospel only cautiously at this time), but also because it principally relies on the four gospels in its reconstruction of the Jesus story.[7] Although it is not entirely certain why Tatian composed his gospel harmony, it seems most probable that Justin's convert, inspired by a similar such harmony used by his mentor at Rome, created the *Diatessaron* for missionary or liturgical purposes. This was at any rate how Tatian's harmony quickly came to be used in the Syriac-speaking church. As far as Tatian and his receptors were concerned, then, the four gospels contained in the *Diatessaron* functioned as an authoritative set. While this may not settle the

---

6. Petersen, *Tatian's Diatessaron*, 426–27.
7. Perrin, "*Diatessaron*," 301–18.

HOW AND WHEN THE FOUR GOSPELS BECAME SCRIPTURE 177

question as to whether the Assyrian composed his harmony with a view to supplanting the four separated gospels, the very composition of the *Diatessaron* speaks to the authority that believers attributed to the four gospels as a mutually interpreting collection of texts. Clearly, Matthew, Mark, Luke, and John were the Assyrian's "fab four."

In the same general period, we also have attestation to the four gospels in the so-called Muratorian Fragment. As for dating this document, we can only approximate on the basis of the remark that Pius I (140–155 CE) had only "very recently" (*nuperrime*) been bishop at Rome, suggesting a window of 170–200 CE or thereabouts.[8] Tantalizingly fragmentary in form, the fragment attests to an original document that had been composed as a kind of an introduction to the four gospels. For our present concern, the two key phrases are: 1) "The third book of the Gospel that is according to Luke," and 2) "The fourth of the gospels is that by John, [one] of the disciples."[9] Quite obviously, if Luke and John represent the third and fourth gospels, then the author must have also had in mind at least two other gospels, to wit, the first and second books of the gospel. And although it cannot be proved beyond all doubt that these two unnamed gospels are Matthew and Mark, it is a natural enough inference, especially giving the papyrological evidence of a four-gospel codex at that time.[10] Thus, between Irenaeus, Tatian, and the Muratorian Fragment, we have strong, mutually corroborating evidence for the authority of the four gospels at least as early as the 170s.

Yet we can move back still earlier when we consider the witness of Tatian's mentor, Justin. Although the written gospels' influence on Justin has been disputed in the past, in the current *status quaestionis* such dependence is virtually beyond question. This is likely true not only for the Synoptic Gospels (though Justin's editorial use of Mark is questionable), but also—though this point has been especially challenged—for the Gospel of John.[11] For his OT sources and gospel sources alike, Justin seems to

---

8. The Muratorian Fragment's dating has been debated for decades now. Its fourth-century setting has been championed most notably by Sundberg, "Canon Muratori," 1–41; as well as by Hahneman, "Muratorian Fragment," 405–15. Persuasive defenses of the traditional late second-century dating include Verheyden, "Canon Muratori," 487–556; Hill, "Debate," 437–52; and Ferguson, "Canon Muratori," 677–83. For a recent overview of the question, see Schnabel, "Muratorian Fragment," 239–53.

9. Lines 3 and 9, respectively, of Metzger, *Canon of the New Testament*, 305.

10. Stanton, "Fourfold Gospel," 326–29, develops this argument, following his own discussion of the Muratorian Fragment.

11. *Dial.* 106.3 ("It is said that he changed the name of one of the apostles to Peter,

draw on a mixture of various texts: in some cases he appears to recur to biblical manuscripts; at other places, he draws on a collection of abstracts and citations, otherwise known as a *testimonium*.[12] The hypothesis of an underlying *testimonium* at any rate better explains Justin's intermittent harmonizing tendencies than the explanation of faulty memory.

While Justin's dependence on the four gospels seems to imply an ascription of authority on some level, dependence by itself does not clarify the exact nature of that authority. Even so, Justin's text has not left us without some important clues. In this connection, the apologist's description of the weekly liturgical practices of his church at Rome is telling, especially where he relates that "the memoirs of the apostles or the writings of the prophets are read for as long as time permits" (*1 Apol.* 67.3). On the warranted assumption that "the memoirs of the apostles" are the written gospels (cf. *1 Apol.* 66.3), his comments are notable in two respects.[13] First, if the gospels were indeed being read in public worship right alongside the inspired Hebrew writings, then this would suggest that these same gospels retained an authority on par with the Scriptures. Second, the fact that this public reading of the gospels (as Scripture) occurred not in some Podunk part of the Empire but in the very hub of mid-second-century Christianity virtually ensures that this liturgical practice had been — or was well on its way to becoming — normalized, at least across the Mediterranean world.

With all this in mind, we are now in a better position to appreciate Justin's *en passant* mention of the fact that the memoirs were composed "by the apostles and those who followed them" (*Dia.* 103.8). Taken at face value, the statement leads us to imagine one of two scenarios. On the one hand, if Justin meant to say that these memoirs/gospels were co-authored by a plurality of apostles and/or apostolic followers, this would involve at least two apostles and at least two apostolic followers in the writing process. Thus, for example, on this reconstruction we might imagine one

---

and it is written in his memories that he changed the names of others, two brothers, the sons of Zebedee, to Boanerges, which means 'sons of thunder'") reflects Justin's awareness of Mark's gospel (cf. Mark 3:16-17) as an apostolic text. Though Justin does not cite John explicitly, various phraseological parallels make it likely he knew the fourth gospel as an authoritative text; see Hill, *Johannine Corpus,* 312–42; Hill, "Was John's Gospel," 88–94.

12. See, above all, Skarsaune, *Proof from Prophecy,* 130–31, 425–34; Albl, *And Scripture Cannot Be Broken,* esp. 101–9; Bobichon, "Composite Features," 158–81.

13. Lacking text-critical support, the proposal that "gospels" at *1 Apol.* 66.3 is a later scribal interpolation strikes me as an exercise in question-begging.

gospel co-authored by two apostles and another one co-authored by several of their successors. Yet given a generally observable rule, whereby gospels—as opposed to epistles—tend to be credited to either single authors or the Twelve as a whole, we are more inclined to imagine that Justin has in view at least four gospels, two written by apostles (namely, Matthew and John) and another two written by those who followed the apostles (namely, Mark and Luke). Although the point cannot be proven with absolute certainty, the surmise irresistibly follows as a matter of inference. Justin's regular recurrence to the gospels—whether directly or in a book of testimonies—is finally to be explained by the premise that he, together with his community, assigned these texts a scriptural status.

On this review, it becomes clear that in the second half of the second century Matthew, Mark, Luke, and John together comprised a special set of writings. Each in their own way, Irenaeus, the Muratorian Fragment, Tatian's *Diatessaron*, and Justin all witness to this reality. Precisely because these four texts were the only four biographies of Jesus to attain scriptural status, they were naturally grouped together in a kind of canon (though not necessarily as a "fixed" canon) within an emerging canon. Only by the time of Irenaeus do we have any evidence of this grouping being officially legitimized as a collection. But even Irenaeus's stipulation seems to have been little more than a way of sanctioning what had already been a long-established standard for many churches.

Epistula Apostolorum

To push our analysis of the four gospels further, we need to take another step or two back in time. Still earlier than Justin's writings is the *Epistula Apostolorum*, a document which, surviving in a fourth to fifth-century CE Coptic and a fourteenth to fifteenth-century Ethiopic recension, was likely composed c. 140 CE.[14] Close to the opening of this fictive conversation between the risen Jesus and the Eleven we find a passage shedding light on the purpose of the *Epistula*, which was

> written because of the false apostles Simon and Cerinthus, that no one should follow them—for in them is deceit with which they kill men—that you may be established and not aver, not be

---

14. Following the argument of Hannah, "Four-Gospel 'Canon,'" 628–32, Hornschuh, *Studien zur Epistula Apostolorum*, 116–19, opts for a date of 120 CE. For further overview, see Hills, *Tradition and Composition*, 1–9.

> shaken and not turn away from the word of the Gospel that you have heard. And we have heard (it), kept (it), and have written (it) for the whole world.[15]

The snippet is illuminating in several respects. First and most immediately, we gather some sense of the author's specific concerns with the heresies of Simonianism and Cerinthianism, consistent with a dating within the first half of the second century, when the soon-to-be more looming concern of Valentinianism had not yet emerged. Second, we are informed the *Epistula* was meant to function as a kind of ecclesial guardrail, designed to encourage the faithful to remain true to the "word of the gospel" taught by Jesus. This "word of the gospel," likely entailing not just the words of Jesus but also the chain of events that would eventually enter into the gospel stories presented by the evangelists, was entrusted to the Eleven, that they might memorize it and write it down for "all the world" (perhaps an allusion to Mark 16:15 ["all the world" τὸν κόσμον ἅπαντα], part of the so-called longer ending).[16] This description of the envisaged transmission ("we have heard it . . . and have written it for the whole world") clarifies the authoritative nature of the documents themselves. In the first place, whereas rabbinic students of the second-century period would memorize and textualize the teachings of their masters *qua* authoritative teachings, the apostles' analogous approach to the "word of the gospel" implies no less authority, either on the part of the oral "word of the gospel" or on the part of the resulting texts.[17] In the second place, that these apostolically authored texts were addressed "to the world," rather than, say, a local community of believers, suggests their universal sweep. The apostles' written accounts of the "word of the gospel" must have been seen as weighty documents indeed.

That the author of the *Epistula* has in mind all four gospels follows from fairly compelling evidence of his use of Matthew, Luke, John, and even the much-neglected Mark. As for signs of Matthew, we need only point to four distinctively Matthean passages in the *Epistula*: the miracle of the coin in the fish's mouth (Matt 17:24–27 [*Ep. Apost.* 4–5]); Jesus' teachings on excommunication and reinstatement (Matt 18:15–17 [*Ep.*

---

15. *Ep. Apost.* 1. This and subsequent translations are from Muller, *New Testament Apocrypha*, 1.249–84.

16. It is possible that the antecedent of the implied direct object of "heard . . . kept . . . and written" (i.e., "have heard (*it*), kept (*it*), and have written (*it*)" is not the "word of the gospel" but the epistle itself. But this is unlikely.

17. The seminal study on the movement from orality to textualization in the rabbinic setting is Gerhardsson, *Memory and Manuscript*, 19–32.

Apost. 48]); Jesus' stipulations regarding the title "rabbi" (Matt 23:28 [*Ep. Apost.* 41]); and the Parable of the Ten Virgins (Matt 25:1–13), a passage which receives extensive treatment in *Ep. Apost.* 43–45.[18] While it is theoretically possible that such materials were mined from an independent source behind Matthew (M), this is rendered improbable by preserved traces of Matthean redaction, not least the detail that the feeding miracles were enjoyed by 5,000 and 4,000 "not counting women and children," a toss-in that only Matthew adds—twice (Matt 14:21; 15:38).

The writer's use of Luke is no less palpable. For example, in *Ep. Apost.* 21 the author records Jesus as saying, "What is impossible on the part of men is possible on the part of the Father," a logion extremely close to Luke 18:27 ("He replied, 'What is impossible for mortals is possible for God.'"). Once again the explanation of a *Sondergut* source (in this case L) is ruled out by the fingerprints of Lukan redaction elsewhere. In *Ep. Apost.* 5's account of the story of the hemorrhaging woman, we find—much as we do in the Synoptic tradition—Jesus' question "who touched me?" as well as his comment, "I know that power has gone out of me." Both phrases are worded precisely as we have them in Luke 8:45–46: "Who touched me? . . . for I noticed that power has gone out from me" Τίς ὁ ἁψάμενός μου; . . . ἐγὼ γὰρ ἔγνων δύναμιν ἐξεληλυθυῖαν ἀπ' ἐμοῦ (Luke 8:45–46). Meanwhile, the parallel phrases in Mark are worded very differently. Although this evidence does not necessarily prove that the hand behind the *Epistula* availed themselves of Luke directly (there may well have been an intermediary text that preserved swathes of final-form Lukan material), it does prove that the third gospel, like Matthew, circulated as an authoritative text.

Language and imagery from the fourth Gospel are so abundant in the *Epistula* that one hardly needs to belabor Johannine influence. For the present purposes, three examples should suffice. First, the author clearly invokes John 1:14 at three different places (*Ep. Apost.* 3, 14, 39). Second, *Ep. Apost.* 4–5 presupposes the uniquely Johannine account of the Wedding at Cana, with near verbatim dependence on John 2:1. Finally, in *Ep. Apost.* 11 the author ruminates on the fourth gospel's famous story of the doubting Thomas (John 20:19–29). The impact of John's Gospel on our text is hardly controversial.

---

18. Not insignificantly, the writer's highly reflective elaboration on the last of these pericopae suggest the possibility that the uniquely Matthean parable had already enjoyed an extensive reception.

The case for dependence on Mark is more difficult, but nevertheless in my view finally sustainable. Of course, since redaction is the sure mark of Synoptic influence, and since we are by the very nature of the case (given the Two-Source Hypothesis) unable to speak of Markan redaction, there is an intrinsic difficulty in demonstrating dependence on the second gospel. For all we know the author of the *Epistula* may have depended on Mark at various points, but in most cases this is impossible to prove, since, again, the corresponding Lukan or Matthean parallels invariably present themselves as equally plausible backdrops. Nevertheless, as Darrell Hannah helpfully points out, where the writer retells the story of the women at the tomb in *Ep. Apost.* 9, "the *Epistula* clearly stands closer to Mark than to Luke," for only the second evangelist and our author specify exactly why the women at the tomb bring their ointments.[19] This observation, together with Hannah's further observations, renders the *Epistula*'s "dependence on Mark 16:1 is all but certain."[20] In summary, then, the *Epistula Apostlorum* shows signs of drawing on all four gospels that would go on to achieve canonical status.

Although the author's use of the four gospels obviously implies some degree of accredited authority, this reliance hardly requires the supposition of a four-fold gospel canon. Even so, a close reading of the *Epistula* seems to point in this very direction, beginning with Jesus' instructions to the Eleven regarding the Apostle Paul, the recipient of apostolic teaching:

> And every word which I have spoken to you and which you have written concerning me, that I am the word of the Father and the Father is in me, so you must become also to that man, as it befits you. Teach and remind (him) what has been said in the Scriptures and fulfilled concerning me, and then he will be for the salvation of the gentiles.[21]

Apparently the forty-day window between the resurrection and the ascension finds the apostles doing some considerable writing about Jesus![22] But what did these writings include? For starters, a rather obvious clue emerges in Jesus' assumption that one of the referenced texts asserts his co-identity with the Word and the Father's location in his own person—propositions uniquely articulated in the Gospel of John (John 1:1, 14;

---

19. Hannah, "Four-Fold 'Canon,'" 617.
20. Hannah, "Four-Fold 'Canon,'" 617.
21. *Ep. Apost.* 31.
22. The notion is not unique to the *Epistula*; see *Apoc. James* 2,8–19 (= NHC I.1).

10:38; 14:10, 11). In the next sentence Jesus goes on to imply that these same textual traditions will also prove useful for teaching and exhortation, activities that are centrally concerned with "what has been said in the Scriptures and fulfilled concerning me." The wording here is plausibly derived from Luke's report of the Emmaus Road incident, where "beginning with Moses and all the prophets, he [Jesus] interpreted to them the things concerning himself in all the Scriptures" (Luke 24:27).[23]

Needless to say, even if the *Epistula*'s Jesus is trading on Lukan language, this does not necessarily mean that the author has a uniquely Lukan concern in mind. After all, the theme of Jesus as the fulfillment of Scriptures is equally a Matthean interest and, though to a lesser extent, a Markan interest as well.[24] All this raises an intriguing possibility, namely, whereas 1) *Ep. Apost.* 31 obviously functions as a summary of the *kerygma*; and whereas 2) the assertion "I am the word of the Father and the Father is in me" is a fitting résumé of *Johannine* Christology (reflecting John's focus on Jesus as Logos and member of the binitarian godhead); and whereas 3) the phrase "what has been said in the Scriptures and fulfilled concerning me" is a defensible condensation of *Synoptic* Christology (reflecting the Synoptic tradition's focus on Jesus as the fulfillment of Scriptures); I suggest that Jesus' precis contained in *Ep. Apost.* 31 is not so much a summary of the gospel story behind the four gospels but rather an aggregated summary of the four gospels themselves. In this case, as far as the author of the *Epistula* is concerned, the four-fold gospels essentially *are* the *kerygma*, and the epistemic shift to a four-fold gospel canon (in a functional rather than an official sense) is already underway. The evidence is suggestive rather than probative.

A final point of interest emerges in *Ep. Apost.* 31's insistence on the logical priority of the Eleven's gospel in relation to Paul's. It is appropriate, Jesus says here, that the Eleven instruct the Apostle to the Gentiles, using both the received oral tradition and the gospel texts they themselves have authored. On one level, in portraying the Eleven as those mandated to share their own eyewitness account with Paul, the narrative corresponds to the historical reality attested by Paul himself (1 Cor 15:3-8; Gal 1:18-19). On another level, since the Pauline letters pre-date the finalized gospel texts, the scenario that Jesus anticipates is obviously anachronistic. Yet neither the *Epistula*'s historical verisimilitude nor its lack thereof detracts

23. NRSV, slightly modified.

24. See, for example, two essays in the same volume: Knowles, "Scripture, History, Messiah," 59–82; Evans, "Beginning of the Good News," 83–103.

from the significance of this early-to-mid-second-century exchange that frames the apostolic inscripturation of the Jesus story as the definitive basis for Paul's gospel. Regardless of the perceived status of the Pauline writings at the time of the *Epistula*'s composition, the subordination of the apostle's writings to the gospels would be difficult to imagine without a prior recognition of the gospels as authoritative books assembled in something approaching an authoritative collection.

While the evidence that the author of the *Epistula Apostolorum* self-consciously availed himself of a four-fold gospel canon is less than conclusive, it is compelling enough to hold out the hypothesis as a reasonably strong possibility. This is significant, not only because it would move our dating for a four-fold gospel canon back *at least* another few decades (surely the author of the *Epistula* is building on assumptions that were already well in place ahead of his own time), yielding a new *terminus a quo* of, say, roughly 130 CE; but also because the *Epistula*'s eastern provenance (with Egypt and Asia Minor leading the pack as candidates) demonstrates that Justin's communities at Rome were by no means idiosyncratic in their high estimation of the four gospels.

2 Clement

Yet perhaps we can move back even further. In the still earlier *2 Clement* (I will postpone the question of how much earlier), we detect no less than two dozen allusions and/or citations of authoritative texts, ranging from the Hebrew prophets to Tobit, from now-canonical gospel texts to apocryphal sources. Within this mix, *Clement* evinces roughly nine parallels with Matthew, Mark, and Luke. Though the author betrays no direct knowledge of the fourth gospel, the significance of this point should not be overly pressed. Since the paucity of Synoptic citations constitutes a slim statistical sample in its own right, the absence of any explicit citation of John does not permit any strong inference that the writer was either ignorant of John or (if he knew the fourth gospel) unimpressed by it. Besides, potential Johannine influence can be discerned, for example, in *2 Clem.* 9:5 ("there is one Christ ... who ... became flesh"), which shows promising parallels to John 1:14, or in *2 Clem.* 9:6 ("let us love another"), mirroring John 13:34.

For my part, I intend to argue that like the author of the *Epistula*, the composer of *2 Clement* demonstrates all but certain knowledge of Matthew and Luke, as well as probable knowledge of Mark and John.

The former point is established at several junctures where the author of 2 *Clement* preserves Matthew and Luke's distinctive markings. For example, a citation occurring in 2 *Clem.* 3:2 ("the one who confesses me before other people, I will confess before my Father") reflects redactional traces unique to Matt 10:32 ("Everyone therefore who acknowledges me before others, I also will acknowledge before my Father in heaven"). Similarly, a parallel between 2 *Clem.* 13:4 ("For when they hear from us that God says, 'It is no credit to you if you love those who love you; but it is a credit to you if you love your enemies and those who hate you'") and Luke 6:32 ("If you love those who love you, what credit is that to you? For even sinners love those who love them"), a characteristically Lukan logion, demonstrates that the author behind 2 *Clement* has availed himself of Luke's finalized text (or some mediating form, oral or written, dependent on Luke). Meanwhile, 2 *Clem.* 6:2 and 9:11 yield impressive enough parallels to Mark 8:36 and 3:35, respectively, though without the decisive proof of redaction. As for John, I suggest that the aforementioned parallel between 2 *Clem.* 9:5 and John 1:14, together with the parallel between 2 *Clem.* 9:6 and John 13:34, together, once again, with the multiple references to the favorite Johannine theme of "eternal life," makes direct or indirect dependence on John more likely than unlikely.[25]

Beyond merely depending on these texts, the author of 2 *Clement* ascribes his gospel sources an authority akin to that of Scripture. The above-cited 2 *Clem.* 13:4 ("For when they hear from us that God says, 'It is no credit to you'"), drawing on Luke 6:32, provides a fascinating case in point, for here the homilist has either entirely collapsed the distinction between Jesus and God, or has so firmly established Luke's gospel as holy writ in his or her own mind that for all intents and purposes to quote the third gospel would be tantamount to quoting God.[26] In the latter case, the author of 2 *Clement* would of course be admitting no principal distinction between the gospel text and the Hebrew Scriptures. In the former case, if Jesus is baldly equated with God, then this would presumably have the effect of conferring scriptural status to at least the dominical citations in Luke's gospel if not the gospel as a whole.

The Gospels' scriptural standing is confirmed elsewhere in 2 *Clement*. Following a citation of Isa 54:1, the author offers another citation at no extra charge: "And another Scripture says, 'I have come not to call the

---

25. Whereas Synoptic Gospels make only sparing use of the phrase, John by contrast mentions "eternal life" 17x.

26. See Tuckett, 2 *Clement*, 243.

righteous, but sinners'" (*2 Clem.* 2:4). While the Greek wording of 2 *Clem.* 2:4 is quite close to Matt 9:13c (unlike *Clement*, Matthew retains a "for" γὰρ), it is identical with Mark 2:17c. Sensitive to the absence of any clear citation of Mark's Gospel in *2 Clement*, some scholars are inclined to see Matt 9:13c in the background rather than Mark 2:17c, despite *2 Clem.* 2:4's exact correspondence with the latter.²⁷ I demur: the one clear-cut allusion to Matthew at *2 Clem.* 3:2 (as opposed to no clear-cut citations of Mark) is a slim basis for preferring Matthew to Mark, especially when the wording of Mark 2:17c (and not Matt 9:13c) provides a perfect match. In my view, the source-critical scales tilt slightly in favor of Mark not Matthew.

Meanwhile, the designation "another Scripture" would seem to presuppose not only the author's *textual* dependence on Mark 2:17c (or possibly Matt 9:13c), but also his according scriptural status to the same logion as part of an inspired text. In other words, the phrase "another Scripture" seems to render Mark (or Matthew) on par with the likes of the venerated book of Isaiah. True, some scholars have balked at this possibility, arguing that the writer had a free-floating oral saying in mind that he carelessly designated as *graphē*, or that, besides, the absence of the article would seem to militate against any pre-understanding of Mark 2:17c (par. Matt 9:13c) as Scripture.²⁸ This line of argumentation has also been generally bolstered by the judgment that, given the context of 2 *Clem.* 2:4, Jesus' call to sinners has at best a hazy connection with any Synoptic context, and correlates even less with Isa 54:1. This being the case, so the reasoning goes, we should avoid attaching too much—indeed any—significance to this *ad hoc*, decontextualized saying carelessly labeled as "another Scripture."²⁹

---

27. Kelhoffer, "Pigeonholing," 284; Tuckett, *2 Clement*, 139n7; Pratscher, *Der zweite Clemensbrief*, 80.

28. For example, following Bultmann and Dibelius, who saw *2 Clem.* 2:4 as incongruous and therefore as the derivative of oral tradition, Donfried, *Setting of Second Clement*, 59–60, suggests "that the author of 2 Clement is not dependent on Matthew or Mark, but rather that he has received this logion from the '*Gemeindetradition*.'" Meanwhile, Lindemann, *Die Clemensbriefe*, 205; and Pratscher, *Der zweite Clemensbrief*, 80; see the anarthrous *graphē* as a decisive indication of the text's non-scriptural status; against this whole line of thought, see Kelhoeffer, "Pigeonholing," 283.

29. Kelhoeffer's "Pigeonholing," 293, summary comments are representative: "Simply put, the texts [of 2 Clement 2] we have analyzed are fuliginous, if not somewhat rambling and incoherent."

Such judgments, however, I fear have more to do with hasty scholarly judgments than a careful consideration of the cited texts: *2 Clement* and Isaiah. Toward properly understanding Clement's method, we need to begin, in the first place, by laying out the full subtext undergirding the citation of Isa 54:1, a passage revolving around the so-called Suffering Servant:

> Out of his anguish he shall see light;
> he shall find satisfaction through his knowledge.
> The righteous one, my servant, shall make many righteous,
> and he shall bear their iniquities.
> Therefore I will allot him a portion with the great,
> and he shall divide the spoil with the strong;
> because he poured out himself to death,
> and was numbered with the transgressors;
> yet he bore the sin of many,
> and made intercession for the transgressors.
>
> Sing, O barren one who did not bear;
> burst into song and shout,
> you who have not been in labor!
> For the children of the desolate woman will be more
> than the children of her that is married, says the Lord.[30]

According to the Isaianic context, the ministry of the Suffering Servant provides the grounds for barren Israel's rejoicing; her children (Isa 54:1) are none other than the transgressors redeemed by the servant himself (53:11). Meanwhile, the saying contained in Mark 2:17 falls within a pericope commonly known as the Calling of Levi, part of a larger unit consisting of five disputes (Mark 2:1–3:6). In the first and fifth of these debates, Mark's Jesus identifies himself as the Son of Man (2:10, 28), a figure who is later implicitly associated with the Suffering Servant (10:45; cf. 12:7; 14:21, 24), even as both figures are tied back to Jesus. Two hints of Jesus' role as the Suffering Servant are also forthcoming in Mark 2:17 itself: 1) Jesus offers himself as physician for the unwell, much as the Suffering Servant offers himself as the one who heals Israel's diseases (Isa 53:4–5); 2) Jesus comes as one who calls "sinners," even as the Suffering Servant identifies himself with "sinners" (Isa 53:11). But these hints would certainly be nothing more than wisps of smoke apart from the

---

30. Isa 53:11—54:1.

larger Markan context, which makes the implicit claim that Jesus is simultaneously the suffering Son of Man and the Suffering Servant of Israel.[31]

Circling back to 2 Clement 2, we are finally in position to make sense of the writer's exposition. Recognizing, first, the Suffering Servant's redemptive ministry (Isa 53) as seminal for Israel's eschatological children (Isa 54:1), and, second, Jesus as both Son of Man *and* Suffering Servant (obliquely announced in Mark 2:17, but only truly manifest in the fuller narrative of Mark's gospel [Mark 10:45; cf. 12:7; 14:21, 24]), the author of 2 Clement sees Isaiah and the gospel as mutually interpreting. (Whether the author of 2 Clement drew on Matt 9:13 or Mark 2:17 effects my argument negligibly, for if Mark's Jesus is identified with the Son of Man and the Suffering Servant simultaneously, the same triangulation occurs in Matthew's gospel as well.)[32] In any case, whether Mark 2:17 or Matt 9:13 stands behind 2 Clem. 2:4, the mysterious "other Scripture" must be one of these two full-length gospels, that is, if we hope to make sense of Mark 2:17//Matt 9:13's collocation alongside Isa 54:1. This would also be consistent with the parallel the author elsewhere draws between "the books [of the prophets]" and "the apostles" (2 Clem. 14:2), the latter term being almost certainly a metonymy for the apostolic writing, inclusive—as it now becomes clear—of at least several if not all of the gospels.[33]

At the same time, this is not to insist that 2 Clement only draws its Synoptic materials from the individual gospels now known as Matthew, Mark, Luke, and John. Indeed, if the author was aware of the discrete gospels, he or she also seems to have been familiar with a compilation of gospel texts, mixed together with sundry sayings falling outside the Synoptic and Johannine traditions:

> For the Lord says in the Gospel, "If you do not keep what is small, who will give you what is great? For I say to you that the one who is faithful in what is very little is also faithful in much."[34]

---

31. One of the earliest studies in this connection is McDowell, *Son of Man*.

32. According to Davies and Allison, *Matthew*, 2.239, the first evangelist wishes "to interpret Jesus with the Christological category of servant" and "that servant is a comprehensive title" pertaining to "Jesus' entire ministry, all that Jesus says and does."

33. Although it is unclear whether the text originally read "books" *simpliciter* (as in C) or "books of the prophets" (as in S), there is perhaps not a great deal of difference between the two options.

34. *2 Clem.* 8:5.

The key phrase is "in the Gospel" (ἐν τῷ εὐαγγελίῳ). Given the obvious allusion to Luke 16:10–12, it may of course be inferred that "the Gospel" in mind is simply Luke's Gospel. However, there are two difficulties with this inference. First, one would have to explain why the author chose to designate Luke as "*the* Gospel," as if the third Gospel had some kind of special status over and against the rest, including the putatively apostolic gospels Matthew and John. Second, given the inclusion of apocryphal material falling under the rubric of "the gospel," it seems patently unlikely that Luke or indeed any of the four now-canonical Gospels as we know them are directly in play. In my view, the best solution is to hypothesize a preexisting compendium of gospel texts that functioned in church life alongside the discrete gospels, carrying a commensurate authority—not necessarily in competition with the four but perhaps as an abridged extension of them. On this scenario, we speculate that the setting of *2 Clement*, like the setting of the later Justin, recognized two legitimate, non-competing modalities for preserving the gospel tradition: one in which the four discrete Gospels were handed down and read as distinct documents, and another in which the four Gospels were combined, piecemeal or as a whole, into a unified *testimonium*, identifiable in Clement's day as "the Gospel."

Up to now, I have delayed consideration of the vexed question surrounding the dating of *2 Clement*. On this question there are a range of options marked out by two extremes. On the late side, Harnack, identifying *2 Clement* as an epistle written by the bishop Soter, has posited a date of c. 166–74 CE.[35] On the early side, Karl P. Donfried, following the lead of Zahn and Lightfoot, has argued for a dating closer to the turn of the first century.[36] In the past fifty years or so, the bulk of current scholarship has taken safe haven in navigating between these two poles, usually proposing a date somewhere in the second quarter of the second century.

While this mediating position is not an unreasonable guess, it is, alas, little more than a guess. For my part, I am gently persuaded that Donfried is essentially right to locate *2 Clement* tentatively at the very beginning of the second century. After all, in the manuscript tradition, *2 Clement* comes down to us alongside *1 Clement*, a text written at the close of the first century and directed to a community of Corinthian believers struggling with schism. Given clear allusion to the athletic contests at *2*

---

35. Harnack, *Die Chronologie*, 1.438–50.
36. Donfried, *Setting of Second Clement*, 1–15.

Clem. 7:1, which includes a remark about sailing to those games (implying a harbor right on location for those games, much as the Corinthian isthmus offered), it is likely that the author of 2 *Clement* is writing to the same Corinthian community, a community that would be delighted by the author's nod to the Isthmian games, not to mention 2 *Clement* 7's allusion to 1 Cor 9, where Paul picks up the image of the Isthmian games to make a point about the Christian life. For such reasons, not to mention the notional continuities between *1* and *2 Clement,* Donfried's case that 2 *Clement* falls close on the heels of *1 Clement* deserves serious consideration. If we go this route (and I do), this places 2 *Clement* at 98–100 CE or shortly thereafter.

All things considered, we have decent—though admittedly not finally compelling—evidence that the four Gospels were being cited authoritatively by the opening decade of the second century, both as discrete documents and, even more remarkably, as distilled texts that had been re-rendered in harmonized form. The practice of compiling the Gospels was certainly underway no later than the composition of Mark's longer ending (c. 130 CE).[37] The text of 2 *Clement* provides evidence that this practice had already been well in place decades earlier. Furthermore, if the Corinthian community recognized individual Gospels as Scripture alongside the Hebrew Scriptures, and if the same community would not have been put off by appeals to a compendium of Gospel texts worthy of the appellation "the Gospel," this speaks, I believe, to all four gospels as having achieved authority by the end of the first century. The early church presumably would not have bothered to reduce the four gospels into an authoritative *testimonium* unless they had also regarded the same discrete Gospels as authoritative.

Conclusion

When did the four gospels come together as an *exclusive* fixed canon? This is difficult to say—certainly no later than the time of Irenaeus. But when did the four Gospels begin to coalesce as an authoritative, mutually interpreting collection of books? We cannot be entirely certain. However, based on the argument I have advanced here, it would not be unreasonable to suppose as soon as the last of the Gospels was composed

---

37. Kelhoffer, *Miracle and Mission,* 169–77; Heckel, *Vom Evangelium des Markus,* 283–85.

and circulated. In this case, D. Moody Smith was likely correct when he broached the possibility that the believing messianic communities received the four gospels as intrinsically authoritative.[38] If so, this also helps us with our "how?" question: how did the Gospels attain to scriptural status? Very simply, on the scenario I am reconstructing, the Gospels most likely "became authoritative" on their initial reception. In fine, there are good historical reasons to believe that the Gospels, unlike other now-canonical books, never achieved authority as Scripture, much less had authority thrust upon them. Rather, the authority of the four-fold collection seems to have been implicitly granted on the basis of the texts themselves, if not also on the basis of their authors' credentials.

Bibliography

Albl, Martin C. *And Scripture Cannot Be Broken: The Form and Function of the Early Christian Testimonia Collections.* Supplements to Novum Testamentum 96. Leiden: Brill, 1999.

Apocalypse of James 2, 8–19 = NHC I.1.

Bobichon, Phillipe. "Composite Features and Citations in Justin Martyr's Textual Composition." In *Composite Citations in Antiquity.* Vol. 1, *Jewish, Graeco-Roman and Early Christian,* edited by Sean A. Adams and Seth M. Ehorn, 158–81. Library of New Testament Studies 525. T. & T. Clark, 2016.

Davies, W. D., and Dale Allison. *Matthew.* 3 vols. Edinburgh: T. & T. Clark, 1997.

Donfried, Karl D. *The Setting of Second Clement in Early Christianity.* Supplements to Novum Testamentum 38. Leiden: Brill, 1974.

Evans, Craig A. "The Beginning of the Good News and the Fulfillment of Scripture in the Gospel of Mark." In *Hearing the Old Testament in the New Testament,* edited by Stanley E. Porter, 83–103. Grand Rapids: Eerdmans, 2006.

Ferguson, Everett. "Canon Muratori: Date and Provenance." *Studia Patristica* 17 (1982) 677–83.

Gerhardsson, Birger. *Memory and Manuscript: Oral Tradition and Written Transmission in Rabbinic Judaism and Early Christianity; with, Tradition and Transmission in Early Christianity.* Edited by Eric J. Sharpe. Biblical Resource Series. Grand Rapids: Eerdmans, 1998.

Hahneman, Geoffrey M. *The Muratorian Fragment and the Development of the Canon.* Oxford Theological Monographs. Oxford: Clarendon, 1992.

———. "The Muratorian Fragment and the Origins of the NT Canon." In *The Canon Debate,* edited by Lee M. McDonald and J. A. Sanders, 405–15. Peabody, MA: Hendrickson, 2002.

---

38. Smith, "When Did the Gospels," 3–20.

Hannah, Darrell D. "The Four-Gospel 'Canon' in the *Epistula Apostolorum*." *Journal of Theological Studies* 59 (2008) 598–633.

Harnack, Adolf von. *Die Chronologie Geschichte der altchristlichen Literatur bis Eusebius.* Leipzig: J. C. Hinrichs, 1897.

Heckel, Theo K. *Vom Evangelium des Markus zum viergestaltigen Evangelium.* WUNT 120. Tübingen: Mohr Siebeck, 1999.

Hill, Charles E. "The Debate Over the Muratorian Fragment and the Development of the Canon." *Westminster Theological Journal* 57 (1995) 437–52.

———. *The Johannine Corpus in the Early Church.* Oxford: Oxford University Press, 2004.

———. "Was John's Gospel Among Justin's Apostolic Memoirs?" In *Justin Martyr and His Worlds*, edited by Sara Parvis and Paul Foster, 88–94. Minneapolis: Fortress, 2007.

Hills, Julian. *Tradition and Composition in the Epistula Apostolorum.* Harvard Theological Studies 57. Cambridge: Harvard University Press, 2008.

Hornschuh, Manfred. *Studien zur Epistula Apostolorum.* Patristische Texte und Studien 5. Berlin: de Gruyter, 1965.

Kelhoffer, James A. "Pigeonholing a Prooftexter? The Citations in 2 *Clement* 2 and Their Allegedly Gnostic Background." *Zeitschrift für die Neutestamentliche Wissenschaft* 107 (2016) 266–95.

———. *Miracle and Mission: The Authentication of Missionaries and Their Message in the Longer Ending of Mark.* WUNT 2.112. Tübingen: Mohr Siebeck, 2000.

Knowles, Michael P. "Scripture, History, Messiah: Scriptural Fulfillment and the Fullness of Time in Matthew's Gospel." In *Hearing the Old Testament in the New Testament*, edited by Stanley E. Porter, 59–82. Grand Rapids: Eerdmans, 2006.

Lindemann, Andreas. *Die Clemensbriefe.* Die apostolischen Väter. 1/HNT 17. Tübingen: Mohr Siebeck, 1992.

McDowell, Edward A. *Son of Man and Suffering Servant.* Nashville: Broadman, 1944.

Metzger, Bruce M. *The Canon of the New Testament: Its Origin, Development, and Significance.* Oxford: Clarendon, 1987.

Muller, C. Detlef G. *New Testament Apocrypha.* 2 vols. Edited by Wilhelm Schneemelcher. Translated by R. M. Wilson. Louisville: Westminster John Knox, 2003.

Perrin, Nicholas. "The *Diatessaron* and the Second-Century Reception of the Gospel of John." In *Legacy of John: Second-Century Reception of the Fourth Gospel.* Supplements to Novum Testamentum 132. Leiden: Brill, 2010.

Petersen, W. L. *Tatian's Diatessaron: Its Creation, Dissemination, Significance, and History in Scholarship.* Supplements to Vigiliae Christianae 25. Leiden: Brill, 1994.

Pratscher, Wilhelm. *Der zweite Clemensbrief: Kommentar zu den apostolischen Vätern.* Göttingen: Vandenhoeck & Ruprecht, 2007.

Schnabel, Eckhard J. "The Muratorian Fragment: The State of Research." *Journal of the Evangelical Theological Society* 57 (2014) 231–64.

Skarsaune, Oskar. *The Proof from Prophecy: A Study in Justin Martyr's Proof-Text Tradition: Text-Type, Provenance, Theological Profile.* Supplements to Novum Testamentum 56. Leiden: Brill, 1987.

Smith, D. Moody. "When Did the Gospels Become Scripture?" *Journal of Biblical Literature* 119 (2000) 3–20.

Stanton, Graham N. "The Fourfold Gospel." *New Testament Studies* 43 (1997) 326–29.

Sundberg, Albert C. "Canon Muratori: A Fourth-Century List." *Harvard Theological Review* 66 (1973) 1–41.

Tuckett C. M. *Nag Hammadi and the Gospel Tradition*. Studies of the New Testament and Its World. Edinburgh: T. & T. Clark, 1986.

———. *2 Clement: Introduction, Text, and Commentary*. Oxford Apostolic Fathers. Oxford: Oxford University Press, 2012.

Verheyden, Joseph. "The Canon Muratori: A Matter of Dispute." In *The Biblical Canons*, edited by J. M. Auwers and H. J. de Jonge, 487–556. Bibliotheca Ephemeridum theologicarum Lovaniensium 163. Leuven: Leuven University Press, 2003.

Watson, Francis. *Gospel Writing: A Canonical Perspective*. Grand Rapids: Eerdmans, 2013.

How and When the Gospels Became Scripture

Respondent: Mark A. Matson

How early did the Gospels begin to be treated as authoritative texts, as "Scripture"? The issue of the use and authority of the Gospels is the central focus of Nicholas Perrin's article. Given the recent publication by Francis Watson of two very different books dealing with the origin and use of our four-gospel canon, this article is a welcome addition to the current focus on the early period of canon formation.[1] Perrin in particular examines some early examples of the use of *all four Gospels*,[2] which can rightly be taken as an incipient indication of a canon taking shape.

One is not surprised that a discussion of Irenaeus's comments about the four-gospel canon serves as an entry point to Perrin's discussion, with Irenaeus pointing to the necessity of four, and only four, Gospels. Irenaeus is often the poster child for the recognition of, or perhaps initial argument for, a four-fold gospel canon. But for Perrin, Irenaeus serves as the end point anchor to his main concern, which is that Irenaeus represent instead the *culmination* of a previously long process of recognition for these four Gospels. His main point, then, is to show that the four canonical Gospels have already been seen and referred to as authoritative Scripture, and that there are indications that these references often included all four of the Gospels, and only these four.

---

1. Watson, *Gospel Writing*; Watson, *Fourfold Gospel*.

2. There are other indications of the use of, or influence by, single gospels. One might think of Ignatius's seeming dependence on Johannine concepts that point to his knowledge of John, and also the Epistle to Diognetus's extensive use of Johannine ideas and phrases. Or in a similar way, we might cite the Didache's seeming reliance on Matthew. Perrin, however, focuses on early instances of where all four gospels seem to be used in a manner that implies scriptural authority.

Perrin's point is bold, and overall quite persuasive. If sustained, he is pushing the recognition of just these four Gospels much earlier in the second century, and in doing so is challenging ideas that the canonical Gospels were but part of a much larger, and possibly undifferentiated, group of Gospels. Instead, Perrin is suggesting that very early on these four Gospels had a special status that was recognized and shared.

As Perrin traces the evidence of the four Gospels backward, he finds first Tatian's Diatessaron, a harmony of the four Gospels using the Fourth Gospel as the organizing framework. This document seems on the face of it to validate the importance of the four canonical Gospels as uniquely authoritative. But does this suggest that Tatian's mentor, Justin Martyr, had also used such a harmony as a handy tool? This, it seems to me, is rather speculative. But it does raise the question of whether Justin nonetheless viewed the four canonical Gospels alone as authoritative testimony about Jesus. If so, then we can move the date of the authority of these four gospels even earlier, perhaps to 160 or 150 CE.

Perrin suggests that the current state of the question in Justin studies now sees that Justin relied on all the Gospels, even John.[3] While I am not as familiar with the larger Justin research, my own reading of Justin does suggest at least knowledge of most of the Gospels. But since many of the references in Justin are allusions, not direct citations, it is possible that Justin had only a harmonizing *testimonium*.

Perrin does, however, want to suggest that Justin's writings acknowledge the Gospels themselves as discreet authoritative texts. So, pointing to *1 Apol* 66.3 where Justin notes that in the church's liturgy the "memoirs of the apostles" are read along with the prophets, Perrin argues that this suggests that the "memoirs" (gospels?) are of equal stature to the prophets, and hence Scripture. I think Perrin is on firm ground here. And, based on *Dial* 103.8, where Justin argues that "the memoirs" were composed by *apostles* and those *who followed them*, Perrin finds evidence for four Gospels: two apostles (hence Matthew and John), and two others (Mark and Luke). This identification is somewhat speculative, and yet Perrin here is following many others who find behind this phrase evidence for the four canonical Gospels. More important, it certainly does point to the

---

3. In support of including John in this he points especially to Hill, *Johannine Corpus*, which is full of well-researched data about the early references to John as well as the other gospels. Perrin also cites another of Hill's books, *Who Chose the Gospels*, which is also a rich source of information.

existence of discrete documents he calls memoirs, which are authoritative and linked to the apostles.

One problem with Justin, however, is the imprecise nature of his citations. References are rarely "word for word," and often are more allusions than citations. Not only does Justin paraphrase broadly, but at times conflates various Gospels. Perrin here suggests that in these instances Justin is drawing on a "collection of abstracts," that is, a *testimonium,* alongside the four Gospels. But do we need to imagine Justin's use of the four Gospels on the one hand (Perrin's main point), but also a *testimonium* which explains much of the paraphrasing? Rather, it seems to be the pattern in many of church fathers to loosely quote or refer to biblical materials, both Gospels and Old Testament. With respect to Justin, for instance, Charles Hill summarizes his use of John in this way: "Despite the lack of formal citation, despite his tendency to paraphrase or summarize, and despite his habit of conflating texts, Justin's knowledge of the Fourth Gospel has to be considered quite secure and really quite comprehensive."[4] The same could be said for Justin's use of other Gospels. It is more likely that Justin simply chooses to paraphrase and combine texts—perhaps under the idea that they are all part of "the gospel"—than that we have two distinct patterns of transmission of the Gospel material.

From the second half of the second century, the Muratorian Fragment also offers Perrin useful data for his thesis. In this document, dated to around the same time as Tatian (c. 170 CE), we have what seems to be an introduction to the Gospels. Moreover, the reference to four Gospels that are enumerated suggests the Gospels we have in the New Testament canon. Due to the fragmentary nature, only Luke and John are specifically named as the third and fourth Gospels, thus strongly suggesting that Matthew and Mark are in view as the first and second Gospels.

Perhaps the most intriguing and early document that Perrin cites for the early recognition of the Gospels as authoritative texts is the *Epistula Apostolorum,* a text now extant in Coptic but variously dated from 120 to 140 CE, Perrin opting for the later date. This document, important in the Ethiopic canon, refers in various ways to the Gospels as written documents ("the word of the Gospel that you have heard . . . and have written for the whole world"), though often they are referred to in the composite as "the gospel."[5] Based on the references to the Gospels, it is

---

4. Hill, *Johannine Corpus,* 337.

5. It should be noted here that this is a key point Watson makes in the *Fourfold Gospel,* that the church referred often to "the gospel" in four witnesses.

clear that at least John, Matthew, and Luke are known to the author of the *Epistula Apostolorum*, and Perrin makes an argument that Mark is known as well, although the similarities between Matthew and Mark make this less certain. Of these, it is noteworthy that the evidence that the author knew the Gospel of John is especially strong.[6] These writings (Gospels) are attributed to the apostles, which gives a strong authority to them as Scripture. And this is the central point Perrin makes, that this document assumes a collection of Gospels that is functioning in a similar way as the later canon: it includes at least three, and possibly all four Gospels, it does not include any non-canonical Gospels, and it ascribes scriptural authority to them.

Finally, Perrin turns to 2 *Clement*, which he also wants to argue shows evidence of the use of the four canonical Gospels, which are cited in such a way as to be authoritative in nature. Here, however, I found Perrin stretching a bit beyond the evidence. Perrin is on sure footing when he notes that the author of 2 *Clement* shows clear signs of knowledge and use of Matthew and Luke. There are sufficient number of quotations and allusions to material that are unique to Matthew or Luke that we can easily see the author's knowledge and use of them. The evidence for 2 *Clement's* reliance on John is less secure. Here he points to a reference that Jesus "became flesh" (2 *Clem*. 9:5//John 1:14) and the hortatory exhortation, "let us love one another" (2 *Clem*. 9:6//John 13:34), although it should be noted that the latter form is closer to 1 John than the Gospel. Perrin also cites the use of the Johannine theme "eternal life." To me, these are not strong indications that 2 *Clement* knew the Gospel, though perhaps it does indicate that Johannine ideas had become somewhat common in the church.

Perrin's evidence for the author's use of Mark is more problematic. Two of the citations he offers as Markan (2 *Clem*. 6:2 and 9:11) could just as easily be Matthean. In addition, Perrin argues that 2 *Clem*. 2:4 is quoting Mark 2:17c; but again the passage is almost identical in Matthew 9:13c, with the latter only having an additional γάρ added. This postpositive particle seems a slim reed to hang 2 *Clement's* use of Mark. But 2 *Clem*. 2:4 is important for Perrin in another way—its use of γραφή in

---

6. See Hill, *Johannine Corpus*, 367–68. "It is not the sheer number of allusions to the Fourth Gospel which reveals the author's high regard for that Gospel. Unlike several of the gnostic texts examined above, he uses that Gospel in a wholly positive way. Despite the apocryphal and pseudonymous nature of this document, it does not seek to supplant or supersede the Church's accepted Gospels" (368).

introducing the Gospel quotation implies that the Gospels have similar authoritative value as Old Testament Scripture. That is, that Matthew/Mark in this verse is considered "Scripture." But of course γραφή could simply refer to something written (i.e., a text). In order to support the idea that here we have a reference to "Scripture" not "writing," Perrin argues that the quotation earlier in 2 *Clem.* 2 from Isa 54:1 and Mark 2:17 mutually interpret one another. To sustain this, he sees the Suffering Servant (the implicit subject of Isa 53–54, though perhaps not the main focus of Isa 54:1) and the Son of Man (the term used by Mark and first introduced in Mark 2:10) as being identified with one another and being a central connection between the two citations. In other words, when 2 *Clement* then refers to "another Scripture" to introduce the Mark/Matthew passage, he means that the first Scripture is Isaiah, and the "other" Scripture then is Mark/Matthew. And this, then, means that γραφή is clearly authoritative Scripture. Yet, as I reread 2 *Clem.* 2, it seems that the linkage is not that apparent; both citations seem to be referring, instead, to the importance of God's call to the desolate, not a connection between Suffering Servant and Son of Man. I am not certain, then, that 2 *Clement* is inherently affirming the Gospels with the same status as Isaiah or the Old Testament. Nor am I clear that either Mark or John are in view in 2 *Clement's* homily.

But the bigger problem with 2 *Clement* is the use of non-canonical material with what seems to be equally authoritative citation formulae. There are clearly non-canonical citations in 2 *Clem.* 5:3–4, 12:2, and 11:2. The 2 *Clem.* 12:2 passage seems to be a citation from the Gospel of Thomas 22. Perrin does acknowledge the use of apocryphal materials in 2 Clement, and suggests they come from some kind of compendium of Gospels texts that included non-canonical texts. As a result, he suggests that what we have here is a dual track pattern of preserving Gospel tradition, similar to what he proposed for Justin: "we begin to suspect that the setting of 2 *Clement*, like the setting of the later Justin, recognized two legitimate, non-competing modalities for preserving the Gospel tradition: one in which the four discrete gospels were handed down and read as discrete documents, and another in which the four gospels were combined, piecemeal, or as a whole into a unified *testimonium*, identifiable in Clement's day as "the gospel." But Perrin has here too-neatly shuffled the non-canonical material into a *testimonium* that includes canonical material. But why might not the apocryphal material also be from "discrete" Gospels, and used as equally authoritative? While Perrin can clearly point to canonical Gospel material (notably Matthew and Luke) being used by *2 Clement*, he must not understate that apocryphal material is even more clearly attested than Mark or John. And while an argument for authority can be made, it is not restricted to the four Gospels that later became canonical.

Perrin makes a strong case that the four canonical Gospels were already being used, authoritatively, earlier than Irenaeus's well-known apology for a four-Gospel unit. The *Diatessaron* is a clear example of the implicit use of the four Gospels in an authoritative way, although without any real appreciation for the discrete nature of the four-fold emerging canon. The Muratorian Fragment also speaks to what seems to be a clearly developing four-fold unit of texts, even if the inclusion of Matthew and Mark must be inferred rather than explicitly seen. Moving back a few decades though, Perrin has identified the same four-fold unit in Justin's alongside a *testimonium*, the evidence for which seems weak to me. Instead, with Justin the case for his reliance simply on the four Gospels now deemed canonical seems more likely, which would line up well with Tatian's reliance only on these four Gospels. And moving just a few decades back to the *Epistula Apostolorum*, again Perrin notes very strong evidence that the four Gospels of the canon were considered authoritative in a way that suggests an early formation of a canonical unit. Perrin's overall thesis that the shaping of a four-Gospel canon began early in the second century seems to be a very strong one, even if we discount the evidence of *2 Clement* as I have suggested.

There is substantial current interest in the role of the Gospels in the formation of the canon, and Perrin's argument adds substantially to that discussion. Francis Watson, in *Gospel Writing*, argued, "The starting point for an account of the emerging four-fold Gospel must be in the late second-century Alexandria," and he then explores the work of Clement of Alexandria, who wrote right at the close of the second century. Yet he seems to have both his dating and his location wrong for the emergence of the Gospel canon. With the evidence Perrin proposes for the use of the four Gospels now considered canonical, and perhaps adding other even earlier use of some of the Gospels by Ignatius and *Ad Diognetum*, it would seem the emergence of a special view of these four Gospels as uniquely authoritative began in the first half of the second century. This, of course, is quite compatible with my own view of an early Gospel of John.[7] Moreover, if sustained, this must influence how we see the role of

---

7. See "Revisiting the Priority of John" elsewhere in this volume.

other gospel materials (e.g., G. Thomas, G. Peter, P. Egerton 2, etc.) in the early church, and certainly with respect to their influence on the Gospels of the canonical tradition.[8] The key witnesses to the emerging canon in Perrin's article are Irenaeus, Justin, Tatian, and *Epistula Apostorum*, all of which can be located in Asia Minor.[9] And if we add to them Ignatius and *Ad Diognetum*, which are also located in Asia Minor, a pattern becomes clear. In addition to its origination earlier than previously thought, the primary location for this canon-shaping activity was not Egypt but Asia Minor.

Bibliography

Hill, Charles E. *The Johannine Corpus in the Early Church*. Oxford: Oxford University Press, 2004.
———. *Who Chose the Gospels?: Probing the Great Gospel Conspiracy*. Oxford: Oxford University Press, 2010.
Watson, Francis. *The Fourfold Gospel*. Grand Rapids: Baker Academic, 2016.
———. *Gospel Writing: A Canonical Perspective*. Grand Rapids: Eerdmans, 2013.

---

8. I note here that I have already at the 2016 SBL responded critically to Francis Watson's proposal that the Gospel of John used P. Egerton 2. The evidence I believe is strongly in favor of P. Egerton being much later and derivative of both Mark and John. In fact, it points to another early valuation of these two gospels, as it seems to be a compilation of materials from already authoritative documents.

9. See Hill, *Johannine Corpus*, 366, on the Asia Minor provenance for *Epistula Apostolorum*. 362.

6

Ben F. Meyer and The Gospels for All Christians

Jonathan Bernier

RICHARD BAUCKHAM'S 1998 EDITED volume, *The Gospels for All Christians* (hereafter abbreviated *GAC*),[1] notably shifted the shape of contemporary scholarly discourse regarding gospel origins. *GAC* constituted a critique of what I have elsewhere described as "community criticism," i.e., that late-twentieth-century approach to reading the Gospels, which supposed programmatically that the Gospels tell the story not of Jesus but rather of the respective communities in which they were written.[2] One significant voice of late-twentieth-century New Testament scholarship was absent from the debates and discussions that ensued,[3] namely that of Ben F. Meyer, who passed away in 1995. This paper is an exercise in the imagination, asking what Meyer might have said had circumstances allowed him to participate in the *GAC* debate. *GAC* consists of the written text of a paper that Bauckham delivered in 1995,[4] followed by contributions from five British New Testament scholars who wrote in support of the thesis developed in said paper, plus one more contribution

---

1. Bauckham, *Gospels for All Christians*.
2. Bernier, Aposynagōgos *and the Historical Jesus*, 5–6.
3. Esler, "Response to Richard," 235–48; Kazen, "Sectarian Gospels," 561–78; Klink, *Audience*; Klink, *Sheep*; Mitchell, "Patristic Counter-Evidence," 36–79; Sim, "Gospels for all Christians?" 3–27.
4. Bauckham, "For Whom," 9–48.

from Bauckham himself.[5] If Meyer had constituted a seventh contributor, what might he have said on the matter?

Under the community-critical regime, the historian's task was to utilize the Gospels to reconstruct putative communities from which the Gospels originated. Community critics utilized the Gospel of Matthew in order to reconstruct the putative Matthean community in which the Gospel of Matthew was produced;[6] the Gospel of Mark to reconstruct the putative Markan community in which the Gospel of Mark was produced;[7] the Gospel of Luke to reconstruct the putative Lukan (or Lucan) community in which the Gospel of Luke was produced;[8] the Gospel of John to reconstruct the putative Johannine community in which the Gospel of John was produced.[9] As I will argue more fully below, this understanding of the historian's task is largely grounded in F. C. Baur's tendency to conceive early Christianity in terms of an antagonism between Petrine and Pauline Christianity that was only reconciled relatively late in the post-apostolic era. This created a vision of an apostolic, sub-apostolic, and early patristic Christianity that is in fact not a Christianity at all, but rather multiple Christianities that related to each other, if at all, via antagonism. From such supposition it was relatively simple to multiple Christianities: no longer just a Petrine and a Pauline, but also a Matthean, Markan, Lukan, Johannine, Thomasine, etc. With the advent of first form

---

5. Alexander, "Ancient Book Production," 70–111; Barton, "Can We Identify," 173–94; Bauckham, "John for Readers," 147–71; Burridge, "About People," 113–45; Thompson, "Holy Internet," 49–70; Watson, "Towards a Literal Reading," 195–217.

6. For examples of Matthean community criticism, cf. Overman, *Matthew's Gospel*; Saldarini, *Matthew's Christian-Jewish Community*; Sim, *Gospel of Matthew*; Stanton, *Gospel for a New People*.

7. For examples of Markan community criticism, cf. Kee, *Community*; Marxsen, *Mark*; Myers, *Binding*; Weeden, *Mark*.

8. For examples of Lukan community criticism, cf. Esler, *Community*. The relative dearth of Lukan community criticism is quite telling. Community criticism supposed in part that the gospels allegorically tell the history of the respective communities in which they were written. This supposition is difficult to sustain in the case of a gospel that has as its sequel an ecclesiastical history, and moreover one that is not focused upon the history of a single community but rather of the broader Christian movement throughout the northeastern Mediterranean region. The empirical reality of Luke-Acts is sufficient reason to question the supposition that gospels by their very nature aim to tell the history of a particular Christian community.

9. For examples of Johannine community criticism cf. Brown, *Community*; Cullmann, *Johannine Circle*; Culpepper, *Johannine School*; Howard-Brook, *Becoming Children*; Martyn, *History and Theology*; Rensberger, *Johannine Faith*.

and then redaction criticism, this supposition became twinned with another, namely that the Gospels provided data primarily not about Jesus' life but rather about the respective communities that produced these writings. The Gospels became not biographies of Jesus but autobiographies of their putative communities.

Against community criticism, Bauckham argued that "[t]he Matthean, Markan, Lukan, and Johannine communities should disappear from the terminology of Gospels scholarship."[10] The bases for this argument will be examined more closely as we move through this contribution. For now, let us state merely that, looking back almost twenty years on, gospel criticism has largely actualized Bauckham's subjunctive. In the 1970s through 1990s it was normal science for Gospels scholars to produce histories of these putative communities. This is no longer the case, and virtually no such histories have been produced in the years following the publication of *GAC*.[11] Indeed, the use of gospel community language seems to be increasingly a mark of antiquated scholarship. Certainly, no one could competently use such language today without demonstrating an awareness of, and engaging carefully with, Bauckham's critique. Community criticism is functionally deceased, hence why I will refer to it in the past tense throughout this contribution. A shift has occurred: quietly, barely heralded, but nonetheless quite real. Any such shift requires reflection upon the form that the new paradigm will take. It is in this context that I ask what insights we might glean from Ben Meyer.

Focus in this contribution will be placed upon two themes in Meyer's later work: 1) his effort to define more precisely the relationship between unity and diversity in early Christianity; and 2) his related effort to define more precisely the development of Christian identity as it progressed from its initial Palestinian Jewish matrix into the world mission. It will be argued throughout this contribution that the framework Meyer was developing can more adequately account for the data relevant for gospel origins than can community criticism; that this framework is

---

10. Bauckham, "Introduction," 4.

11. Kloppenborg Verbin, *Excavating Q*, 214–70. Kloppenborg's reconstruction of a putative Q community has received relatively little support among New Testament scholars. In part, this is because it was published not long after Bauckham's critique called the community critical enterprise into exercise, and in part because it was published not long before the emergence of renewed critiques of the very existence of Q in volumes such as Goodacre, *Case Against Q*; Goodacre and Perrin, *Questioning Q*. Cf. the critiques of Kloppenborg's reconstructed Q community in Dunn, *Jesus Remembered*, 149–52; Freyne, *Jesus Movement*, 250–56.

in general congruent with Bauckham's hypothesis as put forward in the *GAC*; and that Meyer's framework can help fill in certain lacunae that remain in Bauckham's account.

Unity and Diversity

Meyer's brilliance was located perhaps most of all in his remarkable capacity for identifying inescapable heuristic distinctions and then using them to resolve pernicious problems in New Testament studies. One suspects that he would have brought such capacity to bear upon the question of community criticism, and the shift therefrom. *GAC* provides a preliminary sketch for a program of gospel scholarship that dispenses with community criticism. Unfortunately, as is almost invariably the case with such preliminary sketches, hindsight reveals various inadequacies. One such inadequacy is a conceptual imprecision that at times mars the argument. For instance, Bauckham writes that "[w]hatever the influences on an evangelist's work may have been, its *implied readership* is not a specific audience, large or small, but an indefinite readership: any or every church of the late first century to which his Gospel might circulate."[12] As written, this sentence evinces a degree of conceptual imprecision. If the implied readership is delimited to Christians, as Bauckham implies here and argues explicitly elsewhere in the same contribution,[13] then it is not indefinite. This imprecision, however, is hardly fatal to Bauckham's argument, but rather demands that we develop more precise definitions. A hypothetical contribution from Meyer would likely have aimed to provide such definitional precision. As such, the balance of this contribution aims largely to develop the arguments advanced in *GAC* by providing more precise heuristic definitions, beginning with the matter of unity and diversity.

Central to Bauckham's argument is that first-century Christianity was a "network of communities in constant communication."[14] He is clear, however, that

> [t]his picture should not be misunderstood as though it portrayed the Christian movement as entirely harmonious and homogeneous. It does not require the evidence for conflict and

---

12. Bauckham, "For Whom," 45.
13. Bauckham, "For Whom," 9–10.
14. Bauckham, "For Whom," 43.

diversity to be played down. On the contrary, it is clear that this network of communication among the early Christian churches was a vehicle for conflict and disagreement, as well as for fellowship and support.[15]

Bauckham is here articulating implicitly a series of distinctions that Meyer had already articulated explicitly. The early Christians, Meyer argued,

> put a high premium on identity (the principle of unity), quite consciously and deliberately making room for plural self-definitions (the principle of diversity). This means that they found unity and diversity compatible.... The contrary of unity is not diversity but division, just as the contrary of diversity is not unity but uniformity. Unity and division, like uniformity and diversity, were reciprocally exclusive, but there was nothing to prevent unity from coexisting with diversity—and in retrospect one might even say (indeed, should say) that, if unity was an imperative grounded in the gospel itself, diversity was a concrete human, existential, personal and cultural condition of this unity.[16]

Let us use an example drawn from Linnean taxonomy to explicate these terms. A lion is self-evidently not a tiger. They are irreducibly distinct species. If we consider no level of abstraction higher than species, then lions and tigers stand in a relationship of *division* from one another. If, however, we move our analysis to the level of genus, then suddenly we find that they stand in a relationship of *unity*: these two irreducibly distinct species can now be seen to be united in the genus *Panthera*. They remain irreducibly distinct, but nonetheless evince a unity. Reciprocally, we can describe the genus *Panthera* as consisting of a *diversity* of species: the lion and the tiger, as well as the jaguar, the leopard, and the snow leopard. This diversity exists because each of the five species is distinct from one another. If, however, the five species were indistinct, then the genus would consist of *uniformity*, i.e., an absence of difference among its members. Instead of five species there would be just one. If species is the highest level of abstraction that one functionally conceives, then one will be unable to apprehend the unity that evidently exists at the level of genus. Indeed, one will be unable to conceive of any unity but rather only division between the lion and the tiger, no different in principle from the

15. Bauckham, "For Whom," 43.
16. Meyer, *Christus Faber*, 160.

division between lion and bear. Put quite simply, a functional failure to conceive of a higher-level of abstraction than species hobbles one's capacity to genuinely apprehend the relationship between lions and tigers.

Community criticism suffered from a comparable hobbling effect. In practice, if not always in theory, the local community constituted the highest level of abstraction with which community criticism functioned. This is evident when community critics supposed, often spontaneously and with but little apparent reflection, that the particularities of the individual gospels constitute evidence for the particularities specific to the respective community. To use an example presented by Bauckham,[17] let us grant with J. Louis Martyn that John 9 allegorically narratives the expulsion of Christians from synagogues in the 80s or 90s.[18] Contra Martyn, it does not follow that such expulsion would be limited to Christians belonging to the putative Johannine community. Even on Martyn's own account of the passage, there is no reason to exclude the possibility that this was a more widespread phenomenon, which for whatever reason only John reports. Indeed, given that most scholars would date the Gospel of John later than the Synoptic Gospels, it would take little effort to find a perfectly reasonable hypothesis for why John alone reports this phenomenon: it had not yet emerged when the Synoptic Gospels were written. In that case, this Johannine particularity would become a product not of spatial difference but rather temporal. Yet this hypothesis, which is altogether congruent with Martyn's decision to treat John's Gospel as an allegory for early Christian history, seems not to have occurred to Martyn. Consequently, one has reason to suspect the presence of a conceptual impairment.

In principle, of course, community critics recognized that at least some early Christian communities were in contact with each other, and given the nature of the Synoptic problem they could not deny at least indirect contact among the Matthean, Markan, and Lukan communities.[19] Yet, community criticism was able only to conceive of the relationship between communities in terms of division between communities. Unity

---

17. Bauckham, "For Whom," 22–24.

18. As argued in Martyn, *History and Theology*. Cf. the critique of Martyn in Bernier, *Aposynagōgos*.

19. A fact that allows Bauckham, "For Whom," 12–13, to build a powerful "preliminary argument" against the community critical approach: to the extent that one concedes the existence of the Synoptic problem, to at least that extent one must concede that there is a level of abstraction above that of the individual communities.

was excluded as a live conceptual option. This is evident in Esler's response to *GAC*, in which he advances the possibility that "each evangelist primarily shaped his Gospel in accordance with the faith and understanding of his local community . . . but also contemplated the possibility that it would travel further afield, in which case he hoped that his version would compete with and even supplant the unsatisfactory gospels."[20] Leaving aside that this largely concedes the case that Bauckham is endeavoring to make,[21] and that with Esler's proposed model we can no longer place a hermeneutical premium upon the needs and interests of the evangelists' own individual communities, it should be noted that Esler supposes that any aim to circulate a gospel beyond a local community would have entailed communities competing with other communities. And it should be asked: why? Why must we suppose that this was the case?

Bauckham likely hits incidentally upon the ultimate historical source for Esler's supposition of competing communities: "the stress on competition and conflict, which goes back to F. C. Baur."[22] As I have argued elsewhere, the conceptual apparatus for community criticism goes back in large part to F. C. Baur's tendency to conceive of differences among Christians only in terms of divisions between factions.[23] Community criticism, having inherited this conceptual limitation, multiplied divisions, adding Matthean, Markan, Lukan, and Johannine Christianities alongside Petrine and Pauline, but retained the fundamental Baurian model of communities divided from each other and locked in irreducible conflict. Community criticism could not conceive of these communities standing with each other in a relationship of unity, precisely because it lacked a conceptually robust account of the higher-level abstraction in which that unity would be constituted. This conceptual dearth had a hobbling effect on the community critic's historical imagination.[24]

As the Synoptic problem demonstrates well, and as the contributions to *GAC* elaborate more fully, there was in early Christianity a unity above the level of the local community. Bauckham designates this as a

20. Esler, *Community*, 242.
21. As noted by Bauckham, "Response," 249.
22. Bauckham, "Response," 250.
23. Bernier, *Quest*, 97–102.
24. "Historical imagination" being a term borrowed from Collingwood, *Idea of History*, 231–49. Cf. the discussions of Collingwood in Meyer, *Aims of Jesus*, 84–87; and Meyer, *Critical Realism*, 157–72. Cf. now also Ryan, "Jesus at the Crossroads," 66–89.

"network."[25] The undeniable reality of this unity can be demonstrated by reference to the *Hebraioi* and *Hellēnistai*, known to us from Acts 6:1–6, upon which Meyer focused much of his last major work of historical investigation proper.[26] Of course, as Craig Hill has subsequently emphasized, one should avoid the Baurian temptation to imagine that these terms designate competing theological factions.[27] Fortunately for our purposes, Hill's warning requires little correction of Meyer's account, in which the distinction between *Hebraioi* and *Hellēnistai* is largely linguistic and cultural rather than theological.[28] Most important for our purposes is to note that the Jerusalem community was marked by linguistic and cultural diversity from the off. Indeed, Luke provides hints that this linguistic and cultural diversity exceeded that of the *Hebraioi* and the *Hellēnistai* (cf. the Pentecost account in Acts 2, esp. vv. 9–10).[29] Indeed, vis-à-vis their role in the Lukan narrative, the *Hebraioi* and *Hellēnistai* might be best construed as exemplary "figures" that Luke has used to symbolically manage the Jerusalem community's lively diversity.

Acts reports that members of the Jerusalem community were scattered abroad in Judea and Samaria (8:1), and Phoenicia, Cyprus, and Antioch (11:19), and thus can be expected to have spread such diversity with them to these other locales. As early as perhaps eighteen months after Jesus' death, there were Christian communities located throughout the northeastern circum-Mediterranean region.[30] These communities appear to have been characterized by the presence of the sort of persons that Luke described as *Hebraioi* and *Hellēnistai*, and where demographi-

25. Bauckham, "For Whom," 30–44. Cf. Thompson, "Holy Internet."
26. Meyer, *Early Christians*, 53–83.
27. Hill, *Hellenists and Hebrews*.
28. For this reason, the distinction between *Hebraioi* and *Hellēnistai* does not run afoul of the argument put forward in Hengel, *Judaism and Hellenism*, namely that not even the least obviously Hellenized Jewish persons in the Land could escape the influence of Hellenism. The *Hebraioi* are not necessarily persons isolated from or inoculated against Greek (or Roman) language or culture, but rather persons who were more oriented toward a "Hebraic" language and culture. The differences between *Hebraioi* and *Hellēnistai* were probably relative, not absolute.
29. Much of what follows regarding the specifics of the Jerusalem community recapitulates arguments advanced in Bernier, *Quest*, 102–10.
30. Scholars otherwise as diverse as Jewett, *Chronology*, 29–30, and Riesner, *Paul's Early Period*, 64–72, agree that Paul's conversion likely occurred approximately eighteen months after Jesus' death. If this is granted, then the events narrated in Acts 1–8 could conceivably have occurred in that relatively short window.

cally relevant presumably also *Parthoi*, *Mēdoi*, and *Elamitai*, among others (cf. Acts 2:9). What we learn from this data is two-fold. First, we learn that there was likely as much or even greater difference *within* any early given Christian community than *between* such communities. Second, we learn that each such community was likely a microcosm of larger patterns of difference. This does not obviate regional differences. Each community would presumably have evinced different frequencies of *Hebraioi*, *Hellēnistai*, *Parthoi*, *Mēdoi*, *Elamitai*, etc. The salient point is that Bauckham's understanding of early Christianity as a network of diverse communities can readily account for this patterning in the data. The very unity of the network functioned as a vector for spreading that which constituted the basis of diversity within the communities.

Unfortunately for community criticism, it failed to articulate a comparably adequate account. Was the Jerusalem church composed of both *Hebraioi* and *Hellēnistai*? If so, what distinguished this community from other communities that had representatives of both these horizons, such that whatever Gospel they might have produced would be indelibly marked by such distinction as to allow the modern historian to reconstruct the community's particular experience? Alternatively, did the *Hebraioi* and the *Hellēnistai* each constitute a separate community unto themselves? Would such a hypothesis of division adequately account for the report that they appear to have each looked to the same group, namely the Twelve, for governance? And regarding the likelihood that there were *Hebraioi* and *Hellēnistai* in locales beyond Jerusalem, would we now need to describe these communities themselves as trans-local phenomena? Were these communities in fact trans-local networks of *Hebraioi* and *Hellēnistai*? If so, what evidence have we that these constituted separate communities in the various locales in which they were found, especially given that the clearest data that attests their existence shows them apparently united under common leadership? Add in *Parthoi*, *Mēdoi*, and *Elamitai*, as well as the number of other groups mentioned in Acts 2:9, and the relatively simple understanding of "community" supposed by community critics is no longer sufficient to describe the complexity of this earliest known Christian church. If we substitute, for instance, the words "Matthean" and "Lukan" for *Hebraioi* and *Hellēnistai*, then we can see quite clearly the acute difficulty for community criticism. Indeed, such a substitution only serves to heighten the difficulty, for at least the existence of the *Hebraioi* and *Hellēnistai* is attested in our sources. If we preserve the concept of community only by making it a trans-local phenomenon, then have we not virtually conceded Bauckham's argument that the Gospels were written for a wide rather than limited Christian circulation? If Matthew's Gospel was written for any Matthean Christian, and Matthean Christians dwelt alongside and in unity with non-Matthean Christians, then Matthew reasonably could expect it to be read in locales with non-Matthean Christians.

There is, of course, a tradition, dating back to Baur, of seeing reports such as the coexistence between the *Hebraioi* and the *Hellēnistai* as a retrojection of later conditions on to what was a far less united Christian movement. This of course begs the question, supposing that which would remain to be proven: namely that there was greater division than the most relevant data *prima facie* indicates. That having been said, even if it is such a retrojection, given that most scholars would date Acts approximately coeval with the Gospels,[31] it would likely represent a retrojection from around the time at which the Gospels were written. Indeed, if anything, this retrojective hypothesis would likely increase rather than decrease the relevance of these early chapters of Acts for the study of the context in which the Gospels were written. Moreover, this pattern recurs in our data, even prior to the period at which most scholars hold that the Gospels were written. Recurrently in the New Testament material—and not least of all in the Pauline material—we see the distinction between persons with a more "Hebraist" and persons with a more "Hellenist" orientation constituting a major fault line in various Christian communities. Indeed, Baur's entire scheme supposes this recurrent pattern: it is precisely what allowed him to argue that Acts is a retrojection from later conditions. There is little evidence of debates sufficiently particular to a specific community that one could expect to infer such particularity from any gospel texts that they might have hypothetically produced.

---

31. This holds on what we might call the lower chronology (which argues that most or all the canonical gospels were written prior to c. 70 CE), the middle chronology (which argues that most or all were written between c. 70 and c. 100 CE), and the higher chronology (which argues that at least one or more gospels were written at least a decade or more into the second century). For instance, Robinson, *Redating the New Testament*, 254–311, argues that the gospels were composed during the span ranging from c. 40 to c. 65, and he dates the composition of Acts to c. 57–62; on the side of the higher chronology, Pervo, *Dating Acts*, argues that Acts should be dated to c. 110–120, and also wants to date Luke's Gospel to a comparable range. Whether one favors lower, middle, or higher dates, it seems that most scholars are agreed that at least Luke's Gospel and Acts, and probably also John's Gospel, were written in close temporal proximity.

Sim argues that Bauckham's understanding of early Christianity cannot adequately apprehend the reality of diversity.[32] He could not be more mistaken. Indeed, Sim seems to have misapprehended Bauckham. For instance, he writes that "[i]n the light of the diverse and polemical nature of the early Christian factions, it is extremely improbable that any follower of Jesus the Christ would have classified the world, as Bauckham implies, simply into Christian and non-Christian."[33] Not only does Bauckham imply no such thing, he in fact states exactly the opposite, in for instance the quotation cited at the beginning of this section. Bauckham knows quite clearly that the early Christians were a diverse lot. One suspects that Sim's manifest misapprehension of Bauckham's argument results from a prior failure to apprehend the heuristic distinction between what, following Meyer, we here describe as diversity and division. "So intense were these disagreements and divisions within the ranks of Christians that it is perhaps more appropriate to speak of very different Christian movements rather than a single movement," Sim writes.[34] Yet the very example that he adduces to support this conclusion, that of the conflict presented in Gal 2:11–14, places these different movements coexisting in a single community, namely the Antiochene. Exactly what emerges is something more akin to Bauckham's model: yes, there is diversity, there is conflict, but this conflict ranges across a network and recurs throughout various communities. By envisioning early Christianity not as a collection of disparate communities divided from each other but rather a unified field marked by diversity, Bauckham's understanding of early Christianity accounts for diversity far better than does community criticism. Such unity was in principle recognized already in Meyer's work, but he was never able to bring it to bear directly upon the matter of community criticism.

From Community to Horizons

Although Bauckham rightly states that his understanding of early Christianity does not obviate the reality of early Christian diversity and conflict, such matters remain undertheorized in *GAC*. This is not a critique, but rather an observation. It is in the nature of such pioneering sketches

---

32. Sim, "Gospels for All Christians," 9–12.
33. Sim, "Gospels for All Christians," 10.
34. Sim, "Gospels for All Christians," 10.

to leave many matters undertheorized. Indeed, this undertheorizing is in a certain sense welcome, as it provides room for scholars friendly to Bauckham's work to build creatively upon the foundation that he and the other contributors have laid. Meyer's use of "horizon" can be of significant help in so doing.

Meyer derives the concept "horizon" from his teacher, Bernard Lonergan, defining it conceptually as the limits of those things in which one is interested in and knowledgeable about.[35] It is related to such concepts as *Weltanschauung* (and its English calque, "worldview") or *mentalité* (the latter as used in the *Annales* school of historiography), and of course Gadamer's "horizon," insofar as each is trying (with greater or lesser success) to describe the reality that different persons construe the world differently. Lonergan writes, "The scope of one's knowledge and the range of one's interests vary with the period in which one lives, one's social background and milieu, one's education and personal development."[36] Unfortunately, community critics were working with one concept where they should have been working with two. "Community" and what, following Meyer, we have here designated as "horizon," were functionally fused, such that the Matthean community was defined as that Christian community which evinces a Matthean horizon, the Markan community as that which evinces a Markan horizon, the Lukan community as that which evinces a Lukan horizon, and the Johannine community as that which evinces a Johannine horizon. By fusing horizon and community, community criticism functionally defined Christian communities as internally uniform. After Bauckham's intervention, even if we can any longer think in terms of distinctly Matthean, Markan, Lukan, or Johannine communities (and that itself remains dubious), we can no longer treat them as functionally self-identical with putative Matthean, Markan, Lukan, or Johannine horizons.

It remains to be asked, though: how do we discuss community and horizon as distinct from each other? Here we can look again to Meyer for assistance. Meyer's most extensive use of the Lonerganian concept of horizon comes in his discussion of the early Jerusalem community, already discussed in this contribution, in which he defines the distinction between the *Hebraioi* and the *Hellēnistai* as a distinction between differing

---

35. Lonergan, *Method*, 221-23; Meyer, *Reality*, 49-55. Note that by the time this contribution appears in press, there should be in print a revised edition of *Method*, viz. Lonergan, *Method in Theology*.

36. Lonergan, *Method*, 221.

horizons.³⁷ In this work, Meyer begins to develop an understanding of early Christianity marked by a diversity of local communities, each of which in turn are marked by a diversity of horizons. Such is exactly what we find throughout the New Testament. Corinth is perhaps the textbook example here.³⁸ 1 and 2 Corinthians furnish data that strongly indicate the existence of disparate horizons within the Corinthian church. Perhaps the strongest evidence for such disparate horizons comes in 1 Cor 8, wherein Paul aims to mediate a dispute over whether to eat meat sacrificed to idols. Contrary to Baur,³⁹ the evidence is not such that these struggles can be identified (on the basis of 1 Cor 1:12; cf. 3:4–9, 3:22–23) with competing Pauline and Petrine missions, or what in community-critical language would constitute effectively distinct communities. 1 Corinthians is addressed τῇ ἐκκλησίᾳ τοῦ θεοῦ ἐν Κορίνθῳ. Paul seems to have anticipated that not just those who identified with him would hear the letter, but also those who identified with Apollos and Peter. No question, there were a multiplicity of Christian horizons in Corinth, but it seems that they all had the same mailing address.

This appears still to have been the case in Corinth some decades later: 1 Clement writes τῇ ἐκκλησίᾳ τοῦ θεοῦ τῇ παροικούσῃ Κόρινθον not ταῖσ ἐκκλησίαις τοῦ θεοῦ ταῖσ παροικούσαις Κόρινθον, and understands the conflict in Corinth not as between communities or entailing the creation of a new one but rather as dynamic transformations within an existing one (cf. 1 Clem. 44). It would constitute question-begging of the highest degree to assume that Paul or 1 Clement were writing only to those Corinthian assemblies with which they were in communion. A similar pattern seems to exist beyond Corinth. Meyer's former student, Thomas Robinson, argued that the reason Ignatius was so vexed by the existence of theological controversy was not because it represented conflict with communities other than those with which he was associated, but rather precisely because it represented conflict within those communities.⁴⁰ There is precious little evidence of communities divided from each other and defined by their distinctive theologies and locked in sectarian

37. Meyer, *Early Christians*, 53–83. Cf. also Bernier, *Quest*, 102–10.
38. Here I recapitulate much of the discussion in Bernier, *Quest*, 122–25.
39. Cf. the discussion in Baur, *Paulus*, 1:287–343, ET: *Paul*, 268–320.
40. Robinson, *Ignatius of Antioch*, 76–85. Robinson, *Bauer Thesis Examined*, which was written as a dissertation under Meyer's supervision, remains one of the most incisive critiques of the influential model of Christian origins articulated by Bauer, *Rechtgläubigkeit*, ET: *Orthodoxy*.

conflict with one another. Again, the pattern recurs: not controversy between communities but rather within communities. Indeed, perhaps the only example of conflict "between" communities would be those attested from Acts 15 and Gal 2, where Christians with some association with Jerusalem are said to have urged such practices in communities abroad.[41] Yet it would be a double-edged sword to invoke these passages in support of the community-critical paradigm, as they reinforce the conclusion that the most pressing of Christian conflicts recurred throughout various communities. Were these conflicts occurring in the Antiochene, the Galatian, or the Jerusalem churches? The answer is "yes," a fact that undermines fatally the idea that any one of these communities had a particularity that can be reconstructed from narrative texts that state nothing explicit about the locale in which they were written.

The concept of horizon aids us in envisioning the internal diversity of Christian communities. It allows us to integrate questions about how such human distinctions as language and ethnicity and gender and sexuality into our historical accounts in a manner that community criticism simply could not. Such distinctions were functionally epiphenomenal to community criticism, whereas they are the essential engines of a model such as Bauckham's. Put quite simply, Bauckham's model opens up early Christianity to a far wider range of social and cultural analysis than does the blunt conceptual instruments utilized by community criticism. That said, it remains to be asked: how do we connect such questions with the Gospels? For that, we need to consider the matter of translation.

Translation

Meyer writes of the "transposition, or translation" model for explaining early Christian formation, which he defines as "suppos[ing] that every act of meaning is embedded in a context and that the maintenance of meaning is conditioned by the more or less creative act of transposing meaning from one context to another."[42] At the historical fount of Christianity lies a set of experiences: of first the earthly and then the risen Jesus.[43] We need not here determine the ontological status of such experiences,

---

41. Cf. again, the discussion in Sim, "Gospels for All Christians," 9–12.

42. Meyer, *Early Christians*, 190. Cf. the recurring theme of interhorizontal translation in Bernier, *Quest*, 97–158.

43. Cf. Meyer, *Early Christians*, 174–81.

especially those involving the risen Christ: for our purposes it is sufficient to state that in the period following Jesus' death several of his followers and at least one of his opponents (*viz.* Paul of Tarsus) experienced what they understood to be Jesus of Nazareth, in some sense raised from the dead. Given what we know about first-century Galilee, one imagines that most (but not necessarily all) of these came from a horizon that can be broadly defined as aligned with that of Luke's *Hebraioi*.[44] Right from the start, those who had such experiences had to make them intelligible to those who had not, thus inevitably transforming the shared understanding of said experiences. As persons whose horizons Luke grouped under the category *Hellēnistai* began to enter the early Christian community in more substantial numbers, as well as those persons that he describes as the *Parthoi*, *Mēdoi*, and *Elamitai*, we can reasonably infer that such communicative work would all the more constitute a transformative influence. Thus did a process of development begin wherein "something of the old was (both deliberately and indeliberately) lost in the translation and significant new elements were gained."[45] This is a process that in very real ways continues through to the present day.[46]

The diversity among the gospels must be situated within this work of translation. It is not self-evident that the horizons of the author or authors would coincide with those of the intended audience. Indeed, to the extent that the gospels were written as collective projects, it is not self-evident that all those who worked to produce a specific gospel shared closely aligned horizons. Papias tells us that the basis for Mark's Gospel was Peter's oral teaching, and moreover that Mark had served as Peter's translator or interpreter.[47] Thus we find already in our data an

---

44. Our knowledge of first-century Galilee has grown significantly in recent years. Cf. Fiensy and Strange, *Galilee*; Freyne, *Jesus Movement*. For present purposes, cf. esp. Chancey, "Ethnicities of Galileans," as well as the discussion of Meyer's use of "horizon" in Freyne, *Jesus Movement*, 209–213.

45. Meyer, *Early Christians*, 191.

46. Meyer, *Early Christians*, 190, explicitly associates his translation model with the work of John Henry Newman, especially as expressed in the latter's *Essay on the Development of Christian Doctrine*. Combined with Meyer's discussion of ancient Israelite religion, *Early Christians*, 188–189, this presents a sketch for a developmental narrative that could in principle extend from the religions of Canaan through to the twenty-first century. Cf. the earlier discussion of Newman's *Essay* in Meyer, *The Church*, 122–147. For a recent, closely related, Lonerganian approach to specifically Catholic history, cf. Ormerod, *Re-Visioning the Church*, 175–352.

47. *Apud* Eusebius, *Eccl. Hist.* 3.39.15.

explicit statement that Mark's Gospel was the product of translational work, involving persons who apparently evinced distinct linguistic backgrounds, and one imagines also distinct cultural ones. Moreover, if there is any truth to the tradition that Mark wrote in Rome at the behest of the Christian community there, then we might imagine that at least his initial, "commissioning" audience consisted of persons that we might broadly define as *Hellēnistai* and even as *Hellēnes*, i.e., non-Jewish "Greeks."[48] Mark's Gospel is probably the earliest extant narrative source for Jesus' life,[49] and it might even have been the first such text ever written, but he hardly represents the beginning of the work of translation needed to communicate the experiences of the earthly and risen Jesus to those who did not have such experiences themselves. Nor does he represent the last. Certainly, the other canonical gospels constitute further attempts to translate between horizons.

Space and Time

As intimated in the above discussion of Mark's possible Roman provenance, this work of translation took place in space and time. Space and time were almost epiphenomena in community criticism. The communities that were constructed could have existed virtually anywhere or any-when in the early Roman Empire. This is a significant liability for a historiography that claimed interest in identifying the specifics of an ancient community. If one lacks confidence in answering such a basic question as "Where?" it is difficult to suppose that one could have much confidence in answering more advanced questions. Of course, Bauckham's initial articulation also leaves the spatial and temporal questions undertheorized, focusing instead upon the higher-level concept of "network."[50] Yet, one can easily see how the spatial and temporal dimension can be integrated fully into Bauckham's account, an integration that never fully emerged with community criticism. The gospels had to origi-

---

48. Lampe, *From Paul to Valentinus*, 7–65, has shown that the Roman Church originated among Jewish sectors of the city. Given Rome's position in the western Diaspora it seems probable that the church had significantly more persons who could be described as coming from a Hellenist cultural and linguistic background than a Hebraist one.

49. Assuming Markan priority.

50. But see Thompson, "Holy Internet," for a powerful corrective to this undertheorizing.

nate *somewhere* in the network, and at *sometime*. One needs only identify those wheres and whens.

Community criticism struggled to do so because it restricted its data set to the texts of the individual gospels, and moreover impoverished forms of those texts. Community criticism so attenuated the data set that it refused to even consider what we might learn from the traditional attributions of the gospels, which, despite scholarly myth to the contrary, appear to be integral rather than secondary to the respective texts. Hengel observes that "there are still crude judgments [regarding the superscriptions of the gospels]. That may be connected with the fact that even in more recent editions of Nestle-Aland the textual evidence for the *inscriptiones* and *subscriptiones* is in part quite incomplete. These titles are widely attested in a variety of ways: by some of the earliest papyri, by reports in the second- and third-century church fathers, and by the earliest translations."[51] The response, typified by Crossley, namely that Mark's Gospel would not necessarily have been known as the εὐαγγέλιον κατὰ Μᾶρκον until there was at least one other gospel in existence, is really quite speculative, and in any case would apply only to Mark's Gospel and perhaps John's.[52] In the absence of positive evidence that any of the gospels ever circulated absent their putative attributions, we should do best to judge these attributions as coeval with the texts itself.

With that in mind, it is surely of some significance that this gospel is attributed to a person closely associated with the Jerusalem community, just as are the Epistle of James and the Didache,[53] both of which evince clear literary affiliations with the Gospel of Matthew.[54] By comparison, and again despite scholarly myth, there is virtually no data that associates Matthew's Gospel with Antioch. This myth appears to have become established with Streeter. Streeter arrived at this geographical origin through a series of questionable inferences.[55] First, he supposed that the "[t]he

---

51. Hengel, *Four Gospels*, 48.

52. Crossley, *Date of Mark's Gospel*, 16-17.

53. The latter bearing the longer title, διδαχὴ κυρίου διὰ τῶν δώδεκα ἀποστόλων τοῖσ ἔθνεσιν ("the Teaching of Lord through the Twelve Apostles to the Nations"). Whether this is original to the text or not, it does tell us something about how the early Christians apparently understood the Didache's geographical provenance.

54. As explored in, *inter alia*, van de Sandt and Zangenberg, *Matthew, James, and Didache*.

55. Streeter, *Four Gospels*, 500-527. Cf. the discussion of Streeter's formative role in the development of community criticism in Bauckham, "For Whom," 14-15.

anonymity of the Gospel shows that it was written for a definite local church,"[56] a dubious supposition on at least two grounds: 1), as discussed above, there is in fact no evidence that Matthew's Gospel was an initially anonymous work; and 2), such anonymity simply would not demonstrate that it was written for "a definite local church." Second, even if the supposition of anonymity is granted, Streeter arrived at the Antiochene origin by adducing "reasons for excluding Rome, Alexandria, Ephesus, Caesarea—and indeed any Church in Palestine." Thus, "Antioch [is] the only important Church left, and to this there are no objections."[57] Process of elimination is generally not the strongest line of argumentation when establishing geographical provenance. Streeter's positive arguments, which include references to Ignatius and the Didache, are hardly more convincing.[58] Yes, Ignatius was Antiochene, but he was writing to the churches of Asia Minor, and thus that he refers to the Gospel of Matthew as the gospel does not establish that this is a peculiarly Antiochene usage; and the parallels between the Gospel of Matthew and the Didache can only establish the former's Antiochene origin if it has been established for the latter on independent grounds. Moreover, Streeter cannot escape the conclusion that the Matthean *tradition* is ultimately of Jerusalemite origin, and must resort to the hypothesis that it was brought to Antioch by refugees fleeing Judea during the catastrophes of the 60s.[59] Given such a concession from the scholar who cemented the Antiochene hypothesis, we are well-warranted in suggesting that the Gospel of Matthew originated, if not from Jerusalem, at the very least from an author or authors who had close associations with Jerusalem.

The above does not obviate Bauckham's argument that the gospels were written with a general audience in mind. Matthew or Pseudo-Matthew could have written his gospel in Jerusalem, and even have been thinking primarily in terms of communicating to the horizons most characteristic of the Jerusalem community. It would not follow that he did not expect that the gospel would circulate further abroad, nor that he would fail to take that into account as he wrote. It certainly does not follow that we can use his gospel to reconstruct the history of the Jerusalem

---

56. Streeter, *Four Gospels*, 486, cf. 500–501.
57. Streeter, *Four Gospels*, 486, cf. 500–501.
58. Streeter, *Four Gospels*, 504–7.
59. Streeter, *Four Gospels*, 511–13.

church.⁶⁰ Similarly, all the evidence points to Ephesus as the place of origin for John's Gospel, yet this gospel seems to tell us little more about Ephesian Christianity than that the language particular to this gospel was more common in and around the Ephesus area (and the fact that such language is less characteristic of the Revelation might speak against even that hypothesis. At the very least it suggests that there were Christians in the region whose language was not strongly marked by what we see in the Fourth Gospel).⁶¹ And Luke's Gospel, for which we have but the slimmest of evidence related to its geographical origin, can tell us virtually nothing about any particular Christian community that can be located in space and time. The gospels were written in particular spaces, and at particular times. We can often establish these spaces and times with reasonable precision. It does not follow that they are *about* those spaces and times.

Conclusion

The Gospels for All Christians is one of those works that, in retrospect, marks a clear turning point in a discipline. Community criticism had long before moved gospel scholarship from the realm of careful historiography and toward the realm of speculative fiction. *GAC* reversed this movement. I am persuaded that Ben F. Meyer would have welcomed this reversal as a salutary advance. Certainly, it is congruent with the directions in which his scholarship was moving toward the end of his life. This contribution has sought to enrich both the arguments put forth in *GAC* and those put forth by Meyer, by bringing them into mutual dialogue. Building upon both, it aimed to articulate an understanding

---

60. It is interesting to note that while Meyer, *Five Speeches*, 65, affirms that the Gospel of Matthew was likely edited in Antioch, this affirmation appears only in a literally parenthetical comment and does not lead him to reconstruct Antiochene Christianity on the basis of this text.

61. Cf. the discussion of Christian diversity in first-century Ephesus in Trebilco, *Early Christians*. While I would diverge from Trebilco, this is largely a matter of semantics. Trebilco, *Early Christians*, 712, concludes "that the Pauline group and Johannine group were distinct and separate communities, although they maintained non-hostile contact." Although I would be disinclined to use the term "separate communities" to describe the relationship between these groups, precisely because of the unity implied by the term "non-hostile contact," Trebilco's description ably sums up the argument advanced in this contribution: that the Christianity of any given locale was internally diverse. Moreover, if Johannine Christians coexisted in the same city as Pauline Christians, then the possibility that the Johannine author(s) anticipated that the Fourth Gospel would circulate beyond Johannine circles is notably increased.

of early Christianity that can encompass both the macro-scale of inter-community relations (something that community criticism was virtually incapable of doing) and the micro-scale of intra-community dynamics (something that community criticism struggled to accomplish). It has sought to locate the gospels within that understanding. And it does so with profound gratitude to both Ben F. Meyer and Richard Bauckham for their decades of excellent work on Christian origins.

Bibliography

Alexander, Loveday. "Ancient Book Production and the Circulation of the Gospels." In *The Gospels for All Christians*, edited by Richard Bauckham, 70–111. Grand Rapids: Eerdmans, 1997.

Barton, Stephen C. "Can We Identify the Gospel Audiences?" In *The Gospels for All Christians*, edited by Richard Bauckham, 173–94. Grand Rapids: Eerdmans, 1997.

Bauckham, Richard. "For Whom Were Gospels Written?" In *The Gospels for All Christians*, edited by Richard Bauckham, 9–48. Grand Rapids: Eerdmans, 1997.

———. "Introduction." In *The Gospels for All Christians*, edited by Richard Bauckham, 1–8. Grand Rapids: Eerdmans, *1997*.

———. "John for Readers of Mark." In *The Gospels for All Christians*, edited by Richard Bauckham, 147–71. Grand Rapids: Eerdmans, 1997.

———. "Response to Philip Esler." *Scottish Journal of Theology* 51/2 (1998) 249–54.

———, ed. *The Gospels for All Christians: Rethinking the Gospel Audiences*. Grand Rapids: Eerdmans, 1998.

Bauer, Walter. *Rechtgläubigkeit und Ketzerei imältesten Christentum*. Edited by Georg Strecker. 2nd ed. Tübingen: Mohr Siebeck, 1964 [1934]. ET: *Orthodoxy and History in Earliest Christianity*. Translated by Robert A. Kraft. Philadelphia: Fortress, 1971.

Baur, Ferdinand Christian. *Paulus, der Apostel Jesu Christi*. 2 vols. Stuttgart: Becher and Müller, 1845. ET: *Paul: The Apostle of Jesus Christ*. 2 vols. Translated by Allan Menzies. London: Williams and Norgate, 1873–75.

Bernier, Jonathan. *Aposynagōgos and the Historical Jesus in John: Rethinking the Historicity of the Johannine Expulsion Passages*. Biblical Interpretation Series 122 Leiden: Brill, 2013.

———. *The Quest for the Historical Jesus after the Demise of Authenticity*. Bloomsbury: T. & T. Clark, 2016.

Brown, Raymond E. *The Community of the Beloved Disciple: The Life, Loves, and Hates of an Individual Church in New Testament Times*. New York: Paulist, 1979.

Burridge, Richard A. "About People, By People, For People: Gospel Genre and Audiences." In *The Gospels for All Christians*, edited by Richard Bauckham, 113–45. Grand Rapids: Eerdmans, 1997.

Chancey, Mark A. "The Ethnicities of Galileans." In vol. 1 of *Galilee in the Late Second Temple and Mishnaic Periods: Life, Culture, and Society*, edited by David A. Fiensy and James Riley Strange, 112–28. Minneapolis: Fortress Press, 2014.

Collingwood, R. G. *The Idea of History*. Edited by Jan van der Dussen. Oxford: Oxford University Press, 1994.

Crossley, James G. *The Date of Mark's Gospel: Insight from the Law in Earliest Christianity*. London: T. & T. Clark, 2004.

Cullmann, Oscar. *The Johannine Circle*. Translated by John Bowden. Philadelphia: Westminster, 1976.

Culpepper, R. Alan. *The Johannine School: An Evaluation of the Johannine-School Hypothesis Based on an Investigation of the Nature of Ancient Schools*. Missoula, MT: Scholars, 1975.

Dunn, James D. G. *Jesus Remembered, Christianity in the Making*. Grand Rapids: Eerdmans, 2003.

Esler, Philip F. *Community and Gospel in Luke-Acts: The Social and Political Motivations of Lucan Theology*. Cambridge: Cambridge University Press, 1987.

———. "A Response to Richard Bauckham's *Gospels for All Christians*." *Scottish Journal of Theology* 51 (1998) 235–48.

Fiensy, David A., and James Riley Strange, eds. *Galilee in the Late Second Temple and Mishnaic Periods*. 2 vols. Minneapolis: Fortress, 2014–15.

Freyne, Seán. *The Jesus Movement and Its Expansion: Meaning and Mission*. Grand Rapids: Eerdmans, 2014.

Goodacre, Mark. *The Case Against Q: Studies in Markan Priority and the Synoptic Problem*. Harrisburg, PA: Trinity, 2003.

Goodacre, Mark, and Nicholas Perrin, eds. *Questioning Q*. London: SPCK, 2004.

Hengel, Martin. *The Four Gospels and the One Gospel of Jesus Christ: An Investigation into the Collection and Origin of the Canonical Gospels*. Translated by John Bowden. Harrisburg, PA: Trinity, 2000.

———. *Judaism and Hellenism: Studies in Their Encounters in Palestine during the Early Hellenistic Period*. Translated by John Bowden. 2 vols. Philadelphia: Fortress, 1974 [1969].

Hill, Craig C. *Hellenists and Hebrews: Reappraising Division with the Earliest Church*. Minneapolis: Fortress, 1992.

Howard-Brook, Wes. *Becoming Children of God: John's Gospel and Radical Discipleship*. Maryknoll, NY: Orbis, 1994.

Jewett, Robert. *A Chronology of Paul's Life*. Philadelphia: Fortress, 1979.

Kazen, Thomas. "Sectarian Gospels for Some Christians? Intention and Mirror Reading in the Light of Extra-Canonical Texts." *New Testament Studies* 51 (2005) 561–78.

Kee, Howard Clark. *Community of the New Age: Studies in Mark's Gospel*. Philadelphia: Westminster, 1977.

Klink, Edward W., III. *The Sheep of the Fold: The Audience and Origin of the Gospel of John*. Cambridge: Cambridge University Press, 2007.

———, ed. *The Audience of the Gospels: The Origin and Functions of the Gospels in Early Christianity*. London: T. & T. Clark, 2010.

Kloppenborg Verbin, John S. *Excavating Q: The History and Setting of the Sayings Gospel*. Minneapolis: Fortress, 2000.

Lampe, Peter. *From Paul to Valentinus: Christians at Rome in the First Two Centuries.* Translated by Michael Steinhauser. Edited by Marshall D. Johnson. Minneapolis: Fortress, 2003 [1989].

Lonergan, Bernard J. F. *Method in Theology.* Edited by Robert M. Doran and John D. Dadosky. 3rd ed., Collected Works of Bernard Lonergan. 14. Toronto: University of Toronto Press, 2017.

———. *Method in Theology.* 2nd ed. New York: Herder and Herder, 1973 [1972].

Martyn, J. Louis. *History and Theology in the Fourth Gospel.* 3rd ed. Louisville: Westminster John Knox, 2003.

Marxsen, Willi. *Mark the Evangelist: Studies on the Redaction History of the Gospel.* Translated by J. Boyce et al. Nashville: Abingdon, 1969.

Meyer, Ben F. *Aims of Jesus.* London: SCM, 1979.

———. *Christus Faber: The Master-Builder and the House of God.* Allison Park, PA: Pickwick, 1992.

———. *The Church in Three Tenses.* Garden City, NY: Doubleday, 1971.

———. *Critical Realism and the New Testament.* Allison Park, PA: Pickwick, 1989.

———. *The Early Christians: Their World Mission and Self-Discovery.* Wilmington, DE: Michael Glazier, 1986.

———. *Five Speeches that Changed the World.* Collegeville, MN: Liturgical, 1994.

———. *Reality and Illusion in New Testament Scholarship.* Wilmington, DE: Michael Glazier, 1994.

Mitchell, Margaret M. "Patristic Counter-Evidence to the Claim that the 'Gospels Were Written for All Christians.'" *New Testament Studies* 51 (2005) 36–79.

Myers, Ched. *Binding the Strong Man: A Political Reading of Mark's Story of Jesus.* Maryknoll, NY: Orbis, 1994.

Ormerod, Neil. *Re-Visioning the Church: An Experiment in Systematic-Historical Ecclesiology.* Minneapolis: Fortress, 2014.

Overman, J. Andrew. *Matthew's Gospel and Formative Judaism: The Social World of the Matthean Community.* Minneapolis: Fortress, 1990.

Pervo, Richard I. *Dating Acts: Between the Evangelists and the Apostles.* Santa Rosa, CA: Polebridge, 2006.

Rensberger, David. *Johannine Faith and Liberating Community.* Philadelphia: Westminster, 1988.

Riesner, Rainer. *Paul's Early Period: Chronology, Mission Strategy, Theology.* Translated by Doug Stott. Grand Rapids: Eerdmans, 1998.

Robinson, J. A. T. *Redating the New Testament.* London: SCM, 1976.

Robinson, Thomas A. *The Bauer Thesis Examined: The Geography of Heresy in the Early Christian Church.* Lewiston, NY: Edwin Mellen, 1988.

———. *Ignatius of Antioch and the Parting of the Ways: Early Jewish-Christian Relations.* Peabody, MA: Hendrickson, 2009.

Ryan, Jordan. "Jesus at the Crossroads of Inference and Imagination." *Journal for the Study of the Historical Jesus* 13 (2015) 66–89.

Saldarini, Anthony. *Matthew's Christian-Jewish Community.* Chicago: University of Chicago Press, 1994.

Sim, David C. *The Gospel of Matthew and Christian Judaism: The History and Social Setting of the Matthean Community.* Edinburgh: T. & T. Clark, 1998.

———. "The Gospels for All Christians? A Response to Richard Bauckham." *Journal for the Study of the New Testament* 84 (2001) 3–27.

Stanton, Graham. *A Gospel for a New People: Studies in Matthew.* Edinburgh: T. & T. Clark, 1992.

Streeter, B. H. *The Four Gospels: A Study of Origins.* London: Macmillan, 1924.

Thompson, Michael B. "The Holy Internet: Communication Between Churches in the First Christian Generation." In *The Gospels for All Christians*, edited by Richard Bauckham, 49–70. Grand Rapids: Eerdmans, 1997.

Trebilco, Paul. *The Early Christians in Ephesus from Paul to Ignatius.* Grand Rapids: Eerdmans, 2004.

Van de Sandt, Huub, and Jürgen Zangenberg, eds. *Matthew, James, and Didache: Three Related Documents in Their Jewish and Christian Settings.* Symposium Series 45. Leiden: Brill, 2008.

Watson, Francis "Towards a Literal Reading of the Gospels." In *The Gospels for All Christians*, edited by Richard Bauckham, 195–217. Grand Rapids: Eerdmans, 1997.

Weeden, Theodore J., Sr. *Mark: Traditions in Conflict.* Philadelphia: Fortress, 1971.

Ben F. Meyer and The Gospels for All Christians

RESPONDENT: NICHOLAS PERRIN

In a welcome contribution to this volume, Jonathan Bernier puts the late Ben F. Meyer in conversation with the thesis that the gospels were written for audiences spanning the breadth of humanity (as opposed to single communities only), as advanced by Richard Bauckham and others in the collaborative volume, *The Gospels for All Christians*. As Bernier sees it, the arguments of Bauckham and Meyer are mutually reinforcing; accordingly, so our author surmises, Meyer would have assuredly embraced the proposition that the gospel-writers did indeed compose their texts with an eye to local and geographically far-ranging audiences alike. Though by its very nature a "what if?" thought experiment of this kind cannot be proven, Bernier's judgment, rendered succinctly and elegantly, is likely correct. But what I find more promising and ultimately more interesting is the author's fresh critique of the so-called "community criticism" approach, which he registers along the way. Though I may quibble with Bernier on relatively minor points here (for example, I suspect that it may be premature to be drawing up community criticism's death certificate), I am both intrigued and persuaded by the thrust of his critique. And so, by way of grateful response it would seem most productive not to dwell on isolated, trifling points but rather to extend Bernier's argument (at the risk of reiterating it), even as he has done us the service of extending the arguments of Bauckham and Meyer. However one might characterize the diversity of the early Christian movement, its constitutive local communities must have held in common at least *some* practices and beliefs that would have not only marked them off as followers of the Nazarene but also effected at least a unity of a certain kind. Unfortunately, as our author points out, it is precisely at this point that community criticism is inherently blinkered. In Bernier's words, the approach is gravely limited by its failure to provide "a conceptually robust account of the higher-level abstraction in which ... unity [despite social divides] would be constituted." This is an important insight and one that merits more consideration.

In order to understand this lacuna within the community critical approach, it will be helpful in the first instance to recognize this paradigm's filiation from form-criticism. In this connection, we may first think of Hermann Gunkel who in his study of Psalms and Genesis sought to correlate the evolution of form or genre (*Gattungsgeschichte*) with proposed *Sitze im Volksleben* ("settings in the people's life"), i.e., a recurring social setting within Israel's cultic life. According to Gunkel, once the original speaker, the audience, and the aims of the communicative act behind the text are illuminated, the critical scholar is positioned to identify a form and suggest a corresponding setting-in-life. Not many years later, Martin Dibelius would advance Gunkel's study of forms but this time on the premise that oral traditions retained an unwavering staying power resistant to the intrusion of individual tradents. Thus, for Dibelius, "The personal peculiarities of the composer or narrator have little significance; much greater importance attaches to the form in which the tradition is cast by practical necessities, by usage or by origin."[1] The differences between the two figures' approaches is more than superficial. In contrast to Gunkel, who sought to reconstruct the social setting as well as the intentions of the original speaker, Dibelius entirely rejects the relevance of the speaker's individual aims or posture, positing that any given form could be predictably and accurately matched with a specific social setting (*Sitz im Leben*) alone. On this formulation, which would prove to be far more influential than Gunkel's in the course of twentieth-century research, the discrete traditions comprising the gospels can only have been occasioned not by any concern to memorialize history nor by any interest to promulgate dogmatic commitments but rather by certain social agenda, which, in the very nature of the case, could only be hypothesized.

By the mid-twentieth century, redaction critics took over Dibelius's assumptions (initially formulated in the analysis of isolated oral traditions) and applied them without modification to the gospels as a whole, and accordingly looked to the duly reconstructed social setting (*Sitz im Evangelium*) as the singular *explanans* for their origination. Yet here it needs simply to be observed—a point made with astonishing

---

1. Dibelius, *From Tradition to Gospel*, 1.

infrequency—that if form-criticism's exclusive attention to social explanations for the discrete gospel traditions was arguably a precarious move in its own right (as Gunkel in his time insisted), then Redaction Criticism's transfer of the same principles to the very composition of the gospels is even more challenging to sustain. For while there is a certain difficulty in maintaining, as the early form-critics did, a lockstep connection between the social setting and the generation of corresponding oral forms; this difficulty is rendered all the more acute when one moves from isolated traditions to whole gospel compositions that patently reflect the shaping influence of an individual evangelist who, whether in his selection of material or in his decision to compose his gospel in the first place, may—for all we know—*not* have been constrained by any particular social setting. In short, redaction criticism facilely perpetuated Dibelius's working assumptions as if form-critical explanations for isolated traditions could be harnessed without residue in accounting for the contours and very existence of the Gospels. But if twentieth-century research into the Gospels has demonstrated anything, it has shown that the evangelists were in fact very deliberate in their shaping of materials and thus their individual impress can no longer be denied. Because the obvious intrusion of the individual composer problematizes simplistic attempts to draw a straight and unbroken line from social setting to the final form of the Gospels, the burden of warrant now falls more than ever on modern-day community criticism, at least insofar as it attempts to advance the social setting as a comprehensive explanation for the existence of the Gospels.

The interpretative consequences of all this are pernicious. By screening out ahead of time any and all putative purposes for the Gospels that cannot be related back to an immediate social concern, community criticism is virtually forced to conceive the gospel audience as being constituted along the lines of a certain social—as opposed to theological—agenda. On one level, this raises the specter of reductionism. But a further problem here is that community criticism proves to be a blunt instrument when it comes to disentangling the complex, interpenetrating polities that are dimly reflected in the Gospel narratives. To illustrate the point, I return to Bernier's observation that within any early Christian community we cannot deny the possibility, indeed the likelihood, of co-existent self-identifying *Hebraioi* and self-identifying *Hellenistai*. Given Paul's interest in Jew-Gentile relations in Rom 9–11, along with the raised issue of meat-eating that does not seem to be entirely unrelated to taxonomies of *Hebraioi* and *Hellenistai*, we might suppose that the church at Rome was one such place that exhibited a healthy mix of both cultural constituencies. Now if we agree with many scholars that Mark sent his Gospel to the Roman Church as a kind of first destination (setting aside for now the question as to whether Rome was also the Gospel's intended final destination), then we must also agree that the evangelist was self-consciously addressing not an undifferentiated mass of Christ-followers, but an audience composed of both *Hebraioi* and *Hellenistai*. But of course this particular taxonomy speaks only to one kind of diversity. Within the Roman Church there would have been other fault lines as well: gender, political persuasion (pro-Caesar, anti-Caesar, or somewhere in between), social class, slave or free (which though obviously intersecting with concerns of social class is hardly identical with it), halachic sensibility (including prescriptions regarding the eating of meat), to name only some. On applying a mirror reading evenhandedly with all these various constituencies in view, we soon discover that Mark had something to say not only to the *Hebraioi* and *Hellenistai* at Rome (as *Hebraioi* and *Hellenistai*, respectively), but also to the women as women (as suggested, for example, by the very positive characterization of women in this gospel), to the hesitant tax-payers as tax-payers (as suggested by the *Steuerfrage* contained in Mark 12:13–17), and to slaves as slaves (judging by Jesus' demand that his disciples aspire to be "servant of all") (9:35). That Mark contains material relevant to multiple constituencies such as these (and that this manifold relevance finds analogy in the three remaining gospels as well) may not necessarily invalidate the attempt to explain the Gospel with reference to only one constituency and corresponding social concern, but it does give rise to competing explanations which cannot be easily ignored. Who's to say, in other words, that Mark didn't set out to write his Gospel primarily in response to his concern that women (or slaves or tax-payers) were being denigrated? By what criteria do we come to exclude some explanations while foregrounding others?

Furthermore, by turning a blind eye to evidence within the text of a transcendent theological reference point, by which conspicuous social differences within the immediate audience might otherwise be tethered and qualified, community criticism can offer no metric for determining the relative importance of the various sociologies (*Hebraioi* versus *Hellenistai*, male versus female, wealthy versus poor, slave versus free, etc.) in play. Likewise, precisely because this approach emphasizes the text as an occasional piece (written in response to a very specific situation), it inevitably consigns itself to reconstructing a scenario on the basis of a text which, for all we know, may be giving uneven or idiosyncratic expression to the community's presenting issues. Lacking a whole in which the constitutive parts of the Gospel may be integrated, this strategy for reading the gospels is finally forced to make arguments which rely on relative degrees of emphasis within the text rather than the text as a whole.

In my judgment, the surer way forward is to suppose that the Gospels were written not for a single audience with an overarching social agenda, but for a complex amalgamation of overlapping sub-audiences, each with their own set of concerns and pastoral needs. After all, human beings are complex social animals, who have and wear different hats simultaneously, even as they claim membership within multiple demographic profiles. And once we step back to realize that the authors of the NT epistles show every indication of taking this complexity seriously, all the while supposing that the gospel-writers were no different, it becomes very difficult to assume that Gospels were intended for a strictly local audience. Without denying the likelihood that Mark wrote his Gospel primarily with a view to addressing certain social issues that presented themselves in the church at Rome, one can only imagine that Mark would have quickly agreed that his message to these particular constituencies at Rome would have been equally or at least nearly equally as useful to analogous constituencies in other locations. Thus, unless the evangelist was inexplicably short-sighted or ungenerous, one also suspects that the evangelist entertained hope that the pearls of wisdom contained in his gospel would be shared beyond the Gospel's first destination. Of course, it may be theoretically countered that Mark was unaware of communities outside of Rome, but this would be to argue the impossible. On the basis of such reasoning, I concur with Bernier: the Gospels really were indeed written "for all Christians," notwithstanding the specificity of the evangelists' immediate concerns.

This is finally underscored by the evangelistic nature of each of the Gospels (Matt 28:18–20; Mark 8:38; 14:9; Luke 1:1–4; John 20:31). While, generally speaking, community criticism invites us to imagine isolated and introverted communities hunkered down in conflict with competing sects holding to competing ideologies, each of the four gospel-writers seems to have composed on the assumption that his hearers would commend (or "translate" to use Meyer's terminology) the principles articulated in their texts to believers in other settings. In other words, if Mark indeed had something to say to women, slaves, and diffident tax-payers at Rome, we suspect that this same "something" was expected to be seen as relevant to women, slaves, and imperial citizens outside the immediate community, in faraway places such as Corinth or Ephesus. The Gospels contain the seeds of their own universality.

Mark Twain once quipped that the transatlantic reports of his death were merely an exaggeration. While Bernier's report of community criticism's death may perhaps be a slight exaggeration, I agree with him that this approach to reading the Gospels, tending to narrow reductionism, has long outlived its usefulness. Social backgrounds are certainly an important part of understanding the Gospel's genesis but they cannot hope to provide a full account. It's time to move on to a more integrative approach.

Bibliography

Dibelius, Martin. *From Tradition to Gospel*. Translated by Bertram Lee. New York: Scribner, 1935.

7

The Sociological Contours of Pauline Christianity and Implications for the Bauer Thesis

Nicholas Perrin

In his 1934 book *Rechtgläubigkeit und Ketzerei im ältesten Christentum*, Walter Bauer set forth the provocative thesis that the early Christian movement was neither as homogeneous nor as linear in development as standard accounts of the early church had previously imagined.[1] Instead, in the first two centuries of their existence the communities of Jesus-followers, largely siloed from one another across the vast Roman Empire, quickly came to reflect considerable diversity in belief and practice. It was only toward the end of the second century, with the dogmatic resolutions of certain influential figures, preeminently Irenaeus, that Christian belief as we know it today began to take its fundamental form. Toward solidifying their power, Irenaeus and his collaborators sought on the one hand to extol their own belief system as having sole affiliation with the apostles, and, on the other hand, to vilify those sects that failed to toe the new party line as misguided "Gnostics." Hoping to establish a new standard of faith through the imposition of a *regula fidei*, Irenaeus had essentially rewritten the past so as to consolidate the legitimacy of his views.[2]

---

1. The standard English translation is Kraft, *Orthodoxy and Heresy*.
2. Pagels, *Beyond Belief*, 80, for example, summarizes Irenaeus's chief challenge as follows: "Although he knew that they were scattered in many small groups throughout the world, Irenaeus shared Polycarp's hope that Christians everywhere would come

While in the initial years after its publication *Rechtgläubigkeit und Ketzerei* attracted relatively little notice, this all changed with the momentous discovery of the Nag Hammadi codices at the end of World War II, a library of texts that attested to a great diversity of Christian beliefs. Once scholars had undertaken the task of understanding the Gnostic writers on their own terms, Bauer's thesis slowly began to take on a fresh plausibility. In recent decades, with a recursive scholarly emphasis on the diversity of early Christian belief, Bauer's thesis—though not unchallenged—seems to have become the current orthodoxy within the sub-discipline of Christian Origins.[3] If the outmoded model of Christian origins envisioned a sociologically and theologically monolithic trajectory spanning from Pentecost to Nicea, today we prefer to speak of multiple "Christianities" with highly fluid and evolving boundaries. The paradigmatic vision of a trajectory spanning from the apostles to Irenaeus has been all but discarded as the vestige of outdated scholarship bewitched by the all-too tendentious Bishop of Lyons.

Of course in many respects, Bauer's vision has offered a helpful corrective, inasmuch as it has sensitized scholars of second-century Christianity to the fact that the early church was indeed a highly complex, rapidly changing phenomenon. Moreover, the voice of Bauer has effectively and appropriately relieved Irenaeus, as it were, of the duty of writing second-century history on our behalf. History by its very nature demands a critical sifting of the past, which includes a critical posture to those like Irenaeus who have a vested interest in telling their story *their* way, leaving open the possibility and indeed the likelihood of distortion. Now by hearing from both Irenaeus *and* his interlocutors, we are in a better position to make sense of the reality on the ground—not just "reality" according to Irenaeus. The dialectic comparison of sources can only make for more accurate historiography, and indeed in many ways it has.

At the same time, one may be forgiven for wondering whether the present *status quaestionis* has swung the pendulum too far in the opposite

---

to see themselves as members of a single church they called catholic, which means 'universal.'" Similarly, Ehrman, *Lost Christianities*, extends the thesis of Campenhausen (*viz.*, that the proto-orthodox interest in canonization was in direct response to Marcion) and applies it to Irenaeus's injunction.

3. Even so, the accumulated criticisms of Bauer have been substantial. See Hartog, *Orthodoxy and Heresy*; Köstenberger and Kruger, *Heresy of Orthodoxy*; Desjardins, "Bauer and Beyond," 65–82; Robinson, *Bauer Thesis Examined*; McCue, "Orthodoxy and Heresy," 23–44; Betz, "Orthodoxy and Heresy," 299–311; Turner, *Pattern of Christian Truth*.

direction. In other words, with repetitive use of words like "tolerant" and "diverse" in our modern-day descriptions of the second-century milieu (terms that, interestingly enough, are common parlance in contemporary discourse), it may be asked whether modern-day historians have removed the speck from the eye of the heresiologists only to ignore a plank in our own. If the commonly received tradition, so dependent on Irenaeus's narrative of a uniform development, has erroneously tended to interpret first- and second-century Christianity as a monolithic socio-religious entity, how can we be so sure that the current project of correcting this totalizing narrative has not over-compensated?

In this essay, I intend to make a small contribution to this question by examining the social contours of earliest Christianity, insofar as these can be reconstructed from a limited set of sources, namely, the four so-called "capital epistles" of the Apostle Paul (Galatians, 1 Corinthians, 2 Corinthians, and Romans). By restricting myself to these four unquestionably Pauline letters, addressed to three different sets of communities (the churches in Galatia, Corinth, and Rome), I not only limit the scope of my inquiry to manageable proportions but also avoid the inevitable second-guessing (with attendant implications of authorship and dating) that might otherwise bedevil a study of a wider Pauline canon.[4] My thesis is quite simple. Whereas proponents of the Bauer thesis have generally assumed that the earliest Christian movement(s) were characterized by a high degree of autonomy and independence on a local level, with little if any overarching structure that might lend the discrete communities a shared unity, I wish to argue that the situation in Paul's day (the earliest recoverable Christianity) witnesses to a quite different reality. On a sober assessment of the data drawn from these four epistles, it appears that despite the immense geographical and cultural distances separating the churches under Paul's jurisdiction, these same communities exhibited an extraordinarily high degree of interconnectivity, characterized and sustained by a social, theological, and structural unity centered around the apostolic office.

---

4. Perhaps a criticism of this kind might be leveled at Hvalvik, "All Those Who in Every Place," 123–43, who makes use of Acts and a much broader Pauline canon as his evidentiary base. Even so, in many respects my argument and my overall conclusion come close to his. For the purposes of this essay, I will assume standard critical datings of Romans and the Corinthian correspondence, while recusing from the controverted question of Galatians' provenance and dating. None of these factors materially impact my argument.

Social Unity

While each of Paul's local communities obviously constituted a social system in its own right, the question is whether and to what degree these same associations thought of themselves as being meaningfully interconnected with similar bodies formed in the wake of the apostle's missionary activity. Unfortunately, all we have is Paul's side of the conversation, as it were; as a result, history leaves us no *direct* record of how these societies thought about themselves, much less how they reflected on like-minded societies. Even so, within the four capital epistles one cannot go far before stumbling across all kinds of clues pointing to a highly cohesive alliance between the Pauline churches.

The first set of clues relates to Paul's habit of using familial metaphors in reference to his audiences, more specifically, sibling metaphors involving the terms "brother" (ἀδελφός) and "sister" (ἀδελφή). Within Romans, 1 and 2 Corinthians, and Galatians, the former term occurs some 58 times; the latter, 45 times. Needless to say, for Paul as well as for other early Christian writers, "brother(s)" and "sister(s)" served as the standard designations for the messianic adherents; such terms reinforced a fictive kinship that had become fundamental to early Christian self-identity.[5] Paul's sibling language was grounded in the redemptive event, for, according to the apostle, it was precisely through the redemption wrought by Jesus Christ the Son that the Galatian believers received the rights of sonship: "for in Christ Jesus you are all children (υἱοί) of God through faith. As many of you as were baptized into Christ have clothed yourselves with Christ" (Gal 3:26-27). Likewise, if the believers' shared "sonship" retained a Christological significance, it also entailed a pneumatological aspect, for only those "who are led by the Spirit of God are children of God" (Rom 8:14). In Paul's mind, Spirit and sonship were so closely tied that he was even able to refer to the former as the "spirit of adoption (υἱοθεσίας)" (v. 15). Undeniably, the basis for Paul's fraternal relations with the believers at Rome, Corinth, and Galatia was the redemptive action of the triune God.

For Paul this fictive kinship, rather than being tied to a local social structure or otherwise geographically restricted, reflected an objective reality that obtained across the breadth of the churches. This is exactly why

---

5. The scholarship on Paul's fraternal metaphor is not insubstantial; see Punt, "He Is Heavy," 153-71; Hodge, *If Sons, Then Heirs*; Aasgaard, "Role Ethics in Paul," 513-30; Bartchy, "Undermining Ancient Patriarchy, 68-78.

in his correspondence with the Corinthian believers the apostle does not hesitate to call the non-Corinthian Apollos "*our* brother" (1 Cor 16:12). For the same reason, again in correspondence with the Corinthians, Paul readily refers to believers in regions to the north as mutual "brothers" (2 Cor 9:3–5; 11:9). Meanwhile, in his letter to the Galatians, Paul designates his coauthors as "all the brothers [in Judea] with me" (Gal 1:2). My point is very basic but nonetheless important: while Paul's notional family certainly includes his addressees along with himself, his application of sibling language to third parties in other churches implies that the believers across the scope of his mission field are no less fraternally related to one another than they are to Paul.

Not merely a theoretical construct, Paul's notional kinship exerted a shaping force on his ethical vision for the local communities (cf. e.g., Rom 14:1–18), even as it defined relationships between the various churches scattered throughout the Roman Empire, as evident not least in the mutual interest shared by the churches at the apostle's encouragement. When Paul relates that the faith of the Romans is being reported "all over the world" (Rom 1:8), it is unlikely that this means that the masses in the religiously differentiated Roman society were spreading news of the Romans' newfound faith. Rather, such reports would have probably been circulated among the synagogues of the Diaspora, as well as among the Pauline churches "from Jerusalem all the way around to Illyricum" (Rom 15:19). The apostle himself served as a conduit of information between the churches (2 Cor 8:1–7; 9:1–2), as one might expect. But, again, Paul's habit of bringing information from one church to another could have no perceived relevance apart from a preexisting interest on the part of those receiving said information. This in turn implies a preexisting network.[6]

More obvious evidence of such a network is forthcoming in Paul's project of gathering a collection for the saints in Jerusalem.[7] In the Corinthian correspondence, Paul speaks of the collection not as a new item of business but as a highly coordinated effort that had been long in the making (1 Cor 16:1–4). The apostle's passing remarks regarding the contributions of the Galatians (v. 1b) and the Macedonians (2 Cor 8:3–5) likewise indicate that all the churches within his remit had been well apprised of the collection's broad geographical scope. When Paul mentions

---

6. As has been argued out more fully in Thompson, "Holy Internet," 49–70.

7. While I prefer to think of the offering as evidence of preexisting networks, many, like Ogereau, "Jerusalem Collection," 360–78, see Paul's collection as a deliberate strategy for building unity.

the collection to the Romans (Rom 15:25–33), he gives the impression that the Roman believers had already been privy to the project, implying preexistent, effective channels of communication between Rome and her sister churches to its east. The concerted effort of the Jerusalem collection presupposed a concerted chain of communication, sustained in turn by a high-functioning relational network operating between the churches. The collection itself would have only reinforced such links.[8]

The personal greetings that Paul offers in several of his letters underscore the point further. For example, when Paul asks the Romans both to receive Phoebe of Cenchrea (coming as she was from outside of Corinth) (Rom 16:1–2) and to greet Priscilla and Aquila (Rom 16:3), active in Ephesus, this reflects a scenario in which internationally mobile believers from far-flung lands were taking advantage of one another's hospitality. Of course, neither Phoebe nor Priscilla and Aquila are the exception. The laundry list of names in Paul's greeting demonstrates an ongoing exchange of individuals between churches situated at considerable geographical distance from one another. The obvious frequency of such reciprocal movements bespeaks a tight-knit network characterized by high levels of communication and strong inter-ecclesial relationships.

In sum, the historical record confirms that the Pauline churches enjoyed considerable social cohesiveness, as a result of—perhaps among other factors—regular communication and the exchange of personnel. Though this social interconnectivity was obviously encouraged by Paul and enhanced at his initiative, we have the sense that by the early to mid-50s the relationships between the churches seem to have taken on a life of their own, quite apart from apostolic mediation. As best as we can tell, Paul's language of kinship approximated an experiential reality that was being achieved through and apart from his own initiative.

Structural Unity

Whatever the merits of the Bauer thesis, one of its conspicuous weaknesses lies in its failure to account for evidence that the apostles deliberately

---

8. Downs, *Offering of the Gentiles*, 18, similarly observes: "While the monetary collection for Jerusalem undoubtedly exemplified the solidarity of Jewish and Gentile believers, it has not often been observed that the collection also served to strengthen ties between the separate Gentile churches of the Pauline mission spread across the cities of the Eastern Mediterranean." See also Hvalik, "All Those Who in Every Place," 141–42.

set out to integrate local expressions of Christianity within a global organizational structure. Of course, the universal reach of the apostles' vision comes into its own only after the conversion of Saul (Paul), a watershed moment that eventually leads to a parsing of mission fields, leaving Paul and the Gentiles on the one side and the rest of the apostles and Judaism on the other. In his letter to the Galatians, Paul recounts his early exchanges with the Jerusalem-based apostolate:

> On the contrary, when they saw that I had been entrusted with the gospel for the uncircumcised, just as Peter had been entrusted with the gospel for the circumcised (for he who worked through Peter making him an apostle to the circumcised also worked through me in sending me to the Gentiles), and when James and Cephas and John, who were acknowledged pillars, recognized the grace that had been given to me, they gave to Barnabas and me the right hand of fellowship, agreeing that we should go to the Gentiles and they to the circumcised. They asked only one thing, that we remember the poor, which was actually what I was eager to do.[9]

While one might be tempted to interpret this parsing of missional responsibilities as having been driven by purely pragmatic concerns (as if the apostles were merely trying to find a way of avoiding stepping on one another's toes), this would be to overlook the more fundamental redemptive-historical grid through which Paul had come to understand his own conversion and vocation. Earlier in the same epistle, Paul speaks of the God "who set me apart before I was born and called me through his grace" being "pleased to reveal his Son to me, so that I might proclaim him among the Gentiles" (Gal 1:16–17). Whether or not Matthew Harmon is correct in his contention that this phrasing invokes the Servant of Isaiah 49, who is tasked to be a light to the nations, enough commentators have detected Isaianic servant allusions elsewhere in Galatians, not to mention Romans and 2 Corinthians—allusions that identify the servant not with Jesus but with Paul.[10] While I will prescind from the question as to whether Paul's mystical union with the servant (Gal 2:20) was *the* notional point of departure for his mission to the Gentiles, it is enough for the present purposes to show that Isaiah's servant narrative provided an important framework for Paul's apostolic self-understanding.

---

9. Gal 2:7–10.

10. Harmon, *She Must*, 119; Das, *Paul and the Stories*, 235; Gignilliat, "Servant Follower," 98–124; Wagner, *Heralds of the Good News, passim*.

Situating Paul's Gentile mission against the backdrop of Isaiah's servant cycle, we come to appreciate not only the universality of Paul's mission but also its exclusivity. The apostle understood his mission to be *universal* insofar as he, as the embodiment of the Isaianic servant, had been mandated to proclaim the gospel to the nations with a view to bringing about the end of exile and the worldwide worship of the one true God. In the scriptural logic, "the nations" were not a subset within the larger categories of non-Israelite peoples but encompassed the whole gamut of humanity. Accordingly, Paul saw himself as the recipient of "grace and apostleship to bring about the obedience of faith *among all the Gentiles* (ἐν πᾶσιν τοῖς ἔθνεσιν)" (Rom 1:5; cf. v. 13). At the same time, Paul also recognized his role (i.e., as apostle to the Gentiles) as *exclusively* his own. This recognition followed not least from his conviction that, although there was some sense in which he shared his servant identity with the rank and file messianic believers, the mission to the Gentiles ultimately fell uniquely to him, as a singular extension of the suffering and now risen servant, Jesus Christ (Rom 15:15-21).[11] Any and all expressions of Christ-devotion outside the boundaries of ethnic Judaism, therefore, finally fell into Paul's area of responsibility and scope of authority.

Paul's exclusive responsibility for the Gentiles is borne out repeatedly in his writings. For example, in comparing himself with a builder laying a foundation, Paul insists that "each builder must choose with care how to build on it. For no one can lay any foundation other than the one that has been laid . . . Jesus Christ" (1 Cor 3:10b-11). If there is one and only one foundation, then the means by which such building is to be accomplished are likewise unique, namely, the apostolic "grace of God given to me" (v. 10a). In Rom 16, the apostle closes by issuing greetings on behalf of "all the churches of Christ" (Rom 16:16), not, it seems, because the churches had one-by-one actually requested Paul to extend their salutations but because as a matter of course he forthrightly spoke on behalf of all the churches, as their representative head. The same logic seems to be at play in his claim that Gaius is "host to me and to the whole church" (Rom 16:23). I take the construction to be epexegetical, hinting that if the Romans accept the responsibility of hosting Paul *en route* to

---

11. Though I agree with Clarke, "Source and Scope, 3-22, that Paul at many points self-limits the force and scope of his authority, and in this sense Paul's authority is "precisely constrained"; Clarke fails to substantiate—against a raft of counter-evidence—his larger claim that Paul's authority was "neither unique, nor absolute, nor universal" (6).

Spain, they will—like Gaius—by the same token receive the same honor as Gaius, namely, the honor of hosting the whole church incorporated within Paul's person. This is consistent with the apostle's self-presentation in Romans: Paul's personal (perhaps even bodily, cf. Col 1:24) incorporation of the Gentiles is already implied in his priestly role on behalf of the Gentiles (Rom 15:16), for in Jewish thought priests were thought to represent the laity in an incorporative sense.

In practical terms, Paul's apostolic standing established his teaching and way of life as the embodiment of the *kerygma*. This is why he can be so bold as to say, "Be imitators of me, as I am of Christ" (1 Cor 11:1).[12] In the same passage, we further learn that such imitation is meant to include specific practices: "I commend you because you remember me in everything and maintain the traditions (παραδόσεις) just as I handed them on to you" (v. 2). Such traditions obviously include the Lord's Supper (vv. 23–34), but also the practice of head-coverings (vv. 3–16). Paul's instructions regarding the head-coverings are especially illuminating, especially where we find the apostle closing out his argument with this admonition: "But if anyone is disposed to be contentious—we (ἡμεῖς) have no such custom, nor do the churches of God" (v. 16). The apostles' approach to head-coverings, it seems, had become the norm for the "churches of God," and was therefore likewise to function as the norm for the Corinthians' worship. In Paul's mind, the Corinthians' obligation to conform could be settled by an appeal to the intersection of apostolic judgment and ecclesial consensus.

If Paul's apostolic role entailed, in positive terms, an authority to determine boundaries of acceptable practice and belief, it also implied, negatively, the right to excommunicate. Paul threatens no less in the opening line of his letter to the Galatians, when he places an anathema over the heads of those who dare preach "another gospel" (Gal 1:8–9). Far from being a hyperbolic outburst, Paul's language of cursing is an effective speech act by which he intends to ban any and all—humans and angels—should they chose to proclaim an errant gospel. A similar drawing of boundary lines occurs in Paul's invocation of peace on Israel, that is, the true worshipping people of God who resist the Judaizers by

---

12. Ellington, "Imitating Paul's Relationship," 303–15, has rightly argued that Paul's surrendering of rights is at the heart of this imitation. Yet because for Paul these sufferings are part and parcel of his apostolic calling, one suspects there are limits to this imitation, even as they are obvious limits to the apostle's imitation of Christ. See also Dodd, *Paul's Paradigmatic "I"*; Castelli, *Imitating Paul*; DeBoer, *Imitation of Paul*.

eschewing works of the law (Gal 6:16). More explicit reference to excommunication is found in 1 Corinthians, in the case of a man who is having relations with his father's wife (1 Cor 5:1–5). In that case, Paul has "already pronounced judgment" as though he were present (v. 3). Paul's preemptive casting of judgment, quite apart from the actual or potential decision of the Corinthians, suggests that the decisions of local ecclesial courts were in the final analysis but as an extension of apostolic adjudication. As in Galatians, Paul closes this letter with a ban on those who have "no love for the Lord" (16:22), a stern summary of the moral wake-up call Paul has just issued in the substance of 1 Corinthians.

By way of summary, the biblical data suggests that Paul thought of his mission to the Gentiles as being an exclusive undertaking that was all-inclusive in its scope.[13] That Paul would countenance the possibility of Gentile mission apart from his *final* oversight, as Bauer suggests, is belied by the evidence.[14] Paul's apostolic office seems to have entailed the authority not only to set ethical standards of faith and practice, but also to draw the ecclesial boundary lines, so as to separate those who belong from those who do not belong to the Israel of God. In these respects, Paul circumscribed diasporic Christian faith within his own person. Even if the gospel took root in places that had not profited directly from Paul's preaching (at Rome, for example), this hardly obviates the apostle's own conviction that any and all legitimate forms of Diasporic Christianity were necessarily, in a structural sense, extensions of Pauline Christianity.

Cognitive Unity

Having considered evidence of the tight-knit social fabric of the Pauline churches, as well as their subordination beneath the apostle's aegis, it is appropriate to reflect on the distinguishing content of the gospel faith (*fides quae creditur*), at least as far as Paul was concerned. Although there were, one imagines, regional and local differences in how the various churches

---

13. The remarks of Ehrenspreger, *Paul and the Dynamics*, 91, are *a propos*: "Paul does perceive himself and his colleagues as empowered to take on leadership roles within the Christ-movement. This is a claim to power in the sense of exercising power over the communities—but keeping in mind that the message encompasses the proclamation of Christ crucified—and resonates with prophetic topics, the apostles' exercise of power must be analyzed in light of this. Self-enhancement through such an understanding of power then seems contradictory to the context of the message itself."

14. Bauer, *Orthodoxy and Heresy*, 232–37.

expressed their faith, even as Paul allowed some personal latitude in matters of *adiaphora* (e.g., in relation to convictions regarding meat-eating) on an individual level, the capital epistles clearly demonstrate Paul's expectation that believers within his church would subscribe to certain tenets as nonnegotiable articles of faith. While it is beyond the scope of this essay to explore *exactly* how these central beliefs might figure into the larger structure of the apostle's theology (an ongoing enterprise in its own right), it is enough to note their importance, not just for Paul but for individual community members intending to remain in the good graces of the enfranchised leadership.

Returning to the Galatian crisis and Paul's reflections on it, one need only note that for the apostle the stakes involved in the dispute between the "from faith" (ἐκ πίστεως) party and the opposing "from works of the law" (ἐξ ἔργων νόμου) party could not have been greater. The issue at hand was not merely the practice of circumcision, which in Paul's mind was neither here nor there (Gal 5:6a), but the specific theological entailments of the practice, as it was being implemented in the Galatian context. From the apostle's viewpoint, the entailments were indeed so far-reaching and potentially deleterious that the gospel's efficacy among the Galatian convert believers hung in the balance:

> I am astonished that you are so quickly deserting the one who called you in the grace of Christ and are turning to a different gospel—not that there is another gospel, but there are some who are confusing you and want to pervert the gospel of Christ. But even if we or an angel from heaven should proclaim to you a gospel contrary to what we proclaimed to you, let that one be accursed! As we have said before, so now I repeat, if anyone proclaims to you a gospel contrary to what you received, let that one be accursed![15]

By subjecting Gentile converts to the requirement of circumcision, the Judaizers were exchanging Paul's gospel for a false gospel, poised to infiltrate the Galatian churches. To counter this possibility, as noted above, Paul imposes a conditional, solemn execration as a means of implementing a ban on the Judaizers and their supporters. Given the angels' traditionally exalted role as revelatory mediators, especially in apocalyptic Judaism, Paul's hypothetical execration against angels is remarkable (Gal 1:8). Yet perhaps even more striking is the imagined possibility that Paul

---

15. Gal 1:6–9.

and his coworkers ("we") should incur the force of his own curse by preaching a false gospel, for after all, Paul was in some sense the originator of the kerygma received by the Galatians. If nothing else, the terms of the execration reveal that Paul saw the core of his gospel as an objective deposit unconditioned by subsequent apostolic pronouncement. In this sense, Paul's apostolic authority was transcended only by the gospel itself.

Paul's ascription of insuperable authority to the gospel as an objective, self-contained theological assertion renders it extremely difficult to maintain, as the old History of Religions School has done, that the apostle's kerygma was radically shaped by his re-contextualizing the message within the contingent thought-forms of the Hellenistic religions. The same approach is even more difficult to sustain, given the profoundly narratival character of Paul's gospel, especially as it relates to the Corinthians:

> For I handed on to you as of first importance what I in turn had received: that Christ died for our sins in accordance with the Scriptures, and that he was buried, and that he was raised on the third day in accordance with the Scriptures, and that he appeared to Cephas, then to the twelve. Then he appeared to more than five hundred brothers and sisters at one time, most of whom are still alive, though some have died.[16]

The narrative entrusted to Paul clearly operates on two levels. In the first place, Paul insists that the very bedrock of his message consisted of the handed-down, emplotted traditions regarding Jesus' death and resurrection (including post-resurrection appearances). In the second place, the same chain of events also fulfilled a certain prior narrative (or set of narratives) contained in the Hebrew Scriptures. Given Paul's recollection, it appears that the two narratives had already been correlated in the pre-Pauline apostolic traditioning process. And if the Jerusalem community had already interpreted the key events of Jesus' death and resurrection in scriptural terms well before Paul's admission to its ranks, then this interpretative summary would have likewise been infused with an authority to which even the apostle to the Gentiles would have been expected to accede—notwithstanding his insistence to have received his gospel "not from men" but from God (Gal 1:1). Thus, from the very start the gospel contained an irreducible, inviolable content, which Paul could only steward.

---

16. 1 Cor 15:3-6.

Even if scholars disagree as to the precise dating of Paul's early Jerusalem meetings, depending of course on how one chooses to coordinate the reported events of Galatians and Acts, it is nonetheless obvious from 1 Cor 15 that the apostle agreed to integrate the Jerusalem gospel into his own gospel as a matter of "first importance," that is, as an invariable datum immune to subsequent revision. In the course of his missionary journeys, therefore, Paul would presumably recur to the same basic narrative as a kind of common founding narrative for his planted churches. Although Pauline studies may debate the precise content of this pre-established narrative (assuming that 1 Cor 15 only preserves the highlights of much more thorough oral tradition), the very existence of the narrative itself means that the Pauline churches would have been forced, time and time again, to distinguish between its legitimate and illegitimate construals. Such distinctions were necessary in the very nature of the case, given Paul's insistence that accession to the narrative was a *sine qua non* of community membership. On the apostle's description, his very reception of the gospel narrative from the Jerusalem community implied the necessity of carefully perpetuating the account—as a kind of *norma normans non normata*—through an ongoing process of transmission. Whether or not he expected his churches to attend to that perpetuation beyond his own time cannot be proven, but remains, I think, the best surmise.

While Walter Bauer has contended that Paul "scarcely knows what a heretic might be," this contention is certainly hopelessly far from the mark.[17] The historical evidence suggests that Paul not only knew what a heretic might be, but expected his churches to know as well—and to take action accordingly. Not that Paul and his churches had worked out all the boundary lines separating orthodoxy and heresy. But lines there were, and as far as we can tell, these were taken very seriously.

Conclusion

In this essay, I have sought to demonstrate the social, structural, and cognitive unity of the churches that had coalesced under Paul's leadership. By all accounts, the picture that emerges from the so-called capital epistles is one that involves not so much an array of discrete "Christianities" but a fairly monolithic socioreligious reality, more appropriately designated as a singular Pauline Christianity. Obviously, while it cannot be ruled

---

17. Bauer, *Orthodoxy and Heresy*, 234.

out that the gospel seeds sown by Paul may have fallen into fallow fields beyond his reach or awareness, giving rise to separate bodies that thrived outside of the association of churches more directly associated with the apostle; such independent communities, if they existed at all, must have been something of an outlier. The tight mesh connecting the Pauline churches—palpable through their robust intercommunication, shared answerability to apostolic oversight, and enjoined obligation to doctrinal and practical purity—would have naturally induced the apostles and the leading elders stationed at the various churches to flag up such detached communities and enfold them into the existing network. Indeed, nothing less would have been appropriate, given the universal scope of Paul's singular vocation.

Of course, the description of Pauline Christianity offered here would not have obtained for the network of churches as the communities negotiated life in the post-Pauline, post-apostolic era. The void created by Paul's death would have certainly entailed significant structural changes for the churches, in terms of both their self-governance and their mutual relations. As for the nature of those changes, we can only guess, for the transition from apostolic Christianity to the second century remains largely shrouded in mystery. At the same time, if the Bauer thesis is to be credible at all, it must explain how it came about that the Diaspora churches of the late first century chose to forgo its principal commitments, first, to preserve the kerygmatic narrative, and second, to maintain mutual relationships with one another. The Bauer thesis also asks us to believe that the association of Pauline churches had undergone radical balkanization between the apostle's day and the second century. But until evidence for such a transformation is forthcoming, and the Christian literature from the early second century hardly advances this hypothesis, we are best served surmising that early Christianity was not—as we have been so often told in recent years—characterized by a radical diversity, but rather by a diversity expressing itself within a basic sociological unity, notwithstanding the cyclical realities of schism and apostasy. This sociological unity is finally explicable as a result of the theological and structural unity achieved through Paul's ministry in the mid-first century.

Bibliography

Aasgaard, Reidar. "'Role Ethics' in Paul: The Significance of the Sibling Role for Paul's Ethical Thinking." *New Testament Studies* 48 (2002) 513–30.

Bartchy, S. Scott. "Undermining Ancient Patriarchy: The Apostle Paul's Vision of a Society of Siblings." *Biblical Theology Bulletin* 29 (1999) 68–78.

Bauer, Walter. *Orthodoxy and Heresy in Earliest Christianity.* Edited by Robert Kraft and Gerhard Krodels. Philadelphia: Fortress, 1971.

Betz, Hans Dieter. "Orthodoxy and Heresy in Primitive Christianity." *Interpretation* 19 (1965) 299–311.

Castelli, Elizabeth A. *Imitating Paul: A Discourse on Power.* Literary Currents in Biblical Interpretation. Louisville: Westminster John Knox, 1991.

Clarke, Andrew D. "The Source and Scope of Paul's Apostolic Authority." *Criswell Theological Review* 12 (2015), 3–22.

Das, A. Andrew. *Paul and the Stories of Israel: Grand Thematic Narratives in Galatians.* Minneapolis: Fortress, 2016.

DeBoer, Willis Peter. *Imitation of Paul: An Exegetical Study.* Kampen: Kok, 1962.

Desjardins, Michel R. "Bauer and Beyond: On Recent Scholarly Discussions of *Haeresis* in the Early Christian Era." *Second Century* 8 (1991) 65–82.

Dodd, Brian J. *Paul's Paradigmatic "I": Personal Example as Literary Strategy.* Journal for the Study of the New Testament Supplement 177. Sheffield: Sheffield Academic, 1999.

Downs, David J. *The Offering of the Gentiles: Paul's Collection for Jerusalem in Its Chronological, Culture, and Cultic Contexts.* Grand Rapids: Eerdmans, 2016.

Ehrenspreger, Kathy. *Paul and the Dynamics of Power: Communication and Interaction in the Early Christ-Movement.* Library of New Testament Studies 325. London: T. & T. Clark, 2009.

Ehrman, Bart D. *Lost Christianities: The Battle for Scripture and the Faiths We Never Knew.* New York: Oxford University Press, 2003.

Ellington, Dustin Watson. "Imitating Paul's Relationship to the Gospel: 1 Corinthians 8.1–11.1." *Journal for the Study of the New Testament* 33 (2011) 303–15.

Gignilliat, Mark. "A Servant Follower of the Servant: Paul's Eschatological Reading of Isaiah 40–66 in 2 Corinthians 5:14–6:10." *Horizons in Biblical Theology* 26 (2004) 98–124.

Harmon, Matthew S. *She Must and Shall Go Free: Paul's Isaianic Gospel in Galatians.* BZNW 168. Berlin: de Gruyter, 2010.

Hartog, Paul. *Orthodoxy and Heresy in Early Christian Contexts: Reconsidering the Bauer Thesis.* Cambridge: James Clarke, 2015.

Hodge, Caroline E. Johnson. *If Sons, Then Heirs: A Study of Kinship and Ethnicity in the Letters of Paul.* New York: Oxford University Press, 2007.

Hvalvik, Reidar. "All Those Who in Every Place Call on the Name of Our Lord Jesus Christ." In *The Formation of the Early Church*, edited by Jostein Ådna, 123–43. WUNT 183. Tübingen: Mohr Siebeck, 2005.

Köstenberger, Andreas J., and Michael J. Kruger. *The Heresy of Orthodoxy: How Contemporary Culture's Fascination with Diversity Has Reshaped Our Understanding of Early Christianity.* Wheaton, IL: Crossway, 2010.

Kraft, Robert. *Orthodoxy and Heresy in Earliest Christianity*. Philadelphia: Fortress, 1971.

McCue, James F. "Orthodoxy and Heresy: Walter Bauer and the Valentinians." *Vigiliae Christianae* 33 (1979) 118–30.

Norris, Frederick W. "Ignatius, Polycarp, and I Clement: Walter Bauer Reconsidered." *Vigiliae Christianae* 30 (1976) 23–44.

Ogereau, Julien M. "The Jerusalem Collection as Κοινωνία: Paul's Global Politics of Socio-Economic Equality and Solidarity." *New Testament Studies* 58 (2012) 360–78.

Pagels, Elaine. *Beyond Belief: The Secret Gospel of Thomas*. New York: Random House, 2003.

Punt, Jeremy. "He Is Heavy . . . He's My Brother: Unravelling Fraternity in Paul (Galatians)." *Neotestamentica* 46 (2012) 153–71.

Robinson, Thomas A. *The Bauer Thesis Examined: The Geography of Heresy in the Early Christian Church*. Studies in the Bible and Early Christianity. Lewiston, NY: Edwin Mellen, 1988.

Thompson, Michael B. "The Holy Internet: Communication between Churches in the First Christian Generation." In *The Gospels for All Christians: Rethinking the Gospel Audiences*, edited by Richard Bauckham, 49–70. Grand Rapids: Eerdmans, 1998.

Turner, Henry Ernest William. *Pattern of Christian Truth: A Study in the Relations between Orthodoxy and Heresy in the Early Church*. Bampton Lectures. London: Mowbray, 1954.

Wagner, J. Ross. *Heralds of the Good News: Isaiah and Paul "in Concert" in the Letter to the Romans*. Novum Testamentum Supplements 101. Leiden: Brill, 2002.

Pauline Churches: How Diverse? How Homogeneous?

Respondent: John Harrison

Nicholas Perrin takes exception to the popular trend among scholars of early Christianity that has stressed the diversity of Pauline churches to the extent that those churches are customarily imagined as "largely siloed from one another across the vast Roman Empire." This trend Perrin sees as the "current orthodoxy within the sub-discipline of Christian Origins" with its demand that all reconstructions of earliest Christianity be more accurate by acknowledging "Christianities" that were fluid and evolving in faith and doctrine.

Walter Bauer, whom Perrin credits as the original push to accentuate earliest Christianity's diversity, was concerned that historians primarily were giving an uncritical position of authority to those who advocated doctrines that later became known as "orthodoxy." Historians, Bauer believed, were prejudging the diversity of variant representations of Christianity as examples of "heresies" because that is how they were viewed by Irenaeus and other so-called "orthodox" authors. He was challenging the scholarship of earliest Christianity in his day to let the other voices be heard more sympathetically than they were by those deemed to be "church fathers." Bauer argued that it might just be possible that what was later denounced as "heresies" by the dominant figures in the church in the second century were closer in teaching to the original (and only) expression of the Jesus-followers.

More to the point of Perrin's issue with Bauer's approach is what Bauer claimed about the lack of any established orthodoxy even among Pauline churches. Hardly any historian today would claim that every person who confessed Jesus as Lord in the churches associated with Paul believed and thought exactly as Paul did or were expected to do so. That straw man is not even under consideration. But what is questioned is the extent of diversity and homogeneity among them that Paul presupposed and even permitted.

Of course historically diversity among believers had to have existed. It would seem highly improbable that precise uniformity could be enshrined as the gospel moved from group to group even within the same location, not to mention across the regions surrounding the Mediterranean. But has the acceptance of diversity as a common occurrence in various social Christian groups adversely affected New Testament scholars to obscure or minimize evidence of any connections that believers in the one Jesus Christ believed they had? Despite their differing ways of theologizing about who Jesus is, what his death did, how believers should organize themselves as a community, what expectations should be of the Holy Spirit's activities, how they should express their identity as followers of Jesus, and what behaviors were permitted and prohibited for the faithful, what degree of connectedness did believers think they had with other believers in the world? It is not Perrin's aim to contest the existence of diversity among first century believers, but he does contend that the evidence found in Paul's letters shows an interconnectedness despite diversity that argues for a more homogenous relationship than is often expressed by those influenced by Bauer's thesis that challenged previous assumption of widespread uniformity in early Christianity.

The evidence Perrin sees in the undisputed or capital epistles from Paul (Galatians, 1 and 2 Corinthians, and Romans) is not supportive of "siloed" churches but rather is evidence that points to communities of believers who had an "extraordinarily high degree of interconnectivity, characterized and sustained by a social, theological, and structural unity."[1] This unity, he further claims, is centered on the "apostolic office," by which Perrin is not referring to Paul's specific apostolic office (which is

---

1. While I believe Perrin is correct that the evidence in Paul's letters points to a presumed interconnectivity among the Pauline churches, I do not see the parallels for the suggestion that the evidence shows this interconnectivity was of a "high degree" or shows a "highly cohesive alliance." What rubric will have to be adopted by which interconnectivity can be identified in specific degrees? Perrin's essay successfully challenges recent trends to obscure or minimize homogeneity, but he hasn't provided the type of parallels that would demonstrate Paul's understanding of his churches' connectivity is "high" or "higher" in comparison with the connectivity that might have been assumed among other non-Pauline churches, if such evidence could be isolated.

the only office of which Paul typically reminded these letters' recipients)[2] but the office held by all of those who were called to be Christ's apostles.

The evidence that Perrin believes substantiates his claims for more homogeneity among the Pauline churches is separated under three categories: indicators of an existing corporate self-identification of believers in separate locations, indicators of a global organizational structure expected to be accepted and formative upon local church structure, and finally indicators of specific tenets of faith that were treated as nonnegotiable for all believers to uphold and defend. The value of Perrin's essay is that he sheds light on several neglected features within the discussion of how much shared identity the different Christian communities may have experienced. But I want to respond by providing a closer evaluation of the extent the evidence Perrin cites for each category strengthens the validity of his overall argument. Some of the evidence Perrin argues for in his thesis, as I will suggest, is consistent with the direction he takes readers but does not lead to identifying a level of perceived connectedness among Pauline churches that he wants to claim.

Corporate Self-Identity in the Pauline Churches

Does the fraternal language, so common in the capital letters of Paul, indicate that these communities are more homogenous than frequently depicted? Because Christians in Galatia, Corinth, or Rome were expected by Paul to think of themselves as "brothers" or "sisters" (*adelphoi*), did that mean they might have perceived a high level of interconnectedness with believers elsewhere that would have assisted them in preventing substantial theological diversity? The question I am posing is, how does the repeated use of "fictive kinship" language such as "brothers" and "sisters" show that Pauline churches are more homogenous than commonly accepted by the "current orthodoxy"? Put another way, does such language show that the Pauline churches held a "highly cohesive alliance"? Is such language indicative of a unity that Perrin believes was "an objective reality" that would have been acquired by all of the Pauline churches?

"Fictive kinship" language occurs throughout ancient literature.[3] Most occurrences of this language would suggest that a group thought of

---

2. Rom 1:1; 1 Cor 1:1; 2 Cor 1:1; 11:5; Gal 1:1, 11; 2:10.

3. Aasgaard, "Brotherhood in Plutarch and Paul"; Esler, "Keeping It in the Family"; Harland, "Familial Dimensions," 492–93.

itself as bonded together into a small tight-knit community.[4] The idea of their community made up of "brothers" and "sisters" would have generated expectations of solidarity, loyalty, and mutual care. Paul would have most likely expected the same among his converts. But other individuals used the kinship language to promote the idea of certain groups of people seeing themselves connected to others in far more general ways.[5] When Acts 2:37 reports that the apostles' audience of Jews from all over the Mediterranean respond after Peter's speech with the question, "Brothers, what shall we do?," they are not using the fraternal metaphor because they have a very close community with the followers of Jesus. They are merely describing their connection with the apostles as fellow Jews. So what has not yet been shown by Perrin's examples from the capital letters of Paul is the extent of that sense of connectedness believers would have had with others who lived further afield. My hesitation with this particular argument in his thesis is that one person might use kinship language for another person in another location (e.g., a male believer in Corinth might call male and female believers in Rome his *adelphoi*) but may have had very little sense of connectedness to that person in terms of solidarity and loyalty to a whole range of theological issues. In other words, they might share a common belief in who Jesus Christ is (like the audience on Pentecost are connected to the apostles in terms of their identity in Israel) but the designation might not indicate a great deal of solidarity and loyalty with that distant believer as they would more likely have with ones within their immediate community.

Paul's use of kinship metaphors for his small communities of believers in Jesus is similar to those who used it for their smaller and somewhat self-segregated tight-knit communities. While Paul undoubtedly saw this language as useful to describe the reality of believers bonded together in a single identity in Christ even across miles, it is not self-evident how such language proves a homogeneity that goes much beyond this sharing of self-identity in Christ with others. The high level or extent of

---

4. Harland, "Familial Dimensions," 512.

5. As Perrin rightly notes, the literature for understanding the wider social implications of Paul's fraternal metaphor is vast. One of the earliest scholars to help New Testament scholars appreciate the fictive language used by Paul for the interconnected of believers in various locations is Meeks, *First Urban Christians*, 74–110. While it might be debated whether Paul's use of *adelphoi* is meant to be sectarian, its use as a means to suggest a connection with others in different locations appears proven. For a more recent treatment of the language in the letter to the Ephesians, see Darko, "Adopted Siblings," 333–46.

homogeneity that Perrin wants to find in the kinship language of Paul does not follow.

In addition to referring to believers in other locations as the recipients' "brothers" and "sisters," Perrin also argues that Paul indicates the links that his churches had with one another through the collection he was taking up for believers in Jerusalem. The argument is basically that if Paul asks believers in Corinth to financially help believers in Jerusalem, he is doing so either because he presupposes that the Corinthians (and possibly others who may have been asked) would have understood that there existed a link between themselves and those Jerusalem believers or that Paul is using the collection as a means to deepen and appreciate the measure of unity that believers in the two locales should have.[6] This point is a valid one to make. The collection for believers in Jerusalem was no simple act of benevolence for Paul. Rather, as it has been argued before, the collection is Paul's way of demonstrating his ecclesiology that God has created a new people of both Gentiles and Jews as evidenced by the way they financially care for one another as friends or family are expected to do.[7] Through the collection "for the saints" (εἰς τοὺς ἁγίους) in Jerusalem (1 Cor 16:1), Paul hoped to demonstrate to believers in the holy city that they had "brothers" and "sisters" out in the diaspora.

Global Organizational Structure of Pauline Churches

Perrin turns his attention next to identifying the obligations that apostles felt to "integrate local expressions of Christianity within a global organizational structure." Prior to Perrin, others have sought to define to what extent the apostles in Jerusalem exercised authority or control over the various communities of believers. But the scarcity of evidence from the earliest stages of the movement makes any reconstruction of that apostolic influence nearly impossible.[8] However, for Perrin, the one "watershed" episode recounted in Gal 2:7–10 is indicative of the apostle's efforts to exercise control and the responsibility that Paul believed was *"exclusively his own."* When Paul recounts that Peter, James, and John accepted that

---

6. Perrin notes that the former argument is held by Ogereau, "Jerusalem Collection, 360–78.

7. Nickle, *Collection*; Hurtado, "Jerusalem Collection," 46–62.

8. For a recent work from a sociological perspective on the exercise of authority in early Christianity, especially in connection to Paul's authority, see Taylor, *Paul, Antioch and Jerusalem*.

he had been given by Christ the mission to reach the Gentiles, was he implying that there was an understanding that Gentile churches are under Paul's apostolic structural authority as Jewish churches were under Peter's apostolic structural authority?

There is no question that, as Perrin later points out, Paul believed his apostolic calling and authority meant that he could communicate to churches what the ethical standards for faith and practice were. He believed he had the authority to tell even those churches he did not plant (e.g., those in Rome) how they were expected to behave if they were to live lives consistent with the gospel. But does the evidence of apostolic authority by which Paul writes and teaches support Perrin's reading of Galatians to suggest that Paul thought he was the *exclusive* apostle who was allowed reach out to Gentiles?

It does not appear so. In the first place, the Galatians text makes no claim that the Jerusalem leadership recognized Paul as the exclusive apostle who can go out to Gentiles. Secondly, Paul primarily asserted to the Galatians that the pillars of the Jerusalem church have accepted that Paul is an apostle chosen by Christ to go and convert Gentiles without requiring them to become Jewish. What we have in the Galatians text is not evidence of a global structure that divides Jews and Gentiles between apostles who can win them to Christ, but a global recognition that Paul, once a perceived outsider to the fellowship, has been called by Christ and given authority to reach Gentiles. Nothing in the text claims that Paul would have thought that Peter, James, or John would be trampling on his territory if they attempted to reach Gentiles as well. In fact, in 1 Cor 3:4–9, Paul states that what matters is not which apostle does what but God who gives the increase. Paul's concern in Galatians is not about informing his readers which apostle gets to go to which group of people but whether or not the Gentiles have to become Jewish in order to belong to God's people. The global organization structure Perrin hoped to see in Galatians that evidences a high interconnectedness among Pauline churches is readily apparent.

Nonnegotiable Tenets of Faith in Pauline Churches

What Perrin is describing by "nonnegotiable articles of faith" is the core of the gospel that Paul preached. If opponents (similar to those who were in Galatia)⁹ reject his gospel, which included both the narrative of Jesus' death and resurrection and subsequent sightings of him that were handed down in the tradition (1 Cor 15:3–8) as well as the prior narrative espoused by the Hebrew Scriptures, then they are also rejecting Paul's authority. Consequentially, such opponents are denying articles of faith that must not be denied. For those who do so can no longer be associated with all the people who have faith in Christ. These opponents are not simply disassociated from Pauline churches but the entire church, since Paul has gone to Jerusalem and its leadership accepted his kerygma as legitimate.

This portion of Perrin's essay is very helpful. Attempts to stress how diverse first century Pauline churches and their theologies were can be misleading if their reconstructions obfuscate a core theology centered on the narratives that Perrin has pointed out.¹⁰ While I do not believe that Perrin's description of Pauline churches as a "fairly monolitihic social-religious reality"¹¹ is clear enough because "fairly" is too vague and "monolithic" is too misleading, I do think that Perrin is directing the conversation onto the right track. Paul believed that his churches were interconnected because despite their differences they professed a faith in what the God of Israel was revealing about himself and his work in the world through Jesus Christ whom he has raised from the dead and has seated at his right hand. While scholarly efforts to more narrowly define what all was included in Paul's kerygma rightfully persists,¹² we are wandering aimlessly to discover the historical Paul if we start with the position that Paul never taught any kinds of demarcation for what his

---

9. In commenting on Paul's statement to the Galatians that if "an angel from heaven should proclaim to you a gospel contrary to what we proclaimed to you, let that one be accursed" (Gal 1:8), Perrin suggests that Paul's "hypothetical execration against angels" is remarkable given the exalted role angels typically have as revelatory mediators in apocalyptic Judaism. But Paul's potential judgment against angels is not that remarkable when it is noted that he told the Corinthians that they would judge angels in the future (1 Cor 6:3).

10. See the diverse ecclesiologies but shared theologies in Romans, Galatians, and 1 Corinthians in Porter, "Church" ;and Schnabel, "Community," 85–129.

11. Perrin insinuates that the Pauline churches were composed of "leading elders stationed." While Acts 14:23 claims that Paul and Barnabas appointed elders (*presbyteroi*) in the churches they established on their missionary trip, the undisputed Pauline letters do not indicate that these churches were structured with these offices. We might assume that they were because others were, but we could just as well assume that Paul allowed other effective organizational structures (e.g., *episkopoi*) to be in place.

12. For a recent attempt at identifying components of Paul's kerygma, see Hays, *Faith of Jesus Christ*, 116.

followers could and could not believe about the resurrected and exalted Christ Jesus. There were certain beliefs about Jesus that must be held or the faith is vain.

Perrin has reminded readers that the recognition of diversity must not diminish the existence of a perceived connectedness that believers in Jesus in one location would have had with believers in other places. That connectedness would have indeed been articulated in the language of kinship, but the extent of the unity of that connectedness is not accessible from the evidence of Paul's letters. Paul knew that homogeneity among all believers was a reality for all believers because they all exist in the one Christ and therefore all were expected to live according to the traditions of the kerygma they had received, either from Paul himself (as with the Galatians and Corinthians) or from someone else (as with those believers in Rome). Since Paul was an apostle of Christ, whose mission was to go to the Gentiles (but free to persuade any Jew or Gentile that the risen Jesus is the Christ), his authority to teach the ethical implications of the gospel must be acknowledged and accepted. His teaching authority would have provided another layer of interconnectedness upon that which Pauline churches already possessed in Christ. Although the claims of Perrin that the evidence points to a high level or extent of homogeneity and interconnectedness that was perceived by believers addressed in Paul's capital letters is not proven, the three types of unity he has identified as part of the Pauline ecclesiastical cohesion is persuasively laid out and established. Diversity can be claimed without denying that there existed among believers a real perceived unity with other believers in other places. Paul's hope was that the unity believers in one locale should feel with others elsewhere would be reinforced when he used language to suggest a kinship, when he expected submission to ethical instructions through Christ's apostles (especially himself), and when he sought believers' transformation coalescing around the core elements of the apostolic kerygma.

Bauer was right to remind historians to do better at evaluating the evidence on its own merits rather than simply to adopt the evaluation of other forms of Christianity held by the dominant and longer lasting proponents of "orthodoxy." Bauer knew that Paul could spot a heretical view (a different and unacceptable view). He noted that Galatians clearly shows Paul hurling an anathema against people trying to "fasten the yoke of legalism on the necks of liberated gentile Christians."[13] Paul was aware

---

13. Bauer, *Orthodoxy and Heresy*, 236. Though describing the conflict in Galatians

that there were others who taught a different "gospel" than the one he was teaching. But his gospel was the one recognized as legitimate by those leaders in Jerusalem, including James and Peter. It was certainly not the gospel as they would have originally understood it in the days immediately preceding Jesus' ascension (so in this sense it was not "original"), for no one was taking this gospel to the Gentiles themselves. But it became the approved teaching of those who had known Jesus, who were the first to confess his resurrection, and saw themselves as the first ones charged to make the will of God revealed in Christ known.

Even though Bauer, despite what some of his hyperbole implies, recognized that Paul could spot other teachings from so-called followers of Jesus as the Messiah that all believers must reject, Bauer does not read the Pauline evidence on its own merit. In an effort to make sure other neglected voices are heard, Paul's voice gets somewhat stifled. The undisputed letters of Paul express in clear ways that Paul thought of diverse believers as interconnected through a union with Christ. Believers' connections with one another were no doubt expressed to some degree by kinship language and through a shared acknowledgement of Paul's legitimate authority as an apostle of Christ to teach them the ethical implications of the gospel. But more important than "following Paul" or calling one another "brother" or "sister," the primary measure of the homogeneity Paul expected believers to accept, which Bauer was deaf to but Perrin has channeled, is that core teaching about the identity of Jesus Christ as the one risen from the dead, through whom God fulfills his purpose, justifying both Jew and Gentile and forming them into the one people of God.

Bibliography

Aasgaard, R. "Brotherhood in Plutarch and Paul: It's Role and Character." In *Constructing Early Christian Families: Family as Social Reality and Metaphor*, edited by Halvor Moxnes, 166–82. London: Routledge, 1997.

Bauer, Walter. *Orthodoxy and Heresy in Earliest Christianity*. Edited by Robert Kraft and Gerhard Krodels. Philadelphia: Fortress, 1971.

Darko, Daniel K. "Adopted Siblings in the Household of God: Kinship Lexemes in the Social Identity Construction of Ephesians." In *T. & T. Clark Handbook to Social*

---

in terms of fighting against "legalism" as Bauer did is now seen as historically inaccurate and grossly misleading for the concerns of Paul's opponents.

Identity in the New Testament, edited by J. Brian Tucker and Coleman A. Baker, 333–46. London: Bloomsbury, 2016.

Esler, P. "Keeping It in the Family: Culture, Kinship and Identity in 1 Thessalonians and Galatians." In *Families and Family Relations as Represented in Early Judaisms and Early Christianities: Text and Fictions: Papers at a Noster Colloquium in Amsterdam, June 9–11, 1998*, edited by Athalya Brenner and Jan Willem van Henten, 145–84. Leiden: Deo, 2000.

Harland, P. A. "Familial Dimensions of Group Identity: 'Brothers' Adelphoi in Associations of the Greek East." *Journal of Biblical Literature* 124 (2005) 492–93.

Hays, Richard. *The Faith of Jesus Christ: The Narrative substructure of Galatians 3:1—4:11*. Grand Rapids: Eerdmans, 2002.

Hurtado, Larry. "The Jerusalem Collection and the Book of Galatians." *Journal for the Study of the New Testament* 5 (1979) 46–62.

Meeks, Wayne. *The First Urban Christians: The Social World of the Apostle Paul*. New Haven: Yale University Press, 1983.

Nickle, Keith F. *The Collection: A Study in Paul's Strategy*. London: SCM, 1965.

Ogereau, Julien M. "The Jerusalem Collection as Κοινωνία: Paul's Global Politics of Socio-Economic Equality and Solidarity." *New Testament Studies* 58 (2012) 360–78.

Porter, Stanley E. "The Church in Romans and Galatians." In *The New Testament Church: The Challenge of Developing Ecclesiologies*, edited by John Harrison and James D. Dvorak, 85–102. McMaster Biblical Studies Series. Eugene, OR: Pickwick, 2012.

Schnabel, Eckhard J. "The Community of the Followers of Jesus in 1 Corinthians." In *The New Testament Church: The Challenge of Developing Ecclesiologies*, edited by John Harrison and James D. Dvorak, 103–29. McMaster Biblical Studies Series. Eugene, OR: Pickwick, 2012.

Taylor, Nicholas. *Paul, Antioch and Jerusalem: A Study in Relationships and Authority in Earliest Christianity*. London: Bloomsbury, 2015.

Summary and Reflections

Ben Wiebe

The aim in this volume is not to be comprehensive, to present a complete view of this or that theme or to take account of the range and variety of NT "readings." Many of them, within their own appropriate scope, are welcome as contributions. At the same time, on their own in isolation, they are simply inadequate.

The origins of Christianity and the issue of unity and diversity have given rise to a maze of hypotheses.[1] Differences here often are not a matter of knowledge but of prior basic disagreements or differences of horizon. Markus Bockmuehl refers to a loss of orientation and lack of a shared purpose in NT studies.[2] The contributors to this volume take up particular topics dealing with Jesus and Christian origins in order to develop some baselines for interpretation and to illuminate directions toward a new paradigm. If this is clearly grasped there will no doubt be some pertinent questions. To clarify and sum up we will work through some of these questions along with affirmations.

Questions and Affirmations

Question. The point about prior basic differences as an impediment to common understanding is contrary to the assumption that no matter how distant or different any person or tradition may be they can be

---

1. Williams, "Historical Criticism," 216–28, with reference to representative works on historical criticism speaks of a crisis of interpretation, "especially in regard to the Gospels," and goes on to comment, "it is far from clear any longer what counts as a serious argument."

2. Bockmuehl, *Seeing the Word*, 38–39.

understood. All that is required is an "objective" interpreter. If the argument holds that prior basic differences are often at the bottom of our divisions or estrangements, does that not foreclose on the possibility of advance toward common understanding of Jesus or the Gospels?

Affirmation. Yes, it can and often does. Conflicting views in the field of NT studies may be rooted in prior differences about objectivity, values, history, or truth. These are not cases arising from the lack of evidence, which may promptly yield to resolution with the appropriate reception of evidence. To the extent certainly that presuppositions are unwittingly held they may block advance to common understanding.

But no, it does not necessarily close the door to resolution. What should not be overlooked is the fact that all interpreters and all interpretations come from somewhere. We think about the form enquiry takes; it is not the passive registering of this or that, but attention to the particulars of a text, calling for reflection and judgment. These are the acts of a person (subject) taking steps to understand (steps in objectivity). Inquiry calls for the asking and answering of certain kinds of questions in order to move from the known to the unknown. The known provides the means of approach to the unknown. The unknown is selected for the sake of some gain in knowledge with a view to turning the unknown into the known.[3] This holds whether the question is about some historical figure or the date of a NT book. The point is the selection of the unknown to be known is a result of purpose. The history of the inquiry about Jesus' purposes have widely varied. Related to this kind of inquiry such purposes are presuppositions.

Another and second facet with respect to presupposition is the answering of questions. This process moves forward by forming hypotheses or possible answers. The range of possible answers "is established and limited by what the historian conceives as possible. The judgments of possibility are presuppositions."[4] In this sense, inquiry moves forward on the basis of certain matters one presupposes as known (interpretation of the miracles of Jesus, however perceived, has often proceeded on the basis that "we know miracles do not happen because they cannot happen").

Question. If our concern is interpretation of the NT, primary attention to the text is appropriate. It is also the case that the evidence of the

---

3. Meyer, *Aims of Jesus*, 14. Gadamer, *Truth and Method*, 333.

4. Meyer, *Aims of Jesus*, 14. Strauss, *Life of Jesus*, lii, flagged presuppositions as the main barrier to understanding; he saw himself as liberated from them, having "early attained [this] by means of philosophical studies."

early external history about the origins of the NT documents is sometimes fragmentary or lacking, it is therefore important to deal with indications or evidence in the documents as we have them. Why then give so much attention to history?

Affirmation. Yes, the data in the documents is of first importance. In the letters, like Romans, we have reference to Paul as the sender and reference to the addressees (the church at Rome). In context, we have indication of the date for the letter. Furthermore, we have indications and direct evidence about this church as composed of both Jews and Gentiles (e.g., Rom 1:16; 2:9–10, 25–29; 11:13–24; 15:7–12). But no, we do not confine ourselves to the internal evidence. By way of example, to read Romans clearly in historical context the letter form and the purpose the letters served in their setting can aid interpretation.[5]

As to Mark, from the earliest days we have the superscriptions (i.e. "according to Mark" and so on), but otherwise no direct internal evidence of authorship, place of writing, or the addressees. We do have extensive early external evidence for Mark as the author and Rome as the place of writing as well as the first audience for this Gospel. And we can correlate what internal data we have from Mark with certain external data (e.g., Mark serving as interpreter for Peter, and Mark as a work of translation from Aramaic to Greek). To give an important place to evidence of the document itself is not a basis for excluding the external evidence. This also is evidence to be accounted for.

Question. We do not have direct access to the words or deeds of Jesus as we do, for instance, for Paul in his letters. We have the Gospel accounts about Jesus from the evangelists. We are dependent on others for knowledge of Jesus.

Affirmation. In the first instance this poses the question of the relation between event and the data about the event. The inquirer investigates the data and taking account of data develops an interpretation. We recognize that when we read a narrative we do not simply receive it as the event, it represents the event, and we understand it comes to us as an account by way of interpretation. The recent emphasis on the role of eyewitness in the Gospel accounts brings this into our awareness. It is clearly expressed in the title of Dunn's *Jesus Remembered*. The account is not simply to be equated with the event but provides access to the event. This

---

5. Malherbe, *Ancient Epistolary Theorists*.

became the basis for scholars attempting to separate the two and going behind the Gospel accounts with the aim of recovering the "real" Jesus.

Question. One modern response could be that what we have is what participants in the events with Jesus remembered. This is quite subjective, is it not? Would it not be better to hear from observers who were not involved?

Affirmation. Yes, to read the Gospels is reading people attending to and presenting their account of events (in that sense subjective). But no, with reference to ancient historians they certainly did not think so. It was important to hear from participants and to get the testimony of eyewitnesses of the events. For some purposes of history writing today eyewitness testimony is also of primary importance: if we want to understand how it came about and what it was like for Germans when the Berlin Wall came down, we will want to hear from people who were involved in those events. The detached outside observer would probably not know what was important or remember much of it. For that we depend on participants or insiders to the events; without them we simply could not know much. This holds for Jesus and our knowledge of him.

Question. If we take account of the recent emphasis on the Gospel accounts as based on eyewitness testimony, what allows us to identify something from those accounts as coming from eyewitnesses in distinction from development in community or the author's addition or interpretation?

Affirmation. James Dunn, taking actual instances of Jesus teaching and actions in the different Gospels shows that in accord with the transmission of oral tradition, there is the core account and details on either side that may vary. Certain things become clear: 1) key points remain constant; 2) the basic matter from Jesus is generally maintained (see Matt 8:23-27; Mark 4:3-41; Luke 8:22-25). Around this, core stories could be told in concise or more extended form.[6] The substance of the Jesus tradition was treasured and told; the words of Jesus are held in memory more exactly than accounts of his actions. It has long been recognized that the formulation of Jesus' teaching is itself designed to be received and kept in memory (as in the beatitudes, Matt 5:1-12). At the same time there is reason to affirm that Jesus repeated much of his teaching in various settings in somewhat different forms. In those instances of Jesus' words present in multiple sources, there is a strong basis for recognizing the

---

6. Dunn, *Jesus Remembered*, 210-24.

words of Jesus. It remains that there can be variation in accounts and still in substance be from Jesus.

Question. In view of the extended period of oral transmission of the gospel tradition before it was written down, what basis is there for reliance on the Gospel accounts?

Affirmation. Yes, memory can fail. How reliable or accurate memory is depends on the event or subject matter and on how it is received. Of some things we say we will never forget. Memories can thus also be remarkably reliable and accurate. More than this, memory does not function in the abstract; there is the continued presence of the witnesses and the community sustained in the gospel tradition. In a primarily oral culture like the ancient Palestinian culture, there is more importance placed on memory (a person knows something, whether a text or an event, when it is set in the memory). There are people in the community who represent the stories of that community. The memory is thus carried by certain people who know the stories and serve to sustain and to correct if needed.

Further, in the Jewish setting, there is evidence of notebooks used to assist students to learn and memorize the words of their teachers. In the Qumran community we have first-century evidence for the use of Testimonia collections and various other documents. Part of each day was devoted to reading and meditating on Scripture (the result was the writing of some new Psalms and their own writing of commentary on Scripture). This would develop knowledge of Scripture and finally set it in memory. Indeed, Martin Jaffee has noted that in the wider Jewish setting oral communication depended in primary fashion on the knowledge and use of texts. What was presented in oral form (speeches) was often written down and what was written was often delivered in oral form (e.g., Col 4:16).[7]

In the case of Jesus there is reason to believe his teaching and actions formed a strong basis for oral learning. As he moved from place to place in that setting, he would have repeated much of his teaching many times. He also explained his teaching with variation in the circle of his disciples (Mark 4:10), and he sent them out to teach and heal as he had done (Luke 9:1-6). All of this indicates a disciplined reception from Jesus. And what is more, in accord with wider Jewish culture, learning

---

7. Jaffee, *Torah in the Mouth*, 61.

from Jesus may well have been accompanied by the use of notebooks from the beginning.

To follow this up requires our attention to the relation between the disciples as eyewitnesses and as representatives of the gospel tradition in the setting of the early church. That is, the role of the eyewitnesses and the tradition that takes form in the Gospel accounts. The Gospels carry the claim to represent or embody the testimony of eyewitnesses (e.g., Luke 1:1-4; John 19:35; 21:24, 25). And this is not to overlook the process of editing and interpreting as part of the formation of their accounts. They were in direct contact with the eyewitnesses. This goes directly counter to the legacy of twentieth century form-critical thinking that the tradition of Jesus' words and acts passed through a long anonymous process of oral tradition before in the end reaching the writers of the Gospels. Luke and Mark as well, we have noted, give indication of "eyewitnesses" known to them. As Martin Hengel has recently expressed it, "This personal link of the Jesus tradition with particular tradents, or more precisely their memory and missionary preaching . . . is historically undeniable. From the beginning, the recollection of the words (and actions) of the Lord played a role. It refutes the purely form-critical approaches to the Jesus tradition."[8]

This aligns with the recognition that the Gospels were written within the generation of living witness to Jesus. This holds true even if we go by the somewhat later dating more generally accepted for the Gospels. In contrast to the assumption in form-criticism of the anonymous passing on of traditions over generations of time, we think in terms of one generation or within the span of a lifetime. Over this period we have a core group of leaders present and active in the transmission of the gospel tradition. The Gospels take form and embody the testimony of these eyewitnesses. This then serves as a baseline for interpreting them in accord with how we have received them.

Question. To live is to experience change, to leave certain things and to accept other things. This relates to reception history. Interpretation and appropriation of the gospel takes place in the midst of challenges and changes. How can interpretation find a basis in the midst of changing historical events in continuity with Jesus?

Affirmation. The approaches in response have been many and varied. The attempt from Strauss to Schweitzer to Bultmann was to secure a

---

8. Hengel, *Four Gospels*, 143.

basis for faith in Jesus by moving in the end beyond changing historical events. In the endeavor to interpret the NT they explored the historical meaning in order to derive from it some timeless truth. D. F. Strauss early on developed his way of doing this by using the category of "myth" to read the Gospel accounts. Strauss, drawing upon Hegel, distinguished between "representation" (Gospel accounts) and "concept."[9] For him, the concept takes up the essential meaning of the representation on a higher, more adequate level. That is, for Strauss the Gospel account is a representation of truth that can be more adequately expressed in philosophical concepts. Traditional theology is then transcended and can be left behind. The essential matter is not the particular unity of the divine and human in Jesus Christ, but the oneness of God and the world, "the consciousness of the underlying identity of the divine and the human, the infinite and the finite."[10]

Those taking this approach thought to address people in their contemporary situation in ways that the literal sense could not. Lessing is the noted forerunner in the eighteenth century,[11] followed by Bultmann in the twentieth, doing the historical work to derive some ultimate truth from it beyond or above history altogether.[12] This supposes a timeless message, for Lessing an "eternal truth of reason," for Bultmann a timeless call to "decision."

---

9. The development of the "concept" or reason in abstraction from history has early roots in F. C. Baur and G. W. F. Hegel. For D. F. Strauss this defines Gospel interpretation.

10. Strauss, *Life of Jesus*, xiii; Keck, "Introduction," lvi, lvii.

11. Lessing, *Lessing's Theological Writings*, 53–55.

12. Wright, *New Testament*, 20. MacIntyre, *Three Rival Versions*, showed that the question of knowledge (how we know) remains a matter of primary importance with enduring effects within interpretation. In his Gifford Lectures, Alasdair MacIntyre presented what he called the "three rival" forms of inquiry: encyclopaedia, genealogy, and tradition. The main example from MacIntrye of encyclopedic knowledge is the ninth edition of the *Encyclopedia Britannica* (1875–89). He sets out three characteristics: 1) rationality is one and functions with those standards that all without much difficulty can acknowledge; 2) rationality is universal (and basically the same) and by means of the appropriate methods issues in scientific understanding of the whole; 3) rationality is a movement that issues in continuing inevitable progress. This is the progress of reason over time; at the same time reason's discoveries are not historically dependent. They are "timeless truths, in timelessly true principles." Truth is "independent of standpoint . . . can be discovered by any adequately intelligent person, no matter his point of view" MacIntyre, *Three Rival Versions*, 18–23, 78–79.

As it is, this turns out to be an abstraction. We do not need to help Lessing across his ditch; the solid, less particular "truth of reason" is not to be found there. Rather, the mission of Jesus is bound up with actual events in time and place and takes place in the reader's own world. In this relation it is open to question and testing. In this way Christian faith is accountable, and in accord with its own identity does not withdraw into some special sphere to be confined as mere ideology. Their character as *Gospel* accounts does not discount them as historical sources.[13]

Interpretation in accord with the Gospels then does not operate above the text but by taking account of the text. We may know it but easily overlook that no human interpreter is either above history as such, all human reason is "situated." With regard to one's own standpoint and recognizing the Gospels as narratives of events in history, interpretation is required to account for them rather then set them aside. For instance, to abstract the name of Jesus from the web of Christian thought or gospel tradition does not result in some purified understanding of the name, but simply prevents our understanding of the name of Jesus.[14] Interpretation will take up the Gospel narratives and account for them. And in so doing will account for how first century Christians came to believe what they did about Jesus. In line with this we have a concise recent statement from Theissen and Winter in their work, *Quest for the Plausible Jesus*: "What we know of Jesus as a whole must allow him to be recognized within his contemporary Jewish context and must be compatible with the Christian (canonical and noncanonical) history of his effects."[15] The meaning of Jesus' mission and destiny cannot be grasped apart from the interpretations of the Gospel sources.

Conclusion

Here, after engaging the thought of the different contributions, what are the indications for a renewed focus in the study of Jesus and Christian

---

13. Schröter, *Jesus of Nazareth*, 16.

14. MacIntyre, *Three Rival Versions*, 377.

15. Theissen and Winter, *Quest for the Plausible Jesus*, 212. Keith and LeDonne, *Jesus, Criteria, and the Demise*, 201-2. As MacIntyre notes, later editions of the *Encyclopedia Britannica* recognize the limitations of the view from above; there are, in short, rival ways of reasoning. In the fifteenth edition of the encyclopedia the main editor himself acknowledges that knowledge is fragmentary and that contributors speak from various standpoints (56–57).

origins? Christian identity is forged in time and place. This accords with the particular character of the gospel. Christian origins are not reducible to one or another ideology. Access to understanding of the gospel cannot be taken for granted. Amid the confusing and sometimes violent crosswinds of ideology how to open or keep open the path to understanding of the gospel? To begin with, taking full account of the external history in concert with the evidence of the NT documents can serve as a baseline for interpretation. Recognizing the presence of oral tradition in context and taking form in the Gospel accounts has its own importance. Not to be overlooked is the place of eyewitness affirmed in the Gospels (and of memory) for appropriate understanding and interpretation. Again, the early reception history of the Gospels informs our discernment of the "authority" of Jesus in continuity with the church. And taking full account of the four Gospels in their intricate relations of difference and similarity provides both baseline and direction. In and with all this, the conjunction of Jesus' mission and the church is of basic significance in discerning directions toward a new paradigm.

Bibliography

Bernier, Jonathan. *The Quest for the Historical Jesus After the Demise of Authenticity*. London: Bloomsbury, T. & T. Clark, 2016.
Bockmuehl, Markus. *Seeing the Word*. Grand Rapids: Baker Academic, 2006.
Bultmann, Rudolf. *Jesus and the Word*. New York: Scribners, 1958.
Dietrich, Ernst Ludwig. *Sùb Sébut: Die eschatologishche Wiederherstellung bei den Propheten*. Giesen: Töpelmann, 1925.
Dunn, James D. G. *Jesus Remembered*. Grand Rapids: Eerdmans, 2003.
Gadamer, Hans-Georg. *Truth and Method*. New York: Seabury, 1975.
Hengel, Martin. *The Four Gospels and the One Gospel of Jesus Christ*. Translated by John Bowden. Harrisburg: Trinity, 2000.
―――. *Judaism and Hellenism: Studies in Their Encounters in Palestine during the Early Hellenistic Period*. Translated by John Bowden. 2 vols. Philadelphia: Fortress, 1974 [1969].
Jaffee, Martin S. *Torah in the Mouth: Writing and Oral Tradition in Palestinian Judaism, 200 BCE–400 CE*. Oxford: Oxford University Press, 2001.
Keck, Leander. "Introduction." In *The Christ of Faith and the Jesus of History*, by David Friedrich Strauss. Philadelphia: Fortess, 1977.
Keith, Chris, and Anthony LeDonne, eds. *Jesus, Criteria, and the Demise of Authenticity*. London: T. & T. Clark, 2012.
Lessing, G. E. *Lessing's Theological Writings*. Standford: Standford Univeristy Press, 1957.
MacIntyre, Alasdair. *Three Rival Versions of Moral Inquiry*. Notre Dame: Notre Dame University Press, 1990.
Malherbe, Abraham. *Ancient Epistolary Theorists*. Atlanta: Scholars, 1988.
Meyer, Ben F. *Reality and Illusion in New Testament Scholarship*. Wilmington, DE: Michael Glazier, 1994.
Meyer, Ben F. *The Aims of Jesus*. London: SCM, 1979.
Schröter, Jens. *Jesus of Nazareth: Jew from Galilee, Savior of the World*. Waco: Baylor University Press, 2014.
Strauss, D. F. *The Life of Jesus Critically Examined*. London: Chapman, [1835–36] 1846.
Theissen, Gerd, and Dagmar Winter. *The Quest for the Plausible Jesus*. Translated by M. Eugene Boring. Louisville: Westminster, 2002.
Williams, Rowan. "Historical Criticism and Sacred Text." In *Reading Texts, Seeking Wisdom: Scripture and Theology*, edited by G. Stanton and D. F. Ford, 217–29. London: SCM, 2003.
Wright, N. T. *The New Testament and the People of God*. Minneapolis: Fortress, 1992.

Subject Index

Acts, 2, 5, 6, 13, 19–24, 26–32, 38, 57, 94, 97, 168, 210
apostle (see eyewitness), 47, 96, 98, 129, 175, 177–80, 182–83, 195–97, 236–37, 242–43, 250–52
Caligula, 58
canon (formation), 5, 18, 67, 85, 124–26, 173, 176, 179, 183–84, 191, 194–95, 199–200, 231
    Irenaeus 173–76
    Justin Martyr 176–77
    Tatian 176–77
    Epistula Apostolorum 180, 184, 192
    Muratorian Fragment 191–92, 196, 199
    2 *Clement*, 184–86, 188–89, 197–200
church, xi–xiv, xvi, 3, 11–14, 41, 43–48, 56–68, 73, 87, 95–97, 123, 129, 156–57, 173, 204, 226–27, 230
    community, xi–xvii, 46, 52, 55–56, 61, 64, 73, 76, 83, 93, 109, 110, 114, 116, 126–27, 134, 208–9, 211, 240–41, 247–49
    diversity, xiv, 60, 110, 151, 160, 203–5, 208–9, 211, 213–15, 219, 224, 227, 230–31, 243, 246–48, 253, 256

unity, xiv, 47, 204–8, 210–11, 219, 224–25, 232–33, 235, 239, 243, 247–48, 250, 253, 256
Dead Sea Scrolls, xiii, 64, 161, 164
disciples, xi, 37, 48, 61, 74, 77–79, 82–84, 93, 103, 105–10, 152, 227, 261
Ephesians, xvi, 10, 13, 21, 37, 52–54
eyewitness, xvi, 44, 60–61, 79, 83, 88, 97–8, 104–19, 122–27, 130, 139, 140–41, 183, 259, 261, 264
Galilee, 48–49, 62, 142, 150–51, 161
Gnostics, 230
gospel, xiii, 12, 41–50
    community criticism, xviii, 201–9, 210–12, 215–17, 224–26, 228
    form-criticism, 42–48, 57, 80, 124–26, 261
    narratives, 43, 45, 48, 241, 263
    orality, 71–72, 118, 127, 180
    transmission, xiii, xvi–xvii, 67–71, 73–76, 78–84, 87–90, 93, 95, 97, 98, 101, 105–6, 108, 111, 123–27, 180, 196, 242, 259–61
history, xi, xiii–xvi, 1–6, 17, 19, 32, 41–43, 45, 47–50, 57–59, 64, 84, 90–95, 97, 100, 102, 106, 116, 118, 120, 151, 153–54, 172–74, 176, 202, 206, 225, 231, 233, 257–59, 262–64
    ancient Sources, 5, 26, 41, 125

history (*continued*)
  foundations, 6, 7, 14,
  Eusebius, 5, 13, 20–21, 26–28, 30–31, 95–96, 107
  Jamnia, 133, 153, 155, 215
  Occam's Razor, 22, 24, 29, 36, 70
  Papias, 5, 16, 18, 24, 31, 58, 62–64, 94, 96, 107, 215
  Jesus, xi–xiii 17–18, 27, 42–48, 56–58, 61, 64, 67–68, 72, 76, 78, 81, 84, 91, 104–10, 23–24, 126, 130–34, 148–50, 160–62, 170, 188, 195, 202–3, 214–16, 241, 252, 257–58
    mission, 47, 49, 78, 93, 151, 169, 263–64
    christology, 134, 158, 160, 162
    crucifixion, 28, 53, 82, 95, 158, 182
    Nazarenes, 216
    teacher, 12, 43, 70, 73, 76, 84, 106
  Jews, 16, 23, 30, 34, 46, 53, 74, 104–5, 129, 132–33, 143, 148, 155–56, 159–60, 249–51, 258
  Judaism, ix, xii, 46, 64, 71, 94, 113, 131, 133, 145–46, 148–49, 151, 154–55, 159, 237, 241
    Palestinian, 43, 71, 130, 136, 145–146, 203, 260
  John (Gospel of), 14, 48, 49, 61, 95, 97, 110, 123, 125–26, 128–38, 167–71, 173, 176–77, 179, 181–83, 188, 195–97, 219
    and the Synoptics, 209, 221, 223, 225, 257
    geography, 136, 142, 149, 151, 160–61

kingdom of God, xii, 56, 66, 77, 113–14, 116
eschatology, xvi, 8, 12, 54–55
community, xii–x, 46, 51, 55–56, 61, 73, 76, 82–83, 93, 109–13, 117, 122, 126–27, 143, 208, 240–41, 147, 149, 160
Marcion, 173–74, 231
Mark (Gospel of), 41, 44, 47–48, 57–58, 60, 139–40, 179, 196, 206, 217, 227–28, 258
  authorship, 14, 15, 24, 26–27, 29–31, 41, 58–60, 62–64, 95, 215–16, 217, 261
  biography, x, 13, 58–59, 81, 108, 110
  date, 13–19, 24–27, 29–30, 32, 58, 94, 169, 216
Paul, xiv–xvi, xviii–xix, 2, 5, 8–9, 11–12, 14, 20–24, 35, 38, 49, 50–52, 55, 168, 208, 215, 230, 232, 236–37
  Caesarea, 8–10, 11–12, 15, 30–35, 37, 50, 52–54
  early Christianity, 183–84, 202, 207, 232, 245–47, 249–52, 254
  witness, xiv, 56–57, 73, 78–79, 109, 159, 183, 238–42

Author Index

Aasgaard, Reidar, 233, 244, 249, 254
Albl, Martin C., 178n12
Alexander, Loveday, 202n5
Allison, Dale C, xivn12, xx,
Anderson, Paul N.,140, 149, 151, 152, 156, 163
Ashton, John, 147, 148, 163

Bacon, B.W.,144, 145, 163
Bailey, K. E., 81n41, 107
Bartchy, S. Scott, 233n5
Barth, Markus, 54
Barton, Stephen C., 202n5
Bauckham, Richard, xviii, 61 62, 70–87, 96–127, 157–70, 201–24, 244
Bauer, Walter, xviii, 213, 220, 222, 230, 232, 235, 239, 242–45, 246–47, 253–54
Baur , F.C., xvii, xviii, 6, 94, 130, 151, 160, 163, 202, 207–8, 210, 213, 220, 262
Becker, Eve-Marie, 59, 65
Berger, Klaus, 128n3
Bernier, Jonathan, xiii–xx, 59, 64–65, 155, 162–63, 167, 170–71, 201, 206–8, 213–14, 220, 224–25, 228–29, 265
Betz, Hans Dieter, 231n3
Bird, Michael F., 86, 91–92, 102
Bobichon, Phillipe, 178n12
Bockmuehl, Markus, 65, 256, 265
Bousset, Wilhelm, 131, 158, 163
Boyarin, Daniel, 147, 155, 159, 160–63

Brown, Raymond, 24–27, 38, 94, 101, 131, 133, 140, 148–49, 154, 163, 202, 220
Bultmann, Rudolf , xii, xx, 42–43, 58, 65, 103–5, 119, 131–32, 141, 145, 154, 161, 163, 166, 186, 261–62, 265
Burkett, Delbert, 132, 135, 163
Burridge, Richard A., 202n5
Byrskog, Samuel, 73, 80, 84–86, 105–6, 108, 111, 119–21

Cadbury, H. J., 6, 38
Caird, G. B. xii–xx
Casey, Maurice 48, 63–65
Castelli, Elizabeth A., 238n12
Catchpole, David R., 98n35
Chancey, Mark A., 46, 65, 215, 221
Chapman, John, 14–15, 29, 33, 38, 66, 265
Charlesworth, James, 146, 163–64, 165
Chaytor, Henry J., 108n18
Chilton, Bruce, 71
Clanchy, Michael T., 108n18
Collingwood, R. G., 207, 221
Coloe, Mary, 147n53
Crossan, John Dominic, 106, 120
Crossley, James G., 17, 38
Cullman, Oscar, 133, 164, 202, 221
Culpepper, R. Alan, 133, 145, 164, 202, 221, 133, 145

Das, A. Andrew, 237n10
DeBoer, Willis Peter, 238n12

AUTHOR INDEX

Derrenbacker, Robert A., 100n42
Desjardins, Michel R., 231n3
Dibelius, Martin, 42-43, 65, 73, 186, 225-26, 229
Dietrich, Ernst Ludwig, xii, xiv, xx, 265
Dodd, C. H., 7-9, 12, 33, 36, 38, 104, 120, 139, 145, 164, 238, 244
Donfried, Karl P., 186, 189-90, 192
Dormandy, Richard, 8, 9, 13, 37-38
Douglas, Mary, 26
Downs, David J., 235n8
Drury, John, 100n39
Dungan, David L., 38, 68, 85
Dunn, James D. G, xiii, xiv, xx, 44, 50, 65, 81, 85, 106-13, 118, 120, 203, 221, 258-59, 265

Edmundson, George, 16-17, 23, 31, 33-34, 39, 94-95, 102
Ehrenspreger, Kathy, 239n13
Ehrman, Bart, 69, 71, 82, 85, 91, 93-94, 99, 132, 134-35, 164, 231, 244
Ellington, Dustin Watson, 238, 244
Ellis, E. Earle, 4, 16, 24, 29-32, 93-94, 102
Esler, Philip F., 201n3, 202n8, 207
Evans, Craig A., 183n24
Eve, Eric, 72, 75, 78

Farrer, Austin, 28, 89, 94, 98-99, 102, 137
Ferguson, Everett, 177, 191
Fiensy, David A., 215, 221
Fitzpatrick, Joseph, 26n86
Fortna, Robert, 132, 141-43, 163
Foster, Paul, 67, 85
Fotheringham, J. K., 6
Freyne, Seán, 203n11, 215n44
Furnish, Victor Paul, 54, 65

Gadamer, Hans-Georg, 212, 257n3
Gardner-Smith, Percival, 139, 164
Gerhardsson, Birger, xvi, 67-86, 87-89, 92, 95, 97-98, 100, 102, 105-7, 113, 120, 127, 180, 191
Gignilliat, Mark, 236n10
Goodacre, Mark, 5, 39, 67, 85, 205, 221
Gore, Charles, 18
Goulder, M. D., 5, 39, 102
Gunkel, Hermann, 225

Hahneman, Geoffrey M., 177n8
Halbwachs, Maurice, 123n2
Hannah, Darrell D., 179n14
Harland, P. A., 248-49, 255
Harmon, Matthew S., 236
Harnack, A. von, 2, 6, 14, 33, 34, 39, 189, 192
Hartog, Paul, 231, 244
Hays, Richard, 147, 164, 252, 255
Headlam, A. C., 11n32
Heckel, Theo K., 190n37
Hemer, Colin J., 19, 34, 39, 94, 102
Hengel, Martin, xiii, 4, 15-16, 29, 39, 45-47, 59-60, 62, 65,106, 120, 146, 164, 208, 217, 221, 261, 265
Hill, Charles, 179n14, 195-96, n3n4
Hill, Craig, 221
Hills, Julian, 179n14
Hodge, Caroline E. Johnson, 233n5
Hofrichter, Peter, 128n3
Hooker, Morna, 44, 65
Hornschuh, Manfred, 179n14
Horsley, Richard A., 106, 120
Horst, van der, Pieter W.
Hort, F. J. A., 10
Howard-Brook, Wes, 202n9
Humphreys, Colin J., 7, 34
Hurtado, Larry, 90, 158-60, 164
Hvalvik, Reidar, 232n4

Instone-Brewer, David, 155, 164

Jaffee, Martin, 260, 265
Jewett, Robert, 208n30
Johnson, Brian D., 148n54
Johnson, Luke, 131, 145, 148, 164
Junack, Klaus, 109n18

Kazen, Thomas, 201n3
Keck, Leander, 52, 65–66, 262, 265
Keener, Craig, 131, 148, 164
Keith, Chris, 75, 85, 255, 263, 265
Kelber, Werner H., 81, 85–86
Kelhoffer, James A., 186, 190, 192
Kimelman, Reuven, 155
Kirk, Alan, 105, 108, 112, 120
Kittel, Gerhard, 73
Klink, Edward, 154–55, 157, 164
Kloppenborg Verbin, John S, 114–15, 120, 203, 221
Knowles, Michael P., 183n24
Kostenberger, Andreas J., 231, 244
Kraus, Thomas J., 108n20
Kummel, W. G., 4, 26–28, 39, 53, 65

Lampe, Peter, 217n48
Le Donne, Anthony, 91, 102
Lessing, G. E., 68–70, 82, 91, 262–63, 265
Lindemann, Andreas,
Lonergan, Bernard, 50, 65, 170–71, 212, 215, 222

MacIntyre, Alasdair, 262–63, 265
Mack, Burton L., 58, 65
Malherbe, Abraham, 258, 264
Martyn, J. Louis, 132–33, 136, 153–56, 162, 164, 166, 202, 206, 222
Marxsen, Willi, xiii, xx, 201, 222
Matson, Mark A., xii, 128, 192
McCue, James F., 131n3
McDowell, Edward A., 188n31
McGrath, James, 152–53, 160, 165
Meeks, Wayne, 249, 255
Meier, John P., 152
Merton, Thomas, 4, 39
Metzger, 120, 177, 192
Meyer, Ben, xii, xiii, xviii, xx, 5, 50, 59, 65, 170–71, 201–8, 211–16, 219–20, 222, 224, 229, 257, 265
Meyer, Eduard, 5, 8, 17–18, 33, 39, 95, 102
Millard, Alan, 91, 102
Miller, Robert, 142n38

Mitchell, Margaret M., 201n3
Mitton, C. Leslie, 11, 39
Moberly, Robert B., 5, 20, 34–35, 39, 94, 102
Moloney, Francis J., 140, 143, 163, 165
Mosse, Martin, xiv-xvi, 1, 87
Mournet, Terence, 105, 121
Muller, C. Detlef G., 180n15

Neill, Stephen, 2–6, 39, 95, 102
Neirynck, Frans, 139, 165
Neusner, Jacob, 70, 74, 119
Nickle, Keith F., 250, 255

Ogereau, Julien M., 134n7
Ormerod, Neil, 170–71, 222
Overman, J. Andrew, 202n6

Pagels, Elaine, 230, 245
Parker, D. C., 101–2
Perkins, Pheme, 4, 13, 39, 57–58, 62, 66
Perrin, Nicholas, xvii–xviii, 172, 230
Perrin, Norman, xii, xx
Pervo, Richard I., 210, 222
Petersen, W. L., 176n6
Peterson, Brian 147, 165
Peterson, Dwight, 156
Porter, Stanley, 252n10
Powell, Mark Allan, 134, 165
Pratscher, Wilhelm, 186, 192
Punt, Jeremy, 233n5

Rackham, R. B., 98n34
Reimarus, Hermann Samuel, 68–69, 82, 86, 91
Reinhartz, Adele, 148, 156, 165
Riesenfeld, Harald, 71, 86, 107, 121
Riesner, Rainer, xvii, 71, 74–77, 81, 86, 124, 127, 208, 213, 222
Robbins, Vernon, 45, 66
Robinson, J.A.T, xvii, 1–2, 13, 40, 102, 222
Robinson, Thomas, 222, 245
Rodriguez, Rafael, 81n41
Ryan, Jordan, 86, 207, 222

Saldarini, Anthony, 202n6
Sanders, E. P., xiii, 44, 49, 66, 86, 90, 105, 121, 164
Schleiermacher, Friedrich, 130, 166
Schmidt, Karl L., 42n2
Schnabel, Eckhard J., 177, 192, 252, 255
Schnackenburg, Rudolf, 131, 166
Schroter, Jens, 263, 265
Schweizer, 142, 166
Shellard, Barbara, 140n29
Sherwin-White, A. N., 19, 40, 92–94, 97, 102
Sim, David C., 201n3, 211
Skarsaune, Oskar, 178n12
Smith, Moody, 132, 141, 166, 193
Staley, Jeff, 145n45
Stanton, Graham N., 193, 202, 223
Stendahl, Krister, 76n24
Strack, Hermann L., 107n15
Strauss, D. F. xvii, 42, 166, 265
Streeter, B. H., 88–89, 99–100, 102, 217–18, 223, 265
Sundberg, Albert C., 177n8
Sweeny, Armin, 108n18

Talbert, Charles H., 68n4
Taylor, Vincent, 107, 121, 123, 250, 255
Taylor, W. S., 107n12
Theissen, Gerd, 263, 265
Thompson, Michael B., 202, 208, 216, 223, 234, 245
Trebilco, Paul, 219, 223

Tuckett, C. M., 5, 39, 80, 83–84, 86, 98, 100, 102, 174, 185–86, 193
Turner, Henry Ernest William, 231, 244

Underhill, Evelyn, 8, 36, 38

Van de Sandt, Huub, 217n54
Verheyden, Joseph, 177n8
Von Wahlde, Urban, 132, 141–42, 150, 166
Voorwinde, Stephen, 145n45

Waddington, W. Graeme, 7
Wagner, J. Ross, 136n10
Watson, Francis, 173, 192, 194, 196, 199, 200, 202, 223
Weeden, Theodore J., Sr., 202n7
Wenham, John, 16, 34, 40, 93, 100, 103
Wiebe, Ben, 45n9
Williams, Rowan, 256, 264
Wilson, John, 116n42
Windisch, Hans, 138–39, 141, 166
Winter, Dagmar, 263
Witherington, Ben, 57n27
Wright, N. T., 2–6, 39, 43, 48, 66, 95, 102, 262, 265

Yarbrough, Robert W., 94n18